ORTHODOX AND MODERN

ORTHODOX AND MODERN

Studies in the Theology of Karl Barth

Bruce L. McCormack

Baker Academic

a division of Baker Publishing Group

www.BakerAcademic.com

Published by Baker Academic
a division of Baker Publishing Group
P.O. Box 6287, Grand Rapids, MI 49516-6287
www.bakeracademic.com

Printed in the United States of America

Library of Congress Cataloging-in-Publication Data
McCormack, Bruce L.
    Orthodox and modern : studies in the theology of Karl Barth / Bruce L. McCormack.
        p.   cm.
    Includes bibliographical references and index.
    ISBN 978-0-8010-3582-1 (pbk.)
    1. Barth, Karl, 1886–1968. I. Title.
BX4827.B3M38 2008
230'.044'092—dc22   2008019879

Contents

Abbreviations

CD   Karl Barth. *Church Dogmatics*. Edited by Geoffrey Bromiley and Thomas F. Torrance. Translated by G. T. Thomson. 5 vols. in 14 parts. Edinburgh: T&T Clark, 1936–1977

KD   Karl Barth. *Die kirchliche Dogmatik*. 5 vols. in 14 parts. Zollikon, Switz.: Verlag der Evangelischen Buchhandlun, 1932–1970

Introduction

"*Modern . . . and yet orthodox*": for many, such a description will seem to be a contradiction in terms. An explanation why this is not so will require close attention to each term. Perhaps the best place to begin is with a bit of personal biography—which will also shed considerable light on the motives which led to the writing of the essays contained in this volume.

The interpretive traditions in which I find myself most at home as a Barth researcher are European rather than American. This needs to be stated at the outset if the essays in this volume are to be understood well—which is to say, understood contextually and in terms of their basic intentions. In part, this is due to the fact that I first gained entrée to Barth's theology through Eberhard Jüngel's *God's Being Is in Becoming*, which I read in preparation for my doctoral qualifying exams in 1982. For the first time, the whole of Barth's theology was opened up to me in a way that made sense of the details. To that book I owe my most basic commitments as a Barth researcher. This already marks an important difference from those who began their study of Barth under the guidance of Hans Frei, for example—and helps to explain my deviations from the "neo-orthodox" reading, which has shown an impressive ability to reinvent itself in recent years. My starting-point in Jüngel's writings was then further enriched by a Fulbright year at the University of Basel in 1984–1985.

A highlight of that memorable year in Basel was my participation in a German-language *Arbeitsgruppe*—a small circle of friends, led by Niklaus Peter (then a doctoral student at the University of Basel, later managing director of Theologischer Verlag Zürich, and today pastor of the Fraumünster in Zürich). During the winter semester, the object of our study was Barth's book on Anselm, *Fides quaerens intellectum*. The questions which dominated our discussions were finally two: First, is Karl Barth's theology to be regarded as recognizably *modern* in its basic commitments, or is it more rightly understood in terms of a *neoorthodox* repristination of older trains of thought no longer considered viable by the vast majority of European theologians? And second, if Karl Barth's theology, too, is demonstrably modern in character, then what is the meaning of "modernity" in the realm of Christian theology? What is it that makes *any* theology modern rather than ancient?

Where the first of these questions was concerned, leading Barth scholars in Germany at that time were united in the conviction that while Barth's theology might have been many things, "neo-orthodox" was not one of them. Whether the focus of their research was political or more straightforwardly dogmatic, virtually all agreed that Barth's theology constituted a variant within modern theology—Barth's own sharp criticisms of certain tendencies in modern theology notwithstanding.[1] Critics of this central claim were not to be found among adherents but only among those who rejected Barth's theology. And so we wrestled with our questions throughout that semester and on through the remainder of the year.

But obviously, the answer one gives to the first question depends largely upon the answer given to the second. At that time, we looked for answers to the question of what it means to be "modern" in the realm of theology by reading the results of historical research into the intellectual roots of the rise of historical-critical investigation of the Bible. In conjunction with a seminar taught by Uwe Gerber in the university and the discussions spawned by it, I read works by Troeltsch, Ebeling, Scholder, Reventlow, and Hasler, among others.[2] The conviction I came to at that time is one I still hold today: that it was the rise of "historical consciousness"—by which I mean the awareness that all human thinking is conditioned by historical (and cultural) location—that

1. Appreciation of characteristically modern elements in Barth's theology began in earnest in 1972–1973 with the publication of the following: Wolfhart Pannenberg, "Die Subjektivität Gottes und die Trinitätslehre: Ein Beitrag zur Beziehung zwischen Karl Barth und der Philosophie Hegels," in *Grundfragen systematischer Theologie: Gesammelte Aufsätze* (Göttingen: Vandenhoeck & Ruprecht, 1980), 96–111; Trutz Rendtorff, "Radikale Autonomie Gottes: Zum Verständnis der Theologie Karl Barths und ihrer Folgen," in *Theorie des Christentums* (Gütersloh: Gerd Mohn, 1972), 161–81; Friedrich-Wilhelm Marquardt, *Theologie und Sozialismus: Das Beispiel Karl Barths* (Munich: Kaiser, 1972); and Karl Gerhard Steck and Dieter Schellong, *Karl Barth und die Neuzeit* (Munich: Kaiser, 1973). By the time I was studying in Basel, these works had spawned a number of others. See Peter Eicher, *Bürgerliche Religion: Eine theologische Kritik* (Munich: Kösel, 1983); Christoph Gestrich, *Neuzeitliches Denken und die Spaltung der dialektischen Theologie: Zur Frage der natürlichen Theologie* (Tübingen: Mohr, 1977); Wilfried Groll, *Ernst Troeltsch und Karl Barth—Kontinuität im Widerspruch* (Munich: Kaiser, 1976).

2. See Ernst Troeltsch, *Vernunft und Offenbarung bei Johann Gerhard und Melanchthon: Untersuchung zur Geschichte der altprotestantischen Theologie* (Göttingen: Vandenhoeck & Ruprecht, 1891); idem, "Über historische und dogmatische Methode in der Theologie," in *Gesammelte Schriften* (Tübingen: Mohr Siebeck, 1913), 2:729–53; Gerhard Ebeling, "The Significance of the Critical Historical Method for Church and Theology in Protestantism," in *Word and Faith* (London: SCM Press, 1963), 17–61; Klaus Scholder, *Ursprünge und Probleme der historisch-kritischen Theologie* (Munich: Kaiser, 1966); Henning Graf Reventlow, *The Authority of the Bible and the Rise of the Modern World* (London: SCM Press, 1984); Ueli Hasler, *Beherrschte Natur: Die Anpassung der Theologie an die bürgerliche Naturfassung im 19. Jahrhundert (Schleiermacher, Ritschl, Herrmann)* (Bern: Peter Lang, 1982).

was most basic to the emergence of what we tend to think of as "modern" theology today. The most significant preconditions necessary for the emergence of historical consciousness as a culturewide phenomenon in Germany were twofold: first, Kant's limitation of what may be known by the theoretical reason in phenomenal reality and, second, the emergence of early romanticism in Herder and Hamann.[3] It was the confluence of these two developments especially which brought an end to Enlightenment rationalism and made possible the first truly modern theologies. Schleiermacher's relationship to romanticism in his early period is well known. But even Hegel's theology—intended as a reaction to romanticism—embraced its historicizing tendencies to the extent that his "grand meta-narrative" (to borrow the language of the postmodernists) consisted in an understanding of the unfolding of Absolute Spirit which was identified with the history of the world.

Beyond the historicizing tendencies unleashed by the rise of historical consciousness, any truly "modern" theology will also include the following: an acceptance, in principle at the every least, of critical methods for studying the Bible; a recognition of the loss of respect among philosophers for classical metaphysics in all of their (Greek) forms; the recognition of the breakdown of the old Aristotelian-biblical cosmology in the course of the seventeenth century; and acceptance of the necessity of constructing doctrines of creation and providence which find their ground in more modern theological and/or philosophical resources.[4] Negotiable elements (i.e., those found in some "modern" theologians but certainly not in all) include the following: a relatively positive stance towards evolutionary science (the fact that evolutionary theory came into existence only *after* the rise of "modern" theology ought to be sufficient to demonstrate that complete acceptance is not a necessary feature of all modern theologies); and nonfoundationalism and opposition to natural theology. Though many recent postmodern accounts of the "modern" would like to make foundationalism the hallmark of all "modern" theologies and therefore essential to the definition, it is hardly the case that all "modern" theologians were foundationalists. Some among the Hegelians might be argued to be (Ernst Troeltsch comes immediately to mind), but Schleiermacher certainly was not. Nor were the "outsiders" who owed so much to him (e.g., Søren Kierkegaard and J. T. Beck).

Where, then, does Barth stand when measured by the foregoing criteria? The most conspicuous feature of the earliest form of Barth's dialectical theology was its antimetaphysical stance in the matter of theological epistemology. The Barth of the second *Romans* commentary especially was concerned to

---

3. On the importance of Johann Georg Hamann and Johann Gottfried Herder for the emergence of romanticism, see Isaiah Berlin, *The Roots of Romanticism* (Princeton, NJ: Princeton University Press, 1999).

4. On the breakdown of the Aristotelian-biblical synthesis in matters of cosmology, see John Dillenberger, *Protestant Thought and Natural Science: An Historical Interpretation* (Westport, CT: Greenwood, 1977).

overcome what he saw as the domestication of God by "neo-Protestant" or "liberal" theology in the nineteenth century. This concern manifested itself in an attempt to speak of God on the grounds of God's Self-revelation alone rather than on the basis of either classical metaphysics or modern personalist philosophies. The fact that Barth devoted so many pages of his writings in this phase to criticizing neo-Protestant theology tended to conceal the extent to which his antimetaphysical stance was itself a distinctively modern option in theology.

My own contribution to the European discussion of Barth's relation to modernity was to demonstrate the extent to which Kant and the later Marburg neo-Kantianism influenced not only his earliest "liberal" theology (prior to 1915) but also decisively stamped his dialectical theology.[5] From Kant, Barth took the view that human knowing is the consequence of the synthesizing activities of the mind (the combination of intuited sense data with the categories of the understanding). Barth would never see any serious reason to question this basic epistemological commitment later—though his attachment to it was always relative, never absolute. The result was a concept of revelation which laid great emphasis upon the dialectic of divine unveiling in and through the veil of a Self-chosen creaturely medium. Revelation is therefore understood by Barth as an *act* of Self-mediation in the execution of which God remains ontologically other than the chosen medium—and therefore hidden in it. What Barth took from Marburg neo-Kantianism, on the other hand, was his understanding of actualism as having not only an epistemological but an ontological significance. For Hermann Cohen, the founder of Marburg neo-Kantianism, the human simply *is* the sum total of his or her lifetime of knowing activities. Expressed more expansively: the human is what he or she does. It was but a short step from here to reflection upon the divine nature as actualistic—a point which Barth would begin to ground christologically just two and a half years after publishing his second *Romans*.[6]

5. See Bruce L. McCormack, *Karl Barth's Critically Realistic Dialectical Theology: Its Genesis and Development, 1909–1936* (Oxford: Clarendon, 1995), 43–49, 129–30, 207–9, 218–26, 235–40, 245–66, 464–67; idem, "Die theologiegeschichtliche Ort Karl Barths," in *Karl Barth in Deutschland (1921–1935): Aufbruch–Klärung–Widerstand,* ed. Michael Beintker, Christian Link, and Michael Trowitzsch (Zurich: Theologischer Verlag, 2005), 15–40. In the same year in which my book appeared, the question of the influence of neo-Kantianism in particular was addressed more fully in Johann Friedrich Lohmann, *Karl Barth und der Neukantianismus: Die Rezeption des Neukantianismus im "Römerbrief " und ihre Bedeutung für die weitere Ausarbeitung der Theologie Karl Barths* (Berlin and New York: Walter de Gruyter, 1995). Subsequent contributions to this area of investigation include D. Paul LaMontagne, "Barth and Rationality: Critical Realism in Theology" (PhD diss., Princeton Theological Seminary, 2001); Clifford Blake Anderson, "The Crisis of Theological Science: A Contextual Study of the Development of Karl Barth's Concept of Science from 1901–1923" (PhD diss., Princeton Theological Seminary, 2005).

6. See Karl Barth, *The Göttingen Dogmatics: Instruction in the Christian Religion,* trans. Geoffrey Bromiley (Grand Rapids: Eerdmans, 1991), 1:131–67.

Where the other dimensions of the foregoing definition of "modern" theology are concerned, Barth embraced the critical study of the Bible in principle from the very beginning (though he made himself free to be critical of the critics, too!). And he took for granted the breakdown of the older Protestant synthesis of Aristotle and the Bible in his thinking about creation and providence. Beyond these points, where the negotiable items of belief among "modern" theologians were concerned, Barth showed himself to be a member in good standing of the Schleiermacherian tradition in his opposition to natural theology as well as in his "nonfoundationalism." And he saw no merit in seeking to oppose evolution but contented himself with the understanding that this theory belongs to natural science and is not therefore something which a Christian understanding of creation ought either to support or contend against.

The only remaining element in my earlier attempt to establish the meaning of "modernity" in the realm of theology has to do with the tendency to historicize. This element comes more strongly to the fore in the later volumes of the *Church Dogmatics*—after Barth's revision of the doctrine of election in *CD* II/2. The central idea here is that God's eternal election of himself to be God "for us" in Jesus Christ is an act in which God constitutes his being as a being for historical existence (i.e., the incarnate life, death, and resurrection of Jesus of Nazareth). In *CD* IV especially, his thinking about Christology began to draw nearer to Hegel. Barth thereby established both the relative validity and the proper limits of the historicizing tendencies of the previous century and a half. The relative validity lay in God's determination that God's being should be a being in the becoming that is the history of Jesus. The limit—and this is significant—lay in the fact that this act of Self-determination was a *free* act on the part of God, not a necessary one.

The result of this move was that the later volumes of the *Church Dogmatics* are far more explicitly "modern" in their commitments than were the earlier volumes. Still, all of this was but a consistent application of Barth's earlier actualism.

Returning to my personal narrative for just a moment: I came home from Basel in September 1985 to a different theological situation from the one I had left. Almost overnight, American theologians seemed to have decided that "modernity" was over, that we were now in a "postmodern" moment. While my European colleagues and I had been trying to understand the meaning of "modernity," a fair number of Americans had declared "modernity" over and done with! The first indication that this new situation might have an impact on Barth studies had, in fact, appeared before my departure in the form of a dissertation by Steven G. Smith, published in

1983.[7] But the greatest impact of so-called postmodernity on Barth studies lay in the future. Books by Walter Lowe, Graham Ward, and William
Stacy Johnson appeared around the same time as my own.[8] In my view, the
most significant defect in postmodern readings of Barth—aside from the
tendency of its creators to make of "alterity" a principle which is then read
into Barth—is the lack of historical awareness which comes to expression in
them. I regard what is called the "postmodern" in theology to be a variant
of romanticism. But precisely as such, it is not something that comes *after*
modern theology (as its name implies) but something which belongs to one
of the two principal trends of thought which created modern theology in the
first place. It is an inclination towards the fragmentary, the provisional, the
open-ended, the eclectic. This is its link to the romanticism of a Friedrich
Schlegel, for example.[9] The difference is that romanticism in its originating form was characterized by a turn *to* history whereas postmodernism
(in its Anglo-American theological representatives) is engaged in a flight
from history.[10]

7. Steven G. Smith, *The Argument to the Other: Reason beyond Reason in the Thought of
Karl Barth and Emmanuel Levinas* (Chico, CA: Scholars Press, 1983).

8. Walter Lowe, *Theology and Difference: The Wound of Reason* (Bloomington, IN: Indiana
University Press, 1993); Graham Ward, *Barth, Derrida and the Language of Theology* (Cambridge:
Cambridge University Press, 1995); William Stacy Johnson, *The Mystery of God: Karl Barth and
the Postmodern Foundations of Theology* (Louisville: Westminster John Knox, 1997).

9. Jack Forstman has suggested that Friedrich Schlegel's romanticism was born out of a rejection of the harmonies, the sameness, the confident system-building of the Enlightenment. Schlegel
understood human thought to oscillate constantly between two poles: infinite unity on the one side
and infinite chaos on the other. Neither the unity which would be provided by an Absolute ground
nor the pure chaos of a completely disordered mass of particulars is accessible to thought; rather,
they constitute the limits within which thought does its work. That the particulars are thought at
all means that they are thought in combination with other particulars, that coherences between
them are observed and established. But this process can never lead to an absolute ground. "The
consciousness of this as the human condition is the occasion of irony"—the realization that no
matter how far understanding reaches, it will never comprehend reality in any total sense. "The
impulse to understand is inevitable; the impossibility of complete understanding is insuperable.
One must be serious about one's understanding; one can only smile at its feebleness with reference to the infinity of the task. This combination of earnestness and jest, of seriousness and
playfulness is the essence of irony in Schlegel's thought" (Jack Forstman, *A Romantic Triangle:
Schleiermacher and Early German Romanticism* [Missoula, MT: Scholars Press, 1977], 8, 3).

10. The flight from history is rather easily explained where American theologians are concerned. Having spent part of his career in Germany and part in America, Paul Tillich was in a
unique position to explain the major difference between the way theology is done in Europe and
the way it is done here: "If you should come from Europe to America as I did thirty years ago,
you would be astonished at how much more Americans are dependent on the eighteenth century
than Europeans. The reason is very simple. America experienced very little of the romanticist
reaction against the eighteenth century" (*A History of Christian Thought: From Its Judaic and
Hellenistic Origins to Existentialism* [New York: Simon & Schuster, 1967–1968], 299). America
was born in the Enlightenment, and although it had its romantics, romanticism never impacted
its culture in the way it did Europe's. And in any case, we had no past to which to return. We

In response to this newer movement, my own work (after the appea of my book) became much more historical and concerned itself with u..cov-ering antecedents of Barth's theology in the nineteenth century (above all, in Schleiermacher).[11] It also concerned itself with issues surrounding Barth's theological ontology, in the conviction that Barth's superiority to postmodern efforts to provide a theological response to human suffering was demonstrated through his ability to ground in the divine being itself the suffering which brings an end to all suffering. This has led me increasingly to an interest in Christology, election, and Trinity (in that order).[12]

But what of my other term—"orthodox"? In what sense do I mean to employ this term in relation to Barth's theology? "Orthodoxy" means "right teaching" or "right doctrine." But what and who determines what is "right teaching"? The what-question is more easily answered. For any Protestant theologian worth his or her salt, the material norm of what can and must be said within the bounds of Christian dogmatics can be only Holy Scripture. But Scripture must be interpreted—and it is at this point that the who-question becomes pressing. Protestantism in its originating form did not really differ from Catholicism in its insistence that the proper "subject" of theology is finally a church and individuals only as servants of the Word in and for a church—"doctors of the church," in other words. It was for this reason that Calvin could insist that confessions of a church ought not to be written by an individual but by a company of learned pastors. In cases of doctrinal conflict, he wrote, "we indeed willingly concede, if any discussion arises over doctrine, that the best and surest remedy is for a synod of true bishops to be convened, where the doctrine at issue may be examined. Such a definition, upon which the pastors of the church in common, invoking Christ's Spirit, agree, will have much more weight than if each one, having conceived it separately at home, should teach it to the people, or if a few private individuals should compose it. Then, when the bishops are assembled, they can more conveniently deliberate in common what they ought to teach and in what form, lest diversity breed offense."[13] But he could also say, "Whenever the decree of any council is brought forward, I

were forward looking, a country possessed with a "manifest destiny." A well-developed historical consciousness never took root here—not even in the 1960s and 1970s, when interest in hermeneutical questions was high.

11. See the essays contained in part 1 of this volume.

12. See the essays contained in part 3 of this volume. The reader may also wish to consult the following essays: Bruce L. McCormack, "The Actuality of God: Karl Barth in Conversation with Open Theism," in *Engaging the Doctrine of God: Contemporary Protestant Perspectives*, ed. Bruce L. McCormack (Grand Rapids: Baker Academic, 2008), 185–242; idem, "Divine Impassibility or Simply Divine Constancy? Implications of Karl Barth's Later Christology for Debates over Impassibility," in *Divine Impassibility and the Mystery of Human Suffering*, ed. James F. Keating and Thomas Joseph White (Grand Rapids: Eerdmans, 2008).

13. John Calvin, *Institutes of Christian Religion*, ed. John T. McNeill, trans. Ford Lewis Battles (Philadelphia: Westminster, 1975), IV.ix.13.

should like men first of all diligently to ponder at what time it was held, on what issue, and with what intention, what sort of men were present; then to examine by the standard of Scripture what it dealt with—and to do this in such a way that the definition of the council may have its weight and be like a provisional judgment, yet not hinder the examination I have mentioned."[14] Both traditional Protestantism and traditional Catholicism held that a church must finally decide questions of controversy. For both, the ancient councils and their creeds and definitions have a high degree of authority as interpretations of Holy Scripture. But for the older Protestants, the ancient councils were not to be regarded as irreformable—and that marked a major difference from the Catholic view. Protestants also believed that the confessions of their own churches constituted a relatively binding, authoritative interpretation of and/ or addition to the ancient councils and, as a consequence, had to be taken with as much seriousness as the pronouncements of the ecumenical councils.

I say all of this to indicate that even the ecumenical creeds are only provisional statements. They are only relatively binding as definitions of what constitutes "orthodoxy." Ultimately, orthodox teaching is that which conforms *perfectly* to the Word of God as attested in Holy Scripture. But given that such perfection is not attainable in this world, it is understandable that Karl Barth should have regarded "Dogma" as an eschatological concept.[15] The "dogmas" (i.e., the teachings formally adopted and promulgated by individual churches) are witnesses to *the* Dogma and stand in a relation of greater or lesser approximation to it. But they do not attain to it perfectly—hence, the inherent reformability of all "dogmas." Orthodoxy is not therefore a static, fixed reality; it is a body of teachings which have arisen out of, and belong to, a *history* which is as yet incomplete and constantly in need of reevaluation.

All of this is relevant to an evaluation of Karl Barth's "orthodoxy." On the face of it, it would seem to be very hard to deny to anyone who affirms, as Barth does, the doctrine of the Trinity, a two-natures Christology, the virgin birth, the bodily resurrection, the visible return of Christ, the immutability of God, and so on, the honorific of "orthodox." And yet the issue is not quite so simple. The truth is that Barth has not simply taken over unchanged *any* doctrinal formulation of the ancient or the Reformation churches. He has reconstructed the whole of "orthodox" teaching from the ground up. It is not the case that he simply tinkered with the machinery. What he did was to ask, in the case of each piece of authoritative teaching, exactly what Calvin would have him ask: What was at issue? What was the intention? How was it formulated? Did the formulation do justice to the theological subject matter to which it sought to bear witness? And most important, perhaps, is it necessary to affirm the philosophical commitments which aided the ancients and the

14. Ibid., IV.ix.8.
15. CD I/1:269.

Reformers in their efforts to articulate the theological subject matters under consideration? Or may one draw upon more modern philosophies in one's efforts to explain the creeds and confessions today?

My own view is this: what Barth was doing, in the end, was seeking to understand what it means to be orthodox *under the conditions of modernity*. This is the explanation, I think, for the freedom he exhibited over against the decrees of the ecumenical councils and the confessions of his own Reformed tradition. He took the creeds and the confessions seriously—how could he not, believing as he did in the virgin birth and so forth? But he did not follow them slavishly. His was a confessionalism of the spirit and never of the letter. This is why he was willing to think for long stretches with the help of Kant's epistemology and (later) Hegelian ontology. This is why he was willing to set forth an actualistic understanding of divine and human being. Still, I would argue, his reconstruction of Christian orthodoxy succeeded in upholding all of the theological values that were in play in its originating formulations. For this reason, Barth was both modern *and orthodox*.

The essays contained in this volume were all written after the appearance of my book in 1995. Taken together, they constitute a record of how my thinking has progressed and where it is now headed. To that end, revision has been kept to a minimum.

Part 1 begins with an essay on the place of Barth in the discussions of the independence of religion and/or theology which took place at the end of the nineteenth and the beginning of the twentieth centuries. There follow two more essays which seek to assess Barth's relationship to the Schleiermacherian tradition. The fourth essay, on Barth's hermeneutics, helps to locate his work against the background of one of the most seminal developments in German theology in the 1920s.

Part 2 contains responses to postliberal and postmodern readings of Barth. When I wrote these essays, postmodern readings were very much in vogue. Today the tendency of Anglo-American Barth research is decidedly away from the postmodern and towards the postliberal—accompanied by the attempt to make Barth seem more orthodox (in the classical sense of the word) than he actually was. Were I now to write something on postmodern readings of Barth, I think I could afford to be more generous (since they do not pose the threat they once did).

Part 3 contains the essays which have set the course of my most recent work. As this book goes to press, I am still adding to the number of essays in which I seek not only to defend my point of view as a Barth scholar but also to elaborate this point of view more fully in relation to other doctrines treated by Barth after the revision of his doctrine of election in *CD* II/2. The cutting edge of Barth scholarship in the coming years will be centered in contextualized readings of *Church Dogmatics*. The day when *Church Dogmatics* could be read as though it had been written in the space of a single afternoon, as though every part were fully consistent with all the others, is over. The real challenge now is to understand how Barth's mind changed even as he was writing his magnum opus over the thirty-five-year period from 1932 to 1967.

Part 4 contains essays written on various occasions. The occasion for the first was a daylong conference which celebrated the signing of an agreement between the Center for Barth Studies at Princeton Theological Seminary and the Karl Barth-Stiftung and Nachlaßkommission. With the help of a Lilly Grant, Princeton Theological Seminary had paid for the digitizing of materials found in the Karl Barth-Archiv in order to ensure the survival of materials which were suffering degeneration because they had been written on acid-based papers. The Stiftung and the Nachlaßkommission showed their appreciation by giving to Princeton Seminary copies of all digitized materials (including photographs). The agreement ensured protections and proper uses. The second essay in this section was given at an international doctoral colloquium, held at the Friedrich Schiller University in Jena, Germany. The third essay is, as the title clearly indicates, the foreword to the German translation of *Karl Barth's Critically Realistic Dialectical Theology*. In it, I seek to assess the responses the book received in the English-speaking world—in an effort to provide my German friends with a sense of the trajectories of Anglo-American research in the last decade. The collection concludes with two reviews. The first assesses the importance of neo-Kantianism for Barth's theology; the second makes the provocative suggestion that there is indeed a form of an "analogy of being" in Barth's theology.[16]

I wish to express my sincere thanks to Dr. Keith L. Johnson, who did the copyediting and formatting required to turn these essays into a book. My best wishes to Keith as he takes up his duties as assistant professor of theology at Wheaton College this fall.

16. This is a thesis I defended more fully in a paper ("The Analogy of Being: Invention of the Anti-Christ or the Wisdom of God") presented at a Roman Catholic–sponsored colloquium at the Dominican House of Studies and Pope John Paul II Cultural Center in Washington DC on April 4–6, 2008, devoted to the theme of the *analogia entis*.

Part 1

Karl Barth's Relationship to Nineteenth-Century Theology

1

Revelation and History in Transfoundationalist Perspective

Karl Barth's Theological Epistemology in Conversation with a Schleiermacherian Tradition

Introduction

In an essay published in 1924, Rudolf Bultmann made a claim which must surely be startling to most Anglo-American readers today:

> In the polemic of the latest theological movement—a movement which is particularly associated with the names of Barth and Gogarten, the attack against the so-called liberal theology is not to be understood as a repudiation of its own past, but as a discussion with that past. The new movement is not a revival of orthodoxy, but rather a carefully reasoned consideration of the consequences which have resulted from the situation brought about by liberal theology. It is no accident that the latest movement originated not from within orthodoxy but out of liberal theology. Barth was a student at Marburg, Gogarten at Heidelberg, Thurneysen at both.[1]

This essay was originally published in a slightly different form under the title "Revelation and History in Transfoundationalist Perspective: Karl Barth's Theological Epistemology in Conversation with a Schleiermacherian Tradition," in *Journal of Religion* 78 (1998): 18–37. Reprinted by permission.

1. Rudolf Bultmann, "Liberal Theology and the Latest Theological Movement," in *Faith and Understanding* (Philadelphia: Fortress, 1987), 28.

Not surprisingly perhaps, there are those who have been willing to grant the validity of this claim with regard to Gogarten and Bultmann himself. But Barth? Surely Bultmann's reading of Barth rests on a misunderstanding.[2]

Where Barth was concerned, the basis for Bultmann's claim had been laid two years earlier in his review of the second edition of Barth's commentary on Romans, and it is this passage especially that I would like to reflect on for a moment.

> Karl Barth's *Epistle to the Romans* may be characterized by one sentence, the formulation of which he would contest but which would still be valid in terms of the use of language which is customary to this point in time. The book wants to prove *the independence and the absolute nature of religion*. It thus places itself—though in the original form of a commentary—in the same line with such works as Schleiermacher's *Speeches On Religion* and Otto's *The Idea of the Holy*; with modern attempts to demonstrate a religious a priori. . . . However different all these attempts may be in detail, they seek to give verbal expression to the consciousness of the uniqueness and absoluteness of religion.[3]

Bultmann was right: Barth would not have accepted the terms employed in this description.

Barth was not in the least interested in demonstrating a religious a priori; quite the contrary. We might accurately state Barth's concern by saying that he was interested in proclaiming the independence of revelation and, with that, an ineradicable difference between the knowledge of God and the knowledge of creaturely (empirical or nonempirical) reality. Still, Bultmann's reading was not simply mistaken. Barth's attempt to establish the independence of revelation *did* belong to a tradition of thought whose source lay in Friedrich Schleiermacher's effort to make religion independent of metaphysics and ethics.

In what follows, I am going to interpret Karl Barth as a nineteenth-century theologian. But I should point out that such an attempt goes against the grain of much recent Barth research—in the English-speaking world at any rate.[4] At the present, Barth is most often understood as a nonfoundationalist narrative theologian and, for some, as a precursor of postmodern, even

---

2. See Robert Morgan, "Ernst Troeltsch and the Dialectical Theology," in *Ernst Troeltsch and the Future of Theology*, ed. John Powell Clayton (Cambridge: Cambridge University Press, 1976), 33–77.

3. Rudolf Bultmann, "Karl Barths 'Römerbrief' in zweiter Auflage," in *Anfänge der dialektischen Theologie*, ed. Jürgen Moltmann (Munich: Kaiser, 1977), 1:119; translated as "Karl Barth's *Epistle to the Romans* in Its Second Edition," in *The Beginnings of Dialectic Theology*, ed. James M. Robinson (Richmond: John Knox, 1968), 100.

4. The attempt to establish links between Schleiermacher and Barth—even on the methodological level—are not uncommon in European Barth research. See esp. Wolfhart Pannenberg, *Systematic Theology*, trans. Geoffrey Bromiley (Grand Rapids: Eerdmans, 1991), 1:40–48.

deconstructionist tendencies.[5] Against such readings,[6] I would contend that the wealth of problems to which Barth addressed himself were, in many cases, given their characteristic shape as a result of nineteenth-century developments and that even his solutions to those problems often took up elements of nineteenth-century solutions and transformed them by placing them in a different framework of thought. In this essay, I want to direct my attention to just one of those problems: the problem of the independence of religion or, as Barth would have preferred, the independence of revelation.

The argument will be developed in three sections: (1) the independence of religion in Schleiermacher and Herrmann; (2) Barth's transformation of the independence of religion into the independence of revelation by means of a new theological epistemology in his second commentary on *Romans* (1922); and (3) Barth's christological revision of his theological epistemology in his Göttingen lectures on dogmatics (1924–1925). I will conclude with some programmatic suggestions regarding the tasks which a proper understanding of Barth's theological epistemology places on the theological agenda today.

The Independence of Religion in Schleiermacher and Herrmann

As we shall see in a moment, the central problem addressed by the famous second edition of Barth's *Römerbrief* is that of the knowledge of God.[7] It was not just a problem for him, however; the question of whether and how God is known stood at the heart of theological reflection in the modern period.

5. On Barth as a narrative or "intratextual" theologian, see George A. Lindbeck, *The Nature of Doctrine: Religion and Theology in a Postliberal Age* (Philadelphia: Westminster, 1984); idem, "Barth and Textuality," *Theology Today* 43 (1986): 361–76; and (more cautiously) Hans W. Frei, *Types of Christian Theology* (New Haven: Yale University Press, 1992). On the more recent poststructuralist or postmodern reading of Barth, see the following: Stephen Webb, *Refiguring Theology: The Rhetoric of Karl Barth* (Albany: State University of New York Press, 1991); Richard Roberts, *A Theology on Its Way? Essays on Karl Barth* (Edinburgh: T&T Clark, 1991); Walter Lowe, *Theology and Difference: The Wound of Reason* (Bloomington, IN: Indiana University Press, 1993); Graham Ward, "Barth and Postmodernism," *New Blackfriars* 74 (1993): 550–56; and idem, *Barth, Derrida and the Language of Theology* (Cambridge: Cambridge University Press, 1995).

6. This is not the place to mount an argument against such misreadings of Barth. The reader is referred to ch. 5, "Beyond Nonfoundational and Postmodern Readings of Barth: Critically Realistic Dialectical Theology," in this volume. See also Bruce L. McCormack, review of *Barth, Derrida and the Language of Theology*, by Graham Ward, *Scottish Journal of Theology* 49 (1996): 97–109.

7. On the centrality of the problem of the knowledge of God in Karl Barth's theological development, see, above all, Ingrid Spieckermann, *Gotteserkenntnis: Ein Beitrag zur Grundfrage der neuen Theologie Karl Barths* (Munich: Kaiser, 1985). For a systematic discussion of the fundamental importance of the theme for Barth's theology as a whole, see Walter Kreck, *Grundentscheidungen in Karl Barths Dogmatik* (Neukirchen: Neukirchener Verlag, 1978).

The problem had been created by the coincidence of two developments: the rise of biblical criticism with its concomitant distinction of revelation from the Bible and the much celebrated "turn to the subject" which occurred in philosophy from Descartes through Kant. It was, above all, Kant's limitation of theoretical knowing to the intuitable which made knowledge of God so deeply problematic to modern theologians. For if God is a transcendent, wholly spiritual being as the Christian tradition maintained, then God is unintuitable and—if Kant's restriction holds—cannot be known. Moreover, Kant had also shown that the attempt made by traditional metaphysics to overcome this limitation resulted invariably in antinomies. The result was that Kant reduced God to a regulative idea wholly lacking in content, a postulated Guarantor of the meaningfulness of moral behavior.

Schleiermacher's response to this challenge, as is well known, was to assign the origins of religion to a region of human being and existence which he called "feeling." Feeling, as Schleiermacher described it, is not a faculty standing alongside intellect and will. It is distinguished from knowing and doing in two ways. First, unlike knowing and doing—each of which involves a self-movement of the human subject towards something which lies without—feeling "is not effected by the subject, but simply takes place in the subject." Feeling, in other words, belongs wholly to the realm of receptivity.[8] Second, and even more basically, the Source of this feeling does not belong to the series of "objects" known and acted upon by the human subject but is to be fundamentally distinguished from them. That this is so is something Schleiermacher knows through reflection upon the essential content of piety in all its diverse forms of expression. Schleiermacher describes this essential content in a well-known formula: "The self-identical essence of piety is this: the consciousness of being absolutely dependent, or, which is the same thing, of being in relation with God."[9] That humans are conscious of being absolutely dependent upon an Other for the whole of their receptive and active lives sets that Other apart from all other objects of our experience. For with respect to the "world"—that is, the totality of the "objects" belonging to nature or human society—we are not absolutely dependent. Rather, we are relatively dependent (in that such objects or persons can exercise an influence on us) and relatively free (in that we, in turn, can exercise an influence on them). To put it another way, humans stand in a relationship of reciprocity with respect to the "world." Not so with respect to God. God, as the Whence of our feeling of absolute dependence, may not be given directly to us as intuitable objects and persons are given; for in that case, we could exercise a counterinfluence upon God and would not be *absolutely* dependent upon God. "Any possibility of God being in any

8. Friedrich Schleiermacher, *The Christian Faith*, trans. H. R. Mackintosh (Philadelphia: Fortress, 1976), §3,3, p. 8.
9. Ibid., §4 (definition), p. 12.

way *given* is entirely excluded, because anything that is outwardly given must be given as an object exposed to our counter-influence, however slight this may be. The transference of the idea of God to any perceptible object . . . is always a corruption, whether it be a temporary transference, i.e., a theophany, or a constitutive transference, in which God is represented as permanently a particular perceptible existence."[10] So, if it is true that there is a Source of our feeling of absolute dependence, then that Source will have to be—if I may be permitted the phrase—"wholly other" than the totality of intuitable objects.[11] In sum, feeling is to be located at a different level of human being and existence than knowing and doing and is prior to both.

It is clear what Schleiermacher has gained from this move. Kant had made theoretical knowledge of God an impossibility. Schleiermacher has located a point of access to God—or, more accurately, a point in human consciousness of God's access to us—which overcomes the restrictions Kant placed on theoretical knowledge without recourse to practical knowledge. The knowledge of God is a special kind of knowledge which is distinguished from all other acts of knowing by the fact that here a *purely* receptive moment is involved. Knowledge of God, if it is truly to be knowledge, must somehow *include* the theoretical; and yet the limitations of the theoretical are transcended through the exercise of divine power on the level of feeling.

To see how this takes place, we must look at a particular example. In the realm of Christianity, consciousness of God on the level of feeling is aroused and strengthened through the stimulus provided by (1) the hearing of the Word about Jesus proclaimed by the community of faith and (2) the impression made by the lives of the redeemed men and women found in that community. Thus, knowledge of God takes its rise in the coincidence of the external and the internal; theoretical knowledge acts as a spur to enliven a redemptive power which, to this point, had been (unconsciously or consciously) suppressed. To put it another way: revelation has both an objective and a subjective moment. The objective moment is constituted by the impression made by Jesus on the lives of his disciples which is mediated historically by the Christian community. The subjective moment is constituted by the "commandeering" (grasping, enlivening) of a weak (up to then) and undeveloped God-consciousness.

Now it must be conceded with respect to these two moments that the subjective has a certain priority. What occurs on the level of feeling prior to the encounter with the Christian community has, after all, the character of an original revelation.[12] Given that this is so, it will never be possible to completely eliminate the suspicion that the picture of Jesus which has

10. Ibid., §4,4, p. 18.

11. Ibid., p. 16: "This 'Whence' is not the world, in the sense of the totality of temporal existence, and still less is it any single part of the world." Cf. §105, postscript, p. 474: "The difference [*Abstand*] between God and every finite being is infinite."

12. Ibid., §4,4, p. 17.

been found both in the witness of Scripture and in the proclamation of the church has been carefully tailored to the needs of an understanding of redemption whose chief features are the product of a particular philosophical construal of human subjectivity. Still, in fairness to Schleiermacher, it has to be said that he makes every possible effort to confirm his reading of Christian experience of redemption through close attention to Scripture and tradition. Those who, in their own way (I have in mind my fellow Barthians), are equally committed to making theological knowledge a special kind of knowledge will be well advised to proceed charitably with Schleiermacher. For they too will inevitably be regarded with suspicion by those who give priority to secular knowledge and experience in their efforts to defend the rationality of Christian belief.

At the end of the nineteenth century, the theme of the independence of religion underwent a radicalization due, above all, to the work of Wilhelm Herrmann (the chief theological mentor of both Rudolf Bultmann and Karl Barth). The primary source of this radicalization lay in Herrmann's commitment to the so-called Marburg neo-Kantianism of his philosophical colleagues Hermann Cohen and Paul Natorp. The great advance (if that is what it was) of the neo-Kantians over Kant lay in their rejection of his residual realism. For Kant, the content of human knowledge at least, if not the form, came from without and was received through the senses. Over against this, Cohen held that there is nothing given to thought which is not itself the creation of thought. Thought, in other words, provides not only the form of the objects known; it also *generates* the contents of its objects.[13] For Cohen, then, being is a function of thought; his was a wholly constructivist epistemology. For his part, Herrmann was happy to grant the validity of Cohenian epistemology insofar as it touched on knowledge of the "world." But if the being of God were "known" in this way, then it too would be a human construct (full stop) and the objective reality of God would be placed in serious doubt.

For this reason above all, Herrmann followed Schleiermacher in insisting on the independence of religion. But his approach to the problem differed from Schleiermacher's in two ways. First, he did not make "feeling" to be the (created) ground in human consciousness of the relationship to God. He did not deny that feeling was an essential part of consciousness, but he maintained that the source of this feeling was natural law or the unity at the heart of things. It was not the God of faith.[14] Thus, the ground of faith is something that is given by God in the individual's encounter with God. As such, it is not something that is generally available. Second and most important for our

13. Bruce L. McCormack, *Karl Barth's Critically Realistic Dialectical Theology: Its Genesis and Development, 1909–1936* (Oxford: Clarendon, 1995), 44.
14. Ibid., 57.

purposes here, Herrmann repressed the role played by knowledge in revelation more thoroughly than Schleiermacher had. Schleiermacher had not doubted the ability of the historian to identify those features in the life and teachings of Jesus through which he had made a saving impression on his followers. Herrmann, by contrast, drove a wedge between the inner life of Jesus on the one hand and his teachings and works of love on the other, and he did so because he believed that these merely external features belong to the realm governed by the constructivist epistemology of the neo-Kantians.[15] Along similar lines, Schleiermacher had held that the proclamation of the Word (a Word with a more-or-less definite content) played an essential role in the *mediation* of revelation to the individual by the Christian community, whereas Herrmann treated the content of the message as having less significance. For Herrmann, such doctrinal expressions were highly individual in character because the experience that they sought to interpret was highly individual. As such, they could, at most, provide the *occasion* for the religious experience of another. In sum: Herrmann remained as convinced as Schleiermacher that the Christ outside us (whose redemptive influence entered into the stream of history) *is* the Christ in us, but theoretical knowledge played almost no role in the confirmation of this belief. For confirmation, the believer was to be referred to a self-authenticating religious experience. It was not without good reason, then, that Ernst Troeltsch should have seen in Herrmann a radical example of what he called "the agnostic theory of religious knowledge."[16] And on this point at least, Troeltsch was undoubtedly right. It is a mistake to want to banish all that can properly be called "knowledge" from the sphere of religion as Herrmann seemed bent on doing.

To conclude this consideration of Schleiermacher and Herrmann: the theme of the independence of religion was a decisive one for defining a very significant tradition in modern theology, a tradition to which Karl Barth also belonged. In the years prior to the outbreak of the First World War, his solution to the problem followed that of Herrmann in precise detail.[17] After his "break" with Herrmann, the problem continued to be shaped by the challenge originally posed by Kant. But his new solution represented an attempt to relocate the problem and thereby to transcend Kant's restrictions in what Barth believed to be a way less prone to ideological manipulation and distortion.

15. Ibid., 61.

16. Ernst Troeltsch, "Half a Century of Theology: A Review," in *Ernst Troeltsch: Writings in Theology and Religion*, ed. Robert Morgan and Michael Pye (Atlanta: John Knox, 1977), 58.

17. Karl Barth, "Moderne Theologie und Reichgottesarbeit," *Zeitschrift für Theologie und Kirche* 19 (1909): 317–21; idem, "Der christliche Glaube und die Geschichte," *Schweizerische theologische Zeitschrift* 29 (1912): 1–18, 49–72. For reflection on the Herrmannian character of the positions taken in these essays, see McCormack, *Karl Barth's Critically Realistic Dialectical Theology*, 68–77.

The Independence of Revelation: Theological Epistemology in Barth's Second *Römerbrief*

At the heart of Barth's move beyond Herrmann's existentialized Schleiermacherianism in 1915 was the attempt to articulate a theological epistemology which would more fully integrate with theoretical knowing the special kind of knowledge proper to faith. The motivation for the attempt is well known: Barth was deeply shaken by the ease with which German theologians confused war-hysteria with religious experience at the outset of the First World War. The only way he could see to overcome the weaknesses surrounding a starting-point in religious experience was a new *divine-act* "synthesis" of revelation and reason, faith and knowledge. Revelation, Barth now wanted to say, occurs within the realm of theoretical knowing. If it nevertheless remains a "special" kind of knowing (distinguished from all other acts of theoretical knowing), it is because it has its source in an act of God by means of which the human knowing apparatus described by Kant is "commandeered" (laid hold of, grasped) by God from without and made to conform to God as its object.

To put it this way is to suggest that Barth's "break" with Herrmann did not entail a break with the Kantian tradition where questions of philosophical epistemology were concerned. The restrictions placed by Kant on the knowledge of God still had to be overcome, but now Barth would approach the problem on the basis of a new, critically realistic starting-point. Briefly put, the solution now read: *if the unintuitable God is truly to be known, God must make Godself intuitable.* Whereas Kant and Schleiermacher had left God unintuitable, Barth wanted a conception of a God who could make Godself intuitable. For in that case alone would God be truly knowable in the theoretical sense.[18] But it was not enough that God become intuitable. If God were, so to speak, simply transformed into a creature, God would have placed Godself wholly and without reserve at the mercy of the constructive activities of the human knower. God would have become an object like any other—constructed by human epistemic activity and, as such, the clear possession of the human knower. Such a conclusion would not entail any real advance over a starting-point in religious experience. It too would be subject to ideological manipulation. But Barth's solution, as I have stated it thus far, is incomplete. The complete formulation would be this: If the unintuitable God is truly to be known, God must make Godself intuitable. *But God must do so in such a way that the unintuitability proper to God is not set aside.* With this formal description in place, we are now in a position to look more

---

18. The source of Barth's shift to a concern with the more theoretical aspects of religious knowledge is well known and need not be rehearsed at length here. The ease with which German theologians interpreted the sudden emergence of national unity in the face of an external enemy as a work of the Holy Spirit and as evidence of God's favor caused Barth to seek more solid ground for theology than religious experience.

closely at the material character of the theological epistemology found in the second edition of *Romans*.

The relation of revelation and history—and with it, the contours of Barth's theological epistemology in the second edition of *Romans*—is given classic expression in the following passage:

> "*Jesus Christ our Lord,*" that is the message of salvation, that is the meaning of history. In this name, two worlds encounter and separate from one another, two planes intersect, one known and one unknown. . . . The point on the line of intersection, however, has, like the entire unknown plane whose presence it announces, no extension whatsoever on the plane known to us. The emanation or, much rather, the astonishing bomb-craters and depressions by means of which it makes itself noticeable within the realm of historical intuitability, are, even if they be called the "life of Jesus," not the other world which touches our world in Jesus. And insofar as this, our world, is touched in Jesus by another world, it ceases to be historical, temporal, material, directly intuitable. . . . Jesus as the Christ can *only* be understood as a problem, *only* as myth, within the realm of historical intuitability. Jesus as the Christ brings the world of the Father, of which we who stand within the realm of historical intuitability know nothing and never will know anything. The *resurrection* from the dead, however, is the turning-point, the "fitting in" of that point from above and the corresponding insight from below. The resurrection is the *revelation*, the discovery of Jesus as the Christ, the appearance of God and the knowledge of God in Him, the entrance of the necessity of giving God the glory and reckoning with the Unknown and Unintuitable in Jesus.[19]

For the Barth of the second edition of *Romans*, the resurrection event *is* revelation. But the resurrection is an event which is "unhistorical." By this, Barth did not mean that the resurrection occurred in some other realm than that of the space and time in which we live. The resurrection was already understood by him at that time as a "bodily, corporeal, personal" event.[20] That which happens to a body (whether living or dead makes no real difference) happens in space and time. In stressing the "unhistorical" character of the resurrection, then, what Barth meant to say was that it was not an event to be laid alongside other events. It was not an event produced by forces operative in history. History does not produce something like a bodily resurrection—not in our experience, anyway. For that, an act of God is required. But an act of God is just as unintuitable as the being of God. We may see its effects, but we do not see the thing itself; hence, Barth's insistence that the resurrection event has no extension whatsoever on the historical plane known to us; hence, also, his insistence that Jesus *as the Christ* can be understood only as a problem, as a myth. Seen in material terms, Barth's solution to the problem created by Kant

19. Karl Barth, *Der Römerbrief, 1922* (Zurich: Theologischer Verlag, 1940), 5–6.
20. Ibid., 183.

was to suggest that the unintuitable divine power which was at work in raising Jesus from the dead cast a light backwards, so to speak, on an event which is intuitable, namely, the event of the cross.[21] Light is cast on this event, a power is exercised, so that without setting aside or altering the human cognitive apparatus as described by Kant, the limitations inherent to that apparatus are transcended. The unintuitable God is revealed to faith through the medium of an intuitable event. Revelation reaches its goal in the human recipient, and knowledge of God is realized.

The inadequacy of this formulation of Barth's theological epistemology, as measured by his later work, lies in the fact that God has not really become intuitable at all. Barth clearly wanted to say more than he was in a position to say. The problem created by the unintuitability of God has been overcome in the second edition of *Romans* by means of an appeal to divine power. Ironically perhaps, there is nothing in the appeal itself which would secure it from the suspicion that the divine Reality to which it points is anything more than an idea, a postulated Whence of a particular kind of religious experience.[22] Little wonder, then, that Bultmann was able to see in the second edition of *Romans* a work which maintained contact with Herrmann's theology even as it sought to go beyond him. What is missing from Barth's account is a doctrine of the incarnation. Without this, it would not be possible to speak coherently of *God* becoming intuitable without setting aside God's unintuitability.

Still, what Barth had accomplished to this point was a transformation of the theme of the independence of religion into the independence of revelation. And this would remain a permanent feature of his theology.

Christological Revision in Barth's Göttingen Lectures on Dogmatics

It was the discovery of the Reformed version of an anhypostatic-enhypostatic Christology in Heinrich Heppe's textbook of Reformed theology which prompted Barth, in the spring of 1924, to a new articulation of his theological epistemology.[23] For the Barth of the *Göttingen Dogmatics*, the epistemological

21. Ibid., 132–38. For a closer analysis of these passages, see McCormack, *Karl Barth's Critically Realistic Dialectical Theology*, 251–56.
22. It is to be admitted, however, that it would never be possible to eliminate that suspicion entirely—nor would Barth wish to do so. One cannot lay as much stress on the hiddenness of God in his Self-revelation as Barth did (and would continue to do) without granting a sizable role to the experience of faith—if not as a source of theological reflection, then at least as the confirmation of the claims which emerge from this reflection. Still, if it were possible to say more about God's having become intuitable, then the needle might shift from the subjective moment of revelation back to the objective moment, and other criteria, in addition to the experience of faith, might be brought into play in assessing the truth of the knowledge claim in question—as we shall soon see.
23. See McCormack, *Karl Barth's Critically Realistic Dialectical Theology*, 327–28, 358–67.

significance of the incarnation lies in the fact that God has entered into the realm of historical intuitability through the assumption of a human nature while surrendering nothing of the unintuitability proper to God. To put it this way is to acknowledge that the requirements of Barth's theological epistemology controlled to a considerable degree his appropriation of the classically Reformed model of Christology even as that Christology forced him to significantly revise his theological epistemology. What we catch sight of here is a "correlation" of modern epistemological considerations with traditional christological materials or, expressed in a way which captures the extent to which Barth still remained faithful to the spirit of the Schleiermacherian tradition, a mediation of tradition by means of a modern theological epistemology.[24] To explain this correlation in greater detail is the purpose of this section.

The Christology which Barth sought to mediate was the classically Reformed Christology which, judged in terms of more ancient controversies, belonged to the Alexandrian type. To speak of this Christology as Alexandrian is to call attention to the fact that, like Cyril of Alexandria, the Reformed tradition to which Barth made appeal understood the unity of the divine and human natures in Christ to be a unity of Subject. Not the indwelling of a human subject by a divine Subject but the union of two natures in a single divine Subject (the Person of the Logos) is the view Barth wanted to affirm. He explicitly rejected the Nestorian option (to which he thought that Zwingli, unlike Calvin, had come dangerously close).[25] Thus, all of the attributes proper to each nature are rightly ascribed (realistically and not merely figuratively) to the one Person of the Logos.

Now, if all the attributes proper to Christ's human nature are rightly attributed to the Logos, as the Subject in whom this "nature" has its being and existence grounded from the moment of its creation,[26] then the first half of the requirements of Barth's theological epistemology will have been met, and met in a way which does not suffer from the weakness we observed with respect to the formulation found in the second edition of *Romans*. For if that is the case, then what it means is that the Second Person of the Trinity entered fully into history as the Subject of a human life. God, the Logos, lived as humans lived, suffered and died and was raised from the dead. The epistemological significance of this lies in the fact that God is here seen to have entered fully into the subject-object relation which governs our knowledge of things in this

---

24. In describing Barth's view of revelation as modern, I have in mind, above all, the cogent suggestion of Wolfhart Pannenberg that the concept of divine *Self*-revelation has its origins in Hegel and was perhaps taken over by Barth in a form which linked God's Self-revelation with the thought of its unique, once-and-for-all occurrence in Jesus Christ. See Pannenberg, *Systematic Theology*, 1:223.

25. Karl Barth, "Unterricht in der christlichen Religion" III, §28, pp. 40, 48; typed manuscript in the Karl Barth-Archiv, Basel, Switzerland.

26. Ibid., p. 44.

world. God has fully entered the world of intuitability. Whereas in *Romans* Barth could secure intuitability only by means of an appeal to an exercise of divine power which bridges the gap between unintuitability and intuitability, here it is God—and, Barth would add, the whole of God, complete and undivided[27]—who has become intuitable. The life of Jesus of Nazareth is God's life; his intuitability is God's intuitability.

Seen in the light of possibilities resident in the doctrine of the *communicatio idiomatum*, what Barth has done here comes very close to an affirmation of the so-called *genus tapeinoticum* (literally, the genus of humiliation) though he himself does not put it in these terms and would not have wished to associate himself with the implications given to it by nineteenth-century kenoticists. On Barthian soil, it would have to be taken to mean simply the realistic ascription of human attributes to the Person of the Logos—without entailing any self-emptying of divine attributes. Of course, it must be acknowledged that the affirmation of such a communication raises questions about the ontological conditions for its possibility. How is it possible for God to become human without ceasing to be God? How, in other words, is it possible for God to become human without undergoing change and thereby setting aside that immutability which is proper to God as God? Barth had not as yet fully worked out the conception of divine ontology necessary to explain this possibility and would not until he set forth his mature understanding of election (sometime after 1936).[28] It also must be acknowledged that Barth was here moving in a direction which, for those standing in the Schleiermacherian tradition (though not only for them), looked suspiciously Hegelian. Schleiermacher himself could not have approved of the *genus tapeinoticum*, given his own commitment to a more nearly Platonic conception of the immutability, impassibility, and simplicity of God. But on this point at least, it is Schleiermacher who was the more traditional, and Barth, the more modern. The crucial point, however, is that the life of Jesus is God's life, and his intuitability, God's intuitability.

27. See esp. Karl Barth, *Unterricht in der christlichen Religion*, vol. 1, *Prolegomena, 1924*, ed. Hannelotte Reiffen (Zurich: Theologischer Verlag, 1985), 110–14; translated as *The Göttingen Dogmatics*, trans. Geoffrey Bromiley (Grand Rapids: Eerdmans, 1991), 1:91–93.

28. After 1936 Barth would secure the ontological ground for this action of God in time by means of a doctrine of election according to which the eternal being of God is Self-determined being, a being determined precisely for the outcome which we see occurring in the incarnation. By means of a free, eternal decision, the eternal being of God *in se* (in protology) is constituted by way of anticipation by the incarnation of God in time (and, we must add, by the outpouring of the Spirit in time). Given this understanding of divine ontology, the actualization of this primal decision in history entails no alteration of the eternal being; divine immutability is preserved. But as yet, Barth had not fully worked out the ontological preconditions necessary for the affirmation he makes here, namely, that the life of Jesus is the life of God. Still, there are already present in the Göttingen lectures hints of that which was to come—as, for example, when Barth said that God is "a free Lord" not only "over the principle of non-contradiction but also over His own deity" (*Prolegomena*, 166 [*The Göttingen Dogmatics*, 1:136]).

But what, then, of the other requirement? What of the need for God to remain unintuitable even as God becomes intuitable? To explain Barth's handling of this aspect of the problem, it is necessary to take another look at the doctrine of the *communicatio idiomatum*. In sixteenth- and seventeenth-century Lutheran sacramentology, the desire to affirm a local physical presence of the risen humanity of Christ in the elements of bread and wine led to the affirmation of the so-called *genus majestaticum*—the idea that, as a consequence of the hypostatic union of the two natures, the human nature of Christ participates in the attributes of the divine nature (above all, omnipresence but also omnipotence and omniscience). To this, as Barth rightly observed, the Reformed said an emphatic no. Barth followed the Reformed in rejecting all thought of a "divinization" of the human nature of Jesus:[29] "A principled transgression of the limits of the creaturely does *not* take place in all that which is properly attributed to the human nature of Christ, to the historical Jesus as such. For humanity, which is finite, is not capable of the infinite. Therefore His knowledge, for example, however penetrating we may think it to be, is not omniscience; His power is not omnipotence, . . . etc."[30] In adopting this position—for good, sound christological reasons, be it noted—Barth was not unaware of its epistemological significance. If there is no "divinization" of the human nature of Christ, then revelation cannot be read directly "off the face of Jesus" as Werner Elert, for example, maintained in his 1924 book, *Die Lehre des Luthertums im Abriss*.[31] "The life of Jesus does not *in itself* impart the knowledge of God (John 14:8–9). In itself it is instead a riddle, a mystery, a veiling."[32] Thus, God remains unintuitable even as God enters fully into intuitability. God remains unintuitable as the hidden, never directly to be recognized, Subject of the life of Jesus.

The affirmation of the hiddenness of God in the medium of God's Self-revelation creates a new difficulty, of course. If God is to be recognized as the Subject of this life, if the medium of human flesh in which God has veiled Godself is to become transparent, then a third element must be introduced.[33] The Holy Spirit must make the veil transparent by giving us the eyes of faith to see that which is hidden beneath the surface.

29. Barth, "Unterricht in der christlichen Religion" III, §28, p. 52. It is worth noting that Barth says that the rejection of the *theopoiesis* of the human nature of Christ is also, at the same time, a rejection of the *theopoiesis* of history: "That means the cutting off of the way that leads to romanticism, to Hegel, to monism."

30. Ibid., p. 46.

31. Barth, *Unterricht in der christlichen Religion*, vol. 2, *Die Lehre von Gott/Die Lehre vom Menschen, 1924/1925*, ed. Hinrich Stoevesandt (Zurich: Theologischer Verlag, 1990), 22 (*The Göttingen Dogmatics*, 1:334); Werner Elert, *Die Lehre des Luthertum im Abriss* (Munchen: Beck, 1924).

32. Ibid., 23 (*The Göttingen Dogmatics*, 1:334).

33. Ibid., 20 (*The Göttingen Dogmatics*, 1:333).

At first glance, such a solution to the Kantian problem may not seem to have advanced beyond the one offered in *Romans* at all. At the end of the day, Barth is still making appeal to an exercise of the power of God to disclose to us something which is unintuitable to us. Has Barth really made progress here? I would say yes, for the following reason. While it may be true that, for Barth, the true identity of Jesus can be known only through an exercise of the power of the Holy Spirit, it is still the case that the life of Jesus is God's life. Whereas in *Romans* Barth restricted the encounter of the unintuitable God with the realm of historical intuitability to a single mathematical point, without extension on the plane of history, his claim now was that the unintuitable God had *fully*[34] entered the realm of intuitability and lived a life which did have extension on the plane of history. The difference this makes is that if the life of God has become historical, then appeals by the individual theologian to the Holy Spirit are not made in a vacuum. They are made with respect to a reality in history; the *veil* of the divine Self-revelation at least is something to which the church as well as the guild of historians have access. And because this is so, claims to knowledge of this reality can be discussed and debated by church theologians and historians without either side supposing that their method is fully adequate on its own to deal with the reality in question. I will return to this point in a moment.

To conclude this discussion with a critical question: has Kant really been overcome *by means of Kant*? God has become intuitable . . . without becoming intuitable? Is this even a coherent notion? The answer, it seems to me, cannot be decided by philosophers as such; it must be resolved theologically through attention to the Christology and soteriology which make it possible. On the objective side, the coherence of Barth's solution will have to be decided on the basis of the adequacy of his Christology. If there are good and sound theological reasons for advancing precisely this Christology, then the meaningfulness and coherence of Barth's assertion that the intuitability of Jesus is God's intuitability will be guaranteed. On the subjective side (which I have had to leave unexplored here), the coherence of Barth's solution will have to be decided on the basis of the adequacy of his soteriology. If the idea that the work of the Holy Spirit completely reorients our thought without altering our rationality is theologically defensible, then it will not be incoherent to say that God "commandeers" the human knowing apparatus described by Kant without altering it. And finally, if both sides of this theological explanation are successful, then what we have before us is a clear and coherent explanation for the possibility that human knowledge of God can be made by an act of God to conform to God's knowledge of Godself, that the knowledge of

---

34. See Barth, *Prolegomena*, 114 (*The Göttingen Dogmatics*, 1:93): "The *hiddenness* of God, however, His *incomprehensibilitas*, is His hiddenness not next to or behind but precisely *in* His revelation."

God is really *knowledge* (in the theoretical sense), that the revelation of God to us has the character of a Word addressed to human *reason* by means of a historical mediation. Of course, it is true that Kant is no longer Kant by the time Barth has finished with him. Barth's solution is not Kantian. My contention is simply that the *problem* being addressed is described in Kantian terms. For a solution, Barth has had to look, as Schleiermacher did before him, to the divine causality.

Conclusion: Some Programmatic Suggestions

A. It is not at all uncommon to read in recent treatments of the contemporary relevance of Barth's theology that he was a forerunner of the theologies in our day which are sympathetic to the nonfoundationalist philosophies of Wilfrid Sellars, Willard Van Orman Quine, Richard Rorty, and Richard Bernstein. John Thiel places Barth at the head of a tradition which today is represented by the Yale theologians Hans Frei and George Lindbeck together with their former students Ronald Thiemann and Kathryn Tanner.[35] I hope that what I have said here has made it clear that the attempt to establish such a connection is not without its obstacles.

It is quite true that Barth steadfastly refused to find a foundation for theology in anything external to revelation (e.g., in a philosophical anthropology). But to the extent that Barth had and worked with a philosophy, this philosophy was Kantian, and Kantianism is a subjective form of foundationalism (i.e., Kant's analysis of how humans know was thought by Barth to be universally valid). Seen in this light, it is scarcely imaginable to me that he would have sought aid and comfort from the likes of a Richard Rorty.

Theologically, however, Barth was not a foundationalist because he refused to allow his philosophical foundations to provide an ultimate ground for his theological truth-claims. It seems to me that if the attempt is made to bring Barth into conversation with contemporary debates over foundationalism and nonfoundationalism, it would be necessary to coin a new term to describe his position, since the existing terms are all misleading when applied to him. The term I would choose would be "transfoundationalism." Barth was seeking to describe a divine act by means of which the limitations proper to the philosophical foundations he presupposed were transcended. So the *trans-* in my term "transfoundationalism" does not refer to a human act of self-transcendence but, rather, a realistically conceived divine act. The crucial point to be underscored is that Barth's transfoundationalism was not intended to negate the possibility of philosophical foundations. Transfoundationalism, as I have described it, is the result of an attempt to transcend philosophical

35. John Thiel, *Nonfoundationalism* (Minneapolis: Fortress, 1994), ch. 2.

35

foundations *without negating them.* It should be added, however, that insofar as Barth refused to allow his philosophical foundations to become foundational for theology, he was also denying to them any ultimacy. And because they lack ultimacy, philosophical formulations of the foundations of human knowledge must be open-ended and revisable. That is, one might well wish to maintain (and I think Barth would) that philosophical foundations do exist without assuming that any one philosopher has provided *or even can* provide an exhaustively true description of them. Room must be left for taking seriously the role played by the knower in constructing descriptions of "foundations." Only then does philosophy become truly critical. The larger implication of this line of thought is that Barth did not grant and could not have granted to his Kantianism a nonnegotiable status.

That Barth was not absolutely wedded to his Kantianism, that it was, in the final analysis, his Christology which determined both his doctrine of revelation and his use of Kantian categories in explicating it—the proof of this lies in the fact that his Christology could be elaborated and defended without resorting to Kantianism at all. So, however true it may be that, from a genetic standpoint, Barth's Kantianism played a sizable role in helping him to conceptualize the Christology he finally advocated, from a systematic standpoint, his Kantianism could conceivably be revised without serious loss to his Christology. But all of this is to say that the appeal made by theologians to philosophical foundations, if made in an a posteriori manner in an effort to explicate the subject matter of theology, is not inappropriate from a Barthian perspective.[36]

36. The roots of Barth's approach to this nexus of problems is to be found in the neo-Kantianism of Hermann Cohen (who taught Barth philosophy during his student years in Marburg). Cohen's philosophy was intended as a very strict form of foundationalism, in that it sought to provide an account of the *erkenntnistheoretischen* foundations of all the sciences, foundations which he identified with those generative laws of human consciousness by means of which "objects" of human knowledge are given not only their form but even (against Kant) their content. Cohen's "critical idealism" was directed principally against the stabilization and absolutization of the "given" as occurred in empiricism and positivism. But his program was also carried out in principled opposition to the "false apriorism" of speculative idealists such as Fichte and Hegel. It sought to overcome such "dogmatism" through an insistence on the act-structure of all thought (which conceives of the generation of "objects" of knowledge as a never-completed task) as well as through constant attention to the "principles" which, in the present moment, govern the work of empirical sciences, empirical ethics, and empirical art. Certainly, to speak at all of the "reality" dealt with by empirical sciences introduced a good bit of asymmetry into Cohen's constructivist epistemology, but he felt (at least on occasion) constrained to do so by the disrepute into which philosophy had fallen as a result of the dogmatism of the speculative idealists. My point here is that Cohen opened a door, however slightly, to moving away from his own critical idealism in the direction of a critical realism of the kind which Barth would eventually advocate. On these points of Cohen's philosophy, see Johann Friedrich Lohmann, *Karl Barth und der Neukantianismus: Die Rezeption des Neukantianismus im "Römerbrief" und ihre Bedeutung für die weitere Ausarbeitung der Theologie Karl Barths* (Berlin and New York: Walter de Gruyter, 1995), 70–77, 82–84. For a more extensive treatment of what I am call-

B. Given that I have hinted here that Barth might justly be located within the Schleiermacherian tradition of "mediating theology," some comment should be made regarding interpretations of Barth which would like to see him as the sworn enemy of mediating theologies of whatever form. Here again John Thiel provides a useful example. For Thiel, the tradition of mediating theology is treated as largely synonymous with the foundationalist enterprise in theology,[37] and if he is right in this, then, of course, Barth was not a "mediating theologian." But if that tradition was more pluriform than Thiel seems to think, and if, in fact, the priority given by Barth to gospel over law (i.e., to revelation over philosophical foundations) was not altogether without precedent in the nineteenth century, then Barth too was a mediating theologian.[38] Though I cannot demonstrate it here, I am convinced that Wilhelm Herrmann's theology was not foundational-ist any more than Barth's was. And a good case could undoubtedly be made for the later Schleiermacher also in this regard. The attempt to read Barth as a mediating theologian is, obviously, one that would require a great deal more evidence than I have given here. But it is a task well worth undertaking.

C. In a letter to Eduard Thurneysen on New Year's Day 1916, Barth wrote, "My Advent sermon caused me to realize just how frightfully indifferent historical questions have become for me. Of course, that is nothing new for me. Under the influence of Herrmann, I already conceived of criticism only as a means to freedom vis-à-vis the tradition, not, however, as a constitutive factor of a new liberal tradition, as Wernle and company would clearly like to have it."[39] Indifference to historical questions, it should be noted, is not at all the same thing as a principled opposition to them. And so Barth could also claim,

---

ing Barth's "transfoundationalism" in conversation with the so-called Yale theology, see ch. 5, "Beyond Nonfoundational and Postmodern Readings of Barth," in this volume.

37. Thiel, *Nonfoundationalism*, 46.

38. The biggest obstacle to such an interpretation lies, of course, in Barth's humorous but devastating picture of the "type" of the mediating theologian. See Karl Barth, *Protestant Theology in the Nineteenth Century* (London: SCM Press, 1959), 574. The mediating theologian, he says, is a person who "thinks ecclesiastically. He answers questions about the substance of dogmatics by pointing to what was really credible and what was really believed in such and such a year. . . . The *status quo*, understood properly, is thus the measure of all things. The mediating theologian is quite unaware of the pressure to move forwards from it; he is a *beatus possidens* and as such a born churchman." Examined closely, what Barth is opposed to, above all, is the ethos of nineteenth-century attempts at mediation: the all-too-easy rejection of radical extremes, gravitation towards the center in all debated questions as a matter of principle, and the lack of a critical attitude towards modern culture with the result that the synthesis of the biblical thought-world and modernity becomes more or less self-evident. But to acknowledge the pitfalls that surrounded nineteenth-century attempts at mediation does not mean that the program itself was without merit. Nor could Barth have thought so; if he was critically disposed towards Schweizer, he could also find it in himself to grant a great measure of respect to the work of another mediating theologian, I. A. Dorner.

39. Karl Barth to Eduard Thurneysen, January 1, 1916, in Karl Barth, *Briefe*, vol. 2, Karl Barth and Eduard Thurneysen, *Briefwechsel, 1913–1921*, ed. Eduard Thurneysen (Zurich: Theologischer Verlag, 1973), 121.

with justification, that he was not the "sworn enemy of historical-criticism" but only of a historical science which reduced biblical interpretation to a question of historical investigation.[40] Historicism, in other words, not historical investigation, was that to which he was opposed on principle.

Barth was right not to be opposed to historical research. One simply cannot affirm, as Barth did, that the real locus of the meaning of biblical texts is not to be found in the texts as such but rather in a point that lies beyond them (the Self-revelation of God in Jesus Christ, understood as a real event in space and time) and then seek to bar the door to historical work. There is more than a grain of truth in Wolfhart Pannenberg's claim, made over against James Barr's preference for the category of "story" rather than "history" for depicting the true character of biblical narratives: "If we decide for 'story' . . . we make an interest in the reality of what is narrated secondary. But this is not in keeping with the realism of the OT (and NT) traditions. . . . If theology seeks God's historical action in the sequence of events which the Bible records, and as they appear to modern historical judgment and according to their reconstruction on the basis of historical-critical research, it will be closer to the spirit of the biblical traditions than if it treats the texts simply as literature in which the facticity of what is recorded is a secondary matter."[41] Barth would, of course, have wanted to raise a question about Pannenberg's unquestioning acceptance of "modern historical judgment." But this, I would maintain, would be a debate over the theological presuppositions which ought rightly to govern historical investigation; it would not be a debate over the propriety of historical research per se. Under no circumstances would Barth have approved of a hermeneutic which would completely localize meaning in the biblical narratives.[42] I am confident he would have regarded such "literaricism" (if I may coin a word) as just as serious an anthropological reduction in the realm of hermeneutics as the historicism against which he struggled. It seems to me that the most helpful response to the excesses of historical-critics lies not in the kind of flight from history which we see in many literary-critical approaches today but in serious reflection on the adequacy of Troeltsch's segregation of historical method from dogmatic method.[43]

40. Barth, *Der Römerbrief, 1922*, x.

41. Pannenberg, *Systematic Theology*, 1:231.

42. See Mark I. Wallace, "Karl Barth's Hermeneutic: A Way beyond the Impasse," *Journal of Religion* 68 (1988): 396–410.

43. Ernst Troeltsch, "Historical and Dogmatic Method in Theology," in *Religion in History* (Philadelphia: Fortress, 1991), 11–32. In this influential essay written in 1898, Troeltsch argued that a consistent use of historical method requires commitment to three basic postulates: (1) "in the realm of history, there are only judgments of probability" (p. 13); (2) the criterion of probability is "analogy" (or the agreement of the interpretation of events in the past with "normal, customary, or at least frequently attested happenings and conditions as we have experienced them" (ibid.); and (3) "correlation"—"the univocity and total interconnection of historical events" (p. 17)—means that evaluation and judgment of particular events, no less than their explanation and description, must begin with the total context. The implication of this last

It has for some time been recognized that the struggle between Herrmann and Troeltsch was, on one level at least, a struggle over the theological legacy of Schleiermacher. Given the profound changes which had occurred in the theological situation subsequent to Schleiermacher's death, how might his theology be most adequately appropriated? This was one way of putting their (shared) question. It is my contention that Barth too, even after his "break" with Herrmann, continued to be a player in this debate. But in his efforts to go beyond Herrmann, he had assigned a role to history and theoretical knowing which, while not exactly constituting concessions to Troeltsch, certainly brought him a bit closer to Troeltsch's orbit than he had been as a faithful follower of Herrmann. It is a pity that Barth never chose to debate Troeltsch publicly on the subject of theology and history—and could not after the latter's untimely death in 1923. To this day, modern theology remains the poorer because that debate never took place.

In this essay, I have attempted to read Karl Barth as a nineteenth-century theologian. I have even made the suggestion that Barth represented a form of "mediating theology" which is not strictly foundationalist in character (i.e., one which allows for the priority of gospel over law)—though I could not defend it here. In a day in which the theme of "tradition and the modern world" is threatening to become an anachronism (because more and more theologians are treating modern theology as if it too has become part of "the tradition" and, as such, are consigning it to a past which no longer has any obvious relevance for us), it is my fondest hope that more and more Barthians would put aside ancient animosities and find in nineteenth-century theologies the *living* resource for theological reflection that they so richly deserve to be. For only in this way will Barth's theology continue to be the resource it deserves to be.

---

postulate, I take it, is that universal history (understood as the total context for the explanation of historical events) may not be prescinded from—through appeal to a transcendent agency, for example. Now, obviously, it is this third postulate which is the most fundamental of the three. It is the principle of analogy which makes historical-criticism possible; correlation (in Troeltsch's view) provides the justification for the *exclusive* of that postulate. Troeltsch himself, rightly I think, refers to his third postulate as a "metaphysical assumption" (p. 22). What is curious about this is his failure to acknowledge the extent to which his metaphysical assumption constitutes a dogmatic position at least as "authoritarian" (because not testable by historical method) as the "traditional" dogmatic method he rejects. In my judgment, Troeltsch's distinction between historical method and dogmatic method cannot be sustained. Troeltsch's debate with "traditional" dogmatic method (he is really thinking of Julius Kaftan's historical apologetics) turns out to be a contest between two antithetically related dogmatic methods. And what makes them to be antithetically related is finally the very different concepts of God's relation to the world which they presuppose. I point this out not to defend Kaftan at every point but simply to make it clear that the attempt to restrict the use of historical method to the service of one dogmatic scheme to the exclusion of all others threatens to foreclose in advance the more interesting discussion which ought to take place, namely, that of the nature of God and of God's relation to the world.

2

The Sum of the Gospel

The Doctrine of Election in the Theologies of Alexander Schweizer and Karl Barth

The doctrine of election is the sum of the Gospel because of all words that can be said or heard it is the best.

CD II/2:3

Introduction

The jury is still out regarding the question of whether theology has now entered into a "postmodern" period. Certainly, the voices telling us that the modern period in theology is over are many and varied, but as yet the outcome is uncertain. Perhaps the time has come, however, when we can more calmly consider the relative merits of the two most impressive constructive theologies produced in the modern period—those of Friedrich Schleiermacher and Karl Barth—than could a previous generation still caught up in the heat of battle. There are signs that some would like to seek a way "beyond the impasse" between Schleiermacher and Barth. Unfortunately, efforts at seeking points of contact between them have concentrated far too much on questions of method (where little rapprochement may be expected), to the neglect of material questions in dogmatics.[1]

This essay was originally published in a slightly different form under the title "The Sum of the Gospel: The Doctrine of Election in the Theologies of Alexander Schweizer and Karl Barth," in *Toward the Future of Reformed Theology: Tasks, Topics, Traditions*, ed. David Willis and Michael Welker (Grand Rapids: Eerdmans, 1999), 470–93. Reprinted by permission.

1. See the essays contained in James O. Duke and Robert F. Streetman, eds., *Barth and Schleiermacher: Beyond the Impasse?* (Philadelphia: Fortress, 1988).

In this essay, I will examine the doctrine of election and the understanding of its place and importance for constructive theology as a whole in the thought of Alexander Schweizer and Karl Barth. I choose Schweizer—who was arguably Schleiermacher's most gifted student—rather than the master himself because of the Zürcher's vast knowledge of the Reformed tradition and because of his lifelong preoccupation with the doctrine of election. What we will find is that although disagreement will remain between Barth and Schweizer, there is a tremendous convergence of interest which lies in back of their respective formulations of the doctrine. Impulses which gave rise to Schweizer's reflections on the doctrine of election are not simply ignored by Barth but taken up afresh and handled in a different way. What this suggests is that Barth's theology did not constitute a simple repudiation of his "neo-Protestant" forebear but, rather, a fulfillment of many of his deepest concerns in a new framework. And so, if the differences in starting-point and method will not go away, perhaps the realization of shared concerns between Barthians and Schleiermacherians will at least have the effect of teaching both of their need for one another in a vital Reformed theology of the future.

Predestination: "Central Dogma" of the Reformed Churches?

Until the Barthian revolution so dramatically altered the theological landscape in the 1920s, it was widely assumed that the distinguishing feature of Reformed theology in all of its classical forms was the prominence given to the doctrine of predestination. The decisive impetus to this view was given in 1844 by Alexander Schweizer in the first volume of his *Die Glaubenslehre der evangelisch-reformierten Kirche.*[2] The *Glaubenslehre* was a *Lehrbuch*—a textbook of Reformed doctrines, systematically arranged and composed mainly of lengthy citations from sixteenth- and seventeenth-century texts, set forth to illustrate Reformed teaching on the various doctrinal loci of Christian theology. Schweizer's motivation in writing such a work was not purely antiquarian; he had a constructive theological aim throughout. He was a devoted follower of Friedrich Schleiermacher, and his constructive goal was to demonstrate that Schleiermacher's theology represented a revival of the Reformed tradition (albeit in thoroughly modern dress) after it had suffered virtual eclipse in the eighteenth century.

2. Alexander Schweizer, *Die Glaubenslehre der evangelisch-reformierten Kirche, dargestellt und aus den Quellen belegt,* 2 vols. (Zurich: Orell, Füssli, 1844–1847). For a fascinating study of Schweizer and the problems that shall occupy us in this section, see Brian Gerrish, *Tradition and the Modern World: Reformed Theology in the Nineteenth Century* (Chicago: University of Chicago Press, 1978), 99–150. Those familiar with Gerrish's work will immediately recognize the great debt which I owe to him in the interpretation of Schweizer which follows.

In Schweizer's view, what distinguished the theology of the Reformed churches from Lutheran theology was, initially at least, a differing *Grundrichtung*. Lutheran theology concerned itself above all with overcoming and eliminating from the church every last vestige of "judaizing"—the teaching that justification occurs through works. Reformed theology, by contrast, was centrally concerned with the "paganization" of the church through the divinization of the creature (e.g., the fundamentally polytheistic worship of Mary and the saints, the sacralization of nature in the Eucharist by means of the doctrine of transubstantiation, etc.).[3]

Out of this initial difference in *Grundrichtung*, Schweizer argued, there then arose a further difference in "material principle."[4] According to Schweizer, the material principle of Lutheran theology was the doctrine of justification by faith alone whereas for the Reformed churches it was the sense of "absolute dependence upon God alone" (which was articulated dogmatically in the doctrine of predestination). Again, this difference in material principle signals a difference in orientation: the two principles in question are directed to two different basic questions which determine the shape of each theology taken as a whole. The Lutheran question was, What is it in humankind that makes us blessed? and the answer given was faith, not works. The Reformed question looked in a very different direction. It asked, Who blesses or damns, the creature or God alone? and the answer was, of course, God alone. Therefore, Schweizer concluded, the material principle of the Lutheran Church was

---

3. Schweizer, *Die Glaubenslehre der evangelisch-reformierten Kirche*, 1:38–43.

4. The origins of the distinction between the "formal" and the "material" principles of Protestantism (or, alternatively, of Lutheran dogmatics) were carefully researched and presented by Albrecht Ritschl in an essay written in 1876. It was above all August Twesten (one of Schleiermacher's earliest students as well as his successor in Berlin in 1835) whom Ritschl held responsible for coining the formula in the form in which it became commonplace from the mid–nineteenth century on. In his *Vorlesungen über die Dogmatik der evangelisch-lutherischen Kirche*, 2 vols. (Hamburg: Perthes, 1826–1827), Twesten spoke of the authority of Holy Scripture as the "formal principle" of "Protestantism," and of the doctrine of justification by faith as the "material principle" of Lutheran dogmatics. From the beginning, the use of this conceptual pair was plagued by imprecision—a fact that influenced Ritschl to argue for their abandonment. Of the greatest interest for us here are the problems surrounding the notion of a "material principle." Is it to be understood in the bold sense of a *source* from which all other doctrines proceed (in which case, it is not easily reconciled with the notion that Scripture is the sole authoritative source of dogmatics), or is it to be understood in a more modest way, as the one dogma that, more than any other, determines the shape and meaning of the rest? The answer to such a question is not at all self-evident, which means that close attention must be paid to individual usage if an injustice is not to be done to a particular theologian. Schweizer, as we shall see, would have answered in terms of the "softer" sense. See Albrecht Ritschl, "Über die beiden Principien des Protestantismus: Antwort auf eine 25 Jahre alte Frage," in *Gesammelte Aufsätze* (Freiburg: Mohr, 1893), 1:234–47. Cf. idem, *Die christliche Lehre von der Rechtfertigung und Versöhnung* (Bonn: Adolph Marcus, 1870), 1:157–73; translated as *A Critical History of the Christian Doctrine of Justification and Reconciliation*, trans. John S. Black (Edinburgh: Edmonston & Douglas, 1872), 152–67.

anthropological in character; the material principle of the Reformed churches, *theological* in the strictest sense.[5]

Before taking leave of Schweizer's *Glaubenslehre*, we must look more closely at his understanding of the material principle of Reformed theology, for it is precisely at this point that twentieth-century criticism of his historical work has been focused. The Reformed material principle, Schweizer said, differs from its Lutheran counterpart in that it is far less receptive to being cast in the "form of a *Principialsatz*." The feeling of absolute dependence on God is "not one dogma alongside others. . . . It is, much rather, the most heightened religious feeling and consciousness itself, and as a result, it will be everywhere present and will work in the whole of dogmatics as its all-permeating soul."[6] Thus, in its original and pure form, the material principle which Schweizer ascribed to Reformed theology is not a doctrine at all. Dogmatics will inevitably seek to articulate the contents of this apprehension in the form of a doctrine (and did so classically in the locus entitled "the decrees of God"), but this occurs at a second step removed from the original apprehension. The significance of this (thoroughly Schleiermacherian) distinction between the contents of religious consciousness and its doctrinal articulation—as applied to the notion of a material principle—is that, for Schweizer, the value of an articulated material principle was only relative. However central it may be for dogmatics as a whole, a material principle stands under the same reservation to which all doctrine is subjected in a Schleiermacherian framework: it is a thoroughly fallible attempt to articulate the contents of the original apprehension and, as such, stands in constant need of correction. Given all of this, it would have been very surprising indeed if Schweizer had envisioned a *system* of doctrine derived more or less deductively from a single material norm. The critical distance which he maintained from all doctrinal explications of the religious consciousness would never have allowed such a move. And the truth is that he did not take that step. What Schweizer did say was that the material principle—

5. Schweizer, *Die Glaubenslehre der evangelisch-reformierten Kirche*, 1:42. It is hard not to hear in such statements the later judgment of Karl Barth, that the principal difference between the Lutheran and the Reformed views of justification lay in the fact that whereas the Lutherans were interested primarily in the faith which justifies, the Reformed were interested in the God who justifies through faith: "The Reformed faith differs from the Lutheran in that the essence of it is not *fiducia*, though that is part of it: the essence of it is that it is *God's gift*. . . . Here faith has not, as in Lutheranism, the character of a hypostasis mediating between God and humankind; here all Christianity including faith, is a human totality pointing to a Creator and Redeemer; here the final interest is in God and only in God" (Karl Barth, "Reformierte Lehre, ihr Wesen und ihre Aufgabe," in *Das Wort Gottes und die Theologie* [Munich: Kaiser, 1924], 207; translated as "The Doctrinal Task of the Reformed Churches," in *The Word of God and the Word of Man* [Gloucester, MA: Peter Smith, 1978], 263). There can be little question that Barth's interpretation of the Reformed tradition—especially in the formative decade of the 1920s—owed a good deal to the historical work of Alexander Schweizer, though Barth scarcely ever acknowledged the debt.

6. Schweizer, *Die Glaubenslehre der evangelisch-reformierten Kirche*, 1:43.

once articulated—will condition the contents of the other doctrines.[7] But this is not to make of theology a deductive system; it is simply to lay stress on the interconnectedness of all dogmatic thinking.[8]

Schweizer's thesis that predestination constituted the doctrinal articulation of the material principle of Reformed theology was further elaborated and defended ten years later in a genetic-historical study entitled *Die protestantischen Centraldogmen*, and to this day it remains one of the most impressive attempts to trace the evolution of Reformed theology.[9] Certainly, it did much to shape the historiography of classical Reformed theology throughout the remainder of the nineteenth century. In this work Schweizer declared the doctrine of predestination to be the "center" of a constellation of "central doctrines" (shared with Lutheranism) and made this center the focal point of his genetic study. To this extent, we are justified in attributing to Schweizer the view that there was a single "central doctrine" of Reformed theology and that this doctrine was predestination.[10]

With the historical work behind him, Schweizer proceeded in the 1860s to produce his own constructive theology. Already the title is quite significant, for it testifies to Schweizer's deepest-lying ecclesial concerns: *Die christliche Glaubenslehre nach protestantischen Grundsätzen*.[11] What Schweizer was offering was a *Glaubenslehre* for a united church (Reformed and Lutheran) such as had existed in Germany since the Prussian Union of 1817.[12] Drawing upon

7. Ibid., 1:44.

8. The critical distinction between the unthematized contents of the religious consciousness and their subsequent doctrinal articulation had the same significance for Schleiermacher and Schweizer as the critical distinction between the Word and the human words (employed to bear witness to the Word) had for Karl Barth: both distinctions had the effect of relativizing all doctrinal formulations—a move which gave to both approaches to dogmatics a quite definite *un*dogmatic character.

9. Alexander Schweizer, *Die protestantischen Centraldogmen in ihrer Entwicklung innerhalb der reformierten Kirche*, 2 vols. (Zurich: Orell, Füssli, 1854–1856).

10. Brian Gerrish has made much of the fact that Schweizer spoke of "central doctrines" (plural) and not of a single "central doctrine." His goal in doing so is to set aside the mistaken idea that Schweizer believed that there existed a central dogma from which "the rest could be derived or developed" (Gerrish, *Tradition and the Modern World*, 147). Gerrish is absolutely right in insisting that Schweizer did not hold to a central dogma in the sense described. But this does not exclude the possibility that Schweizer held that there was a single central doctrine of Reformed theology in a different sense. The fact is, as Gerrish also readily acknowledges, that Schweizer did believe that the doctrine of predestination was the *Mittelpunkt* around which other "central doctrines" were clustered and, as such, it "determined" their shape and content. See Schweizer, *Die protestantischen Centraldogmen*, 1:16. But if the so-called central doctrines are clustered around one of their number as the center, then surely that doctrine must be "central" in a way that the others are not.

11. Alexander Schweizer, *Die christliche Glaubenslehre nach protestantischen Grundsätzen*, 2nd ed., 2 vols. (Leipzig: Hirzel, 1877). It should be noted that the first volume of the first edition made its appearance in 1863 and the second in 1872.

12. See esp. ibid., 1:4–36.

what he regarded as the best elements of both theological traditions, Schweizer skillfully synthesized them into a coherent whole. As in his previous works, so too here the contribution which the Reformed tradition could make to a united church lay close to his heart. But it was also clear to him that modifications of that tradition would have to occur if its most basic concerns were to be united with those of the Lutheran tradition. And so it happened that Schweizer now set forth as the material principle of the *Evangelical Protestant* Church in terms of the *Grundsatz* that "only in faith in divine grace in Christ is justification to be attained."[13] Historically, this *oberste Materialprinzip*, which was basic to both traditions, was modified by each (according to their differing orientations) and given a slightly different form (which, as before, Schweizer defined as anthropological on the one side and theological on the other).[14] But such modifications were seen by Schweizer to be the result of historical conditions which no longer pertained and which were consequently dispensable. The goal of a contemporary *Glaubenslehre* must be to recast the idea in a purer form. Not surprisingly, this conviction gave to Schweizer a tremendous freedom in his handling of the central doctrine of the Reformed churches. In his hands, the doctrine in its traditional form was subjected to a fairly radical recasting. No longer was it a doctrine of decrees (an idea which Schweizer found insuperably problematic) but a doctrine of "applicative grace"; that is, it provided an answer to the question of how human beings appropriate the redemption actualized in Christ (thereby also answering the question of why some people believe and others do not).[15]

Unfortunately for Schweizer, the timing of the publication of his dogmatics was not propitious. Albrecht Ritschl's more historically-oriented approach to dogmatics was the wave of the future (at least for the last third of the nineteenth century), and this meant that a strict *Bewusstseinstheologie* such as Schweizer's would not attain a great following. And with the onset of the Barthian revolution, the historiography created by Schweizer was also swept aside.

It was Barth himself who laid the theological foundations for what became the standard criticism of Schweizer's historical work. In his first lectures on dogmatics, given in Göttingen in 1924, Barth emphatically rejected the notion of a material principle in dogmatics: "Strictly speaking, there is *no* material principle, *no Fundamentalsatz*."[16] What Barth was rejecting under this heading, however, was the thought of a material dogmatic norm given *in advance* of the encounter with revelation through Scripture (through, let us say, the *experience* of justification) that required

---

13. Ibid., 1:193.

14. Ibid.

15. We will return to a closer examination of Schweizer's doctrine of applicative grace in the next section.

16. Karl Barth, *Unterricht in der christlichen Religion*, vol. 1, *Prolegomena, 1924*, ed. Hannelotte Reiffen (Zurich: Theologischer Verlag, 1985), 365.

only to be validated by means of a *subsequent* appeal to Scripture as the so-called formal norm.

> For the *Lutheran* dogmatician, it is self-evident that dogmatics is constituted through the combination of the formal principle . . . with a so-called *material principle*. . . . On the basis of this content, which in the prolegomena to Lutheran dogmatics is at once stated and established as a so-called basic principle [*Fundamentalsatz*], dogmatics proper will then be analytically developed with the help of the formal principle, usually in the form of a so-called *system*. The system is nothing other than the logical unfolding of the basic principle and its individual parts.[17]

Against such a procedure, Barth said that it is the task of dogmatics to critically test *all* pious words which give expression to the contents of the religious consciousness (and this includes any supposed fundamental doctrine) by the *one* norm of doctrine in the church: the Word of God himself as witnessed to by the canonical Scriptures. God and God alone is the fullness of content, the "formal" principle and the "material" principle in one. The source of doctrine in the church is Scripture alone, for it is only in and through Scripture that the Word is made available in the church. Given the pluriformity of the scriptural witness, it follows quite naturally that a "system" of doctrine will be extremely unlikely and—in Barth's view—is something not to be sought.[18] For these reasons, he opted to organize the contents of dogmatics loosely, along the lines of *loci communes*.[19] Barth was quite confident that in taking this stance he had the Reformed tradition on his side: "The Reformed confessions distinguished themselves from the *Augustana* . . . by placing themselves in a measured distance from the *one object* of all doctrine, not staking everything on *one doctrine* but rather . . . satisfying themselves with relating all doctrine to the one object; leaving it to God to be *the* truth—not their *thoughts* about God but God *Himself*, God *alone* in His *Word*."[20]

---

17. Ibid., 362. Whether Barth was being altogether fair to Lutheran dogmaticians of his time in attributing to them such a bold conception of a material principle (i.e., in the sense of a material norm, distinct from Scripture, which is rightfully employed as a source for the remaining contents of dogmatics) is a question which will have to be left open here. Suffice it to say that there was precedent for the kind of understanding which Barth here describes. C. E. Luthardt, for example, having defined the doctrine of justification by faith as the material principle of "Lutheran Protestantism," went on to say, "The material principle . . . forms the genetic principle of development for dogmatics; the holy Scripture as the documentary report of the saving revelation forms the normative means of proof [*Beweismittel*] for the individual statements of dogmatics" (*Kompendium der Dogmatik*, 3rd ed. [Leipzig: Dörffling & Franke, 1868], 23). It should be noted that Luthardt's "Compendium" was among the works cited by Barth in support of his reading of Lutheran dogmatics.

18. Barth, *Prolegomena*, 368.

19. Karl Barth, *Unterricht in der christlichen Religion*, vol. 2, *Die Lehre von Gott/Die Lehre vom Menschen, 1924/25*, ed. Hinrich Stoevesandt (Zurich: Theologischer Verlag, 1990), 8.

20. Barth, "Reformierte Lehre, ihr Wesen und ihre Aufgabe," 189.

In the decade that followed, Barth's position on these questions moderated to some extent. In large measure, this was due to the fact that with the development of his concept of analogy, he was able to place a much higher valuation on doctrine. In his *Church Dogmatics*, the emphasis would fall not so much on the distance which separates all doctrine from the object to which it testifies but, rather, on the analogical *relation* of the two. And so, it could come about that in *CD* II/2, he could calmly say, "It is a well-known historical fact that more than any other doctrine the doctrine of predestination stamped itself upon the face of the Reformed Church, or rather of 16th and 17th century Reformed theology, thus distinguishing it from others."[21] Such a position did not signal a retreat from his early objections to the notion of a material principle; and he still denied that the doctrine of predestination had served as such a principle in classical Reformed theology.[22] But he had arrived at a more balanced assessment of the importance of the doctrine, not only for the old Reformed but for his own theology as well—an importance which he expressed not in the language of a "material principle" but in the language of "the sum of the Gospel."

In the third section of this essay, we will be looking more closely at what Barth meant in speaking of the doctrine of election as "the sum of the Gospel." The point to be made here, in advance of that discussion, is that in coming to this position, Barth had moved much closer to the view of the importance of the doctrine which had actually been intended by Alexander Schweizer; that is, what Schweizer intended by the language "material principle" and "central doctrine" is quite close to what Barth meant by "sum of the Gospel." And this is a fact which has been largely lost on those influenced by Barth's earliest comments on the problem.

Historians today are by and large united in rejecting the validity of Schweizer's assessment of the importance of the doctrine of predestination for classical Reformed theology—especially as it touches upon Calvin. There are many today who would argue that Calvin's theology had no center at all. Among those who think that there was at least some kind of existential center, the leading candidate is his eucharistic theology and the Christology which underlay it, *not* his doctrine of predestination. It was Wilhelm Niesel, a student of Barth's during his Göttingen period, who first succeeded in marginalizing Calvin's doctrine of predestination vis-à-vis his theology as a whole. In his great work

---

21. *CD* II/2:36.

22. *CD* II/2:77–78: "There can be no historical justification for taking the concept 'central dogma' to mean that the doctrine of predestination was for the older Reformed theologians a kind of speculative key—a basic tenet from which they could deduce all other dogmas. Not even the famous schema of T. Beza was intended in such a sense. Its aim was rather . . . to show the systematic interconnexion of all other dogmas with that of predestination in the then popular graphic fashion. There was no question of making the latter doctrine a derivative principle for the rest. And even in the *Westminster Confession* . . . it was not a matter of deducing all dogmatics from the doctrine of predestination."

on Calvin's theology in 1938, Niesel noted the then still widespread view that predestination was Calvin's central dogma and observed, "If this be the case, then all that we have so far said is false. Then Calvin's doctrines are not like so many signposts pointing through the far-ranging and complex fields of the Bible to the one incarnate God. It would rather be true to say that Calvin's theology is a system of thoughts about God and humankind proceeding from the one thought of the utter dependence of humanity upon God."[23] Niesel's tendency to minimize the importance of Calvin's doctrine of election was given added impetus by François Wendel in 1952. Wendel's argument was based mainly on external considerations of arrangement (the doctrine of predestination only appears at the end of book III of the 1559 *Institutes* and receives scant mention elsewhere).[24] Although there is, no doubt, a great measure of truth in the current consensus on Calvin (it being readily granted that there is no *systematic* center to Calvin's theology), it is a truth whose significance is easily overstated. There is grave danger today that the oft-repeated judgment that predestination was of marginal importance for Calvin might easily lead to the conclusion that it ought to be of marginal importance for Reformed Christians in the present as well. And this would be a great pity, for not only would the errant notion of a double predestination be affected but, along with it, the utterly central truth of the unconditionality of divine grace.

Alexander Schweizer and Karl Barth were as one in the belief that whatever critical corrections may be necessary regarding the form which the doctrine of predestination was given in the sixteenth and seventeenth centuries, the theological intention which lay behind it was essentially correct. For both men, the heart of this intention lay in its emphasis on the unconditionality of grace, and the form (the dualism between elect and reprobate) was a secondary question (and, in their view, easily amended). And they were united in the belief that the doctrine of predestination, rightly interpreted, is of central importance for Christian theology as a whole and, as such, cannot be minimalized without doing serious damage to the Reformed witness to the truth revealed in Jesus Christ. In the exposition which follows, it should become clear that if there is a genuine heir of the most basic theological concerns which lay behind Alexander Schweizer's appropriation of the Reformed tradition, this heir would have to be Karl Barth.[25]

23. Wilhelm Niesel, *The Theology of Calvin*, trans. Harold Knight (Grand Rapids: Baker Academic, 1980), 159–60.

24. François Wendel, *Calvin: Origins and Development of His Religious Thought* (Durham, NC: Labyrinth, 1987), 263–84. Wendel singles out Schweizer as the source of the—in his view—mistaken notion that predestination was the central doctrine in Calvin's theology. But as Brian Gerrish rightly points out, Wendel never bothered to ask what Schweizer meant by a "central doctrine." See Gerrish, *Tradition in the Modern World*, 147.

25. I must leave to one side, at this point, the intriguing question as to the accuracy of Schweizer's historical judgment regarding the Reformed tradition in order to concentrate on the systematic question of the proper place and significance of the doctrine of election in Christian

The Doctrine of God and Applicative Grace: Alexander Schweizer

In his own constructive theology, Alexander Schweizer's reflections on election (or "applicative grace") were everywhere controlled by decisions already made in his doctrine of God. Our task in this section will be to show the extent to which Schweizer's revised doctrine of election was built on a foundation laid in his doctrine of God.

Schweizer built up his doctrine of God in three stages, reflecting his most basic decision that the doctrines taught in the Christian churches should be *Glaubenslehre*—deliverances of the religious consciousness. The most general sphere in which the awareness of absolute dependence on God is discerned by the pious is the world of nature. In this sphere the religious consciousness discerns the world's absolute dependence on God for its existence. In accordance with this awareness, religion posits God as the Creator and Sustainer of the world and accordingly ascribes to God the corresponding attributes of omnipotence (*Allmacht*) and omniscience (*Allwissenheit*). Because, however, the "all" contained in these terms is too indefinite, "pious interest" cannot rest content with them but must press on (through the *via negativa*) to heighten these attributes to the level of the infinite. When this is done, the result is that these two basic attributes are seen to have been at work always and

---

dogmatics. Regarding Schweizer's reading of the tradition, I will only say that I think the question of the importance of the doctrine for Calvin's theology as a whole (or for Zwingli's theology, for that matter) has yet to be treated with the care it deserves. When it is, we may well find that the nineteenth-century historians knew far more than they are usually given credit for and that—in the words of Brian Gerrish—"Schweizer may well offer the most serious alternative—at least in kind—to Barthian historiography of the period" (*Tradition and the Modern World*, 146). The only point to be added is that the most penetrating critic of "Barthian historiography" in the twentieth century is Karl Barth himself! Consider, for example, the following passage, in which Barth, having granted the validity of the protest raised by his Calvin-scholar brother Peter and his student Niesel against the thought that predestination constituted for Calvin "a basic tenet from which all other doctrines may be deduced," raises a caveat against the new "Barthian historiography": "But we must still ask whether in combatting this traditional error some recent writers have not underestimated the function of the doctrine in Calvin's theology." Is not that which Calvin says regarding this doctrine far too important and far too prominent for us to be able to say that this doctrine should not be used, and that Calvin did not mean it to be used, to shed decisive light on all that precedes and follows? Undoubtedly Calvin did not understand or handle the doctrine as a basic tenet. But this does not mean that he placed it on the same level as all the rest. Between these two views there is a third. What Calvin did appear to find in the doctrine of election was this: a final word (and thereby also a first word) concerning the entire reality of the Christian life, a word which tells that the Christian life has its existence, its continuance, and its future utterly and wholly on the basis of the free grace of God. But all Christian doctrine, even that of God at the beginning and that of the Church at the end, deals substantially with this reality of the Christian life, with the life of the person whom God has claimed for Himself in Jesus Christ. And if this be the case, then how can we help thinking of the doctrine of election as the last or first word of the whole of Christian doctrine? (*CD* II/2:86)

everywhere; that is, "the basic attributes of omnipotence and omniscience are *eternal* and *omnipresent* in their efficacy."[26] The second sphere in which the pious subject discerns his or her absolute dependence upon God is that of ethical life. Here God is seen as the One who calls ethical life into existence and rules over it. The attributes which modify the divine causality in the ethical world are goodness and holiness, wisdom and righteousness. Here again these attributes are eternal and omnipresent in their efficacy, which tells us that God is truthfulness and faithfulness in itself (i.e., "eternity" and "omnipresence" carry with them the thought of a "timeless" consistency in God's operations—a faithfulness of God to himself in all times and places). The third and highest sphere in which the pious discerns his or her absolute dependence on God is that of the religious life. Here God is seen to be the sole author of our salvation, and the corresponding attributes which the pious person ascribes to God are love, fatherly wisdom, and forebearing mercy. It should be noted that Schweizer has here moved throughout from the general to the particular (from the lowest or most general level of pious awareness to its most fully developed, redemptive form). Thus, the second stage builds upon the knowledge given in the first, and the third stage builds upon the knowledge given in the first two stages.

The conception of God which emerges from all of this corresponds in most of its details with the God of classical theism. Schweizer wanted nothing to do with pantheism or even with what is widely referred to today as "panentheism" (i.e., process theological conceptions).

> That it [the world] is related to Him [God] . . . as the body is to the soul (God thereby being seen as the world-soul) appears to be an insufficient illustration, for, so far as we know, the body is not absolutely dependent upon the soul. Rather, the body interacts with the soul. Therefore the soul is also dependent upon the body, whereas God is in no way dependent upon the world. The opinion according to which God first comes to consciousness in the course of time by means of the world and perfects himself through the world successively ennobled by him contradicts the religious idea of God, even though one adds by way of explanation that the Self-perfecting of God precedes by an immeasurable distance the perfecting of the world. For a God who, in this way or any other, must first perfect himself, a becoming God, is not the God of the religious consciousness.[27]

---

26. Schweizer, *Die christliche Glaubenslehre*, 1:241. Cf. 240: "The expressions 'eternity' and 'omnipresence' . . . originally want to say that God is unconditioned, not limited by time and space, which can be conceived in two ways. Either He is *allzeitlich* and *allräumlich*, filling all times and spaces—which is the popular though scarcely sufficient conception—or, insofar as time and space are to be considered as the limits and form of worldly being, God is free from existence in time and space, timeless and spaceless, so that these forms of worldly being . . . are excluded from the being of God."

27. Ibid., 1:269–70. Cf. 253.

For Schweizer, God is the sovereign Creator and Ruler of the world who is in no way conditioned by the world.[28] He also rejected every version of emanationism[29] as well as the notion that God created the world as a builder does, out of materials found ready to hand. For him, everything that is (including the so-called chaos of Genesis 1)[30] owes its existence absolutely to the power of God.

But Schweizer also departed from classical theism in two notable ways. He held, first, that the world has no beginning and no end. Did this make the world eternal and therefore undermine the Creator/creature distinction that Schweizer was concerned everywhere else to maintain? No. The fundamental distinction between God and the world for Schweizer is that God alone is "eternal" (in the sense of completely transcending time); the world, however, is structured by time. The word which Schweizer chooses to describe the existence of the world is *Sempiternität*[31] (the attribute of "always existing"—from the Latin *sempiternitas*), a word which suggests something of temporal structure (in the root word *semper*—"always").[32] Schweizer was moved to this conception above all by the belief that if the all-powerful God is eternally and omnipresently effective (as the religious consciousness in the natural sphere says God is), then God must always have created the world. It was unthinkable for Schweizer that an all-powerful God could ever have lacked an object upon which to exercise his omnipotence or that a living God could be conceived of as ever having been completely at rest and only moving into action at a point in time. He buttressed this line of argumentation (which was based on deliverances of the religious consciousness) with the further argument that the idea of a

28. In its *original* usage, the term "panentheism" would not have been inappropriately applied to Schweizer—or to Schleiermacher for that matter. The term was the invention of one Karl Friedrich Christian Krause, a contemporary of Schleiermacher, who used it to describe a view in accordance with which (1) God is understood to transcend the world as the source of its existence (God and the world are not identical) and (2) the "world" is understood to be "in" God, not "outside" God. See Rudolf Eisler, *Wörterbuch der philosophischen Begriffe* (Berlin: Mittler und Sohn, 1910), 2:970. Thus defined, Schweizer (and Schleiermacher) would qualify as panentheists, but to avoid confusion with process theology, it is necessary today to add a modifier. Schweizer and his great mentor might well be styled "*absolute* panentheists" in order to lay stress on their shared conviction that there is no reciprocity in the God-world relation; that is, what happens in the world does not condition God. God—we might accurately say—is the Absolute, the Unconditioned.

29. Schweizer, *Die christliche Glaubenslehre*, 1:245.

30. Ibid., 1:243.

31. Ibid., 1:266.

32. This distinction between "eternity" (as an attribute of God) and *Sempiternität* (as an attribute of the world) is not simply a linguistic trick; it rests on a real distinction between the kind of being God has and the kind of being the world has: "A world without a beginning is still a world, that is, something existing in time and space and therefore structured and divided into parts, at every point conditioned and conditioning, changeable, in all of its particulars transient or mutable, limited or finite through and through. God, however, is the very opposite of all that" (ibid.).

beginning to the world is self-contradictory. If the world had a beginning in time, then there must have been something "before" time. But since one cannot speak of this "before" without projecting the notion of time—which belongs properly to creation—back into a premundane world, then the conception of a beginning of the world leads to irresolvable contradiction. The net effect of these rather Origenistic considerations was that God's creative action must be conceived of as an eternal one, not a temporal one. And this means too that creation was not completed in a moment of time. Creation is a continuous divine activity, according to Schweizer, and cannot finally be separated from God's providential upholding of the world.[33]

Schweizer's other deviation from classical theism lay in his conviction that creation was in a sense necessary for God. It should be noted that he was not altogether happy with the language. Freedom and necessity, he said, are antithetically related only for humans, not for God. Properly formulated, the question should read, Are the works of God accidentally or necessarily related to the being of God? Schweizer noted that even the old Reformed dogmaticians had understood the world planned by God (in the doctrine of the decrees) to be the best of all possible worlds and, as such, a perfect reflection, on the creaturely level, of the divine being—that is, not accidentally but necessarily related to the divine being. The only remaining question, then, is whether God could have chosen not to create at all. Schweizer's answer to this question is already contained in the previous paragraph. God must always have created if he is the eternally omnipotent, all-knowing God. And since the world God created was the expression of God's being, creation was a necessity for God.[34] Schweizer is quick to point out, however, that this "necessity" has its ground in the divine being, not in anything external to God: "One cannot say that God would have had to create the world even if he had not wanted to, as little as one can say that he desired it out of need, to remedy some lack in himself."[35]

How is all of this, then, related to Schweizer's doctrine of election? Schweizer's criticism of the classical doctrine of the decrees, so far as it touches upon election, was already prepared for by his criticism of the same in relation to the doctrine of creation. In both cases the idea of decrees is rejected on the ground that it is too anthropomorphic. It envisions God as a wise man who carefully considers all the options open before him before selecting the best among them and acting. God, said Schweizer, does not have to reflect first on the problem of which of all possible worlds is the best; God knows the best option (the one most in accordance with God's own being) by means of God's perfect and immediate Self-knowledge and does it automatically, by an eternal action. Therefore there can be no temporal or quasi-temporal gap

33. Ibid., 1:244.
34. Ibid., 1:260–63.
35. Ibid., 1:268.

between thought and action, between a so-called world-plan (contained in the doctrine of decrees) and the act of creation. Similarly, in the case of election, God does not have to first reflect on the problem of how best to illustrate his glory—for the simple reason that the problem does not exist for him. God necessarily and immediately does that which is consistent with his being as love. When confronted by sin, God responds graciously. Thus, creation and election stand in a relationship of the most perfect analogy. Both refer to an eternal action, consistent in all times and places.

It should be noted, however, that creation and election have this relation only because they are determined for it in advance by Schweizer's doctrine of God. The foundation for the whole of Schweizer's theology of creation and redemption is laid in the doctrine of the eternally active, omnipotent, and omniscient God (which is to say, in the doctrine of the divine attributes). It is only because God is what he is that creation and election are *necessarily* what they are. But then it must also be noted in turn that Schweizer has built his doctrine of God on a foundation laid by a process of abstraction (i.e., through the *via eminentiae* and the *via negativa*) from alleged deliverances of the religious consciousness in the sphere of nature. Thus, every attribute ascribed to God as the Absolute Cause of the world at the first stage controls and determines in advance what may be said of God at the second and third stages, thereby controlling the doctrine of redemption as well.

The stage is now set for Schweizer's revision of the doctrine of election. The eternal ground of grace is located by Schweizer in the being of God himself rather than in divine "decrees"—it being a fixed principle for him that "what God does in time must be grounded in His eternal being."[36] "Grace" is the divine attribute of love insofar as this love is confronted by sinful human beings. Thus, the word refers to a modification in the divine relating to human beings which occurs as a result of sin. Grace, being a modification of the eternally and omnipresently active divine attribute of love, cannot be contingent upon the presence or absence of faith in men and women. If the love of God is eternally and omnipresently active, then it will (by definition) be universal in its scope. Therefore grace too is universal in its scope.[37]

But then the question arises: if grace is universal, why is it that some believe and others do not? The answer lies in the nature of "applicative grace." Applicative grace, for Schweizer, is not an irresistible, compulsive force.[38] It does not overwhelm the individual but must be willingly received. It works more or less naturally, through the orders of life which have been ordained by God. So, whether a person responds to the grace offered depends on the conditions of life in which that person is found. Some are predisposed to respond in faith;

36. Ibid., 2:307.
37. Ibid., 1:394–400, 406–22.
38. Ibid., 2:313–21.

others are not. That this difference among men and women arises at all is not accidental; it is itself a function of God's providential ruling of the world.

Thus, "in its eternal nature grace is *universal*, but in its historical effects it is *particular*"[39]—and both the universality and the particularity are expressions of the will of God. Is, then, God's will to be gracious towards all frustrated when some do not believe? Schweizer's answer is no; God's grace must ultimately triumph over all human resistance (though this may happen, in many cases, only in an afterlife). There are, of course, problems with this solution. Schweizer has really succeeded only in relocating the irresistibility of the divine willing in the doctrine of providence, not in eliminating it as he clearly wanted to do. If the free decisions of men and women are conditioned by the circumstances of their lives and these circumstances are themselves a function of God's providential rule, then God's will still remains irresistible in the only meaningful sense of the word. Schweizer has simply made election to be a subcategory of providence; the determinism present in his doctrine of providence is the silent presence which presides over his revised doctrine of election.

More serious, however, are the problems which arise as a result of Schweizer's method. What Schweizer did was first to generate a doctrine of God (on the basis of deliverances of the religious consciousness operating in the sphere of nature) and then make the doctrine of election (or applicative grace) to be a function of it. There are at least two problems with this procedure. The first is that it produces an absolute God which can only with great difficulty be reconciled with the God of the Bible. It is this concept of God which then controls all that follows. Second, on an even more basic level, Schweizer's starting-point in the religious consciousness does not allow him to accomplish what he wanted to accomplish in his revision of the classical doctrine of the decrees. Schweizer wanted to show that what God does in time is grounded in God's eternal being. But his method will not yield such a statement in the end. Employed with strict consistency, a theology of religious consciousness will not finally be able to tell us anything about what God is in himself; it will tell us only something about how God relates to human beings. Schweizer tells us as much in the context of his rejection of the doctrine of an ontological Trinity.[40] The so-called attributes of God are, then, not so much attributes of *God* as they are attributes of the relation between an unknown God and human beings.[41] Schweizer has made a herculean effort to narrow the gap between the being of God "in himself" and the being of God "for us" through his repeated insistence that the being of God is pure actuosity; there is no final distinction, he says, between the "attributes" of God (omnipotence and

39. Gerrish, *Tradition and the Modern World*, 141.

40. Schweizer, *Die christliche Glaubenslehre*, 1:404.

41. Ibid., 1:408: "Because all divine attributes are built up as determinations of the divine causality . . . therefore, they should correspond to the *works* of God" (emphasis mine).

omniscience) and the "functions" of God (creation and providence).[42] So, in a real sense, God is what God does. The problem is that Schweizer's method will not really allow him to say this. In order to be in the position to say that God *is* what he does, Schweizer would have to know something of what God is in himself. But Schweizer preferred at the decisive point to remain consistent with his method and disdained all claims to knowledge of God in himself. The effect of these methodological difficulties is that they thoroughly undermine Schweizer's central conviction in the doctrine of applicative grace: that what God does in time is grounded in the eternal being of God. If we follow Schweizer's method to the end, we can never be sure that God really is the gracious God he *appears* to be in his works. In truth, what Schweizer hoped to accomplish with his revision of the doctrine of predestination can be fully realized only with a quite different theological method.

In spite of Schweizer's radical reinterpretation of the doctrine, his belief that something essential to Christian religious consciousness lay behind it was clearly a constant in all of his life's work. The doctrine of predestination, as Brian Gerrish has put it, "answers to quite essential devout feelings, which a purer manner of doctrine must not curtail. The heart of these feelings lies in the humility that ascribes the entire life of salvation wholly to the grace of God as its eternal foundation."[43] The only remaining question, then, is whether Schweizer understood his revised doctrine of election as something like the "central doctrine" of his *Glaubenslehre*. There can be little question but that this was his intention. He did, after all, make grace (and justification) to be the material principle of his "Protestant" theology. And he understood a material principle to be "a governing doctrine, on which other doctrines are dependent." Hence, he could maintain, "the methodological division must . . . lift them [the twin doctrines of grace and justification] up as of decisive importance, which would not be the case if the governing doctrines appear

---

42. Ibid., 1:235–36.

43. Gerrish, *Tradition and the Modern World*, 138. Gerrish is perhaps guilty of overstatement when he writes, "If the earlier, historical studies had already led us to anticipate, not a recital, but a recasting of the old dogmas which would carry him beyond historical analysis, we are scarcely prepared for the radicalness of the final, constructive work. We expect a recasting of the dogma of predestination: what we find is more like a discarding of it" (136). If our expectations based on Schweizer's earlier works are confounded, this might easily be taken to imply that Schweizer changed his mind with regard to his original conviction that the doctrine of predestination had in it an idea that was essential to Christian faith. And this, I think, would be a mistaken reading. It is quite true, of course, that Schweizer abandoned the classical *form* of the doctrine of predestination (i.e., the doctrine of the decrees). But he could not abandon the essential idea that lay behind it, for he continued to regard this idea (viz., that redemption is wholly dependent on divine grace alone) as the (wholly salutary) Reformed contribution to a synthetically conceived material principle of the Protestant churches. See Schweizer, *Die christliche Glaubenslehre*, 1:8–12, 190–208. Schweizer's recasting of the doctrine in the form of a doctrine of grace is radical, but it is a recasting nonetheless and not simply a discarding of the old doctrine.

merely as individuals in a series of others. . . . Much rather, the chief division of the material will already make clear its determination by those governing doctrines as *Prinzipien*."[44] Thus, Schweizer's intention is clear. But it has to be admitted that Schweizer was unable to adequately fulfill this intention. His doctrine of God was almost entirely fleshed out without reference to grace and justification. And when grace is finally introduced as a modification in an essential attribute of God, its content is controlled by that doctrine of God. Thus, if Schweizer's intentions were to be fulfilled, a different framework of thought would be required.

Election and the Doctrine of God: Karl Barth

That election is "the sum of the Gospel" was grounded by Karl Barth in the fundamental claim that the primary object of election is not humankind but God himself. In Barth's view, the primal decision of God (the "decree" if you will) is to never be God apart from humankind. Alternately expressed, God chooses himself for us; God decides himself for grace. In this wholly gracious, wholly free, unconditioned primal decision of God for grace is contained *in nuce* all else that follows in time:[45] the election of the eternal Son for incarnation, suffering, and death on a cross; the election in him of the whole of humanity for communion with God; the outpouring of the Spirit, the creation and upbuilding of a community of believers who represent the whole of humanity. It is at this point that Barth's most original contribution to the historical development of the doctrine of election must be seen to lie. In making God to be not only the subject of election but also its primary object, Barth was making election to be the key to his doctrine of God. Barth would have been in formal agreement with the Schweizerian dictum "What God does in time must be grounded in the eternal being of God"; indeed, it was one of his most cherished convictions. But the material connections in which such a claim stands in Barth's theology as a whole give to it a very different meaning than it had for Alexander Schweizer.

Barth took as the starting-point for all of his dogmatic reflections the Self-revelation of God in the history of Jesus Christ, that is, the incarnation, life,

44. Schweizer, *Die christliche Glaubenslehre*, 1:90.
45. CD II/2:13–14: "The election of grace is the whole of the Gospel, the Gospel *in nuce*. It is the very essence of good news. . . . God is God in His being as the One who loves in freedom. This is revealed as a benefit conferred upon us in the fact which *corresponds to the truth of God's being*, the fact that God elects in His grace, that He moves towards humanity in His dealings within this covenant with the one man Jesus and the people represented by Him. All the joy and benefit of His whole work as Creator, Reconciler and Redeemer . . . all these are grounded and determined in the fact that that God is the God of the eternal election of His grace. In the light of this election the whole of the Gospel is light" (emphasis mine).

death, resurrection, and ascension of the God-man. To put it this way is already to suggest that the starting-point is not simply the man Jesus as he appeared on the surface of history. The starting-point is the God-man as witnessed to in Scripture, and the history of this God-man begins in the way taken by God in taking to himself a fully human life as his very own (in all of its limitations, up to and including death). It is this history which Barth has in mind.

On the basis of this Self-revelation, he then asked, what must God be like if he can do what he has in fact done? What is the condition of the possibility in eternity for the incarnation, death, and resurrection of the Son of God in time? In taking this approach, Barth was taking a principled stance against the more traditional procedure (followed in large measure by Schweizer) of beginning with an "abstract" concept of God (which is to say, one that has been completely fleshed out without reference to God's Self-revelation in Christ) and only then turning to that revelation to find in it confirmation of what was already attributed to God without it. Such a procedure, as we have already seen in relation to Schweizer, determines in advance what revelation in Christ will be allowed to say. Against this procedure employed by theism in all of its forms (classical and neo-Protestant), Barth proposed to work in an a posteriori fashion, beginning not with a general concept of God or a general concept of human being but with a most highly concrete reality, Jesus Christ.[46] And so, if God has in fact done something, it will not do to say that God cannot do it. Theologically responsible reflection will only be able to ask, What is the eternal ground for God's acts in time?

The effect of this procedure on the doctrine of election is as follows. The foundation of the doctrine of election is located by Barth in the single point in which God makes himself to be what he is—that is, in Jesus Christ. When we concentrate our attention on this point, we find that "under this name God himself realized in time, and therefore as an object of human perception, the Self-giving of himself as the covenant partner of the people determined by God from and to all eternity." We find that in what took place in Jesus Christ, "God Himself possesses this people: swearing to it the same fidelity He exercises towards Himself; directing to it a love no less than that with which, in the person of the Son, He loves Himself; fulfilling His will upon earth as it is already fulfilled in heaven, in the eternal decree which precedes everything temporal."[47] We find, in other words, that the reconciliation accomplished in Christ is a wholly gracious event; that is, it is based in a wholly unmerited, free divine decision.

The question now becomes, How can what God has done in Christ be seen to be the Self-revelation of God? How can Jesus Christ be God in this

---

46. Cf. Walter Kreck, *Grundentscheidungen in Karl Barths Dogmatik* (Neukirchen-Vluyn: Neukirchener Verlag, 1978), 188–93; George Hunsinger, *How to Read Karl Barth: The Shape of His Theology* (New York: Oxford University Press, 1991), 32–35.

47. CD II/2:53.

movement, *unless* what God has done in time has its ground in the eternal being of God? And the answer is that the gracious work of God in time is indeed grounded in the divine being.

For Barth, the being of God is Self-determined being; it is a being which God gives to himself in the primal decision in which God determines himself for this gracious relation to humankind. "We cannot go back on this decision if we would know God and speak accurately of God. If we did, we should be betrayed into a false abstraction which sought to speak only of God, not recognizing that when we speak of God, then in consideration of His freedom and of His free decision, we must also speak of this relationship."[48] God is God *only* in this gracious relation to humankind—by God's own act of Self-determination or "Self-ordination."[49] This decision—in which God ordains himself to have his being only in the gracious movement which reaches its climax in the cross and resurrection—is election. God elects himself for us in Jesus Christ. Such a conception of the wholly gracious being of God in relation to the world does not exclude, of course, the element of judgment or reprobation. But it does make comprehensible how and why this element must be the wholly subordinate servant of the purposes of grace. The divine No in which opposition to human sinfulness is expressed is the servant of the divine Yes of grace because grace is the beginning and end of all the ways of God in which God has his being.[50]

Election is the *primal* decision of God.[51] The word "primal" (in German *Urentscheidung*) is meant to exclude every hint of temporality. The word has logical force, describing the "logical origin" behind which it is not possible to inquire further, and as such, it takes the place of the category *Ursprung*, which had been widely used in Barth's two commentaries on Romans. That there is nothing behind this decision means, first of all, that there are no heights or depths in the being of God which lie back of this decision (in which God might somehow be other than the God of this gracious history). It means, second, that there is nothing outside God that could condition this decision; it is the decision from which all the works of God flow (creation, reconciliation, and redemption). "There is no *extra* except that which has its basis and meaning as such in the divine election of grace."[52] Therefore it is a completely free decision.

48. *CD* II/2:6.
49. *CD* II/2:89.
50. *CD* II/2:12–13: "The truth of the doctrine of predestination . . . is not a mixed message of joy and terror, salvation and damnation. Originally and finally it is not dialectical but non-dialectical. It does not proclaim in the same breath both good and evil, both help and destruction, both life and death. It does, of course, throw a shadow. We cannot overlook or ignore this aspect of the matter. In itself, however, it is light and not darkness. . . . The Yes cannot be heard unless the No is also heard. But the No is said for the sake of the Yes and not for its own sake. In substance, therefore, the first and last word is Yes and not No."
51. *CD* II/2:50; cf. *KD* II/2:53.
52. *CD* II/2:95.

It should occasion no surprise that Barth's understanding of the primal character of divine election has enormous implications for his doctrine of God. Whereas, for Schweizer, the doctrine of God determined and shaped his doctrine of election, just the opposite is the case for Barth. It is his doctrine of election which controls the content of his doctrine of God. "The true God is the One whose freedom and love have nothing to do with abstract absoluteness or naked sovereignty, but who in His love and freedom has determined and limited Himself to be God in particular and not in general, and only as such to be omnipotent and sovereign and the possessor of all other perfections."[53] God's perfections are what they are in the service of the divine decision for grace. And so the power of God, for example, is not to be defined in abstraction from the reconciling activity of God (and the eternal decision in which it is grounded). To ascribe "All-power" to God in the light of the divine election of grace is to say that God possesses all the power necessary to carry out his covenantal purposes with humankind. If this be true, it will not do to say, as Schweizer did, that the omnipotence of God must have a "sempiternal" world as an object upon which it can be exercised. Such a claim rests upon an abstract definition of "omnipotence." Rather, the meaning and significance of power in God are defined by God's eternal decision. Therefore whatever use is made of power by God (in eternity as well as in time) will be in accordance with its meaning and significance as grounded in the eternal being of God, since whatever God does will be in accordance with the decision which determines the being of God. Schweizer's other thesis—that God cannot be conceived of as ever having been idle, since (as pure actuosity) God cannot move from rest to action—falls to the ground for the same reason. Pure actuosity was defined by Schweizer in such a way as to allow for no real movement or change in the divine action. But such a definition is a mere abstraction; it bears no relation to the *history* of God's covenantal dealings with humankind as witnessed to in Scripture.

It is not hard to guess what Schweizer's objection to Barth's doctrine of God would be. He would say that Barth's emphasis on decision, on the *freedom* of God in deciding to create, reconcile, and redeem, would make God arbitrary. Barth's answer would be sympathetic up to a point. Schweizer is absolutely correct in asserting that the works of God are not accidentally related to the divine being. But if the decision to create and redeem is already contained in the primal decision in which God's being is itself determined, then the decision to create and redeem is—by definition—fully consonant with the divine being. In fact, they are the expression of that being. Does the freedom of God as expressed in the primal decision mean that God could have decided *not* to create and redeem? Absolutely. God could have decided to be sufficient in himself, to possess in himself (in his triune being) the perfectly sufficient object of his love.

53. CD II/2:49.

The promise contained in the Schweizerian principle that what God does in time must be grounded in the eternal divine being could not be realized by Schweizer himself because he was unable to secure it against doubts that God might not be in himself what God appears to us to be through his works. This promise is realized, however, by Karl Barth. For here it finally becomes clear how the works of God are grounded in the eternal divine being as it really is in and for itself. We can have complete confidence that God will never turn out to be anything other than the God of electing grace.

Conclusion

We have seen that Schweizer's intention of making the doctrine of election to be (at least a part of) the "central doctrine" of Christian theology and to ground everything he says in this doctrine in the eternal being of God could not be realized within the framework provided by his starting-point and method. It was, however, realized within the framework provided by Barth's quite different starting-point and method. The lesson to be drawn from these observations is this: although it remains true that Barth and Schweizer cannot be reconciled on the level of method and that those of us who are confronted by their disagreement in method will inevitably take sides (as I have done here), it nonetheless remains true that they participated in a community of shared theological concerns. At the very least, they were chewing on two ends of the same bone. And this, I think, should have tremendous ramifications for Reformed theology in the present. Reformed theology in the present needs, above all, to have representatives of these two most vital and profound streams within the Reformed tradition of the modern period who can maintain a constant dialogue with one another, seeking to identify their common concerns and searching for doctrinal formulations which will do even greater justice to them than Schweizer and Barth were able to attain. If the representatives of these two great streams continue to ignore one another or continue to engage in the kind of polemic which rests content with questioning one another's character and motives, the Reformed churches of the present will be the losers.

3

What Has Basel to Do with Berlin?

Continuities in the Theologies of Barth
and Schleiermacher

Introduction

Karl Barth and Friedrich Schleiermacher: surely an odd couple if ever there was one![1] What has Basel to do with Berlin? Quite a bit actually, though in some respects I have been fairly slow in realizing it. Of course, it has long been common knowledge that Schleiermacher constituted for Barth, on a deeply personal level, a kind of alter ego, a person with whom he could never be "finished,"[2] a person whose wealth of problems and highly nuanced solutions constantly called into question the adequacy of Barth's criticisms of him. That much I have long understood. And I have also believed for some time that a close investigation of Schleiermacher and Barth on the level of material questions in dogmatics would turn up evidence that the former had exercised

This essay was originally published in a slightly different form under the title "What Has Basel to Do with Berlin? Continuities in the Theologies of Barth and Schleiermacher," in *Princeton Seminary Bulletin* 23 (2002): 146–73. Reprinted by permission.

1. The influence of the monumental work of Brian A. Gerrish on my own reading of Schleiermacher in this essay will be everywhere apparent. It will also be obvious that I have pushed his interpretation in directions that he would not himself wish to go. Still, I dedicate this essay to him in gratitude for all that he has given to me in inspiration, encouragement, and friendship.

2. Barth says of his relationship to his great predecessor, "Although certainly 'against' Schleiermacher in my own way, I for my part was neither so certain nor so completely finished with him as Brunner was after he completed that book [*Die Mystik und das Wort*, 1924]" (Karl Barth, "Concluding Unscientific Postscript on Schleiermacher," trans. George Hunsinger, in *The Theology of Schleiermacher: Lectures at Göttingen, Winter Semester of 1923/24*, ed. Dietrich Ritschl [Grand Rapids: Eerdmans, 1982], 266).

varying degrees of influence on the latter, ranging from the substantial to the less consequential. But for a long time I drew the line when it came to theological method.

On the level of method, I tended for many years to follow the opinion of the vast majority—which meant that I expected no possibility of rapprochement. Indeed, in a review of the well-known volume *Barth and Schleiermacher: Beyond the Impasse?* I referred to Schleiermacher as the "methodological antithesis" of Barth.[3] Looking back, I would have to say that my judgment at that time was understandable (in terms of the consensus shared by specialists in the study of both Schleiermacher and Barth). But I had yet to process the full implications of a truth that was only then dawning on me: that Barth's criticisms of Schleiermacher presupposed an understanding of him which was more accurate where the Schleiermacherianism of Barth's time was concerned than it was for the great Berliner himself. Barth was in this, as in other matters, a child of his times at least as often as he was able to transcend his times. He was the heir of a picture of Schleiermacher that he learned at the feet of his teachers Horst Stephan and Wilhelm Herrmann—a picture which was not without its shortcomings. And when Barth turned against Schleiermacher, it is hard to avoid the impression that he was turning most decisively against that form of Schleiermacherianism whose great advocates at that time were Ernst Troeltsch and Georg Wobbermin.

So where should we begin in our efforts to acquire a more accurate understanding? The question is one that I have been wrestling with as I have been preparing a book on Barth's relationship to Schleiermacher. And the answer I have given to myself has two foci, so to speak. The first has entailed a close reading of Schleiermacher's *Glaubenslehre* in tandem with an equally close study of the history of Schleiermacherianism. The goal of this study has been to ask, "What did the Schleiermacherians take from Schleiermacher? And what did they miss or choose to leave behind?"

The second focus has been tied to the question "Which Barth do I bring into conversation with Schleiermacher?" Do I focus on the later Barth, who seems in the eyes of many to have mellowed in his attitude towards Schleiermacher? This would certainly be one possibility. In the last year of his life, in frustration over his university's decision not to celebrate the two hundredth anniversary of Schleiermacher's birth, he offered a seminar on the *Speeches*. Out of this seminar came Barth's famous "Concluding Unscientific Postscript on Schleiermacher," in which he offered up the provocative suggestion that it might be possible to write "a theology of the third article"—a theology, in other words, in which "everything which needs to be said, considered and

---

3. See Bruce L. McCormack, review of *Barth and Schleiermacher: Beyond the Impasse?* ed. James O. Duke and Robert Streetman, *Scottish Journal of Theology* 44 (1991): 260. I stand by everything else I wrote in that review.

believed about God the Father and God the Son in an understanding of the first and second articles might be shown and illuminated in its foundations through God the Holy Spirit"[4]—and that such a theology might well provide the means of creating a bridge between himself and Schleiermacher. The suggestion remained only tentative and undeveloped. We claim too much for ourselves if we think we can know exactly what Barth meant. The only real clue that he offered, in this context, of what such a theology might look like is that in it the "entire work of God for his creatures, for, in and with human beings, might be made visible in terms of its own teleology in which all contingency is excluded."[5] In other words, the whole would be controlled by eschatology. But reflecting on this possibility has led me to ask, What would a theology written on a foundation laid in the third article and controlled by eschatology look like *if carried out on the soil of Karl Barth's theological commitments*? One possible answer is that it might look very much like Barth's earliest effort at the writing of a dogmatics. In contrast to the christological centering and grounding of doctrines in the *Church Dogmatics*, Barth's earlier *Göttingen Dogmatics* attempts an elaboration of doctrines with constant attention being given to the dialectic of veiling and unveiling in revelation. Not only are such centering and grounding more trinitarian than the later Christocentrism, in that all three moments of revelation come into their own; it is also more nearly "pneumatocentric" in that the situation of the human recipient of revelation stands very close to the heart of Barth's interests. But even more important, the dialectic of givenness and nongivenness in revelation also succeeds in keeping the eschatological reservation which encompasses all dogmatic labor more clearly in view than does the later Christocentrism and gives to the whole a sense of unrest and urgency that contrasts with the calm which surrounds the later unfolding of doctrines from a christological center.

These observations lead quite naturally to a second alternative. One could make the *Göttingen Dogmatics* the centerpiece of a genetic and comparative study, rather than the later *Church Dogmatics*. The *Church Dogmatics* would be brought in only where it became necessary to reflect upon further changes in either the method or the content of Barth's dogmatics.

The Fate of the *Church Dogmatics* in the Schleiermacher Renaissance

The first decade of the twentieth century marked the heyday of the so-called Schleiermacher renaissance. It also saw the breakup of Schleiermacherianism into two main camps, associated preeminently with Ernst Troeltsch on the one side and Wilhelm Herrmann on the other. A close analysis of the issues involved

4. Barth, "Concluding Unscientific Postscript on Schleiermacher," 278.
5. Ibid.

in the split between these two theologians is very instructive for the purposes of my research, for it helps to explain how the picture of Schleiermacher which Barth would eventually rebel against took shape during the years in which he was a student of theology at the Universities of Bern, Berlin, Tübingen, and Marburg. Obviously, I cannot enter into the issues as thoroughly here as would be desired in a book-length treatment. What I can do is to sketch briefly Troeltsch's critical, highly qualified reception of Schleiermacher. To do so will help to make clear just how far the Schleiermacherianism of Barth's day was from the theology of Schleiermacher himself. It will also help to explain why Barth would, from 1915 on to the end of his life, be so critical of Schleiermacher's theology. Notwithstanding the "inner voice" which would, throughout Barth's life, speak to Schleiermacher's advantage,[6] the fact that his critique remained largely unchanged to the very end stands quite possibly as testimony to a worry that Troeltsch might have had Schleiermacher right and that Troeltsch was therefore the most genuine heir of Schleiermacher in a changed theological situation. I turn, then, to Ernst Troeltsch, a sharp-eyed critic of ecclesial dogmatics if ever there was one.

Troeltsch's Reception of Schleiermacher

In a 1908 essay entitled "A Look Back on Half a Century of Theological Science," Troeltsch made clear precisely what he had taken from Schleiermacher and wherein he had to depart from him. The essay offers an analysis of the then current theological situation, whose central problematic, as Troeltsch saw it, lay in the loose, highly conflictual "juxtaposition of a purely scientific historical theology and a practical mediating dogmatics,"[7] both of which had a strong root in Schleiermacher's theology. Troeltsch himself was an ardent defender of the first and highly critical of the second, though he was quick to grant that any truly "scientific theology" would also need to provide support for a living religious preaching. His criticisms of the second possibility, however, mark the limits of his appreciation of Schleiermacher.

The "program of mediation," as Troeltsch saw it, owed its existence to an "agnostic" theory of the nature of religious knowledge.[8] "This dogmatic agnosticism signifies the impossibility of exact and adequate conclusions in the area of religion. The basis for its knowledge is said to reside in its practical, confes-

6. Ibid., 267: "For all my opposition to Schleiermacher, I could never think of him without feeling what Doctor Bartolo so well articulated in *The Marriage of Figaro*: 'An inner voice always spoke to his advantage.'"

7. Ernst Troeltsch, "Rückblick auf ein halbes Jahrhundert der theologischen Wissenschaft," rev. ed. in *Gesammelte Schriften* (Tübingen: Mohr, 1913), 2:221; translated as "Half a Century of Theology: A Review," in idem, *Writings on Theology and Religion*, ed. Robert Morgan and Michael Pye (Atlanta: John Knox, 1977), 76.

8. Ibid., 2:200 ("Half a Century of Theology," 58).

sional and feeling character, and all statements containing or communicating this sort of knowledge are said to be inadequate and symbolic."[9] Of course, for Troeltsch's money, such a "special knowledge" was not really knowledge at all—which is why he calls this an "agnostic theory."

The historical origin of this theory lay quite clearly in Schleiermacher's attempt to locate religion on the level of human consciousness which he denominated "feeling" (in distinction from "knowing" and "doing"). According to Troeltsch, the effect of this move was to reduce dogmatics and ethics to "practical disciplines," without "theoretical" (or, as we might say today, "cognitive") standing. The great virtue of this move, as Troeltsch saw it, lay in the fact that it so completely separated religion from science that the latter was allowed to go its own way, unimpeded by the needs of religion. But it also had the effect, for the time being, of preserving the illusion that was Christian belief in the absoluteness of Christianity. So long as historical science had been unable to challenge Christian belief that the "religious consciousness was perfected in Christianity" and that therefore the redemption accomplished in and through Jesus of Nazareth was final and unsurpassable, the older program of mediation worked well enough. But historical science had come a long way since Schleiermacher's time. The biggest advance lay in the recognition that Christianity is a historical phenomenon which can be studied in a truly "scientific" fashion only by means of a history-of-religions approach which located the origins of Christianity in the historical flux of contemporaneous religious developments (in Judaism, the mystery religions, Hellenistic religions, etc.). A truly "scientific" approach to history would now, Troeltsch claimed, have to be free of Christian presuppositions.[10] But this also put the program of mediation on the defensive. The absoluteness of Christianity could now be maintained only by means of a metaphysically founded apologetic or, as was true in the case of Wilhelm Herrmann, by means of a "subjective mysticism" which regards everything historical as a mere signpost and stimulus for individual religious experience.[11] Either way involved a flight from history. The agnostic theory of religious knowledge had thus brought the older program of mediation into dissolution.

If there was now to be a successful mediation between historical science and dogmatics, it could only happen, Troeltsch thought, where dogmatics as a practical, confessional, ecclesial affair was replaced by a dogmatics which was able to build on a foundation laid in real knowledge. He was quite happy to grant that, on the side of the agnostic theory of religious knowledge, Herrmann was the genuine representative of Schleiermacher. But there was another

9. Ibid. ("Half a Century of Theology," 59).
10. Ibid., 2:211 ("Half a Century of Theology," 68).
11. Ibid., 2:219 ("Half a Century of Theology," 75).

side to Schleiermacher's thought which Troeltsch believed offered a way out of the current impasse.

History and dogmatics must continue to strive against each other unless they are both given a common root and a common presupposition.[12] If the decision regarding such a common root and common presupposition is not to be arbitrary, then it will have to be the result of a "comparative valuation" which flows from an intuition of the whole of historical life. What Troeltsch is clearly suggesting is that the methods of the history-of-religions school offer the key to the entire enterprise. It is their presuppositions that must make possible a reconciliation between history and dogmatics. The history-of-religions approach to the study of Christian origins and development presupposes that the development of the religious consciousness has taken place in accordance with "general laws and tendencies."[13] The elaboration of these general laws and tendencies is the task of what Troeltsch called a "general science of religion" (or "philosophy of religion"). A dogmatics which did not continue to strive against the historical disciplines would, then, also have to be built on the same foundation of the general science of religion.

Now, all of this is spelled out in a terse, programmatic way, and it is not clear (in this essay at least) how Troeltsch would have sought to accomplish this obviously ambitious program in the details. For my purposes here, it is enough to point out that it was precisely in his pursuit of a general science of religion that Troeltsch sought for authorization in Schleiermacher. But the success of this appeal depended entirely on the truth of the claim that Schleiermacher sought to understand the evolution of religious consciousness in terms of *general* laws and tendencies. Clearly, Troeltsch believed that he could have "Schleiermacher's program" without Schleiermacher's alleged "agnostic theory of religious knowledge." He was quick to acknowledge that in the process "scarcely one stone of Schleiermacher's own teaching can remain upon another."[14] But he remained confident that he could carry off this program "in Schleiermacher's sense" even if no one before him (including, apparently, Schleiermacher himself) had managed to do so.

But how accurate is this portrayal of Schleiermacher's theology? The "general laws and tendencies" of an evolving religious consciousness of which Troeltsch speaks must somehow be empirically available for study if they are to provide a demonstrable basis for a "general theory of religion." But the attempt to enlist Schleiermacher in support of such a project could succeed only where Schleiermacher is "psychologized"—where, that is, the subject matter with which Schleiermacher was concerned is reduced to a psychological "given," a datum of the empirical self-consciousness. And as we shall see

12. Ibid., 2:222 ("Half a Century of Theology," 77).
13. Ibid., 2:210 ("Half a Century of Theology," 69).
14. Ibid., 2:225–26 ("Half a Century of Theology," 80).

68

in a moment, this is precisely the move which Troeltsch would later make in his own *Glaubenslehre*. But was Schleiermacher's theology of consciousness guilty of psychologism in this sense? Just how accurate is this portrayal of Schleiermacher's theology? Was Schleiermacher a foundationalist of a subjective kind, as Troeltsch's reading of his "program" would seem to imply? This is the question to which we must now turn.

A More Authentic Schleiermacher

Published three years before his death, the second edition of Schleiermacher's *Christian Faith* is his most mature work. By any standard of assessment, it is a brilliant achievement; unapologetically Christian, explicitly opposed to natural religion, structured throughout by what can rightly be styled the "infinite qualitative difference between God and humanity," it is throughout an exercise in *ecclesial* dogmatics. But this fact has rarely been appreciated. The reason is not simply that the introduction to the *Glaubenslehre* has been read as an *independent* exercise in the philosophy of religion, designed to provide a foundation for the dogmatics which follows in parts 1 and 2. The *Glaubenslehre* most certainly has been read in this way by friends and foes alike. But this is only symptomatic; it is not the root cause of the failure of much Schleiermacherian interpretation. The root cause has to do with a failure to grasp the importance of the unique melding of romantic and idealistic elements in Schleiermacher's thought, a melding which contributed to the construction of a *critical* theology of consciousness.

The truth of the matter is that not all theologies of consciousness are cut from the same piece of cloth. It is the critical nature of the method employed in the construction of Schleiermacher's theology of consciousness which sets him apart from all later imitators and necessitated that the dogmatics which emerged would have the character of "church dogmatics." How this could be missed is an interesting story in its own right, a story which begins with the preoccupation of Schleiermacher's immediate followers with apologetic issues, with the result that they quickly abandoned his romantic category of "feeling" in favor of a foundation laid in Hegel's concept of universal reason. The end point of the story has to do with the psychologism and historicism of Troeltsch and many of his contemporaries (such as Wobbermin). With the weight of scholarly opinion during Barth's student years decidedly in favor of reading Schleiermacher's theology of consciousness in a psychologized fashion, Barth may be forgiven for the interpretive mistakes reflected in his criticisms of Schleiermacher.

What, then, do I mean by a "critical" theology of consciousness? The best place to begin is with an overview of the purpose and method employed in Schleiermacher's introduction. The purpose of the introduction is to identify the "essence of Christianity" so as to have a basis upon which to define the nature of Christian dogmatics and the method(s) appropriate to it. Schleiermacher's strategy for identifying the "essence of Christianity" is to begin with an analysis of human self-consciousness. He commences with a distinction of fundamental and wide-ranging significance—that between "sensible self-consciousness" and "immediate self-consciousness."

"Sensible self-consciousness" refers to what is often identified as empirical or "objective self-consciousness"—the consciousness of self which rises through making the self an "object" to oneself or, at the very least, through the more subconscious awareness of self that accompanies all interaction with the people and things of our experience. The meaning of this category is clear and merits no further comment. "Immediate self-consciousness," however, is a notoriously difficult concept in Schleiermacher's theology; it is easier to say what it is not than to say what it is.[15] What it is not is "objective consciousness"—which means that it entails no production of a "representation of oneself" which is mediated by "self-contemplation."[16] To speak of an "immediate" self-consciousness, then, would be—quite literally—to speak of a form of self-consciousness which is not mediated by representations. But to speak in this way serves only to underscore the elusiveness of the concept. How is it possible to be conscious of self without making oneself, to some degree at least, an "object" to oneself? And does this process not require the production of representations? The two initial examples Schleiermacher gives of states belonging to the immediate form of self-consciousness, namely, joy and sorrow, may indeed be present without reflection upon them. But to admit this much is to tilt "immediate self-consciousness" back in the direction of an unconscious or subconscious state of existence.

Schleiermacher further equates "immediate self-consciousness" with "feeling"—which does not serve to resolve the conceptual difficulties. "Feeling" is defined by Schleiermacher through contrast with knowing and doing. Human life, he says, "is to be conceived as an alteration between an abiding-in-self [*Insichbleiben*] and a passing-beyond-self [*Aussichheraustreten*] on the part of the subject."[17] "Doing" is a pure passing-beyond-self, an action on the part of the subject directed towards an object. "Knowing" entails a mixture of the two. Where "knowing" is taken to mean the act of knowledge in the moment of its actualization (*Erkennen*), it is a passing-beyond-self. Where,

15. Brian Gerrish rightly notes, "'Feeling,' in the sense of 'immediate self-consciousness,' is by definition elusive; a living movement that stops when you stop to look at it. But as long as you leave it alone, it remains indeterminate and you cannot say what it is" ("Nature and the Theatre of Redemption: Schleiermacher on Christian Dogmatics and the Creation Story," in *Continuing the Reformation: Essays on Modern Religious Thought* [Chicago: University of Chicago Press, 1993], 211–12).

16. Friedrich Schleiermacher, *The Christian Faith*, trans. H. R. Mackintosh, 2nd ed. (Philadelphia: Fortress, 1976), §3.2.

17. Ibid., §3.3.

on the other hand, it is taken to refer to acquired knowledge, a having known (*Erkannthaben*), there "knowing" is an abiding-in-self. "Feeling," however, is a pure abiding-in-self. In that it entails no action of any kind on the part of the subject, it is not something that is effected by the subject within himself or herself; it is, rather, something that takes place in the subject, the source of which is to be found outside human consciousness.[18] "Feeling" is thus pure receptivity.

Now, this is not the place to discuss in detail Schleiermacher's philosophical demonstration of the existence of this moment of pure receptivity and his analysis of its most basic content in terms of the so-called feeling of absolute dependence. Much more important for my purposes is the *status* of this "demonstration." Is it intended as an apologetic directed to a non-Christian audience? Is the demonstration thought by Schleiermacher to be of such a nature that it would compel agreement on the part of any "reasonable" reader regardless of what his or her faith commitments might be? And if the answer to this is yes, does this whole train of reflection constitute a "foundation" for the dogmatics to follow? If this were the case, Schleiermacher is much to be pitied, for his effort would in this case have to be judged a dismal failure. Hegel's derisive attitude towards the "feeling of absolute dependence" is symptomatic of the attitude of a good many nineteenth-century philosophers towards Schleiermacher's analysis. But there are good reasons for believing that Schleiermacher had no intention of engaging in this kind of apologetic—not in this work, at any rate.

First, although the feeling of absolute dependence is *in* all people, it is not *recognized* by all. It can undergo defective or arrested development as a consequence of various forms of "godlessness."[19] So, on the face of it, the account given of religion in the introduction could not be expected to make sense to all. But second and even more important, the feeling of absolute dependence does not exist anywhere in reality in a pure form—apart from the consciousness of Jesus of Nazareth, of course. In every individual other than Jesus, it exists only in modified form, that is, in combination with modifications which have been introduced into it through stimuli which have come to the individual from without, entering by way of the "sensible self-consciousness." Indeed, the "peculiar essence of Christianity" consists in the modification of the feeling of absolute dependence by the redemption accomplished in and through Jesus of Nazareth.[20] But if the "essence" of

---

18. Ibid.

19. Ibid., §33.1–2.

20. As Brian Gerrish puts it, "The Christian way of being religious is, in fact, nothing other than faith in Jesus the Redeemer; and it is surely a mistake when [Emil] Brunner interprets Schleiermacher to mean that the feeling of absolute dependence is the essence of Christian faith, the reference to Jesus merely giving its accidental occasion." If it were true that the feeling of absolute dependence is the "essence" of the Christian religion, then the

a given religion consists in the *modifications* which take place in the feeling of absolute dependence and not in this feeling per se, then the various religions cannot be regarded as just so many species of a common genus. Each has an irreducible uniqueness which is not set aside by formal similarities on the level of doctrines or ethical teachings.[21] Third, Schleiermacher is adamant that Christian dogmatics must stand on its own "two feet," so to speak, and not make itself the servant of any philosophy—and this for very sound hermeneutical reasons. "Our dogmatic theology will not, however, stand on its own proper ground and soil with the same assurance with which philosophy has long stood on its own, until the separation of the two types of proposition is so complete that, e.g., so extraordinary a question as whether the same proposition can be true in philosophy and false in Christian theology, and *vice versa*, will no longer be asked, for the simple reason that a proposition cannot appear in the one context precisely as it appears in the other; however similar it sounds, a difference must always be assumed."[22] And so he concludes that dogmatics must at all costs be kept free from speculation. Fourth and finally, Schleiermacher is quite explicit in defining his audience in this work:

> It is obvious that an adherent of some other faith might perhaps be completely convinced by the above account that what we have set forth is really the peculiar essence of Christianity, without being thereby so convinced that Christianity is actually the truth, as to be compelled to accept it. Everything we say in this place is relative to Dogmatics, and Dogmatics is only for Christians; and so this account is only for those who live within the pale of Christianity, and is intended only to give guidance, in the interests of Dogmatics, for determining whether the expressions of any religious consciousness are Christian or not, and whether the Christian quality is strongly expressed in them, or rather doubtfully. We entirely renounce all attempt to prove the truth or necessity of Christianity; and we presuppose, on the contrary, that every Christian, before he enters at all upon inquiries of this kind, has already the inward certainty that his religion cannot take any higher form than this.[23]

Christian religion could only be a subclass of a "universal concept of religion," an "accidental individuation" of that universal and, as such, one possible manifestation of the universal among many others. But this is not Schleiermacher's view. See Brian Gerrish, *Tradition and the Modern World: Reformed Theology in the Nineteenth Century* (Chicago: University of Chicago Press, 1978), 36, 24.

21. In the first of his open letters to his friend Friedrich Lücke, Schleiermacher observes, "I must . . . protest against the view expressed by our friend Nitzsch. . . . He criticizes me for seeking to incorporate what is distinctively Christian into a universal religious knowledge. In my opinion, however, such a knowledge would be nothing other than an abstraction from what is Christian" (Friedrich Schleiermacher, *On the "Glaubenslehre": Two Letters to Dr. Lücke* [Atlanta: Scholars Press, 1981], 52).

22. Schleiermacher, *The Christian Faith*, §16, postscript.

23. Ibid., §11.5.

It is quite true that Schleiermacher is only speaking, in the immediate context in which this passage appears, of the "peculiar essence of Christianity." But since the establishment of this peculiar essence is the goal of the entire first chapter, it is hard to avoid the conclusion that what is said here applies to the whole. And certainly, the statement "We entirely renounce all attempt to prove the truth or necessity of Christianity" is a very bold statement whose significance would be hard to limit if taken at face value.

The conclusion which all of this evidence invites is that Schleiermacher's philosophical derivation of the "feeling of absolute dependence" through an analysis of all human self-consciousness generally is intended for Christians, as a way of supplementing what they know to be true based on their experience of redemption, namely, that they are radically dependent upon God for their redemption and, if radically dependent upon God for redemption, then radically dependent too for their very existence.[24]

But however Schleiermacher may have intended his introduction to be understood, the decisive point for my purposes is this: The elusiveness of the immediate self-consciousness has its ground ultimately in the fact that it is not a psychological *datum* in the same way that the contents of the sensible self-consciousness are. It is not directly available as such; hence, it cannot be separated out from the contents of the sensible self-consciousness in such a way as to allow it to be controlled, mastered, and brought into play at the whim of any individual in whom it is found. If it is to be realized at all, its content (viz., the feeling of absolute dependence) must have mastery over the stimuli which come to the individual from without on the level of sensible self-consciousness.[25] Thus, the feeling of absolute dependence, that original relation of God to the human subject—or "original revelation" as Schleiermacher puts it at one point—is not something that the human subject could ever master in himself or herself. What Schleiermacher has done is to place the God-to-human relation (and the redemptive power which can be released in and through it) at a *critical* distance from all self-reflective human activity, such that control of that relation always remains, at every moment, the prerogative of the divine. Ultimately, the critical difference between divine action and human action, which first announces itself in Schleiermacher's distinction between immediate and sensible self-consciousness, performs the same function in his theology as Barth's distinction between the Word of God and human

24. It is quite true that Schleiermacher says of the first half of his derivation (the portion of the argument which has not yet touched on the feeling of absolute dependence), "To these propositions assent can be unconditionally demanded; and no one will deny them who is capable of a little introspection and can find interest in the subject matter of our present inquires" (ibid., §4.1). Even here, however, the note of "who is capable of a little introspection and can find interest in the subject matter of our present inquires" strongly suggests a reservation. It is quite possible that not everyone will be capable of even this much.

25. Ibid., §5.3.

words performs in his—namely, to overcome the urge within the human subject to seize control of the God-human relation. Absolute dependence is indeed *absolute*; one can, under the impact of divine causality, surrender oneself to its power, but one cannot cause it to be effective.

Such a conclusion finds further support in Schleiermacher's treatment of the God-world relation. A good argument can be made that the central problematic which recurs throughout the *Glaubenslehre*, running through the whole like a red thread, is the problem of the relation of divine causality to the physical causality found in the created universe. This becomes immediately clear at the very outset of the *Glaubenslehre* in the radical distinction which Schleiermacher establishes between God and the world—a distinction which is advanced on the basis of the following train of reflection: vis-à-vis the things and people we encounter in this world, we are relatively free and relatively dependent. That is to say, we exercise on all these people and things, no matter how remote they may be from us in space, an influence, and they, in turn, exercise a counterinfluence upon us. The relationship between all created entities is thus reciprocal. With respect to God alone are we absolutely dependent. But if the dependence of the people and things of this world upon God is truly *absolute*, then God must also be completely free with respect to the world. For Schleiermacher, to bring God into the realm of reciprocal relations would inevitably cancel out or negate the feeling of absolute dependence—which is impossible. "Any possibility of God being in any way *given* is entirely excluded, because anything that is outwardly given must be given as an object exposed to our counter-influence, however slight this may be. The transference of the idea of God to any perceptible object . . . is always a corruption, whether it be a temporary transference, i.e., a theophany, or a constitutive transference, in which God is represented as permanently a particular perceptible existence."[26] Thus, God could not make himself "objective" in this world without entering into the relation of reciprocity that is the inevitable condition of all creaturely relations. Of course, it goes without saying that Schleiermacher's commitment to the absolute freedom of God makes an incarnation as understood in traditional terms a frank impossibility.

But how, then, does the divine causality become effective in this world? God must remain outside the world if God is not to be made subject to the reciprocal relations within that world. In any interaction with the world, God must preserve his "otherness" if he is to be God. He must act from the outside, so to speak, not from within. So how are we to understand divine causality? Schleiermacher holds that "the Absolute Causality to which the feeling of absolute dependence points back can only be described in such a way that, on the one hand, it is differentiated from and thus placed over against everything contained in the system of nature and, on the other hand, it is equated with the

26. Ibid., §4.4.

circumference of the latter."[27] That is, divine causality is equal in compass or breadth to the totality of finite causes at work in the system of nature, but it is to be strictly differentiated from the latter. "The Divine Causality as equal in compass to the totality of the natural is presented in the expression of the divine *omnipotence*. The Divine Causality placed over against the finite and the natural is presented in the expression the divine *eternity*."[28]

But this serves only to underscore the difficulties. If the divine causality is eternal, how does it become effective in time? The closest Schleiermacher can come to an explanation is to speak of the "supernatural becoming natural"— and, of course, doing so in such a way as not to set aside the difference between the two.[29] But, of course, that is not an explanation; it is at most a witness, a pointing to a reality that is extremely difficult to conceptualize. At the time of writing the second edition of his *Romans*, Karl Barth addressed a similar problem by means of a geometrical image: "In the resurrection, the new world of the Holy Spirit touches the old world of the flesh. But it touches as a tangent touches the circle, without touching it and precisely in that it does *not* touch it, touches it as its boundary, as new world."[30] For Barth, this problem was very much a problem of the relation of eternity and time. Can eternity enter time without ceasing to be eternity? Barth's answer in the second *Romans* was no; eternity cannot enter time. But eternity can *encounter* time; it can influence time from beyond, so to speak.[31] Schleiermacher needs something like this in order to be able to speak at all of how the "supernatural becomes natural."[32]

My point here is not to defend any of this, though it must be said that if anyone wished to take issue with any of it, he or she would have to recognize that there is far more to Schleiermacher's understanding of the God-world relation than I have been able to present here. My point is this: The feeling of absolute dependence is the result of a divine act of relating to the human in time, a divine act which is eternal and therefore at most *encounters* the human

---

27. Ibid., §51, introductory proposition.

28. Ibid., §51.1.

29. Ibid., §88.4; 100.3; 117.2; 120.1–2.

30. Karl Barth, *Der Römerbrief, 1922* (Zurich: Theologischer Verlag, 1940), 6.

31. See Bruce L. McCormack, *Karl Barth's Critically Realistic Dialectical Theology: Its Genesis and Development, 1909–1936* (Oxford: Clarendon, 1995), 263–64.

32. Schleiermacher, *The Christian Faith*, §4.3: "Hence a feeling of absolute dependence, strictly speaking, *cannot exist in a single moment as such*, because such a moment is always determined, as regards its total content, by what is *given* to us, and thus by objects towards which we have a feeling of freedom" (initial emphasis is mine). Like Barth's understanding of revelation in the second *Romans*, which occurs in a moment without before and after and therefore without any perduring existence on the plan of history, so also Schleiermacher's conception of the divine act which gives rise to the feeling of absolute dependence is that of a relation the character of whose Whence guarantees that it cannot exist in a single moment as such. How, then, do we gain access to it? Only by means of a kind of transcendental deduction which asks for the conditions for the possibility of the Christian experience of redemption.

in the depth dimensions of his or her being but in no way becomes fixed and stabilized. It is *dandum* and not a *datum,* something which is given at every moment by means of a unitary, supratemporal divine action and not something that is simply in us as a capacity is in us. And certainly it is not something that is at the disposal of the human, to bring into play for purposes we might deign to assign to it. Thus, when I speak of Schleiermacher's theology of consciousness as being *critical* in nature, what I have in mind is the fact that it sets definite limits to the capacities of the human where the knowing and experiencing of God are concerned. Schleiermacher's theology is a theology of limits—one, that is, which limits the human in order to lead him or her to the point where God might establish a redemptive relation with that human.

The final question which needs to be addressed is this: What is the theological method commensurate with a critical theology of consciousness as I have described it? What is the theological method which is best able to honor the elusive, uncontrollable character of immediate self-consciousness and of the feeling of absolute dependence which is its primary content? Far too many interpreters of Schleiermacher speak quite simply of his dogmatics as though it were the result of a fairly straightforward attempt to "read" doctrines off the Christian's religious self-consciousness in the present moment. But this is a fairly drastic oversimplification.

"Dogmatic theology," Schleiermacher says, "is the science which systematizes the doctrine prevalent in a Christian Church at a given time."[33] The central aim of this definition is the overcoming of the purely individual. The subject matter with which dogmatic theology works is not "individual opinions and views"—even if the opinions and views in question be those of the theologians carrying out the exercise. Dogmatic theology is not "private confession" or an individual performance-piece. The subject matter with which dogmatic theology works consists in the shared expressions by means of which religion is communicated *in a church.* The "prevalent doctrine" is thus that which "can be put forward as a presentation of common piety without provoking dissension or schism." That such material includes the doctrinal formulations found in the confessional symbols of a given church is affirmed by Schleiermacher, though he adds that the prevalent doctrine may not be limited to the confessions alone.[34] To put it this way is to suggest that the raw material with which the dogmatician works is highly complex, composed of present elements but also of past elements. It would be a mistake, then, to suppose that Schleiermacher's definition of dogmatic theology represents a kind of tyranny of the present moment.

Not surprisingly, then, the dogmatic method which Schleiermacher advocates is not a method for "thematizing," if you will, the contents of the

33. Ibid., §19, introductory proposition.
34. Ibid., §19.3.

Christian's religious self-consciousness as such. In truth, there is no *method* for doing that. But given that the Christian's religious self-consciousness has already developed in a particular community, that it has already turned up a number of dogmatic propositions, the need arises to bring order into the fragmentary and often chaotic mass of such propositions. To achieve this end, Schleiermacher advocates what he calls a "double method"—a method that is at once systematic and historical, a method that involves *adopting* dogmatic statements and *connecting* them so as to bring out their internal relations. Such a double method must also attend, however, to both the contents of the Christian's religious self-consciousness as it is attaining communal expression in the present moment as well as the contents of the Christian's religious self-consciousness as it attained communal expression in the past. If the statements adopted are to be Christian, they must stand in a demonstrable relation to Scripture; if they are to be Protestant, they must stand in a demonstrable relation to the confessions. *Glaubenslehre*, you see, has a history; it is the history of efforts on the part of the church and its theologians to make a critical selection from amongst the chaotic mass of dogmatic propositions and to find a suitable arrangement of them which would disclose their organic and logical connections.[35] Schleiermacher's method is, in truth, dialectical in nature. He moves back and forth, between past and present—which is why his treatment of a locus of doctrine will typically begin with an appeal to relevant data from the New Testament and the evangelical confessions.

Now, if the need to adopt and connect existing dogmatic propositions (past and present) is to be well served, there is a need for rules of engagement, so to speak. And it is precisely here that the feeling of absolute dependence comes into play. But it is of the utmost importance to remember that the feeling of absolute dependence *as feeling* lies beyond the conceptual grasp of the dogmatician. All the dogmatician has at his or her disposal is a representation of that feeling, constructed by the objective consciousness. And this means that insofar as the feeling of absolute dependence is brought into play in dogmatic theology, what is really being brought into play is the verbal formulation, the construct rendered in didactic form, and not the thing itself. That Schleiermacher is less than explicit about this is not an insuperable argument against the validity of the claim I am making here. For his actual procedure in the elaboration of his various doctrines shows that what he is doing is using the verbal formula to address two needs above all: (1) the need for a critical norm for setting limits to the subject matters and questions which may be validly treated with the dogmatic sphere of reflection (so as to avoid speculation) and (2) the need for a flexibly employed heuristic principle for appropriating

---

35. Ibid., §27, introductory proposition: "All propositions which claim a place in an epitome of Evangelical doctrine must prove themselves; partly through an appeal to the Evangelical confessions . . . and partly through an explanation of their unity with other already acknowledged propositions."

biblical testimony on the one hand and Christian dogmas and confessional statements of faith on the other. *As feeling*, the feeling of absolute dependence is an a priori element proper to human nature as such. *As a verbal formula* employed within the bounds of dogmatic theology, however, it is an a posteriori construct. That this is so follows directly from the nongivenness of the feeling, which we established earlier.

Theology done under these conditions is always an incomplete, fragmentary enterprise. It does not lead to a "system" in the sense suggested by the overused phrase "deductive science." It is certainly systematic, in that the propositions employed are organically related and admit of considerable logical coherence. But done well, a critical theology of consciousness in Schleiermacher's style will always be a theology which places due emphasis on the limits of human knowing.

Troeltsch's Modified Schleiermacherianism

Ernst Troeltsch lectured for two semesters on the subject of *Glaubenslehre* in the summer semester of 1912 and the winter semester of 1912–1913 at the University of Heidelberg.[36] Much had changed since the time of Schleiermacher, above all in the realm of the natural and historical sciences, and these changes were reflected in what Troeltsch took from Schleiermacher and what he felt obligated to leave behind. In the realm of the natural sciences, the advance of scientific materialism (fueled by evolutionary theory) threatened the dignity of the human. In the face of this development, from Ritschl on through Troeltsch, German theology sought to defend the thesis that spirit and matter are incommensurable realities. The realm of the spirit was seen to be the realm of freedom. In view of the high value placed on freedom and its importance for a truly *personal* existence, Schleiermacher's "feeling of absolute dependence" seemed all too pantheistic in a materialistic sense, all too deterministic, and his God indistinguishable from "fate." In the historical sciences, the greatest innovation had been fueled by Troeltsch himself as the theologian of the history-of-religions school. In Troeltsch's view, any attempt to define the "essence of Christianity" from this point on would no longer be able to privilege the originating form of Christianity but would have to attend to the totality of church life in all of its historical manifestations. It would also have to be guided by a recognition that "the essence of Christianity can only be arrived at in so far as Christianity is thought of as a part of an overall religious and cultural development. For every peculiarity of a special area, every special essence, is after all only a particular form of the general development of the

---

36. These lectures were published posthumously by Marta Troeltsch. See Ernst Troeltsch, *Glaubenslehre* (Munich and Leipzig: Duncker & Humblot, 1925); translated as *The Christian Faith*, trans. Garrett E. Paul (Minneapolis: Fortress, 1991).

spiritual life."[37] In practice, this meant that the "essence of Christianity" would no longer be abstracted from the Christian's experience of redemption as per Schleiermacher; it would be identified by means of investigation into the historical development of Christianity in its totality in comparison with the development of other religions.

Gone in Troeltsch's *Glaubenslehre* was the entire apparatus of the religious self-consciousness delineated by Schleiermacher. To the extent that Troeltsch retained a place for "feeling," it had now become a constitutive element of what Schleiermacher had once described as the "sensible self-consciousness," a third faculty on the same level as mind and will that is closely related to imagination (which itself is an active capacity, not a moment of pure receptivity). Gone was the category of immediate self-consciousness and, with that, the first of the two elements which made Schleiermacher's theology of consciousness to be critical. The feeling of absolute dependence had been abandoned. In its place was what Troeltsch called "the Christian principle." Whence did Troeltsch derive this principle? "Formulating the principle itself involves a historical intuition that extends over the entire range of manifestations, but it also involves pointing toward the future direction the principle will take."[38] Historical intuition regarding what has shown itself to be the driving idea which has come to expression in all the totality of church life in its historical development is the key here. And the result? In keeping with his concern to secure the freedom of the individual from determination by the material conditions of life, Troeltsch found this principle in the following formula: "We define the Christian principle—which will serve as the basis for all subsequent discussion—in this way: Christianity is the general, decisive breakthrough in principle to a religion of *personality*, opposed to all naturalistic and anti-personalistic understandings of God."[39] In place of the feeling of absolute dependence, we find in Troeltsch a principle constructed by means of historical study which has been carried out under the guidance of an "intuition" as to the driving idea which is alleged to have come to expression in varied historical manifestations but in fact owes much to what Troeltsch acknowledged to be the modern "worldview."[40]

Gone, finally, is the second decisive element which made Schleiermacher's theology to be critical. Schleiermacher's careful elaboration of an "otherness" of God which would allow for no confusion of God and the world has been replaced by an "interpenetration" (*Ineinander*) of divine spirit and human spirit.[41]

---

37. Ernst Troeltsch, "What Does 'Essence of Christianity' Mean?" in *Writings on Theology and Religion*, 133.

38. Troeltsch, *Glaubenslehre*, 71 (*The Christian Faith*, 63).

39. Ibid.

40. Troeltsch, "What Does 'Essence of Christianity' Mean?" 133.

41. It may seem strange that Troeltsch should contend that "Schleiermacher's dogmatics is everywhere saturated with pantheistic thinking, shot through and through with an atmosphere that breathes heavily of Spinoza and Goethe," (*Glaubenslehre*, 130 [*The Christian Faith*, 113])

Whereas, in Schleiermacher, religion was the result of a moment of pure receptivity on the side of the human—divine causality encountering human causality as a sovereign and free power—in Troeltsch, religion is the result of a coincidence of divine spirit and human spirit which makes the individual to be a person capable of cultivating in himself or herself the values of personality (e.g., dominance over the material conditions of life).[42] And with this loss of the "otherness," the sheer nongivenness of God, there also takes place the loss of any real need for communal discernment. Schleiermacher's theology was ecclesial in the final analysis precisely because it was critical, because he knew that human beings could never simply lay hold of God and that, as a consequence, theology must be communal. It was not just that the experience of redemption was communal because communally mediated. Theology itself *had to be* communal because the process of critical self-correction necessitated by the lack of human control of the subject matter of theology was a process less prone to personal whim when carried out communally and in conversation with Scripture and tradition. But in Troeltsch, *Glaubenslehre* as "church dogmatics" has been replaced by *Glaubenslehre* as a tool for furthering the development of "personality."[43]

What is clear from all of this is that Troeltsch was not wrong when he said that "scarcely one stone of Schleiermacher's own teaching can remain upon another"[44] if Troeltsch's program was to be fulfilled. Where Troeltsch was wrong was in thinking that he could make all of these changes and still be carrying out Schleiermacher's program. What Troeltsch's *Glaubenslehre* shared with Schleiermacher's, at the end of the day, was the name only. To acknowledge this much helps us to understand how Barth could have been so wrong in so many of the criticisms he directed towards Schleiermacher. Barth's critique was, in a good many of its main lines, not valid for Schleiermacher. But it was valid for Troeltsch. Barth's problem was that he never succeeded in distinguishing Schleiermacher from Troeltsch. My own guess is that he suspected that a confusion of this nature was at work; hence, he could never simply reject Schleiermacher as he had, from the very beginning of his studies, rejected Troeltsch.

---

when he himself would appear to have committed himself to a form of pantheism. What keeps his own conception free of pantheism, in Troeltsch's view, however, is the above-mentioned insistence on the incommensurability of matter and spirit. Troeltsch thinks that one has a tendency towards pantheism only where one allows reality to be reduced to materiality. There and there alone do you have a true monism.

42. The concept of revelation which undergirds this conception of religion is that of "an inner stimulation that proceeds from the mysterious connection of the divine and human spirits, which denotes the whole of the inner life, with its religious and ethical convictions and values"— "a breaking-through of a disposition out of the unity of divine and human spirit" which leads to "trust" (Troeltsch, *Glaubenslehre*, 41, 49, 52 [*The Christian Faith*, 41, 47, 49]).

43. Barth would later call "personality" the "idol of the century" (Karl Barth, *Der Römerbrief [Erste Fassung], 1919*, ed. Hermann Schmidt [Zurich: Theologischer Verlag, 1985], 272).

44. See above, footnote 13.

It remains for me now to suggest, in brief outline, why I think that Barth is a more genuine heir of Schleiermacher's real concerns than was Troeltsch. Notice that I do not say that Barth was an heir of Schleiermacher's theology in any direct fashion. Barth's theology was not a theology of consciousness. But his theology was critical, and it is this which joins him so directly to Schleiermacher's concerns and makes him a genuine representative of Schleiermacher.

The Return of "Church Dogmatics" in the Schleiermacherian Tradition

Karl Barth's theology was born of an effort to overcome historicism and psychologism in theology. Central to this effort was the conceptualization of the revelation of God as a *dandum* ("to be given") rather than a *datum* (a "given"), something which must be given anew in each new moment and not a secure possession. And it was precisely here that Barth came within hailing distance of Schleiermacher. For Schleiermacher too, revelation was a "giving," not a "given." It was the consequence of a divine causality which exercised its effect in and through creaturely causality without setting aside the difference between the two.

But, of course, the frame of reference in which this conception of revelation was worked out entailed a fairly dramatic departure from Schleiermacher. Whereas Schleiermacher worked out his concept of revelation in terms of an analysis of the Christian's religious self-consciousness, Barth grounded his conception in the *Göttingen Dogmatics* in Christology. The element of indirection which preserved the divine otherness in the act of revelation was preserved in Barth's thought not by a critical distinction between immediate and sensible self-consciousness but by an actualistic understanding of the ancient anhypostatic-enhypostatic Christology—and this certainly constituted an important shift away from Schleiermacher. Like Troeltsch, Barth too could no longer make use of the category of immediate self-consciousness or the feeling of absolute dependence which comes to expression on that level. But unlike Troeltsch, Barth was able to elaborate a conception of revelation which preserved the critical element which was so basic to Schleiermacher's achievement.

Revelation

The heartbeat of Barth's conception of revelation in the *Göttingen Dogmatics* is the notion of indirectness.[45] God does not reveal himself directly to human beings but only indirectly, through various media of God's choosing.

---

45. The passages to which appeal might be made in support of this claim are legion. The following examples are merely illustrative: Karl Barth, *The Göttingen Dogmatics: Instruction*

The relation of God to these media is that of a unity-in-differentiation, although the basis for the unity in question varies depending on the medium in question. The primary medium of God's Self-revelation, *the* medium through which the Self-mediation of God's knowledge of himself takes place, is, of course, the humanity of Jesus. The unity in this case is understood in terms of the ancient category of a hypostatic union of two natures in a single Subject which is identified with the eternal Logos, the Second Person of the Trinity. Given the intimacy of this form of a unity-in-differentiation, Christology constitutes the basis upon which all of God's other acts of Self-revelation take place—whether in Holy Scripture or in preaching that is based upon Holy Scripture. Jesus Christ is revelation itself. Holy Scripture constitutes the primary *witness* to this revelation; preaching that is based on Holy Scripture constitutes a secondary and derivative witness. The relation of God to these witnesses stands in an analogical and participatory relation to the primary unity-in-differentiation which characterizes the God-human, Jesus Christ. Here we are not dealing with a unity constituted by the singularity of the Subject in which two "natures" are grounded; we are dealing with a unity which arises through a relation of correspondence. Revelation is an act of God's grace in which God takes up the creaturely media of Scripture and preaching and gives to them a capacity which they do not possess in and for themselves to bear adequate witness to God. In that this occurs, the media *correspond* to revelation itself. In this relation of correspondence, they participate actualistically in the primary form of unity-in-differentiation which is Jesus Christ. They obtain a *share* in God's act of Self-revelation.[46]

The element of indirectness which I spoke of a moment ago is a function of the fact that however the element of unity in the complex act of God's Self-revelation is established, the unity in question does not set aside the on-

---

in the Christian Religion, trans. Geoffrey Bromiley (Grand Rapids: Eerdmans, 1991), 1:57–59, 138, 144, 151, 158, 160, 329–39.

46. Already in the *Göttingen Dogmatics*, Barth elaborates a doctrine of the Word of God in a threefold form, and he understands the relation of these three forms (Jesus Christ, Holy Scripture, and preaching) as standing in an analogical relation to the unity-in-differentiation that is the Trinity:

The Word of God on which dogmatics reflects . . . is one in three and three in one: revelation, scripture, and preaching—the Word of God as revelation, the Word of God as scripture, and the Word of God as preaching, neither to be confused nor separated. One Word of God, one authority, one power, and yet not one but three addresses. Three addresses of God in revelation, scripture, and preaching, yet not three Words of God, three authorities, truths, or powers, but one. Scripture is not revelation, but from revelation. Preaching is not revelation or scripture, but from both. But the Word of God is scripture no less than it is revelation, and it is preaching no less than it is scripture. Revelation is from God alone, scripture is from revelation alone, and preaching is from revelation and scripture. Yet there is no first or last, no greater or less. (ibid., 1:15)

tological difference between God and the human medium. God remains God; the medium remains a creaturely medium.[47] As the two "natures" of Christ are unimpaired in their original integrity in the act of hypostatic union,[48] so also God remains ontologically other than the media of Holy Scripture and preaching. It is this difference which creates the indirectness. Our knowledge of God is indirect as opposed to direct—indirect because we do not confront God directly but only in hiddenness, only in a veil, only in concealment.[49] The net effect of this act of veiling is that God can be known only where God grants the eyes of faith to "see" what is hidden beneath the veil. The veil must be lifted. This unveiling of God in and through a creaturely veil constitutes an irreversible relation.[50] God remains the Subject of the event throughout. In that God conceals himself in a veil, God makes himself to be "objective" to the human knower in such a way that God's freedom to be the Subject of the event is preserved.

As with Schleiermacher's conception of revelation, so also with Barth's: revelation itself can never become a direct "given." It is a "giving," ever to be renewed, moment by moment. It is not a "given." "Revelation is not a direct openness on God's part but a becoming open."[51] Now, obviously, important differences of a material nature remain. The biggest difference is that Barth is able to affirm a real incarnation of God—and this is no small matter, obviously. For him, the indirectness of revelation is a function of the mode of God's Self-revelation in time. In Schleiermacher it was a function of the effort to preserve the necessary distinction between the eternal God and temporalized human existence for the sake of safeguarding the feeling of absolute dependence. For this reason, the *content* of Schleiermacher's conception of revelation stood in closest proximity to that found in the second edition of Barth's commentary on *Romans*, not to that found in the *Göttingen Dogmatics*.[52] But this difference

47. Ibid., 1:332: "Directly, plainly, and in itself . . . , our knowledge has to do with a medium. This medium can impart the knowledge of God to us. But this already means indirect impartation. The medium in itself does not impart the knowledge."

48. Ibid., 1:138: "The real deity and the real humanity must be so united that neither can be changed into the other or mixed with it. The relation must be an open and loose one inasmuch as the deity does not pass into the humanity or the humanity become identical with the deity. Otherwise it would no longer be God that meets us, or he would cease to meet us truly. On no side then, can the union become an equation. It must be a union in inequality, in differentation. It must be a strictly dialectical union." Cf. 1:91, where Barth insists that there must be no "deifying of the creature."

49. Among the many passages which could be chosen to illustrate the point, see ibid., 1:329–31.

50. Ibid., 1:330: "God does not set aside or reverse his irremovable and irreversible I. He does not cease to be God in his revelation. But he conceals his I in a relation in which we can share in his self-knowledge, in which he can meet us, in which we can stand before him."

51. Ibid., 1:58.

52. As to the content of revelation, Barth insisted that nothing that is proper to the being of God as God is left behind in the incarnation of the Son and the outpouring of the Spirit in

in content between Schleiermacher's *Glaubenslehre* and Barth's *Göttingen Dogmatics* must not be allowed to blind us to the continuity on the formal level. Both affirm an indirect conception of revelation in the absence of which neither theology could have been "critical" in the sense of limiting the grasp of human knowing in order to make room for divine action in revelation. What this continuity on the level of the critical character of their respective theologies means for the relationship of Barth's dogmatic method in comparison with Schleiermacher's will be the final question I will take up here.

Dogmatic Method(s) in the Göttingen Dogmatics

Barth's discussion of dogmatic method in the *Göttingen Dogmatics* does not prepare us adequately for what he does in doctrinal construction. The method he advocates in his prolegomena is the dialectical method of pitting statement over against counterstatement.[53] This method is employed in the *Dogmatics*, above all in the doctrine of God's attributes. But we will not have come even close to a complete description of Barth's methods—and they really are methods (in the plural)—if we stop there.

In my first book on Barth, I described the methods employed in the *Göttingen Dogmatics* as a combination of a "Sentence Commentary" approach, which substitutes Heinrich Heppe's *Reformed Dogmatics* for Peter Lombard's *Sentences* as the basic text, with the *loci communes* approach of Philip Melanchthon.[54] That interpretation certainly arrived at something central to Barth's approach. But it left one significant factor out of account—which is easily missed because of Barth's protest against the employment of a "material principle" in Christian theology. Barth's protest was not only motivated by a desire to obviate the possibility of speculation in dogmatics, though this too played a role. His real concern was with dogmatics which elevated some one Christian doctrine above the others and sought to deduce the contents of the others from the one which had been made basic. It was the fear of the arbitrary which led Barth to oppose the elevation of one doctrine above the others and to descry the analytical method by means of which its contents would be unfolded. Barth claimed to find this approach in the dogmatics of C. E. Luthardt, Albrecht Ritschl, Julius Kaftan, F. A. B. Nitzsch, and Ernst Troeltsch.[55]

But Barth had a "material principle" in a quite different sense than that against which he raised an objection. My conviction is that Barth substituted

---

time. The presence of God to us in revelation is the presence of God, complete, whole, and entire. "God's hiddenness, his incomprehensibility, is his hiddenness not alongside or behind revelation but *in* it" (ibid., 1:88–95).

53. Ibid., 1:309–12.

54. McCormack, *Karl Barth's Critically Realistic Dialectical Theology*, 349.

55. Barth, *The Göttingen Dogmatics*, 1:300.

for Schleiermacher's feeling of absolute dependence the dialectic of veiling and unveiling in revelation. Like Schleiermacher before him, Barth was very concerned to eliminate any a priori speculative principles from the realm of dogmatics. But he was also convinced that he had learned to understand revelation as indirect in his sense, that is, as occurring by means of a *Realdialektik* of veiling and unveiling, from an attentive and faithful "following-after" of revelation in its actuality. And—this is the truly decisive point—he used his a posteriori "material principle" not analytically but critically and heuristically, just as Schleiermacher had employed his feeling of absolute dependence throughout his *Glaubenslehre*. "Critically": that means as a tool for establishing the limits of what can be said within the realm of dogmatics and avoiding errors in doctrinal construction. "Heuristically": that means as a tool for assimilating the witness of Holy Scripture to particular doctrinal themes and the witness of tradition to that witness. In most cases, both uses are at play in the same context. I will give you one brief example of this.

The example is taken from Barth's doctrine of humanity in "The Human as God's Creature," §22 of the *Göttingen Dogmatics*. The starting-point for reflection is, once again, revelation. And so, when Barth asks already in §4, "What must man be because revelation is?"[56] he has already indicated the methodological course he will pursue in the more material consideration of the doctrine of humanity in §22. What the starting-point in revelation means is that what Barth will be concerned with in the object of his reflections is not the human person as he or she appears in natural-scientific, historical-psychological, or philosophical modes of consideration.[57] The object of his reflection is the human as he or she is addressed by God in revelation. And here a critical use of revelation understood in terms of the dialectic of veiling and unveiling announces itself. Neither the materialist nor the idealist accounts of the human, whatever truths may come to expression in them, may control a truly theological anthropology.[58] If God has deigned to address us in and through creaturely media of God's choosing, then we may not look away from what we are seen to be in this situation as though it had not happened.

Barth's concentration upon the concrete situation of revelation then enables him to make a transcendental move which takes the following form: given that revelation is as I have described it to be, what must we say about the human recipient of revelation? What Barth is trying to gain access to by means of his starting-point in the situation of revelation is an understanding of the human as created: that which the human is "essentially." The move Barth makes here differs in an obvious way from that found in more classical forms of Protestant theology. In those earlier theologies, if one wanted to know something about

---

56. Barth, *The Göttingen Dogmatics*, 1:72.
57. Karl Barth, *Unterricht in der christlichen Religion*, vol. 2, *Die Lehre von Gott/Die Lehre vom Menschen, 1924–25* (Zurich: Theologischer Verlag, 1990), 344.
58. Ibid., 350.

the human as created, one turned immediately to Genesis 1 and 2 and to the passages, scattered through Scripture, which constituted a gloss or commentary on Genesis 1 and 2. But Barth begins with the concrete situation of revelation because, as he contends, "*in* and with the address of God to man in His revelation is given, in the first instance, a definite knowledge of the being [*das Wesen*] of man as such."[59]

What do we learn from the concrete situation of revelation? As God "speaks with me in veiling *and* unveiling, so also I myself am a remarkable parable, a suitable recipient of his Word: visible *and* invisible reality. Just as revelation would not be revelation if it were not both veiling *and* unveiling, not next to one another but rather in and with one another, in the same way man would not be man if he were not body *and* soul."[60] Expressed more expansively: what we learn from the concrete situation of revelation is that the human person belongs with the rest of creation, as having a material nature. The human person stands before a medium of revelation which, in its empirical givenness, its "materiality," constitutes a barrier between oneself and God which this person, in his or her bodily limitations of sense experience, may not penetrate.[61] In this, a person finds that he or she corresponds in one aspect of his or her being to one aspect of the nature of revelation itself.

But in that it takes place that one is also made a recipient of revelation, one learns something more about oneself. The human person learns that he or she is more than his or her bodily existence. Without ceasing to be a veil, the veil is made "transparent" to the person. God is unveiled in and through the veil of human words. And from this the person learns that he or she is also "soul," an act of cognition, a thinking substance as the ancients used to put it, in the mode of thinking and willing. "In that God addresses man, he recognizes himself to have been created by God for the perception and reception of His Word [which is] not only a physical but precisely also a psychic, spiritual operation."[62] What takes place when the veil is "lifted" is that the human receives a word which engages both mind and will, has rational, communicable content, and lays a claim upon one.

Clearly, the transcendental move that I have described belongs to the critical function of the concept of revelation. For, in beginning with the concrete situation of revelation, Barth is ruling out of court other approaches in a theological anthropology.

59. Ibid., 346.
60. Ibid., 350–51.
61. Ibid., 347. The one who is confronted by God in the Self-mediation of knowledge of himself stands on the boundary of his or her creatureliness at the point where an "abyss" between God and oneself opens up and the true transcendence of God begins (a transcendence that is not a human projection but the reality of God in the act of unveiling himself in and through a veil that, in itself, remains a veil).
62. Ibid., 353.

Armed with this understanding of the human, Barth then turns in subsection 3 to a consideration of the Christian tradition as it comes to expression primarily, though not exclusively, in Heinrich Heppe's *Reformed Dogmatics*.[63] It is here that the heuristic use of the dialectic of veiling and unveiling comes into play (in combination with a critical use). Barth uses his understanding of revelation, and the doctrine of the human as created which is entailed by it, in order to critically assimilate traditional teaching, to strip it of certain philosophical elements in order then to find, in its critically received form, a confirmation of the understanding he has advanced to this point. The traditional Reformed understanding of the human as a body-soul unity is affirmed but on a basis quite different from that on which it was originally constructed. The metaphysical-philosophical elements have been stripped away. What remains is a strictly theological account of the human as body and soul. The details of this discussion need not detain us any longer. It is important to point out that the examples could easily be multiplied. It is not just in the doctrine of humanity that the dialectic of veiling and unveiling plays the role that I have described. In doctrine after doctrine, this is the case. So, what I have shown in relation to the doctrine of humanity is meant to be only suggestive.

The dialectic of veiling and unveiling never disappeared from Barth's theology. But with the publication of his revised doctrine of election in *CD* II/2, the critical and heuristic roles that I have pointed to here were taken over by Barth's Christology. The Christocentrism that most people associate with Barth's later theology is a function of his doctrine of election. That the critical and heuristic functions continued to be played by a doctrinal complex at all, however, is proof enough that the methodological lessons learned in Göttingen would not be forgotten in the move to Basel.

Conclusion

So, why should any of this matter? Why should it matter to anyone that Barth's relationship to Schleiermacher was not simply oppositional but also embraced elements of continuity? The historian of doctrine in me would like to answer, "Setting the record straight is reason enough. A historian does not need a bigger reason than that." But the systematic theologian in me will not rest content with this answer.

It is my conviction that the nineteenth century is still with us. It has been chastened in some quarters, but in other quarters has shown surprising resiliency in its originating forms. In relation to the last-named development, I think of the resurgence of interest, in the German-language sphere, in early German idealism: in Fichte, in Schelling, in Hegel, in the early Schleiermacher

---

63. Heinrich Heppe, *Reformed Dogmatics* (Grand Rapids: Baker Academic, 1978).

of the *Speeches*. Even Emanuel Hirsch is once again attracting a good deal of attention. Chastened adherents of nineteenth-century theology will admit that there is a certain point to postmodern criticism of the modern project, but they will not concede that the project was simply wrong. Where postmodernism has taken the step of saying that there are no "grand metanarratives," the death of theology must surely follow. But the true "foundations" of theology are a "giving," not a "given." This may mean the end of foundational*ism*, but it does not mean the end of foundations. The true foundations of all truth claims whatsoever are to be found in the being-in-act of the Triune God. But insofar as these "foundations" always elude the grasp of the human attempt to know and establish them from the human side, they cannot be "demonstrated" philosophically or in any other way.

And it is because this is so that both the later Schleiermacher and the early Barth continue to have so much relevance today. These were theologians who took seriously the limits of human knowing and experiencing. Both passed through a period of serious romantic influence. Both wrote books which reflected this romantic edge—Schleiermacher with his *Speeches* and Barth with his commentaries on Romans. But both also recognized that the churches cannot live on criticism alone. Theology must go on to say something positive if the churches are to be fed and nourished. Without losing sight for a moment of the lessons they had learned in their romantic phases, they both went on to write "church dogmatics" which were, at one and the same time, majestic in their scope and modest in the claims they made for themselves. (Barth's, at least, could probably have afforded to be a little less majestic!)

Neither Schleiermacher nor Barth was "postmodern." But both anticipated in their own ways a number of the valid insights which have emerged in so-called postmodernism. My own guess is that postmodernism is a storm that is already moving off the coast and heading out to sea, where it will simply blow itself out. What will remain are the theologies which are able to combine academic rigor with ecclesial concern in the setting of a modernity that is now more chastened than before. What will remain are theologies like those of Schleiermacher and Barth.

4

The Significance of Karl Barth's Theological Exegesis of Philippians

Introduction

Long before he had earned widespread recognition as the greatest dogmatic theologian since Schleiermacher, Karl Barth was known as a highly innovative exegete of Holy Scripture. The first edition of his commentary on Paul's Epistle to the Romans, published in 1919, won for him an honorary professorship in Reformed confession, doctrine, and church life at the University of Göttingen in the fall of 1921. The more famous second (revised) edition of 1922 catapulted him into the front ranks of the most influential theologians of the day. Written in an expressionistic style replete with military metaphors, characterized by sharply dialectical thought-forms ("the infinite qualitative difference between time and eternity")[1] and a resounding witness to divine judgment on all things human, the second edition struck a deep chord of response in a German culture weary of academic commitments which had done little to prevent the war and much to fuel it, especially the tendency towards the subjective and the individualistic fostered by the neo-Kantian tradition in philosophy. With the collapse of neo-Kantianism, a longing for a return to the "object" and the elevation of community over individualism spread like wildfire throughout Germany—and this is what many found in Barth's

This essay was originally published in a slightly different form under the title "The Significance of Karl Barth's Theological Exegesis of Philippians," in Karl Barth, *Epistle to the Philippians*, 40th anniv. ed. (Louisville: Westminster John Knox, 2002), v–xxv. Reprinted by permission.

1. Karl Barth, *Der Römerbrief, 1922* (Zurich: Theologischer Verlag, 1940), xiii; translated as *The Epistle to the Romans*, trans. Edwyn C. Hoskyns (Oxford: Oxford University Press, 1933), 10.

Romans, even as others were finding it in various forms of phenomenology (Husserl, Scheler, and Heidegger).

From the beginning of his teaching activity in Göttingen, Barth offered exegetical lectures alongside his courses in historical theology and dogmatics. Already in his first semester in the winter of 1921–1922, he taught a course on Ephesians. This was followed by courses on James (winter semester 1922–1923), 1 Corinthians 15 (summer semester 1923), 1 John (winter semester 1923–1924), Philippians (summer semester 1924), Colossians (winter semester 1924–1925), and the Sermon on the Mount (summer semester 1925). In 1925 Barth's contribution to New Testament studies was given formal recognition through his appointment to a combined chair in dogmatics and New Testament exegesis in Münster. Here he lectured on John's Gospel (winter semester 1925–1926), Philippians (winter semester 1926–1927), Colossians (summer semester 1927), and James (winter semester 1928–1929). Subsequent to his move to Bonn in 1930, Barth repeated his courses on James, Philippians, John's Gospel, and the Sermon on the Mount (summer semester 1930, winter semester 1930–1931, summer semester 1933, and winter semester 1933–1934 respectively). His teaching of New Testament exegesis was rounded out by the repetition of his Colossians course in the winter semester of 1937–1938 and a new course on 1 Peter in the summer semester of 1938 (both taught in Basel).[2]

Innovation came at a price—initially at least. Reactions to Barth's *Romans* commentaries were almost uniformly negative where the members of the New Testament guild were concerned. The exceptions were to be found among the small minority of those who, like Rudolf Bultmann, already had a strong interest in hermeneutical issues (both philosophical and theological) before the stir caused by Barth. More typical was the response of Adolf Jülicher, then the dean of New Testament studies in Germany.[3] Jülicher saw already in Barth's

2. From this rather extensive investment in the academic field of New Testament exegetical study, only the lectures on 1 Corinthians 15 and Philippians were published by Barth himself; see Karl Barth, *Die Auferstehung der Toten: Eine akademische Vorlesung über 1. Kor. 15* (Munich: Kaiser, 1924); translated as *The Resurrection of the Dead*, trans. H. J. Stenning (London: Hodder & Stoughton, 1933); *Erklärung des Philipperbriefes* (Munich: Kaiser, 1928); translated as *The Epistle to the Philippians*, trans. James W. Leitch (Richmond: John Knox, 1962). Out of the corpus of lectures unpublished in Barth's lifetime, only the Münster lectures on John 1–8 have been published to date; see Karl Barth, *Erklärung des Johannes-Evangelium (Kapitel 1–8)*, ed. Walther Fürst (Zurich: Theologischer Verlag, 1976). Plans are now under way, however, to produce a critical edition, in two to three volumes, of all the remaining exegetical lectures, together with new critical editions of 1 Corinthians 15 and Philippians. I should add that a critical edition of Barth's famous second edition of *Romans* is also in the planning stages. For more on plans for future volumes in the *Gesamtausgabe*, see Hans-Anton Drewes, "Die Zukunft der Karl Barth-Gesamtausgabe," *Verkündigung und Forschung* 46 (2001): 8.

3. For an exhaustive treatment of the reception of the first edition of Barth's *Romans*, see Richard Ernest Burnett, *Karl Barth's Theological Exegesis: The Hermeneutical Principles of the "Römerbrief" Prefaces* (Tübingen: Mohr Siebeck, 2001), 14–23. This work constitutes a landmark in the history of interpretation of Barth's hermeneutics. What is new in it, beyond

first commentary on Romans an exercise in "practical" exegesis, as opposed to a "strictly scientific" approach. By "practical" he meant an exegesis which "reproduces the basic thoughts of that letter [Romans] in the language of our time, indeed recast in the conceptual world of today," and which "shows its own value in steady confrontation with the religious and moral problems of the present day." Such efforts were deemed necessary in order to provide "a stimulus for the direction which thought must take if it is to keep Paul alive and arouse the spirits of present-day men [*sic*]."[4] Had Barth himself been willing to acknowledge that this was his task and gift, Jülicher would have found no cause for complaint. But Barth actually believed that what he had to say constituted a more adequate understanding of Paul and his message than could be acquired by means of the tools employed in historical-critical research. In the face of this effrontery, Jülicher could not restrain himself: "Much, perhaps even very much, may someday be learned from this book for the understanding of our age, but scarcely anything new for the understanding of the 'historical' Paul." Barth, he said, was a "pneumatic"—a gnostic who believed himself able "to look beyond and through the historical 'into the Spirit of the Bible, which is the eternal Spirit.'"[5] Marcion "proceeded with the same sovereign arbitrariness and assurance of victory, with the same one-sided dualistic approach of enmity to all that comes from the world, culture, or tradition."[6] Barth's book was a manifestation of "a period in the history of culture that is not historically oriented."[7]

Barth responded to these charges in the preface to the second edition. "I am not a 'pneumatic,'" he wrote. He also insisted that he was not the "enemy of historical criticism" which critics such as Jülicher and Hans Lietzmann made him out to be.[8] Historical investigation had, in his view, a significant role to play in any truly adequate exegesis. Its role was that of establishing "what stands in the text"—what the text says. This may well involve an attempt to

---

the immediately obvious fact that the breadth of research upon which its conclusions rest is far more extensive than anything done heretofore, lies in its attempt to demonstrate that Barth operated exegetically with clear hermeneutical "principles" and was not the ad hoc exegete defended by representatives of the so-called Yale school. It will not be possible to provide even an overview here of all of the principles and subprinciples that pass in review in the course of Burnett's exposition. I will content myself with lifting up one or two central ideas which will aid us in understanding what Barth was trying to achieve in his Philippians commentary and why. For the rest, Burnett's work is required reading.

4. Adolf Jülicher, "A Modern Interpreter of Paul," in *The Beginnings of Dialectic Theology*, ed. James M. Robinson (Richmond: John Knox, 1968), 72–73.

5. Ibid., 78. Jülicher is here quoting from the preface to the first edition of Barth's commentary. See Barth, *Der Römerbrief, 1922*, v (*The Epistle to the Romans*, 1).

6. Jülicher, "Modern Interpreter of Paul," 78.

7. Ibid., 81.

8. Barth, *Der Römerbrief, 1922*, xiii (*The Epistle to the Romans*, 9). It should be noted that Edwyn Hoskyns's translation of the word *Pneumatiker* with "esoteric personage" fails to capture the technical significance of the term, drawn as it was by Jülicher from ancient gnostic literature.

reconstruct the text in an order that is historically and psychologically more plausible—though Barth expressed a certain amount of scepticism where such procedures are concerned: "Jülicher and Lietzmann know far better than I do just how uncertain [such work is], just how much historians are guided by assumptions of the most dubious kind already in the determination of what 'stands' in the text."[9] Still, however fraught with difficulty the historical task of establishing what "stands" in the text might be, it is a necessary first step. No attempt to interpret the meaning of what was said is conceivable apart from having first established what was said. Barth's protest was not directed against historical research as such but against the *historicism* of the historians who sought to reduce all valid (truly "scientific") explanation of the biblical texts to historical explanation and that alone.

The tide of theological history was turning against Jülicher even as he wrote his review of the first edition of *Romans*. By the mid-1920s, a romantic reaction had set in which brought the ideals of the academic exegesis defended by Jülicher into question. Like the romantic exegesis which flourished in the age of Schleiermacher as a reaction against the aridity of the university-based, highly rationalistic exegesis found in the Enlightenment, the new hermeneutics laid great emphasis on the need for a "pneumatic exegesis" which—though not intending to eliminate historical exegesis—would somehow complete it.

The Romantic Reaction

Though he had contributed so much to creating the conditions necessary for a renewed consideration of biblical hermeneutics (through his relentless critique of historicism), Barth played no direct role in the debates over "pneumatic exegesis" which remained a prominent feature of theological discussion on into the thirties. Indeed, he refused to be drawn into the discussion—for reasons we will explain momentarily. The debate was launched by Karl Girgensohn, a Lutheran professor of theology in Leipzig with a lifelong interest in giving psychology a role in a science of religion. In an essay written right before his death in 1925, Girgensohn issued a call for renewed attention to pneumatic exegesis.[10] His call quickly drew responses from Otto Procksch,

9. Ibid., x (*The Epistle to the Romans*, 6). Though Barth does not go any further in explaining the pitfalls that surround historical reconstruction of a text, his thinking might well have included some of the following considerations: "Historical reality withdraws itself in a certain sense from the grasp of history; it is not possible to say how it really was. What history can lay hold of is not the naked event, which consists of a chaotic mass of details, but merely the interpretation that the event gives to itself through the context of meaning in which it has its effect. . . . We can know only that which has become meaningful, whereas the formless event is the real limit of historical knowing" (Erich Seeberg, "Zum Problem der pneumatischen Exegese," in *Sellin-Festschrift*, ed. W. F. Albright et al. [Leipzig: Deichert, 1927], 127–28).

10. Karl Girgensohn, *Die Inspiration der heiligen Schrift* (Dresden: Ungelenk, 1925).

Reinhold Seeberg, and Johannes Behm.[11] The appearance in 1926 of the first volume of Joachim Wach's study of the history of hermeneutics in the nineteenth century ensured that all future contributions would have to take Schleiermacher's contribution to a pneumatic exegesis very seriously.[12] Other books and articles followed.[13] A history of the debate as it unfolded would be out of place here. We must content ourselves with a synthetic picture of the chief results.

Most participants in the discussion surrounding pneumatic exegesis were agreed that historical research had done much to increase knowledge of the meaning of particular biblical texts or portions thereof in their original setting. But genuine *understanding* of a text required more than just a knowledge of details. It demanded a grasp of the whole in which the particular passages, letters, and books had their place. The "whole" in question was not identified by most with a canonical principle. What was needed was a more or less intuitive grasp of the "suprahistorical content"[14] of Scripture, that which made the writings of the prophets and apostles to be a whole. The question was: Just what was this suprahistorical content (in whose light the whole of Scripture was then to be understood)? And how was it to be accessed?

One conceivable strategy was for the interpreter to seek to allow the processes at work in the soul of the author which led to the writing of this or that text to be reproduced in himself or herself. "How did he come to form these thoughts? What was happening in him? What did the surrounding world offer him in the way of stimuli, of means of expression? What was he himself feeling as he wrote this? What did he want to achieve with it in his listeners or readers?"[15] This was the "psychological exegesis" derived from Schleiermacher. To experience in one's self the experience which gave rise to a particular text requires that a relation of "congeniality" exist between the one who would understand and the person who would be understood. How this relation comes about was variously explained. Erich Seeberg's explanation was fairly typical at the time. He spoke of a "congenial experiencing-after" (*kongeniale Nacherleben*) on the part of the interpreter,

---

11. Otto Procksch, "Pneumatische Exegese," *Christentum und Wissenschaft* 1 (1925): 145–58; Reinhold Seeberg, "Die Frage nach dem Sinn und Recht einer pneumatischen Schriftauslegung," *Zeitschrift für systematischen Theologie* (1926): 3–59; Johannes Behm, *Pneumatische Exegese? Ein Wort zur Methode der Schriftauslegung* (Schwerin, 1926).

12. Joachim Wach, *Das Verstehen: Grundzüge einer Geschichte der hermeneutischen Theorie im 19. Jahrhundert*, vol. 1, *Die grossen Systeme* (Tübingen: Mohr Siebeck, 1926).

13. The literature is extensive. See esp. Ernst von Dobschütz, "Die pneumatische Exegese, Wissenschaft und Praxis," in *Vom Auslegen des Neuen Testaments: Drei Reden* (Göttingen: Vandenhoeck & Ruprecht, 1927), 49–64; Seeberg, "Zum Problem der pneumatischen Exegese"; and Johannes Schneider, "Historische und pneumatische Exegese," *Neue kirchliche Zeitschrift* 42 (1931): 711–33. For further literature, see Burnett, *Karl Barth's Theological Exegesis*, 30n68.

14. Von Dobschütz, "Die pneumatische Exegese, Wissenschaft und Praxis," 61.

15. Ibid., 53.

which had as its presupposition the transposition of one's own I into that of the author.[16] This, in turn, was made possible by the "irrational creativity" of the exegete—an act which reached beyond rational comprehension.[17] The "whole" in this case, in whose light individual statements and passages are to be read and understood, is the "total personality" of the writer. But was this what was meant by "pneumatic exegesis"? Most preferred to think of "psychological exegesis" as, at most, a "pneumatic moment" in scientific exegesis. Any fully adequate account of scientific exegesis must give attention to both historical and psychological interpretation. All of this was a much-needed preparation for pneumatic exegesis but was not yet the thing itself. But, then, just what is pneumatic exegesis?

According to Karl Girgensohn, a truly "pneumatic" mode of consideration is present where Scripture is read prayerfully and the voice of the living God is heard. But this claim found only a highly qualified approval. There was widespread worry that a fundamental confusion of method and charism was at work in Girgensohn's understanding of pneumatic exegesis.[18] The Holy Spirit is not "an objective principle of a scientific method" that can be brought into play at the discretion of the interpreter.[19] The Spirit is a gift of God which can never be brought under human control. No one wished to diminish the significance of this gift. "A theologian who lacks the charism of interpretation is a bad theologian."[20] But such a gift belongs to a "prescientific" equipping of the interpreter for scientific work; it did not belong to methodological inquiry as such.[21]

A second line of objection was even more significant where a comparison with Barth and the other dialectical theologians is concerned. Pneumatic exegesis in the form in which it was defended by Girgensohn would lead to a "renewal of the doctrine of a double meaning of Scripture" of the kind once found in ancient and medieval allegorizing.[22] It was in order to do away with

16. The concepts denoted by the words "congeniality" and "experiencing-after," as well as the thought of transforming oneself into the author, enjoyed a prominent place in the Schleiermacher-Dilthey tradition in hermeneutics. See Burnett, *Karl Barth's Theological Exegesis*, 177–98.

17. Seeberg, "Zum Problem der pneumatischen Exegese," 131.

18. Von Dobschütz, "Die pneumatische Exegese, Wissenschaft und Praxis," 51.

19. Schneider, "Historische und pneumatische Exegese," 722.

20. Von Dobschütz, "Die pneumatische Exegese, Wissenschaft und Praxis," 52.

21. Schneider, "Historische und pneumatische Exegese," 723. With this contention the dialectical theologians would have been the first to agree. See Friedrich Gogarten, *Theologische Tradition und theologische Arbeit: Geistesgeschichte oder Theologie?* (Leipzig: Hinrichs, 1927), 5: "There is no method which one has at his disposal and which one could employ in order to understand the Bible as the Word of God." And Rudolf Bultmann, "The Problem of a Theological Exegesis of the New Testament," in *The Beginnings of Dialectic Theology*, ed. James M. Robinson (Richmond: John Knox, 1968), 255: "Since there is no direct encounter with God, but his revelation is hidden in the word, there can be no appeal to an inner light for exegesis, no 'pneumatic' exegesis which counts on the pneuma as a possession previously bestowed on the exegete."

22. Schneider, "Historische und pneumatische Exegese," 722.

the kind of arbitrariness in exegesis to which allegorical readings gave rise that Luther had insisted upon the literal meaning alone.[23] Now, there was certainly a valid concern expressed in this objection. If the content of the "Word of God" standing back of Scripture, so to speak, stood in no discernible connection to the content of the biblical texts under consideration, then it would be hard to avoid opening the door to the merely arbitrary.

Still, most were not prepared to simply abandon talk of "pneumatic exegesis." They believed it necessary to press beyond mere historical interpretation to the "suprahistorical." The question was, once again, How? And how to demonstrate a material connection between the historical meaning of a text and the Word to which it might conceivably point? One solution, which received a good bit of attention, was that of Erich Seeberg. Seeberg posited the existence of "something metaphysical, something objective," that comes to expression in all great literature, a content which transcends the thoughts and intentions of its authors. "The eternal productivity of great literature which continues beyond epochal historical shifts and cultural decay, even in those cases where the individual soul from which it proceeded has died out or declined in its effects, is to be explained by this suprapersonal, unconscious, and unwanted power in itself." It is in Seeberg's emphasis on the irrational, the unconscious, and the unwanted that we begin to catch sight of the kind of expressionistic hermeneutics which were also at work in the Stefan George circle at that time (as Seeberg himself admitted).[24] Even where this emphasis was not specifically endorsed, the comparative approach (which was invited by Seeberg's talk of an eternal content which comes to expression in a variety of historical forms) was. The comparison of great works of literature or even only of the writings of a John and a Paul held forth a promise of greater objectivity in the attempt to ascertain what is truly normative in the message of the Bible as a whole and the piety which corresponds to it (the "divine" element).[25]

Clearly, the participants in the pneumatic-exegesis debate were trying to tie the "pneumatic" to the "scientific" so as to reduce the possibility of enthusiastic spiritualism, the free imposition of value judgments on texts which had scarcely been understood. "Pneumatic exegesis" must not, in their view, be confused with "practical application" (i.e., an effort to say something about what the text means for us today). Pneumatic exegesis works in the narrow space between scientific exegesis (what the text meant) and practical

23. Seeberg, "Die Frage nach dem Sinn und Recht einer pneumatischen Schriftauslegung," 39.

24. Seeberg, "Zum Problem der pneumatischen Exegese," 134.

25. Von Dobschütz, "Die pneumatische Exegese, Wissenschaft und Praxis," 53–55. See also 57: "I believe that I am able to find an objective standard for comparison. Value has something of general validity about it. When, for example, a thought about Jesus is to be found in Paul as well as John, in James as well as in the Epistle to the Hebrews, that is important. The thought is important because its significance was generally recognized at an early stage."

application (what it means today). Both what it meant and what it means are historically conditioned. What is sought through pneumatic exegesis are the eternal values (religious and ethical) which came to expression there and ought to come to expression here.[26]

With hindsight, it has to be said that in trying to locate pneumatic exegesis *between* the scientific and the practical, these scholars were preserving a distinction between two things that ought not to have been distinguished in this way. The result was an oscillation between a collapse back into what continued to be thought of as scientific exegesis and an irrational leap into a set of values that were finally a function of the creativity of the exegete. This was not a stable position. The one element in this debate that bore the greatest promise was quickly lost to sight. One of the things Girgensohn had called for was a reevaluation of the very concept of "science" which was presupposed in the accepted understanding of "scientific exegesis." Girgensohn pointed out that the presupposed concept was empiricist and positivistic and should be modified in the direction of a concept which made allowance for the unfinished and open-ended character of all scientific investigation.[27] But this point was dismissed because of fear that a reevaluation of the accepted understanding of "science" might mean the *complete* discrediting of historical work[28]—a fear which was unjustified, in my view. A close examination of the "scientific realism" advocated by a goodly number of those engaged today in discussions of philosophy of science would show that Girgensohn was ahead of his time.[29] And had he but been able to recognize it, Karl Barth had already come much closer to arguing for a concept of "scientific" exegesis which would have overcome the hegemony of positivism in the historical sciences.

For his part, Barth refused to be drawn into the debate. He gave two reasons. First, his own position had been so badly caricatured in reviews of his *Romans* and elsewhere that a fruitful conversation had been rendered very difficult. And second, it seemed to him that the debate had become "bogged

26. Ibid., 61–62.
27. Girgensohn, *Die Inspiration der heiligen Schrift*, 20.
28. Schneider, "Historische und pneumatische Exegese," 720.
29. See D. Paul LaMontagne, "Barth and Rationality: Critical Realism in Theology" (PhD diss., Princeton Theological Seminary, 2001), 29–45. LaMontagne shows that "scientific realism" (one of the dominant—if not the dominant—philosophical epistemologies being defended in philosophy-of-science discussions at the present time) is a chastened, postfoundational form of "critical realism" which, while acknowledging that the "real" can defend itself from the constructivist tendencies of the human knower, insists that it can do so only within limits which emerge solely in the process of investigation and experimentation. As such, scientific realism constitutes a rejection of positivism. I might add that where both of these elements are not brought into a proper balance (a knowledge of the real, on the one side, and the role played by social constructs which mediate the real, on the other), where, in fact, only one side of this dialectic is emphasized, the result must inevitably be either positivism or something like the so-called reader-response theories of interpretation.

down in the sphere of methodological discussions, in which a decision is scarcely to be expected."[30] In Barth's view, hermeneutical discussions had an unfortunate tendency to distract attention from the concrete practice of interpreting biblical texts. Exegesis, he thought, must have priority over hermeneutics. If, on the basis of a concrete engagement with biblical texts, one could then say something about the "hermeneutical principles" which have emerged in the actual practice of exegesis, well and good. Such scruples notwithstanding, Barth had already addressed issues of biblical hermeneutics head-on in a number of places prior to the publication of his commentary on Philippians.

What Is "Scientific" Exegesis?

Barth did not see his exegesis as either a "practical" or a "pneumatic" exercise. For him, as for his comrades in the dialectical-theology movement, the struggle in which they were engaged was for a revised understanding of what constitutes "scientific" exegesis. "Theological exegesis" (their preferred term) was not conceived of by them as an alternative to historical exegesis or even as a complementary task (if such complementarity did not arise out of a more integrated understanding of exegesis in which a chastened historical science—stripped of its historicism and the positivistic understanding of history which lent to historicism a greater credibility—itself became a *theological* discipline).[31]

---

30. Barth, *The Epistle to the Philippians*, 7. It was probably just as well that Barth did not choose to participate; he was not really welcome at this particular party. Ernst von Dobschütz wrote, "I do not wish to count as realization of the Girgensohnian call the exegesis of Karl Barth and the dialectical theologians. It is not a pneumatic grasp of the deepest thoughts of Scripture but rather a violation of Scripture by means of dialectical arts, an imposition of foreign thoughts, a misuse of interpretation. This is true, however much one may acknowledge the religious seriousness of Barth's thoughts. An exegete he is not" ("Die pneumatische Exegese, Wissenschaft und Praxis," 50). And Johannes Schneider added, "What Barth defines as exegesis is not, in truth, interpretation but personal appropriation of the thoughts of the Bible, the obedience of faith and the decision of conscience but not understanding. Barth is also—his own exegetical efforts show this—in danger of reading the thoughts of his own theological system into the texts of the New Testament" ("Historische und pneumatische Exegese," 728).

31. See, e.g., Rudolf Bultmann, "The Significance of 'Dialectical Theology' for the Scientific Study of the New Testament," in *Faith and Understanding* (Philadelphia: Fortress, 1987), 146: "Nor, however, does the term 'dialectical theology' denote a *method of investigation* which ought to displace, say, the historical method. In the area of philosophy there might be a kind of 'dialectical method'; but for the New Testament there can be only *one* method, the *historical*. However, insight into what is really meant by dialectical theology could lead to a deeper insight into the nature of history and thus modify, enrich or clarify the method of historical investigation." With this statement, Barth would have been in basic agreement—although he would not have spoken of the subject matter of which the Bible speaks in terms of a "deeper insight into history." But this only shows that the real dividing point between Barth and Bultmann was not hermeneutical, in the first instance, but *theological*. Still, the measure of agreement between

Theological exegesis was, in their view, scientific exegesis. What they were looking for was, basically, two things: an understanding of historical method which exposed the role played by the socially mediated, constructive efforts of the historian; and a more adequate understanding of the subject matter about which the texts found in the Bible speak and in whose light they are to be understood. Of the two, the latter was the more decisive. But the first was also significant. Barth's famous comment "The historical-critics must become *more critical!*"[32] looked in both of these directions—the "objective" (concerned with the true "subject-matter" of Scripture) and the "subjective" (concerned with the reflective-assimilative labor of the interpreter). Both must become "more critical." We will look first at the "objective" side of the problem.

The goal of exegesis, Barth wrote in 1921, is the measuring of all the words and word groups found in a historical document by means of the *Sache* (the "object," the "subject-matter") of which they speak.[33] This commitment marked a constant in his hermeneutical reflections in all phases of the further development of his thought. What did change from time to time was his description of the one "subject-matter" of which all biblical texts, with greater or lesser clarity, speak.

In the preface to the second *Romans*, Barth described the subject matter of the Bible in terms of the "infinite qualitative difference" between time and eternity, between God and the human.[34] The relation—or, more accurately, the *relating*—of God to the human was understood to be a dialectical one, a dialectic of judgment and redemption. Insofar as redemption is something that we humans still await, the dialectic in question has yet to be overcome. The relation of these two realities—and therefore of the concepts which we use to speak of them—contain an "inner tension," an "inner dialectic."[35] To be confronted by the subject matter of the Bible is to be confronted by this question: What does it mean for the true God to relate to the true (i.e., the fallen) human? This is the "cardinal question"[36] which is embedded in all the particular questions that particular texts seek to address. The goal of exegesis is to wrestle with the text (and here Barth is thinking primarily in terms of large units, of entire letters) until one is confronted by this question and the answer given to it in and through this text. "As little as possible of those blocks

---

Barth and Bultmann in the 1920s on the hermeneutical level was great. Barth, too, could insist that he was not looking for a special method for the study of the New Testament which would not be applicable to other works of literature—to the study of Lao-Tzu and Goethe, for example. See Barth, *Der Römerbrief, 1922*, xv (*The Epistle to the Romans*, 12).

32. Barth, *Der Römerbrief, 1922*, xii (*The Epistle to the Romans*, 8). It is worth pointing out that Barth understood the whole of his exegetical work in *Romans* as an exercise in what he called "critical theology" (xiii [10]).

33. Ibid., xii (*The Epistle to the Romans*, 8).

34. Ibid., xiii (*The Epistle to the Romans*, 10).

35. Ibid.

36. Ibid., xii (*The Epistle to the Romans*, 8).

of merely historical, merely given, merely accidental conceptualities should remain; as much as possible, the relation of the Word to the words must be discovered. I must press on as interpreter to the point where I almost stand only before the enigma of the subject-matter, where I almost do not stand any longer before the enigma of the document; where I, therefore, have almost forgotten that I am not the author, where I have understood him so well that I can allow him to speak in my name and can myself speak in his."[37]

The claim to have understood the author better than he understood himself is one that raised many eyebrows at the time it was made, and continues to do so to this day. It is easily forgotten that, in making it, Barth was taking up an aspect of Schleiermacher's hermeneutics and placing it on a new footing. For Schleiermacher too had made it a goal of exegesis to understand the author better than he understood himself.[38] The difference is that, for Barth, to understand an author better than he understood himself does not require an intuition of the "experience" (however that might be construed) out of which he then wrote; it requires understanding him in the light of that to which he points. It is the understanding of the author as *witness*, not as a subject of interest in his own right.

The description, as set forth by Barth in his second Romans commentary, of the true "subject-matter" witnessed to by the writers of Scripture was not something he felt absolutely wed to even as he wrote it. In the nature of the case, he could not be. Ultimately, the subject matter to be known is God; it is the Word, Jesus Christ, a Reality which must give itself to be known if it is to be known at all. The difficulty—the sheer impossibility, humanly considered—of knowing God is a function not of the limits of human knowing, in the first instance, but of divine election. The object of which Paul speaks is not one we can lay hands on; it is a living Subject who must lay hold of us in the knowing process. But if this be so, then every attempt to describe the true subject matter of the Bible must depend, for its success, on the willingness of God to give himself to the would-be human knower, to allow himself to be brought to expression in human speech. This was already true of the apostles; it remains true of the exegete who would understand the apostles.

In the phase of his second *Romans*, Barth emphasized the *distance* which separates human conceptions from their divine object, the fact that verbal formulations of the subject matter of the Bible were not the thing itself. He very quickly passed on to a more positive construal of the relation of the two. He came to understand it as a relation of analogy, an analogy which is established as a consequence of divine action. The effect of this shift was that it freed Barth to inquire more closely into the relation of the "inner unity"

37. Ibid.
38. Friedrich Schleiermacher, *Hermeneutics and Criticism*, ed. and trans. Andrew Bowie (Cambridge: Cambridge University Press, 1998), 23. On this point, see Burnett, *Karl Barth's Theological Exegesis*, 138–47, 221–48.

of a document to the one "subject-matter" to which all biblical documents point. Already in his commentary on 1 Corinthians 15 in 1924, he laid great stress upon the thematic unity of the epistle. He noted that modern interpretations of 1 Corinthians had tended, to that point in time, to treat the concerns which came to expression in the fifteenth chapter as just haphazardly related to the series of subjects which had been treated in the prior fourteen chapters. Against this Barth asked, "first, whether Paul's *reflections* upon the subjects dealt with in 1 Corinthians 1–14 are as disparate as these subjects themselves, or rather whether a thread cannot be discovered which binds them internally into a whole; and, secondly, whether 1 Corinthians 15 is merely to be comprehended as one theme by the side of many others, or rather whether the thread hitherto followed does not at this point become visible, so that this theme, however much externally it is one theme by the side of many others, should be recognized at the same time as *the* theme of the epistle."[39] But not only is the theme of the resurrection of the dead *the* theme of 1 Corinthians; it is *the* theme of Paul's theology generally. "Here Paul discloses generally his focus, his background, and his assumptions with a definiteness he but seldom uses elsewhere, and with a particularity which he has not done in his other epistles known to us. The Epistles to the Romans, the Philippians, and the Colossians cannot even be understood, unless we keep in mind the sharp accentuation which their contents receive in the light of 1 Corinthians 15, where Paul develops what he elsewhere only indicates and outlines. . . . How vitally important is this chapter, if this be the case, for understanding the testimony of the New Testament generally, I do not need to emphasize."[40] What is happening here is that in giving a description of the "inner unity" of Paul's theology generally, Barth is also providing us with a more useful tool, where the praxis of exegesis is concerned, for interpreting the meaning of texts in the light of their "subject-matter." Indeed, we might best understand the inner unity of Paul's writings as the Pauline version of that subject matter. Where talk of the subject matter of the Bible might have seemed in *Romans* to be cut off from any discernible contact with actual texts, here the description is clearly the result of a broad reading of an epistle in an effort to discern its inner unity, the light which shines through Paul's handling of a myriad of problems and concerns. Bultmann described Barth's effort in this commentary with great accuracy and in a way that is pertinent to the question of what constitutes a truly "scientific" exegesis: "The unity to be looked for is therefore a material [*sachlichen*] unity, i.e., one grounded in the subject-matter, not some sort of 'spiritual' unity which would depend on the unity and individuality of the one author's personality."[41]

39. Barth, *Die Auferstehung der Toten*, 2 (*The Resurrection of the Dead*, 12–13).
40. Ibid., 1 (*The Resurrection of the Dead*, 11).
41. Rudolf Bultmann, "Karl Barth: 'Die Auferstehung der Toten,'" *Theologische Blätter* 5 (1926): 1; translated as "Karl Barth, The Resurrection of the Dead," in *Faith and Understanding*, 66.

In sum, exegesis is not understood in a truly scientific fashion where it is made an independent human activity, isolated from the process of knowing God. For if the texts which the exegete confronts are essentially *witness*, that is, proclamation, then a truly "scientific" approach to exegesis will seek methods and strategies which are in accordance with their true character. It will seek to understand a biblical text in the light of its subject matter. Eventually Barth would come to see that this also means attempting to understand a text as belonging to an ordered structure. To say that God's Word has a threefold form is to make a statement with profound hermeneutical consequences. It means that the Bible *belongs* to the Word of God, that when we try to interpret without reference to its proper object, we falsify at the very first step the nature of the documents that we would understand.

But a "more critical" exegesis also looks in a second, "subjective" direction. The object of criticism here is the interpreter. Barth noted that every interpreter brings assumptions to his or her work; he was no exception.

> When I approach a text like the Epistle to the Romans, I do so with the provisional presupposition that the simple and yet immeasurable significance of that relation [between God and the human] stood just as clearly before Paul's eyes as he formed his concepts as it does before mine as I set myself to carry out an attentive thinking after [*Nachdenken*] of his concepts, just as another exegete works with certain provisional presuppositions of a more pragmatic sort, e.g., when he approaches the text with the assumption that Romans really was written by Paul in the first century. Whether such presuppositions are justified or not can only be shown in the act [of interpreting]; that means, in this case, in the exact investigation and reflection upon the text, verse by verse. Obviously, this justification can always only be a *relative*, more or less certain justification. And my presupposition is naturally also subjected to this rule.[42]

Those presuppositions will prove most fruitful in the act of exegesis which corresponds (with greater or less adequacy) to the presuppositions of the writer. But, then, this also means that any adequate exegesis will be an engaged, participatory exegesis. To be confronted by a Pauline text is to be confronted by a text written by someone who is seeking to bear witness to the very object (the divine Subject) by which (whom!) I also am confronted. Now, Barth was not inclined himself to suggest that such an engagement required special spiritual equipment. He did not think of the Holy Spirit as a possession of the interpreter, a power which the interpreter could readily call into play as often as he or she wished. He saw the Holy Spirit, rather, as the creative power of the Word itself which, when spoken, creates faith and obedience. All that is required on the human side is a willingness to engage in a "relentless and

42. Barth, *Der Römerbrief, 1922*, xiii–xiv (*The Epistle to the Romans*, 10).

elastic dialectical movement"[43] from text to subject matter and back to text again, a movement which can never reach a definitive conclusion (because we do not possess the Holy Spirit) and so must be repeated again and again. "Scientific" exegesis, therefore, is something that anyone can do. It is not the preserve of a special class of *pneumatikoi*. But it does require an engagement that is possible only where the Word has been and is heard.

Such a conception constituted a significant challenge not only to the positivism of the historians. The reigning model in the natural sciences in Barth's day was also positivistic in character. But the historians were, if anything, even more positivistic than the natural scientists, operating as they did with the unacknowledged assumption that historical "facts" could be easily disentangled from those interpretive schemes in whose absence they could not be what they are. And it was this conception of "science" and of a "scientific" exegesis that conformed to it that the dialectical theologians challenged.

The Resurrection of the Dead in Philippians

The test of whether Barth's (or anyone else's) hermeneutical principles are sound lies in actual exegesis. Is the resurrection of the dead the central theme of Philippians? And if it is, how does it find expression in the concrete issues which Paul addresses in this epistle? A defense of the fruitfulness of Barth's theological exegesis of Philippians would not need to show that he is correct in all the details of his exegesis. It would need only show that Philippians as a whole bears vivid witness to Barth's understanding of its "inner unity." And it would need to show that his use of this theme in illuminating the parts has remained sufficiently supple and elastic so that it is not woodenly read into the parts but simply seeks to understand their significance in the light of the whole. Where these criteria are employed in testing Barth's exegesis, we find that his hermeneutical principles are, in truth, justified by the results.

The Epistle to the Philippians is shot through with eschatology. Its writer is a man facing a trial before a Roman judge which will likely result in his freedom but could also result in his death. He cannot be sure. But the outcome is not of any real consequence to him. What he thinks about, in these days, is another trial, an eschatological trial, in which he will stand before his Lord. "The day of Christ Jesus" referred to in Philippians 1:6 (cf. 1:10; 2:16; and, implicitly, 2:9–11) is, above all else, a day in which the glory of the Lord will be definitively revealed (cf. 1 Thess. 5:2 and 2 Thess. 2:2). But we should not deceive ourselves into thinking that the concept of the "day of the Lord" meant only revelation, grace, and mercy for Paul. Far from it. It is the all-embracing day of judgment, associated by him with the general resurrection

43. Ibid., xi–xii (*The Epistle to the Romans*, 8).

of the dead (see 1 Thess. 4:16–17). The judgment which will occur on that day will be a judgment that will fall not only on unbelievers but on believers as well (see esp. 1 Cor. 3:11–15). It is this day that Paul recalls when he thinks of his impending trial before a Roman judge. And thinking of it, he has nothing invested *personally* in the outcome of his earthly trial. Moreover, he sees in his imprisonment only an opportunity to proclaim the gospel (Phil. 1:12–13). He cares not if others take advantage of his imprisonment, using the proclamation of the gospel as a means to personal self-empowerment. So long as the gospel is proclaimed, so long as the gospel continues its steady advance through the world, he is content (1:18). And he takes no personal interest in the fact that the Philippians have sent a monetary gift which will enable him to eat in the days to come. He has learned the secret of being filled and going hungry. He can do all things through Christ who strengthens him. If he is pleased with such giving, it is only because of the profit which accrues to the account of the Philippians in view of the coming day, not because of his own needs, which are as nothing to him (4:10–18). Paul is a man who lives an *eschatological existence*, a radically decentered existence which has been recentered in the Lord whose future glory will mean the complete transformation of the world. All that has been valuable to him, including his own *goodness*, he now considers worthless, something to be left behind in order that he might gain Christ (3:8). He is like an athlete who, in running a race, forgets what lies behind and is wholly preoccupied with stretching forth his hands to receive a prize which is not yet his (3:12–14). If we were to be honest, we would have to admit that the Paul of the Epistle to the Philippians is a stranger to us, and his Christianity utterly alien to ours. Today many of us would consider such single-mindedness evidence of fanaticism, zealotry. We might even wish to categorize him by means of a psychological disorder in order to make him comprehensible. The truth is, if we were not at all tempted in this direction, we would most certainly have misunderstood Philippians. It is a measure of just how well Barth has understood Paul that the strangeness of Paul's eschatological existence shines so clearly through his commentary.

But it is not just in relation to the passages which deal directly with eschatological themes that "the resurrection of the dead" (as a compressed expression for the whole complex of eschatological material) comes to the fore. In Barth's commentary, "the resurrection of the dead" is not simply one of a number of blocks of exegetical material whose discussion is forced upon us by particular texts. It is the hermeneutical "principle" which colors Barth's exegesis of all the details, however significant or insignificant they might be by other standards.

Do the Philippians want to know what has happened to Paul (1:12)? Paul answers their question only by reframing it. His answer does not focus on his circumstances and how he came to be in them. Paul's "apostolic objectivity" (*apostolische Sachlichkeit*) will not allow him to dwell on such things.

He just would not be an apostle if he could speak objectively about his own situation in abstraction from the course of the Gospel, to which he has sacrificed his subjectivity and therewith also all objective interest in his own person. To the question how it is with *him* an apostle *must* react with information as to how it is with the Gospel. And so Paul now answers by declaring that with the Gospel it is at all events *well*. What has happened to him, the apostle, has amounted to an advance, a drive forward, a territorial gain for his message and cause. That amounts to saying that with him, the apostle, whatever his human prospects may be, it is *well*.[44]

Is a threat posed to the Philippians by Christians who would undermine the gospel of the free grace of God in Jesus Christ by making humanly attained righteousness through adherence to laws and ceremonies to be the basis of justification? Barth's Paul will certainly oppose this, and does so in no uncertain terms in Philippians 3:1–14. But it would be a falsification of Paul's insistence in 3:12 that he has *not yet* laid hold of the resurrection to come (and, with it, redemption) if we were to seek to understand the claim "we are the true circumcision" in terms of a this-worldly (here and now) triumph of the right of one group over the wrong of another. Paul does not set the Jewish Christians in opposition to another group of more genuine Christians. The "we" of whom he speaks is an eschatological reality, the people of God as they shall be. So Paul describes the "we" by reference to the subject matter [*Sache*] of the epistle, not by reference to psychologically determined, empirical individuals.[45]

Would we, as readers today, like to know more about the circumstances of Epaphroditus's life in Rome? Barth advises that we exercise a certain textual restraint. Given the inevitability that the most that historical science is capable of in such matters is conjecture, he suggests that we "refuse ourselves the liberty of expanding the written text in the manner of the story-teller" and content ourselves with what is written, lest we "lose the solid ground of the text under our feet."[46] And in any case, such textual conservatism bears a testimony in itself to the importance of Paul's "apostolic objectivity."

The success of Barth's hermeneutics as applied to the Epistle to the Philippians makes his commentary a forceful challenge to the way in which commentaries (both conservative and liberal) are written today. Academic commentaries today typically manifest much greater interest in the details than in the unifying themes, so much so that if originality in just a few details of historical interest can be achieved, this in itself constitutes a justification for writing a very long, often disjointed, treatment of a biblical book, a treatment that tells us more about scholarly opinion than it does about the subject matter

44. Barth, *The Epistle to the Philippians*, 26.
45. Ibid., 94.
46. Ibid., 81.

which absorbed the attention of the writer. The only exceptions to this rule are provided by those "practical" commentaries which, precisely in order to avoid the weaknesses of academic approaches, resort to exegeting the situation of the interpreter and his or her own requirements instead of attaining to a strict concentration on the true subject matter of the Bible. Barth's approach would have us raise serious questions about whether the scientific approach is truly "scientific" and whether the practical can be truly "practical" if it is not also "scientific" in the sense he advocates.

A final word of caution is in order as I conclude. Barth's commentary is not well suited for occasional reading. It is not intended for the reader who would just dip into it for an answer to the question "What does this verse mean?" It is a book, not a loose collection of observations. As such, it is intended to be read as a whole, in its entirety. And when it is, its power as a witness to the kind of eschatological existence which Paul asked the Philippians to imitate (3:17) will, I am confident, be felt and understood.

Part 2

Karl Barth's Relationship
to Postliberalism and Postmodernism

5

Beyond Nonfoundational and Postmodern Readings of Barth

Critically Realistic Dialectical Theology

My goal in this essay is to identify and critically reflect upon the leading tendencies in recent English-language Barth research.[1] I will not attempt to treat each and every publication which has emerged in the last decade or so. Instead I will focus my attention on the seminal works which have defined (or are in the process of doing so) clear and distinct trends in Barth studies in the Anglo-American world today. But before turning to this task, it is important at the outset that I make clear the material norm which I will employ in my attempt to engage these movements critically. Such a norm—if effective—could have been elaborated only *after* close study of these works; if it were done in advance, it might miss what is of decisive importance in them altogether. Hence, although I advance this norm here, it should be noted, by way of introduction, that the suitability of this norm was decided upon only after lengthy reflection.

Introduction: On the Critical Importance of Barth's Doctrine of Revelation

At the heart of Karl Barth's doctrine of revelation, in the form in which it was first given a relatively full and positive elaboration in the Göttingen lectures

This essay was originally published in a slightly different form under the title "Beyond Non-foundational and Postmodern Readings of Barth: Critically Realistic Dialectical Theology," in *Zeitschrift für dialektische Theologie* 13 (1997): 67–95, 170–94.

1. Sincere thanks are due my good friend, James J. Buckley, whose criticisms in response to an earlier draft of this essay have made it better than it otherwise would have been.

on dogmatics, lies the concept of "indirect identity": in revealing himself, God makes himself to be indirectly identical with a creaturely medium of that revelation.[2] Such a relation is *indirect* because the use made by God of the creaturely medium entails no "divinisation" of it.[3] The veil in and through which God unveils himself remains a veil. And yet it must also be said that in the act of Self-revelation, God is indirectly *identical* with the creaturely medium. That is to say, the presence of God in the medium of revelation—however *hidden* it may be outwardly, to normal perception—is the presence of *God*, complete, whole and entire (without division or diminution).[4] The hiddenness of God in revelation is not to be likened to the hiddenness of the submerged portion of an iceberg. It is not as though *part* of God is revealed directly while *part* of God remains hidden to view. No, Barth makes it quite clear that if revelation is *Self*-revelation (and it is), then revelation means the revelation of God in his entirety—*but* the whole being of God *hidden* in a creaturely veil. Nothing of God is known directly; God remains altogether hidden. And yet, where God is truly known in his hiddenness, it is the whole of God which is known and not "part" of God.

Expressed christologically: the process by means of which God takes on human nature and becomes the Subject of a human life in our history entails no impartation of divine attributes or perfections to that human nature. And therefore revelation is not made to be a predicate of the human nature of Jesus; revelation may not be read directly "off the face of Jesus."[5] And yet it remains true that God (complete, whole, and entire) is the Subject of this human life. God, without ceasing to be God, becomes human and lives a human life, suffers, and dies.

The principle consequence of this conception of an indirect revelation for theological epistemology is that God is the Subject of the knowledge of God. Human beings can know God only by being given a knowledge which corresponds to God's Self-knowledge. This occurs in that human beings are given the eyes of faith with which to discern that which lies hidden in the veil. Thus conceived, revelation is seen to have two moments: an objective moment (God veils himself in a creaturely medium) and a subjective moment (God gives us faith to know and understand what is hidden in

2. Karl Barth, *Unterricht in der christlichen Religion*, vol. 2, *Die Lehre von Gott/Die Lehre vom Menschen*, 1924/1925, ed. Hinrich Stoevesandt (Zurich: Theologischer Verlag, 1990), 11–18; translated as *The Göttingen Dogmatics: Instruction in the Christian Religion*, trans. Geoffrey Bromiley (Grand Rapids: Eerdmans, 1991), 1:325–31.

3. Karl Barth, "Unterricht in der christlichen Religion" III, §28, p. 52; typed manuscript in the Karl Barth-Archiv, Basel.

4. Karl Barth, *Unterricht in der christlichen Religion*, vol. 1, *Prolegomena, 1924*, ed. Hannelotte Reiffen (Zurich: Theologischer Verlag, 1985), 110–14; translated as *The Göttingen Dogmatics*, 1:91–93.

5. Barth, *Die Lehre von Gott/Die Lehre vom Menschen*, 22 (*The Göttingen Dogmatics*, 1:334).

the veil). The objective moment is christological; the subjective moment, pneumatological.

In the Göttingen lectures, the Kantian assumptions with which Barth works in explicating this point of view are especially clear. With Kant, Barth believes that human knowledge is limited to the intuitable, phenomenal realm. And this means that if God (who is unintuitable) is nevertheless to be intuited (and therefore *known* in the strict, theoretical sense), God must make himself to be phenomenal, that is, God must assume creaturely form. But at this point a further problem arises. In making himself phenomenal, God has entered into the subject-object relation in which the constructive role played by the Kantian categories of the understanding make the human knower the "master" in any and every knowledge relation.[6] So the problem is this: How can God remain God (i.e., the Subject of the knowledge of God) even *as* God takes on phenomenal form? The answer has everything to do with the fact that God does not make himself directly identical with a phenomenal magnitude but only indirectly so.[7] What occurs in revelation is that the divine Subject lays hold of or grasps the human knowing apparatus through the phenomena from the other side. In this way, the limitations placed on human knowing by the Kantian subject-object split are overcome by a transcendent, divine act.

It should be added that Barth secures the lordship ("mastery") of God in this knowledge relation by insisting on its actualistic character. It is not the case that God unveils himself through the veil once and for all, as a completed act. If it were so, then God would have ceased to act; nothing more would need to be done. But such a view could be coherently explicated only by the thought that although God was once only indirectly identical with a medium

---

6. Ibid., 17 (*The Göttingen Dogmatics*, 1:330): "That truly God truly reveals Himself to human beings, that presupposes: 1) that God *encounters* man, 2) that man stands before *God*. But for our problem that means that God becomes the *object* of knowledge and man becomes the *subject*. God becomes the *object* of knowledge in that He becomes man, in Christ. Man becomes the *subject of knowledge* through faith and obedience.... In this condition, in this simple subject-object relation, God becomes knowable. Whoever would contest the fact that God enters into this condition, into this subject-object relation, becoming knowable in it, must deny revelation."

7. Ibid., 13–14 (*The Göttingen Dogmatics*, 1:327): "God's *deity* or *Person* is never a mere object, never merely His being an It or a He but rather His being an I. In His revelation, precisely in His revelation, God is an unsublateable [*unaufhebbares*] Subject, to be confused with no object.... The revelation of God consists precisely in His decisive refusal to become a He or an It, an object. Hallowed be Thy name! Positively expressed: the revelation of God consists in the fact that God Himself encounters man, that man sees himself placed before God *Himself*, but that this Self is indissoluble. It is not to be reduced to something material [*etwas Dingliches*] that He Himself is not." The paradoxicality of the proximity of this statement to the one cited in the note just above is obvious. But the two statements do not contradict one another. The resolution of the paradox lies in Barth's repeated emphasis on the fact that God never becomes a *mere* object. Of course, God also becomes an object; how else could revelation reach its goal with human beings? But in becoming an object, God remains Subject (i.e., God never becomes directly identical with an object).

of revelation, at some point in time God became directly identical with it. In this view, nothing further need occur from the divine side. The epistemic relation between God and the human knower would have become fixed, stabilized. Having begun in a relation of absolute epistemic dependency, the human knower would once again have attained the mastery in this relation. To all of this, Barth said no. God is indirectly identical with the medium of his Self-revelation not only before revelation occurs but during the revelation event and after it. Thus Barth could consistently overcome the limitations placed by Kant on the knowledge of God only by insisting upon the actualistic nature of the epistemic relation.

One final clarification: for those of us who are "disciples at second hand," the place at which God finds access to us (and therefore we to God) is no longer Jesus of Nazareth (who has "ascended on high"); it is, rather, through the medium of the witness of Holy Scripture that God continues to unveil himself. For us, knowledge of God occurs when and where God takes up the language of the biblical witness and bears witness to himself in and through its witness (the objective moment) *and* awakens in us the faith needed to comprehend that witness (the subjective moment). In that this occurs, a relation of correspondence (the so-called *analogia fidei*) is established (actualistically!) between God's knowledge of himself and human knowledge of God. Thus it is quite clear that the motor that drives Barth's theological epistemology is the *Realdialektik* of the divine veiling and unveiling.

For Karl Barth, theology is, humanly speaking, an impossibility; where it nevertheless becomes possible, it does so only as a divine possibility. A theology which has truly understood this will be one which finds its basis—not once, but again and again—in the *Realdialektik* of the divine veiling and unveiling. It will be a theology which takes seriously the *reality* of divine action not only on the level of the theological epistemology it presupposes but also on the level of the theological method it employs. On the other hand, the employment of a method which could succeed in the tasks appointed for it by its human practitioners whether God exists or not—which, in fact, would not be altered in the least by a confession of the nonexistence of God—would reduce theology to something humanly achievable, manipulable, controllable. It would reduce theology to a regular, bourgeois science alongside all the other sciences. "What does one really know of 'being placed in question' on the soil of scepticism, for there the question of whether God exists is left open. Is it not so that this question . . . leaves one fundamentally by himself and unshaken in himself? Is it not so that things only really become life-threatening *if* and *because* God is, . . . ?"[8]

8. Karl Barth to Peter Barth, 29 April 1932, cited by Eberhard Busch, *Karl Barths Lebenslauf: Nach seinen Briefen und autobiographischen Texten* (Munich: Kaiser, 1975), 103; translated as

It is my conviction that the interpretation of Barth in the Anglo-American world has rarely been able to grasp the convictions I have just sketched here. Whether it was because of the inadequacy of Sir Edwin Hoskyns's translation of the second edition of *Romans* (which managed to obscure the influence of Kant), or because of developmental theories which drove a wedge between the early "dialectical" Barth and a later, all-too-positive, "neo-orthodox" Barth, or simply because the all-too-human desire to retain control of all epistemic relations made Barth's dialectical theology finally unassimilable even for its most ardent admirers, or perhaps because of a combination of all of these factors— the fact is that Barth's theology has been poorly understood in America and Great Britain. In failing to grasp the *Realdialektik* which is fundamental to Barth's concept of revelation, English-language interpretation of his theology has tended to move in one of two directions: either to so emphasize the *givenness* of God in revelation (e.g., through collapsing revelation into the text of the biblical witness) that Barth is made into a revelational positivist or to so emphasize the *nongivenness* of God in revelation (as occurs in certain readings of the language of "wholly otherness") that Barth is made into a theological sceptic. The irony is that both interpretations wind up with much the same result: an utterly and completely undialectical Barth.

In what follows, I propose to offer a critical analysis of two recent trends in English-language Barth interpretation. The first of these is the "postliberal" and nonfoundationalist interpretation advocated by the Yale theologians Hans Frei and George Lindbeck. The second is the postmodern reading offered by Walter Lowe and Graham Ward. The essay will conclude with reflections on the gradual emergence of a new orientation in Anglo-American Barth interpretation: an orientation which I will call "critically realistic dialectical theology."

Nonfoundational Readings of Barth in Yale "Postliberalism"

Whether there is such a thing as a Yale school in American theology is matter for debate. Certainly, for those standing outside the immediate sphere of influence of the late Hans Frei and his Yale colleagues George Lindbeck and David Kelsey, the extent to which the Yale theologians and their former students[9] work out of a shared orientation is obvious. Common to them are

---

Karl Barth: His Life from Letters and Autobiographical Texts, trans. John Bowden (London: SCM Press; Philadelphia: Fortress, 1976), 91.

9. Literature emerging from this group, which will not be treated here but would be found in a more complete survey of "postliberal" theology, includes the following: James J. Buckley, "Doctrine in the Diaspora," *Thomist* 49 (1985): 443–59; idem, "A Field of Living Fire: Karl Barth on the Holy Spirit and the Church," *Modern Theology* 10 (1994): 81–102; James J. Buckley and William McF. Wilson, "A Dialogue with Barth and Farrer on Theological Method," *Heythrop*

the following elements: (1) a relatively nonfoundational approach to theology which would eschew every attempt to find an ultimate ground for the intelligibility, coherence, and truth of theological statements in some philosophically construed aspect of "reality" (e.g., in rationally inferred first-principles or perhaps in a phenomenologically described "religious" dimension of human being and existence); and (2) as the positive corollary of the negations proper to their nonfoundationalism, a tendency to define Christian theology as a highly contextual exercise in communal self-description. In practice, such a definition gives to the Yale theology a highly formal character insofar as it fosters a preoccupation with identifying and elaborating the *internal logic* of "first-order" theological statements (defined as the language of Christian confession or witness to God, Christ, the world, etc.) while largely suspending questions of reality-reference (i.e., questions of whether anything corresponding to the language of Christian confession actually exists). Such an investigation is called by Frei "second-order"[10] reflection on "first-order" language, and ultimately it involves the attempt to critically evaluate the success or

---

Journal 26 (1985): 274–93; Mary Kathleen Cunningham, *What Is Theological Exegesis? Interpretation and Use of Scripture in Barth's Doctrine of Election* (Valley Forge, PA: Trinity Press International, 1995); David Ford, *Barth and God's Story: Biblical Narrative and the Theological Method of Karl Barth in the "Church Dogmatics"* (Frankfurt am Main: Peter Lang, 1981); idem, "On Being Theologically Hospitable to Jesus Christ: Hans Frei's Achievement (a Review Article of Hans Frei, *Types of Christian Theology*)," *Journal of Theological Studies* 46 (1995): 532–46; Garrett Green, ed., *Scriptural Authority and Narrative Interpretation* (Philadelphia: Fortress, 1987); George Hunsinger, "Beyond Literalism and Expressivism: Karl Barth's Hermeneutical Realism," *Modern Theology* 3 (1987): 209–23; idem, "Where the Battle Rages: Confessing Christ in America Today," *Dialog* 26 (1987): 264–74; David H. Kelsey, *The Uses of Scripture in Recent Theology* (Philadelphia: Fortress, 1975); Bruce D. Marshall, "Aquinas as Postliberal Theologian," *Thomist* 53 (1989): 353–402; idem, *Christology in Conflict: The Identity of a Savior in Rahner and Barth* (Oxford: Basil Blackwell, 1987); idem, "What Is Truth?" *Pro Ecclesia* 4 (1995): 404–30; idem, ed. *Theology and Dialogue: Essays in Conversation with George Lindbeck* (Notre Dame, IN: University of Notre Dame Press, 1990); Paul McGlasson, *Jesus and Judas: Biblical Exegesis in Barth* (Atlanta: Scholars Press, 1991); William C. Placher, *Unapologetical Theology: A Christian Voice in a Pluralistic Conversation* (Louisville: Westminster/John Knox, 1989); idem, "Postliberal Theology," in *The Modern Theologians: An Introduction to Christian Theology in the Twentieth Century*, ed. David Ford (Oxford: Basil Blackwell, 1989), 2:115–28; Kathryn Tanner, *God and Creation in Christian Theology: Tyranny or Empowerment?* (Oxford: Basil Blackwell, 1988); Ronald Thiemann, *Revelation and Theology: The Gospel as Narrated Promise* (Notre Dame, IN: University of Notre Dame Press, 1985); William Werpehowski, "Command and History in the Ethics of Karl Barth," *Journal of Religious Ethics* 9 (1981): 298–320; idem, "Divine Commands, Philosophical Dilemmas: The Case of Karl Barth," *Dialogue* 201 (1981): 20–25; idem, "Ad hoc Apologetics," *Journal of Religion* 66 (1986): 282–301; Charles Wood, *The Formation of Christian Understanding: An Essay in Theological Hermeneutics* (Philadelphia: Westminster, 1981).

10. Frei can even speak of a "third-order" exercise in which the rules governing the use of language in Christian theology are compared and contrasted with rules found in other, non-Christian, religious communities. See Hans W. Frei, *Types of Christian Theology*, ed. George Hunsinger and William Placher (New Haven and London: Yale University Press, 1992), 20–21.

failure of such language in terms of a norm or set of norms acknowledged by a Christian community. Furthermore, it seems quite clear that the motivation for bracketing off questions of reality-reference arises, in part at least, out of a powerful reaction against the modern use of the Bible as historical source. If the reality behind the text were regarded either as inaccessible on principle or even simply as theologically uninteresting, then historical-critical approaches to the Bible would be devalued accordingly—which is clearly one of the central goals of the Yale theologians. Given this motive, it is not surprising that these theologians prefer to approach the Bible as literature and look to literary theory (and a cultural anthropology favorable to it) as the ancillary discipline most congenial to theological investigation. Still, however true it may be that the Yale theologians share a common orientation, there are interesting differences which arise here and there, making themselves felt in the way Karl Barth's theology is understood and used. In what follows, my primary interest is not in the Yale theology per se but in the use they make of Barth's theology in promoting their own goals.

Hans Frei

The guiding spirit of the Yale theology was, and continues to be even in death, Hans Wilhelm Frei (1922–1988). Frei first came to the attention of the theological public in America through his dissertation on the theological development of Karl Barth, completed in 1956. Though the dissertation was never published,[11] Frei quickly came to be regarded as the premier Barth specialist on this side of the Atlantic. His first great work, *The Eclipse of Biblical Narrative*,[12] established him (in the minds of most members of the theological guild, at any rate) as the leading defender of a movement which many critics had declared moribund—namely, "neoorthodoxy."[13] Thus, from at least 1974 (if not earlier) right down to the present day, the word "Barthianism" has been understood by the great majority in American theological circles to be virtually synonymous with the views of Hans Frei and his associates. Frei's ongoing

11. Portions of the dissertation were revised and published in a Festschrift for Frei's mentor, H. Richard Niebuhr, as Hans W. Frei, "The Theology of H. Richard Niebuhr," in *Faith and Ethics*, ed. Paul Ramsey (New York: Harper & Row, 1957), 9–65.

12. Hans W. Frei, *The Eclipse of Biblical Narrative: A Study in Eighteenth and Nineteenth Century Hermeneutics* (New Haven: Yale University Press, 1974).

13. Frei himself could be fairly critical of the term and was quite content to describe Barth's theology simply as "modern." For evidence of his critical attitude towards the term "neoorthodoxy," see Hans W. Frei, "Eberhard Busch's Biography of Barth," in *Types of Christian Theology*, 147. For an assessment of Barth's relationship to "modern theology," see Frei's little 1968 essay "Karl Barth: Theologian," written on the occasion of Barth's death and reprinted in Hans W. Frei, *Theology and Narrative: Selected Essays*, ed. George Hunsinger and William Placher (New York: Oxford University Press, 1993), 167–76. Though Lindbeck, too, lays no claim to the term, it will be shown that it is far more appropriately applied to his work. See below, 134–37.

influence has been assured by the posthumous publication of two books: the first, a collection of essays and lectures (some of which were unpublished in Frei's lifetime);[14] and the second, a typology of modern Christian theologies which was intended to provide a prolegomenon to a much larger work on the history of Christology in the modern period.[15] In any event, Frei did not live to write his great work, and even his typology remained relatively unpolished.[16] Notwithstanding its unfinished character, it is the latter work especially that I am interested in here, for it effectively works as a kind of apologia on behalf of Barth's theology and, in so doing, provides a fine introduction to Frei's mature understanding of Barth's significance.[17]

Considered on the most general level, Frei's types of modern theologies (they are five in number) constitute a spectrum of possible answers to the question of how theology is related to philosophy—though there are several subordinate questions which the typology was also seeking, with greater and lesser degrees of success, to address.[18] To a significant degree, the differentiation of types is controlled by the logical possibilities that Frei thinks to exist; that is, the

14. See Frei, *Theology and Narrative*.

15. See Frei, *Types of Christian Theology*.

16. According to one of its editors, Frei's *Types of Christian Theology* is most accurately described as "little more than a pastiche of posthumous fragments put together by his editors." See George Hunsinger, "Afterword: Hans Frei as Theologian," in Frei, *Theology and Narrative*, 260.

17. As background, in Frei's corpus of writings, to this typology and the terms in which it is elaborated, see Hans W. Frei, "Eberhard Busch's Biography of Karl Barth," review of *Karl Barth: His Life from Letters and Autobiographical Texts*, by Eberhard Busch, reprinted in Frei, *Types of Christian Theology*, 147–63.

18. Hunsinger identifies four interrelated questions being addressed by Frei's typology:

> (1) What criteria of meaning, intelligibility, and truth are pertinent in Christian theology? Are they (to use Frei's terms) "general" or "specific," field-encompassing or singular? (2) What modes of descriptive analysis are theologically pertinent for Christianity as a religion? Are they "external" or "internal," logically independent of Christian beliefs or logically dependent upon them? (3) What use of language predominates in Christian discourse? Is the language of faith primarily descriptive, objective, and cognitive (*fides quae creditur*); or confessional, self-involving, and performative (*fides qua creditur*)? (4) Finally—and here is what Frei calls his "central topic" (p. 5)—what mode of interpretation or reading is theologically pertinent in the case of biblical texts, especially the New Testament narratives about Jesus? Is the sense of those narratives to be taken as "literal" or "symbolic," as ascribing certain predicates exclusively to Jesus as an unsubstitutable person, regardless of the status of that ascription in reality, or else as ascribing certain predicates to some other subject (such as human nature in general) by way of "Jesus" as an essentially symbolic figure? (*Theology and Narrative*, 260).

My own view would be that it is the first question which is truly basic, for it establishes both the nature and the parameters of the typology. The other questions are brought into play only in order to identify nuances of difference between the less extreme (or pure) positions considered.

individuals chosen as representatives of the types at times fit the given category only imperfectly. The exceptions are types 2 and 4, where David Tracy and Karl Barth give definition to their types rather than being made to fit them.[19]

The poles of this spectrum of opinion are constituted by the two most extreme answers to the question: pure foundationalism, on the one hand, and pure nonfoundationalism, on the other. On the one pole (type 1) lies the view which holds that "theology as a philosophical discipline in the academy takes complete priority over Christian self-description within the religious community called the Church, and Christian self-description, in its subordinate place, tends to emulate the philosophical character of academic theology by being as general as possible or as little specific about Christianity as it can be, and the distinction between external and internal description is basically unimportant."[20]

Presupposed by this approach to theology is the conviction that "*Christian theology is an instance of a general class or generic type and is therefore to be subsumed under general criteria of intelligibility, coherence, and truth that it must share with other academic disciplines.*" The foundationalist assumption that philosophy is capable of successfully articulating "rules of correct thought" which are "invariant and all-fields-encompassing" is taken for granted.[21] Frei's primary example here is the Harvard theologian Gordon Kaufman. In his *Essay on Theological Method*, Kaufman argues that "God" is a construct of the social imagination. There is no divine "reality" corresponding to this term. Only when this is realized can Christian theologians undertake the only possible task left to theologians, namely, that of identifying the function which God-language plays in society or, to put it another way, learning what it is we are trying to achieve with such language and then seeking ways in which those goals might be better realized.

> The concept "God" arises *formally* as ground and limit of the concept "world," and *materially* it arises out of the richness of human experience: for example, the experience of creativity, but also that of need and desire. God must be the ultimate reference point for human cultural and moral concerns. The two functions of the concept of "God" thus are the relativizing and the humanizing of the world. Since the concept "God" is not a report on information, and since the concepts that theology scrutinizes are employed to help us solve problems of meaningful moral and cultural living, theology is a practical rather than a theoretical discipline.[22]

The influence of Immanuel Kant on Kaufman's perspective should be clear.

19. Given that my interest here is ultimately in Frei's reading of Barth, I will not pursue the question of the validity of his reading of any other figure but will simply sketch his interpretation of them to the extent necessary to locate Barth on his map.

20. Frei, *Types of Christian Theology*, 28.

21. Ibid., 20.

22. Ibid., 28.

At the other extreme pole (type 5) lies what I am calling "pure non-foundationalism":[23] the view which maintains that "*Theology* is an aspect of Christianity and is therefore partly or wholly defined by its relation to the cultural or semiotic system that constitutes that religion. . . . What is at stake . . . is understanding a specific symbol system interpretively rather than reductively."[24] The philosophical outlook which undergirds this understanding has the following features:

> General theory is not pertinent to Christian self-description because there really is no such thing in any grand manner in the first place. "Languages" and their "grammars" always function in specific contexts. One learns the internal logic of any such context as one would a new language, through the acquisition of the appropriate conceptual skills, which are as much be-havioral or dispositional as they are linguistic or descriptive. There is no formal, context-independent or independently describable set of transcen-dental conditions governing that internal logic. Christian theology is strictly the grammar of faith, a procedure in self-description for which there is no external correlative.[25]

The close proximity of such views to the nonfoundationalist philosophies of Richard Rorty, Wilfred Sellars, Willard Van Orman Quine, and Richard Bernstein is due to the principled rejection of the possibility of general, uni-versally valid theories of explanation which would cover all fields.[26] In this view, correspondence theories of truth are rejected in favor of performance theories. "Type 5 is reduced to . . . simply repeating the scriptural statements and then, instead of interpreting them under a literal (or some other) reading, claiming that 'understanding' these statements is simply equivalent to acquir-ing the (religious) skill or capacity to use them in the appropriate manner."[27] As exemplars of this type, Frei adduces the so-called Wittgensteinian fideists, the chief representative of which is the British philosopher of religion D. Z. Phillips.[28] At this end of Frei's spectrum, theology is a discipline which benefits from philosophy only insofar as philosophy is willing to disavow all capability for evaluating the Christian language-game.

23. This is my term, not Frei's.
24. Frei, *Types of Christian Theology*, 2.
25. Ibid., 4.
26. Frei himself draws the analogy to Rorty (see ibid., 50). For a more extensive comparison of the Yale school with these nonfoundationalist philosophies, see John E. Thiel, *Nonfounda-tionalism* (Minneapolis: Fortress, 1994).
27. Frei, *Types of Christian Theology*, 6.
28. I will not sketch the views of Phillips here. Suffice it to say that Frei himself was a bit unsure as to how well Phillips fit the "type" he was describing. For our purposes here, the description of the type is vastly more important than the question of whether Phillips belongs, for, in Frei's rejection of it, we catch sight of the very real limits to which he is willing to go in committing himself to a nonfoundationalist approach to theology.

Before turning to the remaining three types, it is worth pointing out the extent to which extremes meet in this typology. However true it may be that type 1 holds optimistically to the existence of theoretical foundations for all knowledge claims while type 5 adamantly denies such a possibility on principle, both wind up with a nonreferential, wholly performative understanding of the meaningfulness of theological language. And thus Frei's spectrum becomes, as he himself suspected, "like a snake curled in on itself."[29] To clarify why this should be so, I would suggest that it has everything to do with an insistence on the nonreferential character of theological language. It is only where theological language is understood to be referential, where (in other words) the "reality" described by Christian theologians and philosophers is thought to *overlap*, that the problem of the relation of external description to internal description can arise at all. As we shall see, it is the latter question and the range of answers given to it which will differentiate types 2, 3, and 4.

The early David Tracy of *Blessed Rage for Order* is the figure who gives definition to Frei's second type.[30] For Tracy, like Kaufman, there are "statable, general, and fields-encompassing criteria for meaning (internal conceptual coherence), meaningfulness (language that discloses actual experience), and truth (transcendental or metaphysical explication of the condition of possibility of common human experience)."[31] So type 2 is like type 1 to the extent that both are strictly foundationalist. But a difference arises—on the formal level, at any rate—at the point at which Tracy wants to take Christianity seriously as a concrete religion. Theology does not involve simply the adjustment of theological language to general criteria; Tracy believes that it also entails an "explication of the Christian religion or the Christian 'fact,' which has a real specificity of its own and in its integrity has to be *correlated* to common human experience, the other source of theological reflection, for their mutual compatibility."[32]

In practice, however, the desire to honor the integrity of the historical givenness of Christian faith (and its object, Jesus of Nazareth) is undermined by Tracy's procedure. His goal is to "correlate" (i.e., to show the thorough compatibility of) the religious symbols which arise from two sources: "common human experience," on the one hand, and classical Christian texts (Scripture and tradition), on the other. The first group of symbols he seeks to articulate (or "thematize") through a phenomenological analysis of an allegedly religious dimension of secular experience. The focus here is, above all, the "basic confidence" which Tracy believes to be an ineradicable feature of all human existence (the confidence that life is worth living). For Tracy, the survival of basic confidence in the midst of certain "limit situations" (i.e., the wholly

---

29. Frei, *Types of Christian Theology*, 51.
30. David Tracy, *Blessed Rage for Order* (New York: Seabury, 1975).
31. Frei, *Types of Christian Theology*, 30.
32. Ibid., 31.

negative experiences of guilt, anxiety, etc.) demonstrates its ineradicability and raises the question of its ground. He concludes that "basic confidence" has implied within it the cognitive claim that "God" is the ground of that confidence; that is, the only adequate symbolization of that ground is theistic. Tracy then turns to his second source and finds there a "limit language" which is disclosive not only of the very situation which was just thematized through phenomenological analysis but also of a Referent which holds forth the promise that life is indeed meaningful when lived in total commitment to the gracious God of Jesus the Christ.

Though Frei himself does not put it this way, I think it would be fair to say that his principal problem with Tracy's "theology of correlation" is that no true correlation can ever arise on the foundations laid by him. Christian self-description (the language of Scripture and tradition) has been thoroughly subsumed into the religious symbols attained through phenomenological analysis of "religious dimensions" of human being and existence. And this can happen only because the results of the philosophical analysis are made to be *the* interpretive key for unlocking the meaning of the New Testament. So Frei is not in the least surprised that Tracy has found in the New Testament precisely what he was looking for; his procedure has guaranteed the outcome in advance.[33] External description and Christian self-description turn out to be one and the same, identical in content. A correlation of two overlapping but distinguishable descriptions is rendered unnecessary. What is most decisive in defining Frei's type 2 is the fact that the subsumption of Christian self-description into external description has been made possible by a universally valid integrative theory (which in Tracy's case is ultimately grounded in a general philosophical anthropology).[34]

As we move to type 3, we move out of the realm of foundationalism. A true "theology of correlation" first appears here, and it does so because external description and Christian self-description are not understood to be completely identical in content. And this, in turn, is because no universally valid integrative theory is advanced which would guarantee such an outcome. Frei's example here is the later Schleiermacher of the *Glaubenslehre*. Here the correlation of external description (which is achieved by means of a series of propositions borrowed from ethics, philosophy of religion, and apologetics) and Christian self-description arrives at a complete convergence only to the extent that a formulistic definition of the "essence of Christianity" is offered which Christians and non-Christians might well agree on. But Schleiermacher also makes it quite clear that dogmatic theology is carried on for those who stand within the church. "Theology is second-order reflection on what Schleiermacher calls *Glaubensaussagen*: first-order statements that are

33. Ibid., 32–33.
34. Ibid., 31.

themselves internal expressions of the wedding of a universal human condition (religion, or the feeling of absolute dependence) with a specific 'positive' or cultural form which provides the only way in which such a condition may be present."[35] Insofar as the material content of all dogmatic statements comes through the modifications wrought in the feeling of absolute dependence by the redemption wrought by Jesus of Nazareth, it follows that "the language of the Church is always community-specific and can never be dissolved . . . into a more general cultural or, for that matter, a philosophical-technical vocabulary."[36] Theology is a function of the church. The principal difference between Tracy and Schleiermacher is that the latter substitutes the church for a general "meaning structure" as the location of Christian self-description. It is the church (its theological traditions, etc.) which structures Christian self-description. But given that the church is not infallible, its traditions must themselves be subjected to critical scrutiny. The consequence is that what shapes Christian self-description is not itself fixed, finished. It is subject to revision. Hence correlations between external description and Christian self-description are indeed possible, but they will necessarily take place on an ad hoc basis (subject to the ebb and flow of modifications in Christian self-description).[37] "There is a real reciprocal relationship between philosophy and theology," but Schleiermacher also "insisted on the autonomy of theology from philosophy, which cannot serve as a foundational discipline for theology."[38]

The picture I have drawn here of the third type is a bit tidier than that set forth by Frei himself. Frei could also say that the correlation in question was one between an academic (university-based) theology and Christian self-description (ecclesial dogmatics). And when he did, he tended to suggest that university-based theology was carried out in accordance with "formal, universal, and transcendental criteria for valid thinking." Just what these criteria are and how they differ from a covering theory which would accomplish the integration of external description and Christian self-description (and thereby from type 2) Frei does not say. What he does say is that there occurs in Schleiermacher a correlation of academic theology (which is subject to universally valid criteria) with Christian self-description *in the absence of a covering theory*. It seems clear that Frei had a certain ambivalence about Schleiermacher and was never quite sure where to locate him. The tidy picture I presented in the previous paragraph would make it very difficult to distinguish Schleiermacher from Barth (and thereby type 3 from type 4). When Frei turns his attention to distinguishing them, a more incoherent picture emerges. What Frei has accomplished through leaving the tensions in his portrait unresolved is to bring

35. Ibid., 35.
36. Ibid., 37.
37. Ibid., 3.
38. Ibid., 38.

Schleiermacher closer to Barth, and this, no doubt, was his goal: to make Schleiermacher an ally of Barth rather than Tracy.

As we move to type 4, we find that the principal difference between Schleiermacher and Barth (i.e., between types 3 and 4) lies, for Frei, in Barth's view that "theology has its own rules of what makes it a science." That is to say, theology is not an academic discipline at all *if* this is taken to mean one which is subjected to "a set of universal, formal criteria which are certain and all fields-encompassing" and can "be stated apart from the context of specific application."[39] Granted, Barth too thinks that theology is an academic discipline, for the use of philosophical criteria for coherence, meaningfulness, and truth are never, in his view, simply dispensable. But such use is "governed by the specific theological issue at hand, and by the general rule that absolute priority be given to Christian theology as Christian self-description within the religious community called the Church."[40] For this reason, Barth refuses on principle to advance a formal theory which would explain when and how such "correlations" should take place. Thus the difference between Schleiermacher and Barth turns out to be one of degree; Barth goes further than Schleiermacher did in insisting on the priority of Christian self-description over external description.

But Barth did not think about Christian theology in merely academic terms. Equally, if not more, important to him was the fact that "all Christian language is self-involving, existential; that whether it is directed towards God or the neighbour, it is the learning and exercising of concepts in a performative manner."[41] Theology, in this light, might well be seen as concerned primarily with the business of teaching and/or learning the grammar which shapes the beliefs and practices of a particular community (and would be so seen by Frei's colleague George Lindbeck). But does such an account do justice to Barth's theology?

At this point in his account, Frei displays a certain ambivalence. He is well aware of Barth's profound concern for the referential aspect of Christian doctrine. He notes (almost in passing) that, for Barth, "the Church is accountable to God for its discourse about God. . . . The Church must undertake a critique and correction of her discourse in the light of the norm she sees as the presence of God to the Church, in obedience to God's grace. . . . The criterion of Christian discourse is the being of the Church, and the being of the Church for him is Jesus Christ, God in his presence or turning to humanity. The question is, Does Christian discourse come from him and move toward him, and is it in accordance with him?"[42] In spite of this rather straightforward affirmation of what I would call the realism of Barth's theology, such elements do not

39. Ibid., 39.
40. Ibid., 41.
41. Ibid., 42.
42. Ibid., 39.

receive the kind of attention one might have expected. And if reason were to be sought for Frei's reticence to emphasize Barth's theological realism, I would hazard the guess that it had a good deal to do with Frei's social location. Frei's teaching career was spent in a divinity school attached to a major university, where the need to justify one's existence (and the academic credentials of his discipline) was a pressing one. But this tended to place him in a bind, since he was not satisfied with previous efforts undertaken by modern theologians who looked to philosophy for help. It seemed to him that such efforts had succeeded only in robbing Christian faith of its integrity. What better way out of the bind, then, than to appeal to a rather different auxiliary discipline—that of cultural anthropology—in order to justify claims for the irreducibility of the Christian language-game, its highly contextual character, and the importance of the internal logic of that language-game for an understanding of the Christian religion.[43] The consequence is to make the study of Christian theology an aspect of the study of the Christian religion and to find the proper location for such an endeavor in a university department of religious studies. Frei, I am suggesting, is not simply interpreting Barth; he is making use of him for his own purposes.[44] There is nothing wrong with this in principle, of course—so long as one makes it clear that this is what is taking place. But Frei did not make it as clear as he ought to have. In locating Barth on a spectrum of opinion whose more nearly confessional pole is defined in terms of "Christian *self*-description," Frei opened the door to an understanding of Barth in which questions of reality-reference will be suppressed in favor of a concentration on the internal logic of theological statements.[45] Indeed, the door has even

43. Frei finds the help he needs in the work of the noted anthropologist Clifford Geertz.

44. If I were asked to identify the most fundamental difference between Barth and Frei, the point at which all further departures find their root, I would say that it lies in Frei's rejection of Barth's contention that, for any science, the reality to be known determines the way taken to knowledge of it. See Frei, *Types of Christian Theology*, 80: "Such an understanding of *Wissenschaft* in terms of its object came to be dismissed, and rightly so, because no self-respecting academic discipline has its method strictly specified by the object or data; at best it is an understanding of the data *under* a method or theory. The theory, not the object, has priority when you ask what kind of explanations make a given discipline a coherent field of study. What Barth might have said instead of 'object of knowledge' is 'conceptual referent within a specific conceptual or cultural-linguistic structure.'" Consistent with this view, Frei would like to understand Barth to be saying, "We don't have more than our concepts of God; we don't have a separate intuition, a pre-conceptual or pre-linguistic apprehension or grasp of God in his reality. . . . But we don't need it either; for the reality of God is given in, with, and under the concept and not separably, and that is adequate for us" (79). Frei is quite right to say that, for Barth, "we don't have . . . a pre-conceptual or pre-linguistic apprehension or grasp of God in his reality." But the dialectical relation of the being of God and the language used to bear witness to God is dangerously flattened out by talk of an "in, with, and under." For Barth, God makes the language of the biblical witness conform to himself and, in that God does so, we do indeed grasp God in his reality. Method in theology is or should be a witness to this fact.

45. Such an understanding of Barth's theological method could, with good reason, make an appeal to his 1931 book on Anselm. For there Barth does indeed set forth a description of

been opened to making an appeal to Barth for a view which would seek the norm(s) governing the Christian language-game in the language itself rather than in the presence of God to the church in Jesus Christ. But I will postpone consideration of the latter possibility for a moment. What I would like to do first is to offer some reflection on the limitations of Frei's typology for an understanding of Barth.

Critique of Frei's Typology

Students of Barth in the English-speaking world owe a tremendous debt to Hans Frei. At a time when Barth's theology had undergone an almost complete eclipse (in the United States, at any rate), Frei stood virtually alone in his willingness to identify himself publicly with Barth's theology. Had he not done so, it is unlikely that there would be the kind of significant interest in Barth's theology which is now emerging. Still, a recognition of indebtedness should not make one blind to weaknesses in Frei's reading of Barth.

---

theology as the attempt to investigate the meaning of a particular article of faith found in the Creed (which, for the purposes of the investigation, is treated as an unknown x), given that the remaining articles are assumed to be true. See Karl Barth, *Fides quaerens intellectum: Anselms Beweis der Existenz Gottes im Zusammenhang seines theologischen Programms*, ed. Eberhard Jüngel and Ingolf Ulrich Dalferth (Zurich: Theologischer Verlag, 1981), 54. But as I have argued elsewhere, the description of theological method set forth in the Anselm book scarcely does justice to the far more elaborate discussion provided in *CD* I/1 and I/2. What is missing in the Anselm book, from the point of view of the *Church Dogmatics*, is an adequate emphasis on the network of dogmatic assumptions which would prevent the theological "science" described in the earlier book from becoming just one more complacent, bourgeois discipline, namely, (1) attention to the fact that theology can succeed in its task of speaking adequately of God only if God *does* something and (2) the comprehension of this realistic emphasis on divine action in terms of a *Realdialektik* of veiling and unveiling, which would locate the reality of God in a realm beyond that accessible by means of direct intuition and thereby make clear the fact that the reality of God cannot simply be grasped, controlled, manipulated. It is this set of dogmatic presuppositions which would forever make theology, for Barth, a *human* impossibility. It is possible as a divine possibility, or it is not possible at all. Not for Karl Barth a definition of theology in terms of the learning of a linguistic skill! Frei seems to have understood all of this with regard to the early Barth of the second edition of *Romans*. He can, for example, in his exposition of the early Barth, make appeal to Barth's statement "Don't things get dangerous only *if* and *because* God is?" (Frei, "Eberhard Busch's Biography of Karl Barth," 152). But Frei believed that the Anselm book constituted a methodological "revolution" in Barth's thought. And I suspect that the misreading of Barth's development contributed to Busch's tendency to take the Anselm book as something more than it was originally intended to be (an exposition of *Anselm's* method) and to see in it a fully adequate guide to the method employed in the *Church Dogmatics* as well. Now, obviously, in an attempt to justify such an interpretation, Frei could also have made appeal to the sweeping claims made with reference to the importance of the Anselm book by Barth himself. But for a complete discussion of why Barth's rather late assessment of the Anselm book ought to be handled critically, see Bruce L. McCormack, *Karl Barth's Critically Realistic Dialectical Theology: Its Genesis and Development, 1909–1936* (Oxford: Clarendon, 1995), 421–48.

The effect of Frei's typology is to place Barth on a spectrum of opinion which is determined by the struggle between foundationalism and nonfoundationalism. In my own view, such a procedure is not only anachronistic (in that Barth could not have foreseen this development); the great weakness in it is that it fails to catch sight of the only possible answer to this debate which he might have given had he lived to see it. Barth was no *theological* foundationalist; this much should be beyond debate. He believed that revelation is self-authenticating and would not allow its claim to meaningfulness and truth to be grounded outside itself, for example, in a philosophical account of the religious dimensions of human being. But Barth was not strictly a nonfoundationalist either. The truth of the matter is that Barth's theological epistemology could never be adequately envisioned if our options were limited by the terms used to set up Frei's typology.

The central problem of Barth's theology was one he shared with all modern theologians, namely, how to understand the nature of, and the grounds for, human knowledge (in the strict sense of *Erkenntnis*) of God. And like a good many other modern theologians, he took for granted the validity of the epistemological "turn to the subject" which had occurred in philosophy (from Descartes to Kant). As I have already noted in the introduction to this essay, insofar as Barth had and made use of a philosophy, it was Kantian.[46] The crucial point to be made in this context is that Kant's epistemology represented a very powerful form of subjective foundationalism (i.e., the synthetic operations of the mind in combining the categories of the understanding with the intuition of sense data were understood by Kant to be universally valid). And Barth was willing to grant all of that—*insofar as it touches upon our knowledge of empirical reality*. But he also believed that God was not directly identical with any element of the reality which is known in this way. God is "wholly other" than the reality which is known by Kant. Given that this is so, *Barth could not allow his philosophical foundations to be made foundational for theology*. What he did instead was to affirm (on Kantian grounds) that if genuine *knowledge* of God (rather than a mere experience of God) were to be possible, then God must enter into the realm of intuitability. God must make himself to be phenomenal. And yet, if the "wholly otherness" of God were not to be sacrificed in the process, then God must never become directly identical with any one medium of his Self-revelation. He must take up the medium in such a way that the ontological difference between God's being and the being of the creaturely medium is not for a moment set aside. No "divinization" of the creaturely occurs in this process; God remains God and world remains world.

Now, all that I have said to this point might seem to suggest that Barth was working with an a priori *Erkenntnistheorie* and tailoring his Christology to it.

46. See McCormack, *Karl Barth's Critically Realistic Dialectical Theology*, 43–49, 58–63, 129–30, 207–9, 218–26, 245–62.

But in fact, just the opposite is the case. Talk of what God "must" do if God is to reveal himself rests upon an a posteriori reflection on what "must" be the case if God has done what God is said to have done in Jesus Christ by the New Testament witness. Thus, I would argue, Barth's anhypostatic-enhypostatic Christology ultimately controlled his use of Kantian categories. Kantian epistemology is brought into play in order to explicate the *erkenntnistheoretischen* implications of his Christology. The significance of that fact is this: if a day were to arrive when Kant's epistemology could no longer be considered valid at every point, Barth's *theological* epistemology would not necessarily suffer. As stated, Barth never allowed his philosophical foundations to become foundational for his theology. His appeal to philosophy was always ad hoc and eclectic. And therefore it could be the case that a new philosophical epistemology which is less strictly foundationalist than the one to which Barth looked would have to be devised in order to explicate Barth's theological epistemology in terms which would be more acceptable to philosophy today.

To sum up: philosophically, Barth was a "foundationalist." As such, he could not possibly have sought an alliance with forms of philosophy that seek to do away with "foundations" altogether (i.e., it is scarcely imaginable to me that he would have found any sympathy with Rorty, Bernstein, et al.).[47] He would have insisted on the human character of all formulations of philosophical "foundations" and would therefore have been open to revising formulations of them. In the ultimate sense, he would say, the *true* "foundations" of all human knowledge consist in the being-in-act of the Triune God. What philosophers call foundations are, at best, approximations of the true foundations. So philosophical foundations are open-ended and revisable. But Barth could not have rejected the attempt to articulate foundations altogether without ceasing to be "Barthian." Thus he was clearly not a nonfoundationalist.

Nevertheless, given that he would not allow his philosophical foundations to become foundations for theology, he would not have located himself on the foundationalist end of the spectrum either. If I were pressed to say how I think Barth would have located his position in relation to the debate depicted by Frei's typology, I would need to coin a new term to describe it. The term I would choose would be "*trans*foundationalism." Barth was seeking to explicate a theological epistemology which transcends the terms set by this debate. That is to say, the truly "foundational" element in his theological epistemology lies in an act of God by which the limitations placed on human knowing by Kant's philosophical epistemology are transcended. Thus the *trans-* in my phrase "transfoundationalism" does not refer to a human act of self-transcendence; it refers, rather, to a realistically conceived divine act. In revelation God takes up a creaturely magnitude and bears witness to himself

47. For a reading of the Yale theologians which would make them allies of the nonfoundationalist philosophers, see Thiel, *Nonfoundationalism*.

in and through it without setting aside the ontological difference. The great weakness of Frei's typology for presenting Barth's theology should now be abundantly clear. The typology leaves out of consideration Barth's most basic problem (the knowledge of God). And in doing so, it lends itself all too easily to a reduction of Barth's theology to a matter of clarifying the internal logic governing the relations of certain doctrinal statements without ever raising the most decisive question, namely, that of the (grace given!) adequacy of those statements for *referring* to God.

But having said all of this, there is still a strength in Frei's typology. For in locating Barth in his type 4, he is at least acknowledging that Barth is not adequately described as a "nonfoundationalist." Put more positively, he is acknowledging that, for Barth, correlations with modern philosophies are not merely possible but, in many cases, desirable. And this, as we shall now see, differentiates his reading of Barth from the one George Lindbeck thinks himself to have learned from him.

George Lindbeck

It must be acknowledged at the outset that George Lindbeck has made no claim to be a Barth scholar. On the contrary, he has explicitly told his readers that what he knows of Barth he learned primarily from his colleague Hans Frei.[48] So what we have now to consider is, in fact, a reading of a reading of Barth—an interpretation of Barth at second hand. Given that this is so, I will first treat Lindbeck on his own terms and only then ask what use he has made of Barth in the process.

In his much-discussed book *The Nature of Doctrine*, Lindbeck offers an argument for a particular theory of religion, a conception of truth and an understanding of doctrine which is commensurate with this theory, and, finally, a theological method. The theory of religion he calls "cultural linguistic"; the understanding of truth, "performative"; the understanding of doctrine, "regulative"; and the theological method, "intratextuality." I will treat each of these elements in turn.

The "cultural-linguistic" model of religion is defined by Lindbeck in reference to two other, competing theories: the "cognitive" and the "experiential-expressive." How the term "cognitive" is thought by Lindbeck to be adequate for describing a full-orbed theory of religion is not altogether clear. It remains relatively undeveloped, in all likelihood, for two reasons: first, because Lindbeck regards it as largely outdated, and second, because his real interest lies in opposing what he regards as the dominant view—the "experiential-expressive." The most that can be said is that a "cognitive" theory is one which lays great

48. See George Lindbeck, *The Nature of Doctrine: Religion and Theology in a Postliberal Age* (Philadelphia: Westminster, 1984), 138n35.

emphasis upon the intellectual dimensions of religious experience and, as a corollary of this emphasis, regards doctrines as propositions which set forth truth claims about objective realities. The theory of truth which supports such a view is normally a "correspondence theory."

But it is the "experiential-expressive" theory which absorbs Lindbeck's attention. At the heart of the experiential-expressive model, as he understands it, lies the conviction that all religion arises out of a prereflective, prelinguistic experience of the "divine"; indeed, the different religions are simply diverse expressions or objectifications of a common core experience which is thought to be present in all human beings—though the nonreligious are less than fully conscious of it. "Truth," in this view, has to do with the effectiveness of symbols in communicating the inner experience of the divine. And this means that the norm which finally decides the adequacy or inadequacy of any particular symbolization is the core experience itself (be it termed the "feeling of absolute dependence" or whatever). Everything that Lindbeck says about the "cultural-linguistic" theory is designed to counter each of these points.

As the name given to it suggests, the cultural-linguistic model finds the closest analogue to religion in a linguistically formed culture. A religion is a semiotic system, a comprehensive interpretive scheme which structures or gives shape to human experience.[49] In this view, there is no such thing as raw, uninterpreted experience. Indeed, without language, it would be impossible to have experience. Language provides the categories needed to make sense of that which is experienced, to assimilate it. That which is not so assimilated is not truly experienced. "There are numberless thoughts we cannot think, sentiments we cannot have, and realities we cannot perceive unless we learn to use the appropriate symbol systems."[50] So, contrary to the experiential-expressivist view, it is language which is primordial, not experience. Experience is derivative of language.[51]

To become religious, then, "involves becoming skilled in the language of the symbol system of a given religion. To become a Christian involves learning the story of Israel and of Jesus well enough to interpret and experience oneself and one's world in its terms. A religion is above all an external word, a *verbum externum*, that molds and shapes the self and its world, rather than an expression or thematization of a preexisting self or of preconceptual experience."[52] *Becoming* religious is a matter of socialization into the use of a communal language, a socialization that occurs either naturally (through upbringing in a community of faith) or through catechesis. *Being* religious (and doing it well) is a matter of being skilled in the use of that language. It should be noted that language is here understood primarily to shape forms

49. Ibid., 32.
50. Ibid., 34.
51. Ibid., 35.
52. Ibid., 34.

of life and *not* (in the first instance at least) to refer to objective realities. "A comprehensive scheme or story used to structure all dimensions of existence is not primarily a set of propositions to be believed, but is rather the medium in which one moves, a set of skills that one employs in living one's life. . . . Thus while a religion's truth claims are often of the utmost importance to it (as in the case of Christianity), it is, nevertheless, the conceptual vocabulary and the syntax or inner logic which determines the kind of truth claims the religion can make. The cognitive aspect, while often important, is not primary."[53]

Given the priorities registered in this passage, it is not surprising that Lindbeck would see "truth" primarily in terms of the "use" which is made of religious or theological language. There is, in fact, a "right use" of religious utterances—certain "forms of life" or patterns of behavior that are commensurate with those utterances when interpreted against the background of the complete linguistic system within which they have their meaning. In the absence of the right use of an utterance, it is not simply the case that its meaning is rendered unintelligible or wrongly intelligible; the statement itself is actually made to be false. Lindbeck gives the following example: "The crusader's cry '*Christus est Dominus*' . . . is false when used to authorize cleaving the skull of the infidel (even though the same words in other contexts may be a true utterance)."[54] What, then, of the status of religious statements in relation to the realities they ostensibly seek to describe? Lindbeck acknowledges that correspondence to reality has a role to play in any fully adequate account of "truth," but he holds that, in the case of religious statements, "their correspondence to reality . . . is not an attribute that they have when considered in and of themselves, but is only a function of their role in constituting a form of life, a way of being in the world, which itself corresponds to the Most Important, the Ultimately Real. Medieval scholastics spoke of truth as an adequation of the mind to the thing (*adequatio mentis ad rem*), but in the religious domain, this mental isomorphism of the knowing and the known can be pictured as part and parcel of a wider conformity of the self to God.[55] Thus "it is only through the performatory use of religious utterances that they acquire propositional force."[56]

53. Ibid., 35.
54. Ibid., 64.
55. Ibid., 65.
56. Ibid., 66. Lindbeck goes so far as to say that "this performatory conformity of the self to God can also be pictured in epistemologically realistic fashion as involving a correspondence of the mind to divine reality." But it is hard to understand how this could be so, given the example he offers by way of explanation. Lindbeck appeals to Thomas, who, he argues, held that whereas "in statements about God the human mode of signifying (*modus significandi*) does not correspond to anything in the divine being, the signified (*significatum*) does. Thus, for example, when we say that God is good, we do not affirm that any of our concepts of goodness (*modi significandi*) apply to him, but rather that there is a concept of goodness unavailable to us, viz., God's understanding of his own goodness, which does apply. What we

The third major element in Lindbeck's project has to do with his under-standing of the nature of doctrine. Lindbeck has a very specific interest here. His concern is not with doctrines in general, with each and every doctrinal statement found in theological books. He is concerned, rather, with "church doctrines." "Church doctrines are communally authoritative teachings regarding beliefs and practices that are considered essential to the identity or welfare of the group in question." Such doctrines may be officially promulgated in the form of dogmas or they may be only informally operative, but in any case,

---

assert, in other words, is that 'God is good' is meaningful and true, but without knowing the meaning of 'God is good.'" I am not interested here in passing judgment on what Lindbeck calls his "agnostic" reading of Thomas. I would simply point out that if it is true that our concepts *as we understand them* do not—under any circumstances?—correspond to anything in the divine being and if it then follows that our concepts may in truth correspond to the divine being only in cases where we do not understand their meaning, then it is hard to see how a correspondence of a concept or statement to the divine reality entails a correspondence of the *mind* to the divine reality. Logically, it would appear that just the opposite is the case. Surely, the mind can correspond to divine reality only where its understanding of concepts does apply to God—*or is made to by a gracious divine action*. It would appear that all that is left standing from a correspondence theory of truth is a conformity of human behavior to God, but in the absence of real knowledge of God, it is impossible even to know where and when such conformity exists. And this impression seems to be confirmed when Lindbeck goes on to make the somewhat astonishing claim that "despite its informational vacuity, the claim that God is truly good in himself is of utmost importance because it authorizes responding *as if* he were good in the ways indicated by the stories of creation, providence, and redemption which shape believers' thoughts and actions" (ibid., 67 [emphasis mine]). Once the appeal has been made to act "as if" God were good, little discernable difference remains between Lindbeck's "performative" analysis of truth and the fictionalist account of a Karl Friedrich Forberg. See B. A. Gerrish, "Practical Belief: Friedrich Karl Forberg (1770–1848) and the Fictionalist View of Religious Language," in *Probing the Reformed Tradition: Historical Studies in Honor of Edward A. Dowey, Jr.*, ed. Elsie Anne McKee and Brian Armstrong (Louisville: Westminster/John Knox, 1989), 367–85.

I do not think myself that this is a consequence Lindbeck intended. What he seems finally to want to say is that theological propositions can indeed be bearers of "ontological truth" (i.e., they can refer more or less adequately to objective realities) but only within "determinate settings"—namely, within the contexts of worship and pastoral care. And he adds,

> This rarely if ever happens on the pages of theological treatises or in the course of doctrinal discussions. . . . Technical theology and official doctrine . . . are second-order discourse about the first-intentional uses of religious language. Here, in contrast to the common supposition, one rarely if ever succeeds in making affirmations with ontological import, but rather engages in explaining, defending, analyzing, and regulating the liturgical, kerygmatic, and ethical modes of speech and action within which such affirmations from time to time occur. Just as grammar by itself affirms nothing either true or false regarding the world in which language is used, but only about language, so theology and doctrine, to the extent that they are second-order activities, assert nothing either true or false about God and his relation to creatures, but only speak about such assertions. (Lindbeck, *The Nature of Doctrine*, 68–69)

Clearly, Lindbeck's concept of truth has contributed directly to his understanding of the nature of doctrine, and it is to this problem that we now turn.

they serve to "indicate what constitutes faithful adherence to a community."[57] With this restricted focus in mind, Lindbeck then advances what he calls a "rule theory" (or, alternatively, a "regulative theory") which defines church doctrines as "second-order rather than first-order propositions" which "affirm nothing about extra-linguistic or extra-human reality." For a rule theory, doctrines "make . . . intrasystematic rather than ontological claims." Lindbeck leaves open the possibility that other kinds of doctrinal statements—those found in the *Church Dogmatics* perhaps?—will be first-order descriptions of objective realities, but where this occurs, the doctrine in question "is not being used as a church doctrine."[58]

Clearly, in defining doctrine in this way, Lindbeck has bracketed off certain possibilities still resident in his concept of truth. In speaking of truth, he maintained that the correct "performatory use" of a theological statement would enable it to "correspond to reality." Now, however, in limiting himself to defining church doctrine rather than doctrine in general, he has put aside any concern for "correspondence." The only doctrines he is interested in are those which (he thinks) function solely and strictly in an intrasystematic fashion—that is, those which make no ontological claims whatsoever. There are reasons, of course, for the restriction to church doctrines, reasons which we have not chosen to enter into here—the chief one being his concern to unravel problems which have arisen in ecumenical dialogue. What is crucial, for our purposes, is to see that Lindbeck's "rule theory" has reduced doctrine to a grammar which governs the way in which certain lexical elements supplied by Bible and tradition are used in the church (or, in some cases, to illustrations of the correct use of that grammar). For a rule theory, however, doctrines "affirm nothing about extra-linguistic or extra-human reality."

The final element in Lindbeck's program is his "intratextual" approach to theology. It is here that he first makes an appeal to Karl Barth as one who—in some places in the *Church Dogmatics* at least—adumbrated the approach which he now advocates.[59] The task of a systematic or dogmatic theology, as Lindbeck understands it, is "to give a normative explication of the meaning a religion has for its adherents." Cognitivists and experiential-expressivists locate this meaning "outside the text or semiotic system either in the objective realities to which it refers or in the experiences which it symbolizes." For this reason, Lindbeck characterizes both approaches as "extratextual." Cultural linguists, on the other hand, locate the meaning of a religion within the semiotic system; meaning for them is immanent. Therefore "theological description in the cultural-linguistic mode is intrasemiotic or intratextual."[60]

57. Lindbeck, *The Nature of Doctrine*, 74.

58. Ibid., 80.

59. Ibid., 135. For a fuller treatment of Barth as an "intratextual theologian," see George Lindbeck, "Barth and Textuality," *Theology Today* 43 (1986): 361–76.

60. Lindbeck, *The Nature of Doctrine*, 114.

KARL BARTH'S RELATIONSHIP TO POSTLIBERALISM AND POSTMODERNISM

Such an approach to theology flows quite naturally out of the prior commitment to a rule theory of doctrine. But it also coheres nicely, Lindbeck thinks, with the fact that "all the world's major faiths . . . have relatively fixed canons of writings that they treat as exemplary of normative instantiations of their semiotic codes. One test of faithfulness for all of them is the degree to which descriptions correspond to the semiotic universe paradigmatically encoded in holy writ."[61] The canonical Scriptures—or, which seems more likely, the biblical narratives interrelated in ways specified by church doctrines—provide "the framework and medium within which Christians know and experience."[62] "For those who are steeped in them [i.e., the canonical writings], no world is more real than the ones they create. A scriptural world is thus able to absorb the universe. It supplies the interpretive framework within which believers seek to live their lives and understand reality."[63]

So understood, "intratextual" theology is, above all, a practice. It is a skill which is acquired initially through the process of being socialized into the language of a given community of faith (through either upbringing or catechesis), and it is a skill in which one may even become expert through repeated use. The practice, in this case, is ostensibly the use of biblical categories to describe extrascriptural realities and experiences. But it must be remembered that it is language which makes experience possible. So it is not the case that those extrascriptural realities act as judges of would-be descriptions. What we are left with, apparently, is simply the question of whether a particular use of biblical categories stands in a recognizable conformity to the biblical usage of them.

What is most striking about Lindbeck's theological program when seen in the light of Frei's typology is the extent to which it fits better in type 5 than in type 4. To recall Frei's definition of type 5, it had the following features: it rejected the possibility of a "general theory" of explanation which could ground all disciplines (including theology). It held that Christian "self-description" involves the highly contextual (communal) use of a language which has been learned as any language is learned—through mastery of its grammar and socialization into its idioms. "Christian theology is strictly the grammar of faith, a procedure in self-description for which there is no external correlative."[64] Now, the last sentence alone would appear to prevent location of Lindbeck in Frei's type 5. Certainly, in his consideration of the concept of truth, he has held out the possibility of a correspondence of the self to God (albeit inconsistently). But by the time he has set forth his understanding of doctrine and his discussion of "faithfulness" in theology, every last vestige of a vision of a theology which

61. Ibid., 116. Though Lindbeck says in this passage that conformity to the semiotic universe encoded in Scripture is "one" test of the faithfulness of a theology, he does not advance any others.

62. Ibid., 84; cf. 80.

63. Ibid., 117.

64. See above, p. 118.

makes truth claims about external realities seems to have disappeared. By the end of this small but influential monograph, Lindbeck finds himself willy-nilly in type 5. As a representative of this type, Lindbeck constitutes a far more consistent form of nonfoundationalist theological thinking than Frei ever did.

He is also prone to the charge of a "positivism of revelation"—at least in its original sense—in a way that Karl Barth never was. For Dietrich Bonhoeffer, who coined the term precisely in order to describe Barth, the latter's positivism of revelation consisted in his (alleged) tendency to continue to remint traditional language forms *after* the death of every metaphysical scheme which would make such language meaningful. Barth himself, so Bonhoeffer's reading of him goes, had set out to say good-bye to all metaphysically-based religion. But Barth was unable to carry these insights through to completion and wound up instead using the ancient creedal language forms which had been made possible by metaphysical assumptions.[65] In the absence of the metaphysics which made this language meaningful and gave to it a certain plausability, all Barth was left with was the language itself and a voluntaristic appeal to "take it or leave it" (or, in more colloquial German, "eat, bird, or die").[66] Bonhoeffer was right about one thing: Barth had indeed said good-bye to all metaphysically-based religion. But at no point did he simply fall back on the biblical or creedal language as an unimpeachable *given* and say, "Take it or leave it." What he did instead was to elaborate a nonmetaphysical, actualistic (divine and human) ontology which took the place of the classical metaphysics of being and the modern metaphysics of the religious a priori and which completed this language and made it meaningful in a new and different way. Lindbeck, by contrast, by bracketing off questions of ontology, reality-reference, revelation, and knowledge of God, *is* left with nothing but the biblical and creedal language and the admonition "take it or leave it." Lindbeck may not have set out to collapse revelation into the texts of Bible and Creed, but his refusal to address questions of revelation, ontology, and so on, has amounted to the same thing.

What, then, of the use of Barth in the promotion of Lindbeck's program? In *The Nature of Doctrine*, Barth is simply mentioned in passing. In a later essay, "Barth and Textuality," Lindbeck expands a bit on his reading of Barth. Picking up a theme from Barth's 1917 lecture "The New World within the Bible," he notes that although Barth had not yet at that time learned to read his Bible in an intratextual fashion (i.e., without reference to God, the world, history, metaphysics—anything outside or beyond the text), "as time went on, the strange new world becomes ever more intratextual, firmly located within the biblical text itself."[67] Of course, Lindbeck's attempt to read Barth in this

---

65. Dietrich Bonhoeffer, *Widerstand und Ergebung: Briefe und Aufzeichnungen aus der Haft*, ed. Eberhard Bethge with an afterword by Christian Gremmels (Munich: Kaiser, 1990), 140; translated as *Letters and Papers from Prison*, 3rd ed. (London: SCM Press, 1967), 153.

66. Ibid., 143 (*Letters and Papers from Prison*, 157).

67. Lindbeck, "Barth and Textuality," 362.

fashion has an immense obstacle in its path in the form of the latter's doctrine of revelation. To his credit, Lindbeck recognizes this, but his solution is simply to isolate what he perceives to be Barth's exegetical practice from his concept of revelation and to jettison the latter. Barth's concept of revelation, he says, does not derive from Scripture as Barth thought. It "has been baptized into the world of Scripture and treated as if it had been born there." The truth of the matter, as he sees it, is that Barth's doctrine of revelation "trades heavily on mistaken descriptions of knowledge and science." Barth has done a "good job of baptizing bad epistemology."[68] Still, Lindbeck holds out the hope that readers will not be put off by their inability "to make sense of what appears to be the foundation of the whole *Church Dogmatics*" (i.e., I/1 and I/2) and realize that "the heart of the enterprise is a retrieval of the Reformation version of the way of reading the Bible which already begins with the New Testament writers with their typological and christological appropriation of Hebrew Scriptures, and that this hermeneutics is logically independent of the apparent starting-point."[69] What this "retrieval" shows, I think, is that it was never Lindbeck's intention to extend Barth's thought, to draw out its possible implications (and here he differs from Frei). What he has done instead is simply to make an ad hoc use of Barth by way of explicating his own theological program. It goes without saying that once Barth's hermeneutics have been cut off in this way from their theological "foundations," the later Barth of *CD* IV/2 has been made to be a nonfoundationalist theologian of the Lindbeckian persuasion.

Critique of Lindbeck's Reading of Barth

As this is an essay on readings of Barth, I will not enter into a lengthy critique of Lindbeck's theological proposal but content myself with the following observation: it is my belief—though I cannot seek to demonstrate it in full here—that Lindbeck's program is best understood as an expression of American neoorthodoxy reinventing itself in a changed situation. The change to which I refer has to do with the dramatic decline in fortunes which neoorthodoxy underwent in the 1960s. Throughout the middle third of this century, neoorthodoxy had been the most powerful theological movement in America. But in the early 1960s, the movement experienced a dramatic loss of prestige; accustomed to a position at the center of things, neoorthodoxy awakened one day to find itself on the periphery, in a defensive posture. The catalyst for this shift was the appearance in 1961 of a devastating critique by

68. Ibid., 368. As Lindbeck provides no supporting argumentation for these assertions, there is no point in trying to respond to them.

69. Ibid. I suspect that Lindbeck's way of understanding Barth's exegetical practice and his preoccupation with it to the exclusion of other elements in Barth's thought which might force him to modify it owes at least as much (if not more) to David Kelsey than it does to Hans Frei. On this point, see Kelsey, *The Uses of Scripture in Recent Theology*, 39–50.

a one-time member of the movement, Langdon Gilkey.[70] The nub of Gilkey's criticism was that neoorthodoxy made sweeping use of biblical language without committing itself to the ontology and cosmology which such language presupposed. Since, in the areas of ontology and cosmology, neoorthodoxy was as committed to modern understandings as the liberalism it opposed, the result was that questions of reality-reference were simply bracketed off and the use of biblical language made to be an end in itself. Twenty-four years later, Lindbeck accomplished much the same thing; the principle difference is that he mounted a spirited defense for doing so with the aid of the cultural anthropology of Clifford Geertz and an occasional nod to nonfoundationalist philosophies.[71] It is this defense alone which justifies the name Lindbeck has given to his program, namely, that of "postliberalism." But as he himself suggests, the intratextual approach to theology which he advocates and which he thinks himself to find in Barth is "in most respects thoroughly pre-modern."[72] Seen from the vantage point of Barth's theology, it is also much too undialectical. Intratextual theology is an all-too-positive science.

For my purposes here, the crucial point to be made is that Lindbeck's appeal to Barth in support of his intratextual theology has had the unintended effect of perpetuating the myth of the neoorthodox Barth.[73] Such an effect was unintended because Lindbeck has always made it clear not only that he is not a Barth scholar but that his use of Barth is just that—a use, and one which does not entail agreement with the dogmatic underpinnings of Barth's exegetical practices. Still, such disclaimers have not prevented critics—and even some would-be "Barthians"—from equating Lindbeck's revised neoorthodoxy with "Barthianism." David Tracy spoke for many when he said of *The Nature of Doctrine*, "The hands may be the hands of Wittgenstein and Geertz but the voice is the voice of Karl Barth."[74] In my judgment, the only possible response

70. Langdon Gilkey, "Cosmology, Ontology, and the Travail of Biblical Language," *Journal of Religion* 41 (1961): 194–205.

71. Lindbeck, *The Nature of Doctrine*, 129: "Postliberals are bound to be sceptical . . . about apologetics and foundations. To the degree that religions are like languages and cultures, they can no more be taught by means of translation than can Chinese or French. . . . Resistance to translation [into another idiom than the biblical one] does not wholly exclude apologetics, but this must be of an ad hoc and nonfoundational variety rather than standing at the center of theology. . . . In short, religions, like languages, can be understood only in their own terms, not by transposing them into an alien speech."

72. Lindbeck, "Barth and Textuality," 366.

73. See McCormack, *Karl Barth's Critically Realistic Dialectical Theology*, 1–28. It is my conviction that Barth's influence on the rise of American neoorthodoxy was much more negligible than most scholars realize. The Barth who influenced those found in this movement was himself a product of a neoorthodox reading of him. The neoorthodox Barth was a stripped-down version of the original—an inoffensive, thoroughly domesticated, positive theologian who had completely left his origins in dialectical theology behind him.

74. David Tracy, "Lindbeck's New Program for Theology: A Reflection," *Thomist* 49 (1985): 465.

to such a claim must be: no, the voice is the voice of American neoorthodoxy in an evangelical-Catholic form.

A critique of Lindbeck's program from the perspective of Barth's theology has already been carried out by George Hunsinger.[75] The most telling element in Hunsinger's argument lies in his observation that "what is finally decisive for Barth in any consideration of the performative aspect of theological truth is not the human but the divine mode of involvement."[76] That is to say, what gives to theological statements their truth is the use that is made of them by God in revealing himself. Theological statements have no intrinsic capacity for bearing adequate witness to God (not even those found in Scripture). But in that God takes up the scriptural witness and bears witness to himself in and through its witness, God gives to it by grace a capacity which it lacks by nature. In revealing himself to the church though Holy Scripture, God gives himself to Scripture as its Referent. God makes theological statements to correspond to the Reality that he is. "It is the miracle of grace, not use in accordance with a correlative form of life that is decisive for the correspondence of a theological utterance with reality."[77]

The immediate consequence of this view of truth for an evaluation of Lindbeck's typology of possible understandings of the nature of doctrine is that Barth's view would be most naturally located under the heading of "propositionalism"—*if* (and this is crucial) the understanding of "propositionalism" was controlled by the *analogia fidei*. It is, of course, quite true that Barth is not a propositionalist as Lindbeck defines the term. Lindbeck understands the term to entail a commitment to the view that propositions are "eternally true or false," admitting of "no degrees or variations."[78] But such a definition would apply only to pre–Vatican II Roman Catholics (and, even in their case, not to all) and misses a wide variety of possible construals of the propositionalist view[79]—including Barth's. That Barth could also treat church doctrines as "regulative" (in the sense of ascribing to them a relatively binding, *human* authority) is not to be denied. But such use of doctrine had its place only within the framework provided by Barth's highly actualistic (and, I would say, "cognitivist")[80] account of revelation and the unique version of a propositionalist understanding of doctrine which it engendered.

---

75. George Hunsinger, "Truth as Self-Involving: Barth and Lindbeck on the Cognitive and Performative Aspects of Truth in Theological Discourse," *Journal of the American Academy of Religion* 61 (1993): 41–56.

76. Ibid., 48.

77. Ibid.

78. Lindbeck, *The Nature of Doctrine*, 47.

79. See B. A. Gerrish, review of *The Nature of Doctrine*, by George Lindbeck, *Journal of Religion* 68 (1988): 88.

80. Here I am thinking of Barth's statement in *CD* I/1:135: "Speech, including God's speech, is the form in which reason communicates with reason and person with person. The utter inconceivability of this event is obvious. But reason with reason, person with person, is primarily

In sum, Lindbeck's understanding of truth and the theory of doctrine which he finds commensurate with it are far too decisively controlled by anthropological considerations to do justice to Barth's concerns.[81] And because this is so, his valiant struggle against the experiential-expressivists looks, from a Barthian perspective, like an in-house debate.

Final Assessment

The nonfoundationalist reading of Barth—as it is found in Lindbeck, above all—succeeds only by means of some fairly radical surgery. The whole of Barth's transfoundationalist doctrine of revelation has been cut out of his theology and set aside. What is left is a theology which has been generated out of a strict concentration on certain of Barth's exegetical practices to the exclusion of the larger framework in which those practices do their work. Seen from this vantage point, the attempt to place Barth in a theological lineage whose characteristic features are stamped more by the postliberal intratextuality of George Lindbeck than anything else must be regarded as a doubtful enterprise.[82]

Postmodern Readings of Barth

At first glance, the move from the Yale theology of Frei and Lindbeck to the writings of "postmodernists"[83] such as Walter Lowe and Graham Ward[84]

---

analogous to what happens in the spiritual realm of creation, not the natural and physical realm. The Word of God . . . is a rational and not an irrational event."

81. See Hunsinger, "Truth as Self-Involving," 47.

82. I am thinking here of Thiel, *Nonfoundationalism*. It is striking that although Thiel claims that "it would not be an exaggeration to say that Frei has had the single greatest influence on the development of the nonfoundational perspective in the field of theology" (67), Frei is treated only *after* Lindbeck in Thiel's sketch and, I would maintain, read in the light of Lindbeck's program. It is quite true that Lindbeck correctly identified a strand of Frei's thought (and of his reading of Barth) and made consistent use of it. But it was only one strand of Frei's thought. There is another Frei to whom I will make appeal in the concluding section of this essay.

83. The terminological distinction adopted here ("nonfoundationalism" on the one side and "postmodernism" on the other) is, admittedly, not an altogether happy one. For many today, nonfoundationalism is one of the hallmarks of postmodernism—which means that Frei and Lindbeck are, in some sense at least, postmodern (although this is a retrospective judgment). Still, in spite of the fact that the thinkers now to be considered share some concerns with Frei and Lindbeck, pronounced differences between the two groups remain, differences which may be summed up in terms of the Yale theologians' preoccupation with biblical language and the (later) postmodern preoccupation with what might be called the problem of alterity. Thus it is not finally the terminology which is of decisive importance here but the material differences.

84. Other interpreters who might have been treated under the heading of "postmodern" readers of Barth include the following (together with their major work): Steven G. Smith, *The Argument to the Other: Reason beyond Reason in the Thought of Karl Barth and Emmanuel Levinas* (Chico, CA: Scholars Press, 1983); Stephen H. Webb, *Re-figuring Theology: The Rhetoric*

might appear to entail a movement backwards in time, a movement from the supposedly neoorthodox Barth of the *Church Dogmatics* to the critical theology of the second edition of *Romans*. For, surely, what one catches sight of in the latter is nothing less than a recrudescence of the emphasis of the early Barth on the "wholly otherness" of God. Whether, in fact, it is a genuine reappropriation of the early Barth which is under way here and not, much rather, the elaboration of an idealistic postulate—a principle of critical negation (in Lowe's case) or a principle of alterity (in Ward's case)—is the central question to be addressed here.

Walter Lowe

In *Theology and Difference* Walter Lowe has written one of the more fascinating books on Barth to appear in recent years.[85] The fascination lies in the fact that although Lowe has produced what is ultimately a misreading of Barth of a rather fundamental nature, it is a very intelligent, well-informed misreading and one which leads him to results that the early Barth at least would probably have greeted warmly.

Theology and Difference can, on one level, be read as a kind of revised and updated Kantian prolegomenon to any future metaphysic. The revision takes place by means of an appeal to the deconstructive philosophy of Jacques Derrida. The proximate goal is to generate a conception of "otherness" which is "non-oppositional" in character—which does not, in other words, eliminate or even only suppress "difference" but rather establishes it. Of decisive importance in the working out of this theme is the role played by theoretical reason. Whereas a good deal of recent philosophical reflection has made "technical" or "instrumental reason" to be the source of the mass violence of the twentieth century (through its reduction of everything—including women and men—to the level of objects), Lowe believes that reason also has within itself the "capacity to intimate the existence of something more,"[86] an Other whose difference from the world would itself be the ground of salutary differences on the creaturely plane.

---

of Karl Barth (Albany: State University of New York Press, 1991); and Richard Roberts, *A Theology on Its Way? Essays on Karl Barth* (Edinburgh: T&T Clark, 1991). The decision to treat Lowe and Ward here to the exclusion of other possible candidates is based on the belief that their works are the most formidable (philosophically and theologically) and therefore the most likely to exercise an ongoing influence. It goes without saying that they can be regarded as only representative figures, the treatment of whom by no means exhausts what we might think of as postmodern interpretations of Barth.

85. Walter Lowe, *Theology and Difference: The Wound of Reason* (Bloomington, IN: Indiana University Press, 1993). Cf. also an earlier essay (portions of which were incorporated in Lowe's book), "Barth as a Critic of Dualism: Re-reading *Der Römerbrief*," *Scottish Journal of Theology* 41 (1988): 377–95.

86. Lowe, *Theology and Difference*, 11.

The larger goal to be served by this project is that of providing a theoretical ground for the elimination of the hierarchical relations within the created order which engender and often justify violence. Thus Lowe can describe *Theology and Difference* as a contribution to a political theology along the lines of Johann Baptist Metz—with the qualification that Lowe is working primarily within the realm of theoretical rather than practical reason.[87] In pursuing these closely related goals, Lowe's central figures are Kant and Derrida. Barth is brought into play as the representative of the kind of theology which is commensurate with the demands of the project as I have described it; or more accurately, it is the theology of the second edition of *Romans* which Lowe finds most helpful.

Given that Lowe's stated intention is to read the second edition of *Romans* under the guidance of Derridean categories,[88] it would perhaps be most helpful to begin our analysis of his reading of Barth with a brief look at his appropriation of Derrida:

> Derrida's thought amounts to a series of strategies for undercutting or "deconstructing" the twofold lure of metaphysical monism (which collapses difference into one) and metaphysical dualism (which dichotomizes difference, creating opposition). Derrida deals with the threat of monism by speaking of a pervasive desire for "*presence.*" The term "presence" in this context refers to any reality which is taken to be autonomous and self-sufficient, and which is regarded as being at some point accessible in a direct, unmediated fashion. . . . As for the second lure, that of dualism: Derrida speaks of a widespread penchant for *oppositional* structures of language and thought, and, related to this, a penchant for oppositional or adversarial ways of relating to the world at large.[89]

Both monism and dualism are productive of the kinds of oppositional, hierarchical relations within the created order which Lowe would like to see overcome. Monism does so in that a particular element of the created order is made, in a speculative fashion, to be the key for understanding reality as a whole. Dualism, while radically distinguishing the so-called infinite from all things finite, achieves the same end in those cases where a particular element in the created order is identified with the "absent" infinite. What is needed is to find a way beyond monism and dualism. The solution to the problem lies, it would seem, in the conception of an altogether different *kind* of dualism, a distinction between the infinite and the finite which is *not* oppositional in nature.

87. Ibid., 10. See Johann Baptist Metz, *Glaube in Geschichte und Gesellschaft: Studien zu einer praktischen Fundamentaltheologie* (Mainz: Matthias Grünewald, 1977); translated as *Faith in History and Society: Toward a Practical Fundamental Theology* (New York: Seabury, 1980).

88. Lowe, *Theology and Difference*, 12.

89. Ibid., 13.

Read in the light of these requirements, what the second edition of *Romans* set forth was a view of the relationship of God to creation which only *appeared* to be dualistic in the bad sense but, in fact, entailed a clear recognition of "the most fundamental difference, which is carefully kept from becoming oppositional." With this "qualitative distinction" firmly in place, it then became possible for Barth to "honour, in appropriate ways, the lesser distinctions within the created order."[90] The nineteenth-century theology criticized by Barth had blurred the fundamental difference between God and the world, with the result that, inevitably, some one element of finite reality was elevated above all others "as idol, as presence, as point of contact with the divine," and where this occurred, opposition was introduced into the created order and justified. Against such a tendency, Barth succeeded in distinguishing the infinite from the finite in a truly fundamental way which had a leveling effect on all things finite.

Now, Lowe is quite aware that there will be those who would want to question the use of Derrida to encourage the "strong distinction" which Lowe finds in the second edition of *Romans* (i.e., the God/world distinction). He is quite candid in admitting that if such an objection could be sustained, then he would be confronted with a "stark either/or. We would virtually have to choose between doing deconstruction and doing theology."[91] To this objection he responds,

> But is the alternative position so obvious and desirable—viz., the position which tacitly assumes that all differences should ultimately be of the same order, of the same sort? Derrida himself makes a strong distinction between *différance* and any other category of thought; he has even been accused (unjustly, I think) of making that notion into an absolute. Any discourse is going to have its strong, orienting concepts: its god terms, so to speak. . . . The question is not the existence of such terms, but *how* they function; whether they function in such a way as to suggest that they are not simply distinctive and important, but self-evident and unquestionable. The question in short is not whether they are present, but whether they function as *presences*. And that is a relational question, to be resolved not by considering the strong term in isolation, rejecting a text when it seems to contain such a term; but by looking to the *relation or dialectic between* that difference and the larger field of differences.[92]

Lowe devotes an entire chapter to the problem of Derrida's stance towards the truth-question, which is designed to demonstrate that Derrida is not a nihilist and is wrongly employed when appealed to for nihilistic purposes. I will not enter into the details of this portion of Lowe's argument. Suffice it

90. Ibid., 44.
91. Ibid., 47.
92. Ibid.

to say, first of all, that Lowe understands Derrida's critique of *presence* to be a critique of anything "which asks to be considered as self-explanatory . . . having meaning in and of itself"—which leaves open the possibility that Derrida's move away from the object (defined as the "simply given") is a move towards a deeper-lying objectivity.[93] Second, Lowe focuses upon an oft-cited essay by Derrida, "Structure, Sign and Play in the Discourse of the Human Sciences," wherein Derrida distinguishes two interpretations of interpretation. "The first, represented in that essay by structuralism, 'has dreamed of full presence, the reassuring foundation, the origin and the end of play.' The second has entered unreservedly into the Nietzschean *affirmation*, that is the joyous affirmation of the play of the world . . . , the affirmation of a world of signs without fault, without truth and without origin which is offered to an active participation."[94] Decisive for Lowe is the fact that Derrida himself resisted being forced to choose between the two options. Against the more nearly nihilistic interpretation of him (which would take the second option to be his own), Derrida said, "I do not believe that today there is any question of *choosing*. Rather, given the difference and the irreducibility of the two positions, 'we must first try to conceive of the common ground, and the *différance* of this irreducible difference.'"[95] For Lowe, "the refusal to choose is not a simple entry into free play; there remains the quest for common ground. Yet the common ground itself is not a 'presence,' to be invoked and chosen by an easy eclecticism."[96] Lowe's treatment of Derrida ends with the observation that in refusing to choose between his two options, Derrida has made "undecidability" to be a characteristic feature of the human situation. In the situation of undecidability, the truth question does not simply disappear as some postmodern advocates of Derrida would have it. Undecidability "*opens* the field of decision or of decidability; it is the 'necessary condition' *for* decision and responsibility."[97]

Whether Lowe has understood Derrida aright is a question which lies beyond the scope of this paper. What is crucial for our purposes is the fact that Lowe believes that recent criticisms of foundationalism have all too often been naive and uncritical.

> This giving up on the foundationalist project, this simple letting go, is worthy neither of the transcendental tradition nor of poststructuralism. It is not worthy of the former because it fails to comprehend that what is true of Kant and Husserl, what virtually defines their common effort, was that their philosophy

93. Ibid., 58.
94. Ibid., 72.
95. Jacques Derrida, *Writing and Difference* (Chicago: Universtiy of Chicago Press, 1978), 292.
96. Lowe, *Theology and Difference*, 72.
97. Ibid., 128.

believed that it could be foundational *because* it was truly critical; and that its being critical was inseparable from its effort after foundations. . . . Nor is the disavowal worthy of the best of poststructuralism. . . . The best of post-structuralism realizes that what is disavowed cannot be simply disavowed; that it reappears in subtle and unexpected guises; and that it is therefore essential to exercise a certain hermeneutic of suspicion. *But the moment one does this, one has already moved away from the pure relativism implicit within much of anti-foundationalism.*[98]

"Anti-foundationalism," Lowe says at another point, "stands in a long lineage which has consistently assumed that the enlightened can distinguish relatively easily between bad thinking, which is 'metaphysical' and good thinking, which is in some sense 'critical.' Once again we observe the inveterate impulse toward a purified linguistic domain. My proposal is a corollary of the failure of such edicts of linguistic hygiene. If it has been impossible to segregate 'critical' from 'metaphysical,' it may be because the critical requires the metaphysical, as a supplement."[99] Clearly, what Lowe is seeking to do is to deconstruct the "deconstructionists" (*not* Derrida), to interject a bit more humility into the enterprise of deconstructing "metaphysics." He does this not so much in the interests of providing a refurbished form of foundationalism (though he will not exclude the possibility of the existence of "foundations" which have "an irreducible elusiveness"[100] about them); rather, he pushes his critique of "anti-foundationalism" in order, first, to insist that undecidability is the leading characteristic of our situation and, second, having accomplished that, to create an open space in which thinking may become truly critical.

It is at this point that we come to the heart of Lowe's project. It must be remembered that he presents his work as a contribution to a political theology. At the dawn of modern times, Lowe contends, it became necessary—in the interests of rationalizing and ordering human existence—to posit a framework within which nature (the realm of order) and history (the realm of disorder) might be unified.

At one level this might be put simply as an aspiration, a hoped-for *telos*, that one day human doings might become harmonious and our alienation from nature be overcome. But in order to make that hope something more than wistful, to give it some grounding in reality, it is altogether natural, and perhaps logically necessary, to posit a confirmation, an actual unity, at some place in the present or some time in the past. From this it is a small step to a fullblown narrative which proceeds in three parts: the *archē* of a primal unity, an original innocence; the division or fall into disunity and alienation; and the *telos*, whether assured or

98. Ibid., 71 (emphasis mine).
99. Ibid., 21.
100. Ibid., 73.

merely hoped for, of restoration and reunification. Unity, separation, reunion: a three-part story—or, figuratively, a diamond.[101]

This "idealist diamond" carried within it an implicit theodicy. To make this clear, it need only be added that "the restoration is not simply a restoration; but that the final state of things is all the richer and more real for having passed through the second stage, the stage of estrangement and conflict. . . . Growth into maturity requires the chaos and conflict of adolescence; and as with the individual, so with the human race. In retrospect the pain is positive, by virtue of what it contributes to individuation and growth."[102] The effect of the "idealist diamond," then, is to provide a "quasi-metaphysical justification for the sufferings undergone" and, to that extent, "a flight from history's open-ended reality."[103] The suffering of oppressed peoples in history, as Metz observed, often makes no discernible contribution to later generations, and even if it did, "the happiness of the descendants cannot compensate for the sufferings of the ancestors and social progress cannot make up for the injustice done to the dead."[104] What is the solution, then? To reject the notions of an *archē* and a *telos* out of hand? According to Lowe, such an effort to "purify the linguistic domain" is not only an impossibility; it is actually counterproductive, for it fails to recognize that "the tenacity of this thought form [i.e., the 'idealist diamond'] does not spring from sheer perversity. The thought form reflects an aspiration and a question which—*as* aspiration and *as* question—is profoundly human, profoundly justified. The trick is to affirm the notions of *archē* and *telos* as aspiration/question—neither more nor less."[105] It is here that Lowe finds Kant most helpful. Kant, he says, did not seek to proscribe all talk of *archē* and *telos*. He recognized that it was no accident that human beings have continually produced such images. "The images respond to a practical moral need. Critical thought is not asked to rebuff this legitimate need, but it is charged with the task of keeping firmly in mind that . . . that to which the need gives access is no assured metaphysical reality, but simply a postulate or idea. Far from being resolved, the issue of whether those ideas do signify a reality persists as an ever-present question, which is the question of theodicy."[106] Hence, as a metaphysical *assumption*, the diamond functions to prevent thought from becoming truly critical—which means seeking to become effective in promoting real change in the situation. But as a question, the diamond can be productive of critical thought. Thus Kant is understood by Lowe to have arrived at the same point Derrida did: the affirmation of an

101. Ibid., 25.
102. Ibid., 25–26.
103. Ibid.
104. Ibid., 9.
105. Ibid., 129.
106. Ibid.

ultimate undecidability with regard to the metaphysical. And it is only on this basis, he thinks, that theology can be done.

Thus far our exposition of Lowe's argument. Now, it is crucial to the critique which will follow to notice that the ideas of *archē* and *telos* cannot function to generate truly critical thinking for Lowe *unless* they are treated as Kant treated them: as "simply a postulate or idea." Notwithstanding the critique of idealism which runs throughout *Theology and Difference*, what Lowe has finally produced is a form of idealism. The idealism of which he is critical is finally Hegel's "ontotheology." But the Kantianism which he has envisioned with the help of Derrida is sufficiently open-ended to avoid the pitfalls found in Hegel. And it is this Kantianism which he thinks himself to have found in the second edition of *Romans*. The question is this: Did the Barth of the second edition of *Romans* really treat the *Ursprung*, for example, as an idea? Or did he not, much rather, treat it as a reality, as *the* Reality?

Critique of Lowe's "Critical Idealism"

Theology and Difference is a book with a number of strengths. Lowe refuses to acknowledge the restrictions currently being laid upon theology by "anti-foundationalists"—and this has to be considered a strength. That he appeals to Derrida in doing so seems to me to be a plausible and strategically interesting move. Lowe also has a dialectical relation to the history of philosophy in the modern period (neither uncritically affirming nor uncritically rejecting) which other Anglo-American theologians would do well to recover.

The great problem with Lowe's project is that the "wound of reason" which he believes is needed if thinking is to be genuinely critical is a wound which, in the final analysis, reason inflicts upon itself through its act of positing an *archē* and *telos* which cannot be comprehended by human thought.[107] And it is this which distinguishes Lowe's thought from that of the Barth of the second edition of *Romans*. Lowe's thought moves *wholly* within the confines of Kant's epistemology; Barth presupposed the validity of that epistemology insofar as it touches upon our knowledge of empirical reality in order then to transcend its limitations in describing our knowledge of God. Kant's "God" need not be known at all in order to perform its "contextualizing" function; indeed, Kant's "God" can perform this function "without needing to exist."[108] For all of this to occur, God need only be *thought*. But this could never be said of the God of the second edition of *Romans*. The early Barth did not regard the *Ursprung* as a postulated idea; he understood it to be the divine Reality and,

---

107. Though I have not treated the realm of the ethical here, a similar thing occurs there as well. The categorical imperative, in Lowe's view, is something which "emerges *from 'within'* the subject" and, as such, "'exceeds' the subject, contextualizing it" (ibid., 111).

108. Ibid., 101.

as such, as that which is more real than all that we normally understand to be real. Lowe is quite right to insist that the early Barth understood the relation of God to the world in terms of neither pure presence nor pure absence. But Barth's refusal of these false options was rooted in his conviction that the divine act of revelation establishes an *indirect* identity with the creaturely medium through which it occurs. Thus the truth of the proposition that God is neither purely present (a relation of immediacy) nor purely absent (a denial of even a mediated presence) depends upon an act of God and not upon an idealistic understanding of reason wounding itself. From the point of view of the second edition of *Romans*, the highest wisdom would not consist in the view that "metaphysics at its best" serves to "contextualize" human thinking.[109] Such an idea might indeed have a certain utility; it might help to clear the ground of a variety of misunderstandings. But it would not be the highest wisdom. The highest wisdom consists in the recognition that it is God who "contextualizes" human thinking; it is the divine Reality which "wounds" (disrupts, breaks into, breaks off, limits) human reason. It is the reality of God which holds human thinking open and thereby makes it truly critical. At the outset, I said that a theological method which could succeed in its assigned tasks regardless of whether God exists or not would render theology a regular, bourgeois science. And this must be the final judgment on Lowe's project.

A second and closely related point of criticism is that Lowe tends to treat the question of truth—or should we say, the question of God?—as something which is inherent to the human situation: "The 'postmodernist' position realized that truth is not something which can be grasped. Therefore it concluded that the question of truth must be let go. What it failed to realize is that the *question* of truth is more than a question: it is a reality. And it is a reality which has hold of *us*."[110] As an interpretation of the second edition of *Romans*, such a statement would be correct *if* it were intended to describe a divine act by means of which we are laid hold of in a revelation event. But it is not at all clear that this is what Lowe intends by the statement. It seems, rather, to be an anthropological judgment—a statement about the human condition as such. Such an interpretation would impute to the early Barth a kind of negative natural theology (dressed out with a "point of contact," etc.). Such an interpretation of the early Barth would not be new, of course; but it was no more successful in its earlier versions.

Notwithstanding the serious shortcomings of Lowe's reading of Barth, I have little doubt but that the early Barth would have found much in *Theology and Difference* in which he could rejoice. In fact, he would probably have regarded Lowe as an ally. In the early 1920s Barth was quite ready to make common cause with anyone whose work could be appealed to for *critical*

109. Ibid., 21.
110. Ibid., 74; cf. 142.

purposes. It was for this reason that he greeted his philosopher brother Heinrich's work with appreciation. Indeed, Karl's reaction to his brother's 1919 lecture "Gotteserkenntnis" provides an excellent clue for estimating how he would have responded to Lowe. For the truth is that Lowe's reflections have a much firmer connection with Heinrich Barth's philosophical theology than they do with the second edition of *Romans*.[111]

In conclusion, it should be noted that the label "postmodernist" is one which Walter Lowe would probably reject for himself—and justifiably so. Not only is he very resistant to the relativistic/nihilistic reception of Derrida; he clearly wants to locate himself within the transcendental philosophical tradition (in its late "critical" phase?). If I have chosen, nevertheless, to treat him under this heading, it is solely because his emphasis on the radical otherness of God places him within hailing distance of Graham Ward, a thinker who does want to claim the label "postmodern" for his reception of Barth. Still, the differences between Lowe and Ward are significant and must be kept in view as we now turn to Ward.

Graham Ward

The most conspicuous differences between Walter Lowe and Graham Ward are two. First and most important, they are motivated by different concerns.

111. The proximity of Lowe's position (it is not just a reading of Karl Barth) to Heinrich Barth's philosophy is clearly seen through a focus on the latter's understanding of God (or the *Ursprung*) as a principle of "critical negation" which functions to make idealism truly critical (thereby surpassing the dogmatic idealism of Hegel, Fichte, and Schelling).

> In order to find the liberating way out of all [the problems caused by materialism, empiricism, and positivism], we must make a radical break with the categories of a material-dynamic way of thinking. . . . If we are to speak of God and the divine, then it must be a matter of something completely New, of an unconditionally Superior, of a fundamental surpassing of that way of thinking. It is not as though metaphysics cannot also speak of God; we would not think of contesting its place of honor in intellectual history. Metaphysics speaks of God in spite of itself insofar as it is more than a mere superstructure to physics, to a doctrine of nature. It represents the spiritual insofar as it does not withhold from the Spirit its original right of thought and creative act. In order to get ahold of this, its truth, we will proceed from a simple logical principle which we ourselves will use as a lever, so to speak, in order, first of all, to rock the natural world and the sublimated supernatural world in their mutual security. This is the epistemic principle of *critical negation*. (Heinrich Barth, "Gotteserkenntnis," in *Anfänge der dialektischen Theologie*, ed. Jürgen Moltmann [Munich: Kaiser, 1977], 1:236)

As for Lowe, so also for Heinrich Barth: the move beyond the metaphysics of the speculative idealists to a truly critical idealism, which is advocated in this passage, has political implications. "The entirety of social life is placed, in principle, under the standpoint of revolution. . . . An orientation to the *Ursprung* means a continuous breaking with that which has become" (ibid., 238). Still, the differences between Heinrich Barth's philosophy and Karl Barth's theology in this period must be not overlooked. For a critical comparison of the two, see McCormack, *Karl Barth's Critically Realistic Dialectical Theology*, 218–26.

Whereas Lowe's central problematic was political theology and theodicy, Ward is preoccupied with what he refers to, in formulaic fashion, as the "crisis of representation."[112] For him, it is the nature of language itself which raises the question of God; the place of anthropology (which in Lowe had served to thematize the truth-question as an essential, ineradicable feature of human existence) has been replaced by language theory. Second, Ward's attempt to demonstrate parallels between Barth and Derrida focuses upon the later Barth of the *Church Dogmatics* and not, as was the case with Lowe, upon the early "dialectical" Barth of the second edition of *Romans*. It is this decision, above all, which makes Ward's work provocative, even audacious—and that has been sufficient reason for some to doubt his central thesis.[113] Less conspicuous perhaps is a third difference which has only begun to emerge in Ward's writings subsequent to his much-discussed book on Barth and Derrida. Ward would probably regard Lowe's work as "liberal," to the extent that Lowe engages in a kind of correlation method which finds its basis in anthropology. And Ward clearly would like to place himself on the side of what he calls "conservative postmodern theologies."[114] I will return to an assessment of these judgments in concluding this section.

In lapidary form, Ward's thesis is twofold. First, Barth's "central problematic" (as registered in his explication of theological epistemology in *CD* II/1) is identical to that of Jacques Derrida, namely, the attempt to elucidate the transcendental conditions for the meaningfulness of language generally.[115] Alternately expressed: both thinkers are concerned with the problem created by an awareness of an "ineradicable otherness which haunts discourse and yet the impossibility of transcending metaphoricity and positing a real presence."[116] The difference between them lies in the fact that Barth reads this problematic theologically, as the problem of how the Word of God comes to expression in human words. Second, Barth's attempt to resolve his theological problem of the Word in the words ends in incoherence. To be rendered more coherent requires a "philosophical supplement" which, for Ward, is

112. See Graham Ward, "Barth and Postmodernism," *New Blackfriars* 74 (1993): 550–56; idem, "Theology and the Crisis of Representation," in *Literature and Theology at Century's End*, ed. Gregory Salyer and Robert Detweiler (Atlanta: Scholars Press, 1995), 131–58; and esp. idem, *Barth, Derrida and the Language of Theology* (Cambridge: Cambridge University Press, 1995).

113. Richard H. Roberts calls into question the strategy of seeking to identify "the ontologized textuality of the later Barth with the anti-ontology of deconstruction." A "truer analogue of Derrida," he suggests, would be found in the "dialectical" Barth (review of *Barth, Derrida and the Language of Theology*, by Graham Ward, *Journal of Theological Studies* n.s. 48 [1997]: 347–51, here 348, 350).

114. See Graham Ward, "Postmodern Theology," in *The Modern Theologians: An Introduction to Christian Theology in the Twentieth Century*, ed. David Ford, 2nd ed. (Oxford: Blackwell, 1996), 585–601.

115. Ward, *Barth, Derrida and the Language of Theology*, 102.

116. Ibid., 247.

supplied by Derrida. The result is the creation of the conditions needed for the elaboration of a "postmodern theology of the Word"[117]—though this task lies beyond the limits of Ward's first book, *Barth, Derrida and the Language of Theology*.[118] This is Ward's thesis in outline. In what follows, I will try to explicate its various elements more fully, identifying problematic features as I go along and concluding with a fuller critique. In conclusion, an attempt will be made to say something about the limits of "postmodern readings" of Barth as practiced by both Lowe and Ward.

The context out of which Ward understands Barth's theology to have emerged is the "crisis of representation," which, Ward believes, was a characteristic feature of the post-war Weimar culture.[119] The "crisis" in question had to do with the widespread suspicion that the modern belief that language gives us immediate access to reality is a mistaken one.[120] In the words of Walter Benjamin: "What does language communicate? . . . Language communicates the linguistic being of things. The clearest manifestation of this being, however, is language itself. The answer to the question 'What does language communicate?' is therefore 'All language communicates itself.'"[121] The implication is that "epistemology and ontology" are to be understood "not as reflections upon our relationship with the world, but as the effects of tropology or rhetoric."[122] Now, Ward in no way means to suggest that Barth's response to the "crisis" is the same as Benjamin's; it is not. Barth's response is a dialectical one which affirms "the necessity of assuming that words name while also countering that assumption."[123] Ward's point is simply that the same cultural situation produced both Benjamin's reflections on language theory and Barth's reflections on the relationship of the Word of God to human words. Still, as we shall now see, the comparison with Benjamin (not to mention Derrida) is not without its problems.

At the heart of Ward's reading of Barth lies his claim that Barth's central concern in chapter 5 of *CD* II/1 was to elaborate a "theology of language." In support of this claim, Ward notes that however true it might be that Barth's doctrine of analogy affirms a divine selection among human words and statements in the act of Self-revelation, such a selection is possible only because *all* language is said by Barth to be originally and properly God's. Barth's horizon

---

117. Ibid., 103.
118. Ibid., 256.
119. Richard Roberts has referred to the culture of Weimar Germany (1919–1933) as the "first postmodernity." Though not himself engaging in comparative cultural analysis, Ward seems to agree with Roberts that a parallel exists between Weimar culture and our own "postmodern" society. See Roberts, *A Theology on Its Way?* 170; Ward, "Barth and Postmodernism," 550, 555.
120. Ward, "Barth and Postmodernism," 551: "The mind does not mirror nature; truth is not an equivalence between reality and its representation."
121. Ward, *Barth, Derrida and the Language of Theology*, 3.
122. Ward, "Barth and Postmodernism," 552.
123. Ward, *Barth, Derrida and the Language of Theology*, 5.

of interest, he says, extends well beyond a theology of scriptural discourse. "For the doctrine of analogy does not require a doctrine of inspiration, in that it takes as its basis for explanation a God-given correlation between human logic, the order of creation and divine reasoning. A doctrine of analogy does not demand a doctrine of punctiliar revelation which bypasses human cognition, for a doctrine of analogical correspondence *is* a doctrine of general revelation."[124] And so "Barth does not wish to reduce the operation of the Word simply to Scripture." What he is interested in, finally, is "a theology of discourse generally."[125] *How* does the Word come to expression in human language?—*that* is Barth's central problematic.

Ward's entrée into Barth's "theology of language" lies through an analysis of his doctrine of revelation. What happens in revelation? "God redeems human beings from that Kantian transcendental consciousness which divorced objects out there from one's perception and conceptions of them. The true correspondence or analogy is restored."[126] Two observations are pertinent here. First, the relevance of Kant's epistemology is restricted to describing the knowing of the *fallen* human. In Ward's view, this means that, apart from revelation, "there can only be semantic agnosticism—for all acts of signification make arbitrary connection between words and what is."[127] Ward refers to this model of language as the "semiotic model." "Without revelation we occupy a world of circulating semiotics."[128] Second, what takes place in revelation, then, is that language is restored to its original, divine meaning. The model of language at work here Ward calls a "communication model" based on a "nomenclatural theory." "Barth adopts a nomenclatural or passive-copy theory of language as the model of correspondence between perception, conception and language in the act of revelation whilst simultaneously rejecting such a theory of language as a description of discourse outside the act of revelation."[129]

It would be helpful to pause for a moment in our exposition of Ward's argument to take note of two problems which have surfaced in his reading of Barth to this point, for they will have a tremendous bearing on where his argument goes from here. The first has to do with Ward's ascription to Barth of a "nomenclatural model" of language in speaking of the divine "speech-act." The problem with this ascription is that it regards the human knower as passive in the revelation relationship. And because the human knower is passive, the degree of correspondence between language and the reality of which it speaks becomes the highest possible: namely, perfection. Ward notes, "The nomenclatural theory of language has always aspired to the ideal of a

124. Ibid., 21–22.
125. Ibid., 22.
126. Ibid., 27.
127. Ibid., 29.
128. Ibid.
129. Ibid., 28.

perfect correspondence between language and the world, to a universal and philosophical language."[130] And for Ward, such aspirations have finally been fulfilled in Barth's doctrine of revelation. "The model of language here, developed upon a nomenclatural theory of language, is of the ideal speech act: a pure communication without ambivalence or excess of meaning."[131] Now, if this were really an apt description of Barth's "language theory," Barth could scarcely have spoken of the result of a divine "speech act" in the modest term of analogy. Analogy, after all, even the "analogy of faith," means not only *similitudo* but also *dissimilitudo*, not a "pure communication without ambivalence or excess of meaning." A pure communication might indeed be possible if it were true that the human knower is altogether passive in the revelation relationship, but he or she is not. And this leads us to the second problem. Ward's description of the "language model" pertinent to the employment of language *outside* the revelation relationship is also strained to the breaking point. It is quite true that Barth appeals to Kant's epistemology to describe the knowing process outside the revelation relationship. But to describe the language theory which is commensurate with this epistemology in terms of "semantic agnosticism" takes us well beyond Kant. However true it might be, on the basis of Kant's epistemology, that the form of human knowledge depends upon the influence of the categories of the understanding and that (as a consequence) knowledge of the "thing-in-itself" is an impossibility, it nevertheless remains the case that the *content* of human knowledge comes from without. Kant (and Barth following him) was sufficiently realistic in his epistemology to avoid making the connection between language and reality *purely* arbitrary. On Kantian soil, the human knower is *not* caught in "semantic agnosticism."

What Ward has done here is to exaggerate and distort Barth's descriptions of the use of language both inside and outside the revelation relationship to the point where the relationship between the two is one of antithesis. "Barth's distinction between human language and God's *Ursprache* is described in terms of two antithetical models of language."[132] The result (and at this point, we have reached the next stage in Ward's argument) is that Barth's theological epistemology as a whole has been rendered incoherent. "The communication model (where words adequately represent and communicate their objects) cannot be accommodated within a model of language which understands words as constructing the reality of objects. Similarly, the semiotic model of language (which emphasizes the mediation of a 'meaning' which forever lies beyond it) cannot accommodate the possibility of unmediated, direct disclosure. Knowledge of God, then, becomes either impossible or contradictory,

130. Ibid., 27.
131. Ibid., 28.
132. Ibid.

for each model is the other's radical alternative."[133] Barth therefore has no coherent account of how the Word comes to expression in human words.

According to Ward, Barth tried to remedy the defect created by the "aporia between two antithetical models for the operation of language" by means of an appeal to Christology. "A keystone analogy holds up the edifice of Barth's theology, the *analogia Christi*: the Word is to Jesus of Nazareth as the Word is to the words of human beings."[134] But Barth's effort fails for the following reason: if, in an effort to make the *analogia Christi* work, Barth's Christology were to be developed in accordance with the "communication model,"

> Christ would be the full and immediate revelation of God as words unambiguously disclose their objects. But the greater the clarity of the disclosure the less emphasis there is upon the means whereby that disclosure has taken place. The signifier dissolves into its direct relationship to the signified. By analogy, the human and historical contingency of Jesus is only then significant in so far as it effaces itself. The Christology analogous to this would be a docetic one in which incarnation is not taken seriously at all. . . . Where the human and semiotic body is taken seriously, as in the second model of language, then exactly the opposite occurs and the divine and transcendent is dissolved into the creaturely and immanent. To hold both models in paradoxical tension—language and the nature of Christ, the nature of Christ as analogous to the nature of language—is a linguistic form of Nestorianism.[135]

Barth is left with a linguistic form of Nestorianism which (apparently) wreaks havoc on his Christology. I say "apparently" because Ward never makes clear with what model of ancient Christology he believes Barth to have most closely allied himself. "Christology, as a theology of the Word, itself demands a coherent theology of language if it too is not to split irredeemably the divine from the human."[136] Nestorianism, whether of the linguistic or the christological variety, would seem, on the basis of this passage, to be a bad thing. But such a conclusion might well be premature. For Ward, the way forward to a coherent theology of language can be obtained only through the elaboration of a model of language that would account for the interplay between Barth's two antithetical models.[137] And this is what Derrida's "philosophical supplement" is expected to provide.

Up to this point in his argument, Ward has led us to expect that the Derridean supplement will show how tension between the two models of language may be resolved (thereby preventing the splitting off of the divine from the human). We have been led to expect that the coherence sought will be a logical

133. Ibid., 30.
134. Ibid., 31.
135. Ibid., 32.
136. Ibid.
137. Ibid., 33.

one. As it turns out, however, "coherence" seems to mean something more like "intelligibility" to a particular cultural mindset (in this case, the postmodern mindset). In other words, the Derridean supplement is not going to resolve the tension between the alleged use of two models of language at all, nor does Ward intend that it should. Divine Self-representation takes place in an *Ursprache* not our own; hence it *cannot* come to expression in ordinary human language. What the appeal to Derrida makes clear—or so Ward seems to think—is that Barth's theological discourse is simply a "rhetorical strategy presenting both the need to do and the impossibility of doing theology."[138] It is Derrida's analysis of "the crisis of logocentrism, the crisis of representation, fostered by postmodernism,"[139] which renders Barth's theology of the Word intelligible (i.e., in Ward's sense, gives it "coherence").

Ward's argument, at this final stage of his presentation, is that Karl Barth's "theology of the Word in relation to words—his *analogia fidei*, his Christology and incarnational theology—are theological readings of a law of textuality, a law of performance and repetition described by Derrida as the economy of *différance*."[140] A law of textuality: Ward has in mind the thought of an ineradicable "trace" of otherness which, on the basis of a close analysis of Derrida, may be said to "haunt" all discourse, the indirect (and therefore unavailable) presence of a final meaning lying beyond the chain of verbal signifiers in which all attempts at representation are caught. The image of "haunting" seems meant to suggest that the "presence" even of such a "trace" is never simply affirmed by Derrida; at most, Ward seems to see Derrida as leaving open the question of such an indirect presence—the "haunting" of discourse by a question which will not go away. Derrida cannot tell us what lies beyond language; his program of deconstruction merely keeps the question open. And this, for Ward, points to the boundary between philosophy and theology. Philosophy keeps the question of an "outside" to language open while theology names that "outside" God.[141] Thus Barth offers a theological supplement to Derrida, even as Derrida offers a philosophical supplement to him.

The net result of all of this for Ward's "postmodern Barthianism"[142] is that the presence of God to human language—*all* human language—is the presence of an Absence. Ward can cite Barth: "Knowing God, we necessarily know His hiddenness." What is crucial here is what Ward makes of this statement: "What we 'know' (and what legitimacy does this word 'know' have when it is really a not-knowing?) is an absence. More specifically, this absence becomes a positive property of God. The absence refers to, points to, is an index for, God. . . . The revelation, the truth, which is described in a rhetoric

---

138. Ibid., 247.
139. Ibid., 256.
140. Ibid., 9.
141. Ibid., 225.
142. Ward, "Postmodern Theology," 593.

connoting immediate and direct communication, is that God is absent, but it is an absence that Barth presents in positivist metaphors and reads theologically as the *incomprehensibilitas Dei*."[143] Whether Ward is justified in assuming that the hiddenness of God for Barth equals the absence of God is a point I will return to by way of critique. At this point it is sufficient to observe that, in the passage just cited, the dovetailing of Barth and Derrida seems to be complete. Barth's "God" turns out to be Derrida's principle of the presence of an Absence which haunts discourse.

One final comment by way of concluding this exposition: it is hard to avoid the impression that Ward has succumbed to the very temptation which he ascribes to "liberal" versions of postmodern theology—"apologetics, correlation, and local expressions of a universal condition."[144] It really matters little that language theory has been substituted for anthropology as the basis for the correlation of theology with philosophy; the effect is the same. Ward's argument leads to the conclusion that "language is always and ineradicably theological,"[145] that is, that the question of God is inevitably raised by a truly adequate language theory. Barth's theology of the Word merely gives the proper name to the "presence" which, as Derrida has shown, "haunts" all discourse by its absence. Such a move would seem to be apologetic by any other name, and given the universality of the alleged transcendental condition of language generally, a powerful program of correlation would seem to be involved as well.

Critique of Ward's "Theology of Language"

There are a number of flaws in Ward's argument which could be mentioned.[146] Here I will deal only with those relevant to the central theme of this essay, namely, the effects of misreadings of Barth's doctrine of revelation. Before turning to the critique, however, it would be helpful to review some elements set forth in the introduction to this essay and to draw out a few more threads which will be relevant in assessing Ward's analysis.

Revelation, as Barth views it, is not a "given" in any straightforward sense. At every point in the process of revealing himself, God remains "other" than the medium of revelation. *Self*-revelation does not mean that God becomes directly available to human perception. God remains *hidden* precisely in the revelation event. And this is what gives to Ward's *Barth, Derrida and the Language of Theology* its air of plausibility and possibly helps to explain

143. Ward, *Barth, Derrida and the Language of Theology*, 24.
144. Ward, "Postmodern Theology," 586.
145. Ward, *Barth, Derrida and the Language of Theology*, 9.
146. I have already published an extensive critique of Ward's work elsewhere. See Bruce L. McCormack, review of *Barth, Derrida and the Language of Theology*, by Graham Ward, *Scottish Journal of Theology* 49 (1996): 97–109.

the positive echo it has found among readers.[147] But the hiddenness of God in revelation is in no way equatable with the absence of God. The hiddenness of God is precisely the presence of God—complete, whole, and entire—the presence of God in the veil of creaturely flesh as the hidden Subject of a human life. It is for this reason that Barth can say, "No relativism, no scepticism, no personal shyness, may hinder us from speaking of God with all the naivete, with all of the certainty, with all of the obviousness, with which one speaks precisely of a *given*. God *is* given in the revelation-relation through the Spirit. Well unto us, if we *for that reason* speak so certainly of Him, in the Spirit! And woe unto us, if we do *not* do so!"[148] God is *given*, but only indirectly so. God is fully and completely *present* in the veil of creaturely flesh.

The claim that God is fully present is made coherent (I speak here of coherence in the logical sense, not in Ward's acculturated sense) through an elaboration of what in later years Barth called "the humanity of God." The ontological ground of the "humanity of God" lies, for Barth, in election. Election means, finally, that God is sovereign even over his own being. God is a Self-determining Subject who, in a primal decision, assigned to himself the being God would have for all eternity. The content of this primal decision was and is and will be the covenant of grace. God chose to be a God "for us" humans and to be God in no other way. And this entails the further claim that God chose to be God as Jesus Christ. To put it another way, God freely determined that his eternal being would be, already in eternity-past, constituted, *by way of anticipation*, by the incarnation of the "Son" in time (and the outpouring of the Spirit in time).[149] And so the incarnation is the manifestation/realization of the eternal being of God in time. That God is "fully present" in Jesus of Nazareth means, then, that the Subject that God is, is a Subject determined by all that happens in time in the birth, life, death, and resurrection of Jesus of Nazareth. Cast in terms of the classical doctrine of the *communicatio idiomatum*, a Christology which finds its ontological ground in Barth's doctrine of election requires the affirmation of the so-called *genus tapeinoticum*. All that belongs to the human nature of Christ is properly ascribed to the Subject of the hypostatic union, that is, to God.

Now if, in spite of the fact that God is fully present in history as the Subject of a human life, God remains hidden to creaturely perception, the explanation will be found in the fact that Barth's doctrine of election does *not* require

---

147. See esp. Andrew J. McKenna, "Derrida, Death, and Forgiveness," *First Things* 71 (1997): 34–37. See also the reviews by Norman Wirzba, *Christian Century* (September 11–18, 1996): 870–71; and Stephen Webb, *Modern Theology* 12 (1996): 265–67.

148. Barth, *Die Lehre von Gott/Die Lehre vom Menschen*, 18 (*The Göttingen Dogmatics*, 1:331).

149. A full presentation of Barth's doctrine of revelation would obviously require greater attention to its pneumatological dimensions. If I focus here on the christological, it is because it is at this point that the fundamental defect in Ward's interpretation becomes most apparent.

a Christology which affirms the so-called *genus majestaticum*. There is no communication of the attributes of the divine majesty to the human nature. The human nature of Christ is not "divinized" through its assumption by the Logos. It is for this reason that there can be no direct perception of the divine Subject of the human life denominated "Jesus of Nazareth." So, the hiddenness of God is preserved in Barth's Christology, but it is the hiddenness of a fully present Subject. It is not absence.[150]

When we move from a consideration of Christology to revelation in and through human language (i.e., from the situation of disciples at first hand to disciples at second hand), we find that here, too, there is no "divinization" of the creaturely medium of revelation. To this extent, there is a relationship of identity between the first form of revelation and the second. So this is not the point of Barth's analogy. The analogy has to do with the similar and yet different ways in which the creaturely medium is made by grace to "correspond" to God. In the first case, what is in view is a hypostatic union which gives rise to an *ontological* grounding of the creaturely medium (i.e., the humanity of Jesus) in God. One might tease this out more fully by noting that the human "Jesus" corresponds to God by means of his willed obedience. Revelation in and through language, however, entails no hypostatic union, and it certainly entails no willed obedience on the side of the creaturely medium. Language is simply "commandeered" by God and made to point to him. As Eberhard Jüngel rightly observed, "Where such 'commandeering' of the language by revelation for revelation becomes event, there is a *gain to language*. The gain consists in the fact that God *as God* comes to speech."[151] The result of such commandeering is the "analogy of faith"; divine meaning and human meaning stand in a relationship of analogy, and what is more, it is an analogy that is highly positive in character. Still, in that this occurs, the gain which accrues to language is not a permanent one. Revelation never becomes a predicate of the language commandeered by God for the simple reason that the relationship between revelation and language is not a stable but an actualistic one. We are now in a better position to advance a clear critique of Ward.

150. Ward either does not know or has chosen to ignore the relevance of Barth's doctrine of election and his Christology for a fuller comprehension of his treatment of the problem of revelation in and through language. It is possible, though he never quite says it, that Ward regards all of this as "onto-theology." If so, I will not object to the term (no matter how pejorative it may be in the mouths of "postmodernists") so long as it is made clear that Barth's ontology is not the product of speculative metaphysics (ancient or modern). But it should also be noted that Ward's failure to assess the relevance of these doctrines for understanding the *analogia Christi* of which he speaks constitutes an overturning of Barth's priorities. For Barth, noetic *ratio* finds its ground in, and must follow upon, ontic *ratio*. See Barth, *Fides quaerens intellectum*, 53.

151. Eberhard Jüngel, *Gottes Sein ist im Werden*, 3rd ed. (Tübingen: Mohr, 1976), 22; translated as *The Doctrine of the Trinity: God's Being Is in Becoming* (Grand Rapids: Eerdmans, 1976), 11.

It is Ward's view that no synthesis can occur between what he calls the divine *Ursprache* and human language. And if Barth really worked with the two models of language which Ward ascribes to him, Ward would be right. But Barth did not. Granted, Ward is right to insist that words have a different meaning inside the revelation-relation than they do outside it. But the relation of these two meanings (divine and human) is not one of antithesis as Ward suggests. If it were, the relation could be described only as one of "disparity" (*Ungleichheit*)—a position which Barth rejects.[152] No, the relation is rightly described by the word "analogy." Of course, Barth then adds that the "analogy" in question is unforeseeable in its content in advance of a revelation event. But an analogy exists nonetheless between divine meaning and human meaning. Hence we lean too far in the direction of "disparity" if we attribute to Barth two models of language. God, for Barth, does not reveal himself in a metalanguage which does not and cannot come to expression to ordinary human language. Barth never ascribes to God an "ideal speech act." On the contrary, God reveals himself in and through ordinary human discourse. And the result is that the analogy between divine meaning and human meaning gives rise (actualistically) to an analogy between God's Self-knowing and human knowledge of God. The truth is that Barth employs only one model of language, not two—a model which is neither "nomenclatural" nor "semiotic." It is a model of appropriation. Revelation lays hold of ordinary language; ordinary language does not lay hold of revelation.

The corollary to this first point is that appropriation occurs through an act of God; it is not a consequence of the creatureliness of language. Ward seriously mistakes Barth's understanding of language in relation to the revelation event when he supposes that all language is ineradicably theological by virtue of its createdness. Language *becomes* a vehicle of revelation where and when God uses it for that purpose. And this means that revelation always involves a selection on God's part among the words employed by would-be human witnesses. It is most unlikely, therefore, that Barth would have shown any interest in the idea that all discourse is "haunted" by an "ineradicable otherness"; certainly, he would not have identified such "otherness" with the God and Father of our Lord Jesus Christ.[153] And it is at this point that we catch sight of the most basic defect in Ward's reading of Barth. Barth was interested in the role played by language in a highly concrete event. He was not interested in advancing a language theory or even a "theology of language" where the latter is understood to embrace all language whatsoever. What is missing in Ward's account is any appreciation of Barth's particularism.

152. *KD* II/1 253 (*CD* II/1 225).

153. If the Barth of the second edition of *Romans* might still have found in Walter Lowe a useful ally, the case is different with Ward because Ward is making appeal to Barth at a quite different stage of Ward's career.

Ward's other mistakes flow from this most basic one. Barth's "analogy of faith" cannot be identified with Derrida's "economy of *différance*." Barth's analogy of faith describes the *result* of a revelation event, not the *economy* of it. Certainly, the doctrine of analogy is no mere "rhetorical strategy," calculated to testify to "the need to do and the impossibility of doing theology." Theology is not impossible on Barthian soil. Even Barth's famous saying "As theologians, we ought to speak of God. We are, however, human and as such cannot speak of God. We ought therefore to recognize both our obligation and our inability and by that very recognition give God the glory" was not intended by him (at the time it was enunciated) to suggest that theology is a frank impossibility. Theology is possible—by God's grace. It is a divine possibility, not a human one.

Final Assessment

In the final analysis, the fatal flaw in Lowe and Ward is the same. Both miss the particularity of the *Realdialektik* of the divine unveiling in a veil. Both make "God" the answer to a problematic which is generally accessible and described in universal terms. The result is that "God" is an idealistic postulate, generated to provide an explanation for the phenomena under investigation. In Lowe's case, what is postulated is a principle of critical negation; in Ward's case, it is a principle of alterity. What the examples of Lowe and Ward demonstrate, I think, is that the consequence of failing to grasp Barth's particularism is that his dialectic is broken—and broken, in the case of these "postmodern" readers, in the direction of "wholly otherness," nongivenness. And in generating a concept of God tailored to the requirements of anthropology or linguistic theory, they have also missed the particularity of the divine action in which God alone is truly God. The incomprehensibility of God, which these men are (in all likelihood) striving to protect, turns out to be identical with the limits of human knowing—a region in which, as Barth rightly saw, the human knower is still the master of the epistemic relation.[154] God will be the master of the epistemic relation only in that theology which depends for its life on divine action. But this does not happen here.

A Third Alternative? Critically Realistic Dialectical Theology

The Barth interpreters to be treated in this final section belong to no existing school. If scholars have been slow to see a relationship between and among them, it is because their writings are diverse, being devoted to a variety of

154. See Barth, *Die Lehre von Gott/Die Lehre vom Menschen*, 54–60 (*The Göttingen Dogmatics*, 1:356–61).

themes in Barth's theology and displaying a variety of approaches. What distinguishes them from the scholars already treated is the fact that they manage to avoid breaking Barth's dialectic, either in the direction of a positivistic biblicism (the final outcome of the Yale school) or in the direction of an idealistic principle of "wholly otherness" (the postmodern interpretations of Lowe and Ward). For just this reason, those now to be treated hold forth the promise of the birth, for the first time in the Anglo-American reception of Barth, of what I tend to think of as an "authentic" Barthianism. That no dawn of a Barthian scholasticism is intended by this comment is a point I will return to by way of conclusion.

I have chosen to lump the interpreters treated in this section together under the rubric of "critically realistic dialectical theology." Obviously, the phrase is one of my own devising, and its use carries with it the risk that the interpreters treated here will not wish to affirm all that the phrase connotes for me. If I, nevertheless, choose to employ it as a descriptive label, it is because each of the scholars treated here has, in his own way, successfully removed the impediment to recognizing what has eluded the awareness of both Barth's critics and proponents in the English-speaking sphere for more than sixty years: that "dialectic" was not simply a characteristic of Barth's early theology but—rightly interpreted!—left its stamp on the mature Barth of the *Dogmatics* as well. Each has gotten Barth's doctrine of revelation right and, in getting it right, has also grasped the actualistic character of Barth's ontology (divine and human). Therefore each *ought* to be able to go a long way in thinking himself into the position which I have chosen to describe as "critically realistic dialectical theology." The interpreters whom I would regard as meeting this criterion are George Hunsinger and John Webster. I will begin here with a brief discussion of what I mean by "critically realistic" dialectical theology. I will then treat briefly the early Hans Frei (whose influence on Hunsinger seems at least as important as that of the later Frei) before concluding with Hunsinger and Webster.

On "Critically Realistic" Dialectical Theology

As my book *Karl Barth's Critically Realistic Dialectical Theology* has received rather thorough attention in the pages of *Zeitschrift für dialektische Theologie*, it will not be necessary here to rehearse its argument(s).[155] Instead, I will confine myself to the task of giving further clarification to my use of the phrase "critical realism."

Although my prior book takes the form of a genetic-history of Barth's theological development, historical excavation was never conceived of as an end in itself. The real goal was a systematic one with a contemporary edge

---

155. See Dietrich Korsch, review of *Karl Barth's Critically Realistic Dialectical Theology*, by Bruce L. McCormack, *Zeitschrift für dialektische Theologie* 12 (1996): 211–18.

to it. It is my view that Barth's theology has an enormous relevance for contemporary issues in theological epistemology, discussions of rationality, and so on, but the recognition of such relevance in the English-speaking world has been rendered very difficult (if not impossible) by the "neoorthodox" misreading of Barth. What I have tried to make clear is that the alleged turn to a positive, neoorthodox theology never took place, that Barth was, not only in his so-called dialectical phase but in the *Church Dogmatics* as well, a dialectical theologian. The adjective "critically realistic" is meant to get at the uniqueness of Barth's version of dialectical theology—that is, that which distinguishes it from the more nearly idealistic versions advanced during the course of the 1920s by Bultmann and Tillich.

The first half of the phrase "critically realistic" is intended, in the first instance, to say something about the relationship of Barth's theological epistemology to the philosophical epistemology of Kant.[156] "Critical" here refers to the fact that Barth used Kant's critical attempt to establish the limits of human knowing in order to "locate" the being of God beyond the reach of human knowing. "Realism," then, means that the being of God is something complete, whole and entire in itself, apart from and prior to all human knowledge of it. That is, the Reality of God is not a construct of the human imagination; it is more real than the "objects" of human knowing which are "constructed" in the way described by Kant. But if this be true, then the word "critical" takes on another, even more profound significance. It does not only refer us to Kant's epistemology in our efforts to understand Barth's theological epistemology, for Kant's reflections on epistemology (as it turns out) were never more than a secular parable of what Barth wanted finally to say.

What truly brings the limits of the constructive activities of the human knower into question is not Kant's First Critique but the Reality of a God who, in revealing himself, makes himself "object" to the human knower without ceasing to be Subject. In other words, it is the hiddenness of the God who is fully present in revelation which calls into question the constructive activities of the human knower and, at the same time, establishes them. God calls human knowing into question by withholding himself from immediate contact with the recipient of revelation. God establishes human knowing by giving to the recipient of revelation the knowledge of something he or she would never possess in the case of any other "object"—that is, a knowledge of the "noumenal" reality that God is. True knowledge of the God-human entails not only a knowledge of the "phenomenon" that we call Jesus of Nazareth but also a Spirit-given knowledge of the "hidden" Subject of this life. (Were this a critical essay on Barth's theology and not just on readings of Barth, this would be the appropriate place to say that Barth's theological epistemology stood in need of greater attention to the category of religious experience than he himself was able to provide.) In sum,

156. See the introduction to this essay, pp. 109–13.

159

that Barth's realism is described as "critical" refers only penultimately to Kant. Ultimately, it refers us to that of which Barth understood Kant to be a witness, namely, the divine Self-speaking which alone is *truly* critical.

The Early Hans Frei

The theology of Hans Frei constitutes a highly creative synthesis of a number of influences. William Placher, who has written a brief description of Frei's theological development, mentions Barth as an influence but devotes the lion's share of his attention to Erich Auerbach and Gilbert Ryle.[157] The diversity of these influences warns us against making too quick an equation of Frei's theology with "Barthianism."[158] But before Frei began, in the 1970s, to bring his own theology before an admiring public, he had already established himself as an influential Barth scholar. Although Frei's youthful work on Barth suggests that his grasp of the significance of dialectic for Barth's mature doctrine of revelation was shaky,[159] it does at least show him to be appreciative of the "ontic *ratio*" in which Barth strove to ground his theology.[160] To this extent, Frei's early reading of Barth opened the door to a much more adequate and penetrating work, that of George Hunsinger.

George Hunsinger

At first glance, George Hunsinger's[161] *How to Read Karl Barth* appears to be a typical product of the "Yale school."[162] It is intended to help students of Barth to

157. See William Placher, introduction to Frei, *Theology and Narrative*, 5–14.

158: For a recent analysis of the differences between Barth and Frei on the level of biblical hermeneutics, see David E. Demson, *Hans Frei and Karl Barth: Different Ways of Reading Scripture* (Grand Rapids: Eerdmans, 1997).

159. On the one hand, Frei could speak of the Anselm book in 1931 as having wrought a "revolution" in Barth's thought and could find evidence for this in an alleged retreat from actualism in the doctrine of God (though what he meant by the latter point is not especially clear) ("The Doctrine of Revelation in the Thought of Karl Barth, 1909 to 1922: The Nature of Barth's Break with Liberalism" [PhD diss., Yale University], 194, 197). And yet Frei is also well aware that the mature Barth of the *Dogmatics* continued to insist that God is revealed in hiddenness, in the givenness of an object with which God is not identical (201).

160. See, e.g., Frei's address on the occasion of Barth's death, where he says of Barth's procedure, "The ground of the actuality of the incarnation, of its ontological possibility, and of our being able to think about it, are one and the same. That God related himself to us means that it was possible, that he must be himself eternally in a way that is congruent with his relating himself to us contingently. . . . The possibility follows from the actuality" ("Karl Barth," in *Theology and Narrative*, 171).

161. George Hunsinger is the Hazel Thompson McCord Chair of Systematic Theology at Princeton Theological Seminary, Princeton, New Jersey.

162. George Hunsinger, *How to Read Karl Barth: The Shape of His Theology* (New York: Oxford University Press, 1991).

acquire a "set of skills"[163] which will enable them to become better (more discerning) readers of the *Church Dogmatics*. The "skills" which Hunsinger wishes to teach have to do with what he calls "pattern recognition."[164] It is his contention that Barth's theology is shaped by the recurrence of certain motifs which, taken collectively, constitute a kind of "depth grammar" in the *Dogmatics*. Since the motifs recur in various combinations throughout the *Dogmatics*, the reader who has mastered them will be in a better position to understand the nuances of Barth's argument at any given point. The motifs are actualism, particularism, objectivism, personalism, realism, and rationalism. The highly formal character of the work, its preoccupation with reading skills, and its internal logic are all features which we have come to expect from theologians trained at Yale. And yet the work succeeds in "breaking the mold" in surprising ways.

Given the formal character of the motifs, one might reasonably worry that their relationship to the material elements of Barth's theology might become a bit strained and artificial—indeed, that there exists here a danger that philosophical principles are being imposed upon Barth's theological subject matter from without. But such worries are groundless in Hunsinger's case. In truth, his definitions of the motifs show them to arise out of a very close *material* analysis of Barth's dogmatics.

"Actualism," as Hunsinger defines it, is the motif which "governs Barth's complex conception of being and time. Being is always an event and often an act (always an act whenever an agent capable of decision is concerned)."[165] Thus, by implication, actualism is not merely a way of describing the event-character of revelation. The ontology presupposed by Barth's doctrine of revelation is itself actualistic. Although Hunsinger does not explore in any thorough way the relation between God's being and the mode of revelation, we might justly draw the conclusion that God's being-in-revelation *corresponds* to his eternal being precisely because God's eternal being was/is/will be "constituted" by the eternal decision for a being-in-revelation. The second motif is "particularism," a category which says that God's being-in-revelation is utterly unique in kind and that because this is so, every concept used in dogmatic theology must "be defined on the basis of a particular event called Jesus Christ."[166] "Objectivism" describes the means by which revelation/salvation occurs—that is, "through the mediation of ordinary creaturely objects, so that the divine self-enactment in our midst lies hidden within them. The status of this self-enactment is also thought in some strong sense to be objective—that is, real, valid, and effective—whether it is acknowledged and received by the creature or not. Revelation and salvation are events objectively mediated by the creaturely sphere and grounded in the sovereignty of God."[167] It is Hunsinger's first three

163. Ibid., vii.
164. Ibid.
165. Ibid., 4.
166. Ibid.
167. Ibid., 4–5.

motifs, taken together, which render impossible a breaking of Barth's *Realdialektik* either in the direction of a positivistic biblicism or in the direction of an idealistic principle of "wholly otherness." It is not surprising, then, that Hunsinger's fuller exposition of Barth's doctrine of revelation (found in chapter 4 of his book) is entirely in accord with the description given in these pages. "Personalism" refers to the fact that "God's objective self-manifestation in revelation and salvation comes to the creature in the form of personal address. The creature is encountered by this address in such a way that it is affirmed, condemned, and made capable of fellowship with God."[168] "Realism," which customarily is used in theological and philosophical discourse to refer to what Hunsinger ascribes to "objectivism," is used by him to speak of Barth's conception of theological language. "Theological language is conceived as the vehicle of analogical reference. In itself it is radically unlike the extralinguistic object to which it refers (God), but by grace it is made to transcend itself. Through transcending itself by grace, theological language attains sufficient likeness or adequacy to its object for reference truly and actually to occur."[169] Hunsinger is well aware that Barth's conception of truth will not be adequately described in terms of a coherentist conception alone; a kind of top-down correspondence theory is also at work.[170] Finally, "rationalism" refers to the fact that theological language "is understood to include an important rational or cognitive component."[171] The distance separating Hunsinger from Lindbeck is evident throughout but is quite conspicuous here. Where Scripture is understood to be, by God's grace, the medium of a rational communication between the divine Person and human persons (divine *ratio* speaking to human *ratio*), there it is perfectly proper to conclude that "doctrines may be derived beyond the surface content of scripture"[172] through analysis of the presuppositions and consequences of the content to which witness is borne by Scripture.

In all of these definitions, there is nothing to which an objection might be raised. If I have any reservations at all about Hunsinger's book, they have to do with his contention that there is no single problem or principle which lends unity to Barth's *Dogmatics*, that Hunsinger's six motifs constitute a series of closely related "thought-forms" which, taken together, do a more adequate job of describing the "shape" of Barth's theology than do alternatives suggested by von Balthasar, Berkouwer, and so forth. Certainly, it is true that Barth repeatedly admonished us against making "system" an end in itself, and Hunsinger also has on his side Barth's early image of Christian doctrines as constituting a circle whose center is left open. But it seems to me that there is greater material unity to Barth's theology than these largely formal categories are able to indicate, a unity which is best grasped through his concentrating

168. Ibid., 5.
169. Ibid.
170. Ibid., 281n1.
171. Ibid., 5.
172. Ibid.

(developmentally and systematically) on the problem of knowing God, the problem of revelation, as I have done here.

This reservation notwithstanding, what Hunsinger's reading of Barth shows—among other things—is that Barth's theology cannot be adequately addressed without taking seriously its reality-referential character. Postmodern suspicions of "ontotheology" are, no doubt, justified insofar as this term is used to describe doctrines of God which depend for their existence on metaphysics (classical or Hegelian). But Barth shows us that a nonmetaphysical version of ontotheology is not only possible but also necessary—if we are to continue to do Christian theology. And this, I think, is one of the principal lessons of Hunsinger's fine book.

John Webster

Most writers on Barth's theological ethics in the English-speaking world take note of their inclusion in his dogmatics; very few really understand *why* they are so included. And this is, of course, why so many think it possible to criticize Barth's ethics without reference to the dogmatic edifice in which they find their home. What sets John Webster's study apart from others in the field is his ability to demonstrate why the only possible outcome of *this* dogmatics had to be ethics—and, indeed, ethics of the kind Barth advocates.[173] To put it this way is to call attention to the fact that Webster's is much more than a study of the posthumously published fragment from *CD* IV/4.[174] Ultimately, it is a work on what Webster calls Barth's "moral ontology," that is, an investigation into the ontological dimensions of Barth's divine command ethic.[175] Such a lofty goal requires close attention to the fundamental doctrines (revelation, election, the being of God) which provide the grounds for Barth's careful integration of dogmatics and ethics. As Webster rightly observes, "We cannot begin to understand Barth's theological ethics until we see that he construes both the human agent and the sphere within which human agency occurs by reference to an entire vision of reality of which the centre is the manifestation of God's creative and regenerative purposes in the history of Jesus Christ."[176] The lucid description which Webster then gives, in chapters 1–3, of Barth's most fundamental doctrinal decisions constitutes as fine a brief introduction to the *Church Dogmatics* as now exists in English.

The great strength of Webster's discussion of revelation lies in his ability to distinguish carefully between the theological realism resident in Barth's

---

173. See John Webster, *Barth's Ethics of Reconciliation* (Cambridge: Cambridge University Press, 1995).

174. This refers to the volume published in English as *The Christian Life: Church Dogmatics IV, Part 4, Lecture Fragments*, translated by Geoffrey Bromiley (Grand Rapids: Eerdmans, 1981).

175. For a fuller exposition and critique of Webster's book, see Bruce L. McCormack, review of *Barth's Ethics of Reconciliation*, by John Webster, *Modern Theology* 13 (1997): 273–76.

176. Webster, *Barth's Ethics of Reconciliation*, 20.

doctrine of the *analogia fidei* and the Yale school's "nonfoundational" preoccupation with "intratextuality."[177] If he has a weakness, it lies in the fact that the dialectic in Barth's doctrine of revelation is not given the prominence which it merits, with the result that—at times—Webster's Barth can come across as a bit too "premodern" (i.e., his realism is not sufficiently distinguished from that of classical metaphysics). Still, even though the question does not arise for Webster, all the elements needed for an affirmation of what I have been calling "critically realistic dialectical theology" are present in his book, so that I have no hesitation in including his work under this rubric. One could not, with any consistency, set forth Barth's doctrines of election, God, and Christology as Webster does and break Barth's dialectic.

Conclusion

The influence of a great theologian—where it has truly been significant—will never consist in the mere repetition of his ideas. There are two ways in which influence can make itself felt, neither of which entails simple repetition (repristination). The first, which we may think of as a direct influence, rests on understanding. Genuine understanding takes place only where not only the words in which ideas have been expressed are appropriated but also the realities to which they seek to bear witness have been seen, acknowledged, and, indeed, loved. Where this occurs, it will seldom be the case that the one so influenced will bear witness to those realities in the same words—or even by means of the same conceptual apparatus—as the mentor. Love for the "object" will drive one to express oneself in one's own words—and in ways comprehensible to one's own place and time. The second form of influence is more indirect and much harder to assess. Such influence does not require love for the subject matter to which witness has been born; *it does not even require understanding of it.* It may be the case that the reading of a great theologian has sparked something in the reader which has set him or her in motion, evoked in the reader a response which stands in no outwardly discernible relation to what was actually there in the texts he or she read. One thinks immediately of Karl Barth's relationship to Franz Overbeck. The reading of Overbeck was a tremendous spur to Barth's further development. But it is also beyond doubt that Barth misunderstood Overbeck in significant ways.

The thinkers treated in the first two sections of this essay are all indebted in some way to the theology of Karl Barth. Each has, in some sense, been influenced by him. Indeed, for many in the English-speaking world, the influence is so obvious as to justify equating just these figures with "Barthianism" in our time. But as should be obvious from the critiques which I have advanced against

177. Ibid., 26–33, 84–85, 102, 219–21.

these interpreters, the influence in each case—with the possible exception of the early Hans Frei—has been more indirect than direct. Each involves degrees of misunderstanding. No doubt, each thinks of himself (or thought of himself) as simply drawing out the implications of Barth's theology, extending his thinking to bring it into contact with questions and problems he could not have foreseen. In my judgment, the truth of such claims is doubtful. Now, obviously, there is nothing wrong with extending and correcting Barth's thought. Indeed, this ought to be the goal of all Barth research. Barth's dogmatics is not a completed scholastic house in which it is our fate to dwell unto eternity. My point is simply that a proper "use" (either positively or negatively, whether constructively or by way of criticism) lays upon us the burden of genuine understanding.

There has been a marked tendency in much English-language research to move much too quickly to "use" of Barth's theology before having acquired a proper understanding. The daring (to put the matter charitably) entailed in such enterprises will always make it interesting to Europeans who, having grown weary of the customary *Sachlichkeit* of German-language interpreters, are able to see in the latter only a kind of Barthian "scholasticism." But the question we ought to be asking ourselves is, What price are we willing to pay for daring and novelty? Where *Sachlichkeit*—that is, a respect for texts and a willingness to investigate them thoroughly and in all of their interconnections—suffers a decline, one has to wonder how long theology will be able to retain its scientific, academic level. In truth, the trends described in the first two sections of this chapter represent a fairly predictable outcome in an American culture which has never been characterized by a well-developed historical consciousness, which has always prized the novel, the new, as an end in itself, and an English culture which has increasingly looked to America and France, rather than German-speaking countries, for intellectual stimulation. Fascination with problems of hermeneutics (the study of which has rarely made effective readers out of those who undertake it) has also been a factor. What is needed, if Barth's theology is to be deeply engaged in the English-speaking world, is more of the kind of work described in the third section. Until the day comes when the fruit of such work attains the level of a common currency in English-language theological education, widespread criticism or affirmation of Barth will remain premature.[178]

---

178. George Hunsinger's defense of his decision not to advance a critique of Barth's theology is worth noting: "Reading what the critics have to say of Barth's theology is usually like looking at an old map, the kind drafted before the dawn of modern cartography in the eighteenth century. Certain basic aspects of graphic features may be present, but the distortion factor is high. Topographic features may be lacking in detail. Whole promontories may be absent or diminished. Monsters, lions, and swash lines may do duty for factual content. The task of responsible criticism presupposes a more reliable depiction of the overall terrain, as well as of the proportional relationships among the various segments, than has usually been the case. A quest for better cartography would seem to be the place to begin" (*How to Read Karl Barth*, x).

6

"The Limits of the Knowledge of God"

Theses on the Theological Epistemology of Karl Barth

In its consequences it is nothing more nor less than a denial of Jesus Christ and blasphemy against the Holy Spirit, resembling the act of the servant who took and hid the talent entrusted to him, if we try to value our incapacity more highly than the capacity which God Himself in His revelation confers upon our incapacity.

CD II/1:201

Church Dogmatics §27 is the locus classicus in that work for two themes which must be central to any evaluation of recent attempts to find in Barth resources for a "postmodern" theology of the Word: the hiddenness of God and the *analogia fidei*. It is in and through the combination of the two that any adequate response must be given. The material which follows will be divided into two sections—(1) material presuppositions of this paragraph, and (2) critical exposition—and is followed by a conclusion.

This essay was originally published in a slightly different form under the title "Paragraph 27 'The Limits of the Knowledge of God': Theses on the Theological Epistemology of Karl Barth," in *Zeitschrift für dialektische Theologie* 15 (1999): 75–86. Reprinted by permission. The original occasion for this essay was a lecture given at the Kampen-Princeton Barth Consultation on January 16, 1999.

Material Presuppositions

■ **Thesis 1:** The single most decisive material presupposition of the argument advanced in this paragraph is the trinitarian structure of God's Self-revelation.
Explanation: A. At the very outset of §27, Barth says,

> We are speaking of the knowledge of God whose subject is God the Father and God the Son through the Holy Spirit. But we men [and women] are taken up into this event as secondary, subsequent subjects. Therefore we are not speaking only of an event which takes place on high, in the mystery of the divine Trinity. We are indeed speaking of this event, and the force of anything that is said about the knowledge of God consists in the fact that we speak also and first of this event. But we are now speaking of the revelation of this event on high and therefore of our participation in it. We are speaking of the human knowledge of God on the basis of this revelation and therefore of an event which formally and technically cannot be distinguished from what we call knowledge in other connexions, from human cognition.[1]

Barth is making two decisive points in this passage. The first constitutes the background of the inquiry he is undertaking in this paragraph; the second is central to the inquiry itself. First, the Subject of the knowledge of God is, in the first instance, the Triune God. Second, the fact that knowledge of God has God as its Subject does not mean the absence of the human from this event. It does not mean "the abrogation, abolition or alteration of human cognition as such, and therefore of its formal and technical characteristics as human cognition."[2] We will return to the second point in the section below ("Exposition"). For now, we will stay with the first point.

B. To speak of God's revelation as trinitarian in structure is to be reminded of Barth's elaboration of the doctrine of revelation in *CD* I/1 and I/2. Revelation proceeds from the Father, is fulfilled *objectively* in the Son, and is fulfilled *subjectively* (in us) by the Holy Spirit.[3] The Father addresses us in the Son, and the Holy Spirit receives that address *in us*. The Holy Spirit does not do this without us, in the absence of full and complete human participation in this event. But it is the Holy Spirit who is the primary Subject of all hearing of the Word of God addressed to us in Jesus Christ. All of this is entailed in the primary claim that revelation is a trinitarian event in which we humans, too, participate.

■ **Thesis 2:** Revelation is, for Barth, a rational event, that is, one that occurs in the realm of human *ratio* through the normal process of human cognition.
Explanation: "Speech, including God's speech, is the form in which reason communicates with reason and person with person. To be sure, it is the divine

---

1. *CD* II/1:181.
2. Ibid.
3. *CD* I/2:1.

reason communicating with the human reason and the divine person with the human person. The utter inconceivability of this event is obvious. But reason with reason, person with person, is primarily analogous to what happens in the spiritual realm of creation, not the natural and physical realm. The Word of God—and at this point we should not evade a term so much tabooed today—is a rational and not an irrational event."[4]

■ **Thesis 3:** If revelation is a rational event, one which takes the form of divine reason communicating to human reason via the medium of speech, then the distinction often found in literature contemporaneous to Barth's work between personal revelation and propositional revelation (Brunner!) must be abandoned. Such distinctions rest on making a particular datum of human experience provide the starting-point for how divine communication is to be understood. Barth's claim is that in God the personal is propositional. Or more accurately, the Word of God (Jesus Christ, the objective reality and possibility of revelation) is intrinsically verbal—his person is a content-ful reality that is communicable in views, concepts, and words.

Explanation: This means that to speak of revelation as a trinitarian event, an event which occurs "on high" in the inner-trinitarian life of God in which we humans *participate* by grace, and as address (as verbal communication) is not to employ two irreconcilable models of revelation. Of course, to make this claim lays upon us the burden of explaining the nature of *participation*—which we will do in due course.

■ **Thesis 4:** It is because revelation is intrinsically verbal in itself that the primary witness to it takes the form of words (i.e., the witness of Holy Scripture). It is through this verbal witness that God's revelation comes to us disciples "at second hand." God reveals himself to the Church today by taking up the witness of the apostles and the prophets and bearing witness to himself in and through their witness. It is this understanding of revelation that gives rise to the need for a careful inquiry into the relationship between God (as the object of human cognition) and human views, concepts, and words—which is the primary focus of §27.

Exposition

■ **Thesis 5:** Barth's claim is that the knowledge of God is formally and technically indistinguishable from human cognition of any other piece of "world-reality."

Explanation: Knowledge of God is a cognition which is "fulfilled in views and concepts. Views are the images in which we perceive objects as such.

4. *CD* I/1:135.

Concepts are the counter-images with which we make these images of perception our own by thinking them, i.e., arranging them."[5] If we, then, out of responsibility to others for the knowledge of God granted to us, seek to communicate our thought, we will do so in the form of words.

■ **Thesis 6:** The human attempt to bring God's revelation to expression in the form of views, concepts, and words is surrounded by a twofold limitation, an "external limitation" and an "internal limitation."[6] What Barth calls the "external limitation" is the hiddenness of God in his Self-revelation in Jesus Christ. The "internal limitation" has to do with the intrinsic *in*capacity of human thought and language to bear adequate witness to God.

■ **Thesis 7:** The hiddenness of God (the "external limitation") is *not* to be identified with, or in any way made to be, a function of the limitations proper to human knowing.

Explanation: A. Again, from §27:

> The hiddenness of God as introduced and represented here has no connexion with a general theory of human knowledge. . . . Nothing can be more misleading than the opinion that the theological statement of the hiddenness of God says roughly the same thing as the Platonic or Kantian statement, according to which the supreme being is to be understood as a rational idea withdrawn from all perception and understanding. . . . The God who encounters humans in His revelation is never a non-objective entity, or one who is objective only in intention. He is the substance of all objectivity. . . . God's hiddenness is not the content of a last word of human self-knowledge. . . . When we say that God is hidden, we are not speaking of ourselves, but, taught by God's revelation alone, of God.[7]
>
> We must not, therefore, base the hiddenness of God on the inapprehensibility of the infinite, the absolute, that which exists in and of itself, etc. For all this in itself and as such (whether it is or not, and whatever it may be) is the product of human reason, in spite of and in its supposed inapprehensibility.[8]

B. In other words, the elaboration of concepts such as the Absolute takes place through a process of rational extrapolation or inference from some datum of human being or experience. To speak of the being of God even in wholly negative terms of this kind is (ironically, perhaps) to apprehend God, to bring him under epistemic control by means of constructs of human reason. "The God who is something in contrast to something else, pole versus counter-pole, Yes versus No, the God who is not altogether free, alone, superior, victorious, is No-God, the God of this world."[9] "God is not the Infinite! The Infinite is

5. *CD* II/1:181.
6. *CD* II/1:195.
7. *CD* II/1:183.
8. *CD* II/1:188.
9. Karl Barth, *Der Römerbrief, 1922* (Zurich: Theologischer Verlag, 1940), 213.

only a projection of the finite, stripped of all its limitations and projected on to a higher being. But because it is a projection, it always remains *inseparably bound* to the finite as its antithesis, its mirror opposite."[10] To speak of God's hiddenness by this means is to speak, Barth says, not of God at all but of "the *ineffabile* of man."[11]

C. To dismiss only the terms which derive from natural, physical life as inappropriate for speaking of God on the grounds that they are too "anthropomorphic" misses the point. All human words—including allegedly "spiritual" words such as "being," "absolute," and so forth—are anthropomorphic in the very nature of the case.[12] All derive from the sphere of ordinary human discourse. If we are going to use any words rightly, we must be taught by God how to do so. More on that in a moment.

■ **Thesis 8:** Positively, the hiddenness of God is a hiddenness of a highly concrete and particular kind, a hiddenness made known in revelation because it is a hiddenness *in revelation*. It is the hiddenness of the Second Person of the Trinity in the veil of creaturely flesh.

Explanation: "In His revelation, in Jesus Christ, the hidden God has indeed made Himself apprehensible. Not directly, but indirectly. Not to sight, but to faith. Not in His being, but in sign. Not, then, by the dissolution of His hiddenness—but apprehensibly."[13] The explanation of this paradoxical series of statements is to be found in the Christology outlined in *CD* I/2, especially pages 159–71. The significance of this Christology for our purposes here lies in the fact that when God unites himself to human nature in the incarnation, God does so in such a way that no abrogation, abolition, or alteration of that nature takes place. The human nature is *human* precisely *in* its union with the divine. As such, it remains a veil *even as God unveils himself to human eyewitnesses in and through it*—by the testimony of the Holy Spirit to them. Hence the Subject of this human life is never given to direct perception. What the disciples apprehend *of themselves* is therefore the humanity of Jesus and it alone. *That* is the hiddenness of God in revelation. "Knowing the true God in His revelation, we apprehend Him in His hiddenness."[14]

■ **Thesis 9:** The hiddenness of God in revelation is the hiddenness of *God*—complete, whole, and undivided. However partial and incomplete our reception of revelation may be, revelation is not partial on the side of God's act. God reveals himself by appearing *in person*, as the Subject of a human life in history. Nothing of God is left behind in this personal act. The hiddenness of

10. Bruce L. McCormack, *Karl Barth's Critically Realistic Dialectical Theology: Its Genesis and Development, 1909–1936* (Oxford: Clarendon, 1995), 247.

11. *CD* II/1:221.

12. *CD* II/1:222.

13. *CD* II/1:199.

14. *CD* II/1:194.

God in revelation is thus not to be conceived of as though it entailed a division in God—part of God revealed, part of God hidden. The being of God may not be quantified in this way.

Explanation: "'The content of revelation is *wholly* God.' The point here is simply that God is not just half revealed or partly revealed, so that another part of his being or attributes or acts will have to remain hidden or will have to be imparted in some other way than by revelation."[15] "A God who reveals Himself quantitatively is not God. . . . God's hiddenness, His incomprehensibility, is His hiddenness not alongside or behind revelation, but in it."[16] "In the revelation of God, there is no hidden God, no *Deus absconditus*, at the back of His revelation, with whose existence and activity we have also occasionally to reckon beyond His Word and Spirit, and whom we also have to fear and honour behind His revelation."[17]

Implication: Postmodern critiques of "metaphysical presences" must be tested (first and foremost) in the light of what God has done in taking on human flesh. Before we ever get to the question of the relation of God to human language, we must first think about the incarnation. If God can hypostatically unite himself to a human "nature," then God can also "indwell" human language.[18]

■ **Thesis 10:** Revelation takes place not only in the "sign" of the flesh of Jesus. "This is the first, original and controlling sign of all signs. In relation to this sign, as the sign of this sign, there is also creaturely testimony to His eternal Word, not everywhere, but where His eternal Word has chosen, called and created for Himself witnesses."[19] It is in this transition from *the sign* to the signs of that sign that the transition from the revelation to witnesses to revelation takes place and, with that, the transition from a consideration of Christology to a consideration of the relation of God to human language. We come, then, to Barth's discussion of the "internal limitation" proper to language and its overcoming by grace.

■ **Thesis 11:** In connection with the problem of the relation of God to human language, Barth's first (critical) point is that human language has no intrinsic (natural) capacity to participate in the truthfulness of God's revelation, to speak—in other words—correctly of God.

Explanation: A. Of itself and as such, human language is applicable only to the creaturely realm.[20] There is no language that is exempt from this limitation,

15. Karl Barth, *The Göttingen Dogmatics: Instruction in the Christian Religion*, trans. Geoffrey Bromiley (Grand Rapids: Eerdmans, 1991), 1:91.
16. Ibid., 1:93.
17. *CD* II/1:210.
18. *CD* II/1:212.
19. *CD* II/1:199.
20. *CD* II/1:227.

neither the language of dogma nor the language of the Bible itself. All human language stands under "the crisis of the hiddenness of God."[21] It is this to which Barth is referring when he speaks of the "inner limitation" of language: the *natural* incapacity of language to speak of a God who is indeed "present" in the world-reality, but present in a way that is qualitatively different from the way in which all other elements in that world-reality are "present" to the human knower.[22]

B. But this is only one side of a dialectic which Barth is constructing. We would make a serious error if we stopped with any of the rather sharp (and even one-sided) statements Barth makes in connection with the *natural* incapacity of language to participate in the truthfulness of God's revelation. Of great interest here is the fact that the dialectical *Denkform* that was given classical expression in Barth's *Das Wort Gottes und die Theologie* resurfaces in this context.[23] But it does so not to describe the presuppositions of genuinely Christian theology but, rather, as a description of what would be the case—*apart from grace!*

> By the grace of God we are like Him, master of Him, one with Him. . . . But as such we shall honour and acknowledge the revelation of the judgment of truth, according to which we *of ourselves* are not these things. We shall, therefore, renounce the capacity to conceive of God—or rather, we shall be forced to know that this renunciation is imposed upon us. When we think the being of this God, God in Jesus Christ, as we can and must, the possibilities of our apprehending do in fact break apart, and we do not really know what we are saying when we say "God," no matter whether we try to express it by this word or by any other word. And this is the point at which we ourselves must and will avow that this is so, necessarily recognizing and confessing the incapacity of our apprehending, and therefore God's hiddenness.[24]

The point is that the "possibilities of our apprehending," when judged in and for themselves as possibilities and capacities, are incapacities where speech about God is concerned. In and of ourselves, our language must "break apart." In and of ourselves, we do not know what we are saying when we say "God." But this is only one side of Barth's *Realdialektik*. His goal in this paragraph is to speak of the capacity which God grants by grace to our incapacity. "God is actually apprehensible in His revelation. He is so in such a way that He makes Himself apprehensible to those who cannot apprehend Him of themselves. But He is still apprehensible."[25] Were we to deny that this is so, were we to stop

21. *CD* II/1:195.
22. *CD* II/1:190.
23. See Karl Barth, "Das Wort Gottes als Aufgabe der Theologie," in *Das Wort Gottes und die Theologie* (Munich: Kaiser, 1925), 171–75.
24. *CD* II/1:189, emphasis mine.
25. *CD* II/1:196–97.

with the first side of the dialectic—the negation of human possibilities—we might well wind up with some form of "postmodern" Barth. But we may not stop here.

C. The truth of the matter is that the incapacity of human speech to be a bearer of divine revelation is not identical with the limitations of human knowing generally but, rather, is a function of the mode of divine self-revelation (the "external limitation"). Thus the true "incapacity" can be known only through the apprehension of God. All talk of human incapacity which does not rest upon a real apprehension of God is *not* talk of the incapacity for revelation.

Thesis 12: By an act of God, human views, concepts, and words can be legitimately applied to God and genuinely describe God.[26] The capacity which is conferred on human language by this act is real and not merely notional. "We do not attribute to our views, concepts, and words a purely fictional capacity, so that the use we make of them is always hedged by the reservation of an 'as if.'"[27] Barth's task in what follows is to say something about how this takes place and what its results are. We will confine ourselves here to saying something about the "how" of this event.

Further elaboration: A. Barth does not fall completely silent where the "how" of the event of revelation in and through human language is concerned. But it is characteristic of his thought generally that he will become very circumspect about addressing the "how" of divine activity. God acts as God acts—by Word and Spirit. This is probably the most that can be said about God's role in this event (or any other). Anything beyond this is a metaphor whose capacity for witnessing to the action of God is annulled if taken literally. Chief among these is the metaphor of "indwelling." Barth says that the "narrowness"—meaning the "inner limitation" of our views, concepts, and words—is not so great as to render it impossible for God to "take up His dwelling in this narrowness."[28] The "divine indwelling" in our views, concepts, and words, however, "does not involve a magical transformation of man, or a supernatural enlargement of his capacity, so that now he can do what before he could not do. He cannot do it afterwards any more than he could do it before. But he is taken up by the grace of God and determined to participation in the veracity of the revelation of God."[29] The very real capacity which is granted to human language, in other words, is not a permanent grant. The "indwelling" of God in human language honors the distinction between the two and in no way annuls it. What occurs in the event in which revelation takes place through the medium of language is that a capacity which remains God's capacity is set up in the midst of an incapacity which remains. Less metaphorically expressed: the meaning of our words is

26. *CD* II/1:227.
27. *CD* II/1:228.
28. *CD* II/1:212.
29. *CD* II/1:212–13.

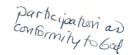
Participation as conformity to God

made to conform to the meaning contained in God's revelation (a revelation which Barth does not hesitate to describe in terms of "authentic information about God"[30]). This relationship of conformity *is* the "participation" of our concepts in words in the truthfulness of God's revelation. "Participation" is here employed as a synonym for "conformity."

B. Barth also has a good bit to say about the posture or attitude of the recipient of revelation. Our "participation" in God's revelation, he says, consists in giving thanks, acknowledgment, joy, and wondering awe.[31]

Thesis 13: The relationship of the content and meaning of human words as applied to God (in the event of revelation) and as applied to creatures is not a relationship of simple identity (*Gleichheit*). Nor is it a relationship of difference (*Ungleichheit*). It is, rather, a relationship of analogy.

Further elaboration: Barth is quite concerned in this context to avoid giving the impression that the meaning of human language is simply turned upside down when applied legitimately to God. Barth seeks to shore up this claim by means of a further one, namely, that all language is originally God's. God therefore does not do something "improper" when God commands us to use our concepts and words to speak of him. Nor does God change our language and its meaning into something altogether different in making use of it. What is truly significant in this context is not Barth's "theory" of the origins of language but simply the fact that he is rejecting the possibility that the relationship between "divine meaning" (the meaning which attaches itself to the words employed in any speaking of God which participates in the truthfulness of revelation) and customary "human meaning" (the meaning which attaches itself to the same words when used for other purposes than for speaking of God) will be a relationship of *equivocation.*

But at this point we must register a critical demurral. As a theory of the origins of language (and of particular words), Barth's reflections here are not beyond criticism. But to acknowledge this does no harm to his essential point about equivocation. It is quite true, as Barth says in this context, that we do not speak "as if" when we use words such as "Father" and "Son" in speaking of God. But to say that the use of these *words* to describe the relationship between the first and second members of the Trinity restores them to their "original" meaning goes too far. What is true, it seems to me, is that the ontological relationship between the Father and the Son is the original *relation* against which all that we call father-son relations on the human plane must be judged and measured. But the human *language* used to speak of this original relation or its analogue on the human plane will very likely have originated as constructs of human social imagination. We are going too far onto the grounds of speculation to take either side in this debate. We do not need an

30. *CD* II/1:210.
31. *CD* II/1:216–20.

"original language." What has clearly driven Barth to this piece of speculation is his worry over the *analogia entis*.

What Barth wants to say is that the "overplus of meaning" which accrues to human language *in* its use by God in a revelation event does not contradict or overturn its ordinary human meaning. If he were to have said that it did, we would be in a situation of equivocation and we could not possibly know what we mean when we apply words to God. Barth knows this—hence the emphatic rejection of equivocation. But he is afraid to simply say that the meaning of those human words which are taken up by God in bearing witness to himself in a revelation event *already* stand in a relationship of analogy to the meaning they will have in God's use of them—even *before* a revelation event takes place—because, if he does so, he seems to open the door to a possible *analogia entis*. Hence the reason for the speculative theoretical discussion about the origins of language. The truth, however, is that the *analogia fidei* is possible only because there is an analogy between the being of God and the being of the redeemed creature. Granted, this cannot possibly be the *analogia entis* of which sixteenth- and nineteenth-century Catholics dreamt. In his 1929 monograph *The Holy Spirit and the Christian Life*, Barth spoke calmly of "true *analogia entis*," which is a predicate not of human being as created but of "the Creator *in his relation* to the creature." Such an analogy is not an "original endowment" bestowed upon the human creature in his or her creation but takes its rise in God's revelational/redemptive dealings with human beings.[32] And if this analogy is already effective in some way even before God addresses any particular individual, it is not because a gift of creation is somehow still effective even after the fall but because divine election is already effective on the ontological plane of the reality of the covenant of grace even before it has an effect on the phenomenal human. What God has eternally chosen us to be is what we truly are even under the conditions of the fall. Now, if this claim be allowed, then Barth no longer need worry about a false *analogia entis*, and his supposed need for a theory of the origins of language disappears.

What remains true is that the *analogia fidei* is not something whose content can be ascertained independently of revelation (in Barth's sense). And the true *analogia entis* is something that is actualized in and through the actuality of the revelation event—which means that realization of the *analogia fidei* is the means by which God also makes the true *analogia entis* effective in the here and now. If, then, I say that the true *analogia entis* is the ground of the realization of the *analogia fidei*, I am speaking protologically and eschatologically of the

32. Karl Barth, *The Holy Spirit and the Christian Life: The Theological Basis of Ethics*, trans. R. Birch Hoyle with a foreword by Robin W. Lovin (Louisville: Westminster/John Knox, 1993), 5.

true *analogia entis* (as it was determined by God in eternity-past, is realized actualistically in the present, and will be fully established in the eschaton).

■ **Thesis 14:** Barth agrees with Andreas Quenstedt that the analogy between human word and divine being is of the nature of an *analogia attributionis* (i.e., "a similarity between two objects which consists in the fact that what is common to them exists first and properly in the one, and then, because the second is dependent upon it, in the second"[33]). Barth agrees that in this relationship, God (or the aspect of divine being which is under consideration) is to be understood as the *analogans* and the creature (and the similar aspect found in it) as the *analogatum*. But at this point the agreement breaks down. For Quenstedt, the analogy is most completely defined as an *analogia attributionis instrinsecae*. That is to say, the terms of the analogy describe attributes or features that are proper to both God and the creature *inwardly*. Barth, on the other hand, wants to define the analogy in question more closely as an *analogia attributionis extrinsecae*. The "analogy" in question is not a predicate of creaturely being, even if only in a dependent and derivative way. The analogy *exists* in the revelation-relation and in it only. What makes the creature the *analogatum* of God is, in other words, *not* something that is found "in" the creature. It is found, rather, in the revelation-relation, in the correspondence established in that relation between God and the creature, a correspondence which depends for its existence on an always-to-be-renewed act of graciousness. *Extrinsecae* means that "the analogy of the *analogatum* and therefore of the creature is proper to the creature only externally in the existence and form of its relationship to the *analogans*, that is, to God, but internally it is proper only to this *analogans* as such."[34]

Further elaboration: It is clear why Barth is concerned about making the analogy rest on something "intrinsic" to the creature. If this is done, it will not matter that we also say the attribute under consideration belongs to the creature only derivatively and in dependence on God. Once it has been made "intrinsic" to the creature, it will then be a fixed datum, something that can be apprehended and used to reason from the *analogatum* to the *analogans*. God, in other words, may be known from the creature. So Barth is concerned throughout to close the door to all natural theology. I think myself that Barth's concern here is a wholly justified one. If I then go on to challenge his handling of the *analogia attributionis* (as I am going to do), I do not want to do so in a way that overturns his objections to Quenstedt.

■ **Thesis 15:** Judged internally (in terms of his own doctrinal constructions and their ontological implications), Barth made a mistake in taking up Quenstedt's distinction between an *analogia attributionis extrinsecae* and an *analogia*

33. *CD* II/1:238.
34. Ibid.

attributionis intrinsecae and defending only one of them. What he ought to have done was to challenge the distinction through a redefinition of the *intrinsecae* which would have made it clear that that which we humans truly are "inwardly" (i.e., properly) is *not* a function of our createdness per se. The *intrinsecae* finds its home, on Barthian soil, not in the doctrine of creation but in the doctrines of election and eschatology (redemption).

Further elaboration: Barth ought to have insisted that the *analogia attributionis extrinsecae* as realized in history presupposes the existence (protologically and eschatologically) of an *analogia attributionis intrinsecae*. And on this basis, he should have said that the realization of the *analogia attributionis extrinsecae* in time, in history, means the momentary actualization of that *analogia attributionis intrinsecae* (since that which we are "internally"—properly—is, at every moment in time, a function of the "external" relation). In putting it this way, I am also suggesting that there is a sense in which the relation between God and the human is "fixed and stable." But this is a truth that remains "hidden with Christ in God" (Col. 3:3), in the divine election. And since (on Barthian grounds) we do not know whether the election of all will result in the salvation of all, we cannot ourselves make use of the "fixed and stable" element in the relation. Our portion is our relation with God in history and that alone.

The real point of divergence between Barth and Quenstedt lies in the presupposed distinction of absolute and relative being implicit in the latter's reflections. Barth could have thought through the ontological implications of his own concept of "analogy" more clearly had he kept his focus on the necessary opposition to this concept of "being" (rather than concentrating on the *analogia attributionis intrinsecae*—an analogy which may be erected on different grounds than that of the kind of *analogia entis* Barth opposes). In putting it this way, I am once again trying to suggest that not all "analogies of being" are bad. Only those "analogies of being" are detrimental to Christian dogmatics which presuppose the ordering of divine being and human being together under the heading of "absolute and relative being" (which would make "being" something common to both God and the creature, thereby establishing a firm basis for natural theology). Barth's ontology, by contrast, is covenantal (in that it has its ground in the covenant of grace for which God determines himself and the creature from eternity) and actualistic (in that the realization of the covenant-relation in time is never, for us, simply a past event, something which has been achieved once and for all times, but always, in every moment, an ever-to-be-renewed event). In sum, Barth's conception of the *analogia fidei* in terms of an *analogia attributionis extrinsecae* is never simply "external"; it has at every point ontological implications which Barth would have done well to clarify. A Barthian version of the *analogia entis* would not fall prey to natural theology, since it would provide no grounds for knowing God from the creature. The instability of the covenant-relation *in time* would ensure that it does not.

I should add that at least part of the reason for Barth's mistake here lies in the fact that he had yet to think through the ontological implications of the revolution which occurred in his doctrine of election, beginning in 1936.

Thesis 16: Barth's doctrine of the *analogia attributionis extrinsecae* is intended to serve the *Realdialektik* of the divine veiling and unveiling in revelation. Univocity in the relation between human word and divine being would mean that the veiling of God in revelation is denied. Equivocity in the relation would mean that the unveiling of God is denied. The analogy in question thus serves to preserve the proper dialectic.

Thesis 17: The relationship of veiling and unveiling is not one of a static equilibrium. Veiling is ordered towards unveiling as its goal.[35] This does not mean that God's hiddenness is ever set aside. Not even in eternity is this the case.[36] The "unveiling" to which Barth refers is an unveiling in and through a veil (the flesh of Jesus or human words) which does not cease to be a veil even as it is used by God for this purpose. Hence unveiling does not succeed veiling in a temporal ordering. The ordering of veiling to unveiling as its goal is not meant to suggest this. What is intended, rather, is the understanding that the moments in which unveiling takes place through a veil stand together in an ordered history. Such moments are not to be conceived of as so many beads on a string without the string. They belong together as parts of an ordered whole.

Substantiation: "The relationship between veiling and unveiling is not symmetrical, equivocal, vacillating or obscure, nor is it a reversal and alternation dependent on the arbitrariness of God or man. If we want to describe the relationship between these two concepts, and therefore the explanation of the concept of analogy, as dialectical, we must always note that what is involved is an ordered dialectic, and indeed one which is teleologically ordered."[37]

Implications: The *analogia fidei* is wrongly construed where it is taken to imply what Jerome Hamer once called "occasionalism." It is not as though the revelation events of which Barth speaks do not stand in some kind of ordered relation. The importance of this lies in the fact that what God has said to the church in the past is not to be dispensed with in our efforts to hear the Word of God in our present moment. Granted, repetition of earlier words is no guarantee that they will be understood in relation to their source (viz., God). But by the same token, the teleologically ordered dialectic of which Barth speaks does not close the door on the possibility that God's speaking to us may lay

35. *CD* II/1:236.
36. *CD* II/1:209.
37. *CD* II/1:236.

upon us the requirement that we speak of God in our time and on our own responsibility in the terms provided by earlier words. Hence repristination may be neither exalted nor completely denigrated.

Conclusion

Thesis 18: Because, in Barth's view, the true hiddenness of God is known only where the veil has been lifted and God has revealed himself; because, second, the capacity which is conferred on human incapacity makes possible a real knowledge of God (analogically related to God's knowledge of himself); because, third, such knowledge is grounded in the very being of God (i.e., divine ontology is the ground and presupposition of theological epistemology); and because, fourth, such knowledge cannot be brought into any meaningful relationship to an allegedly apophatic knowledge of God, therefore Barth's theological epistemology is drastically distorted if read as a precursor to "postmodern" theological epistemologies.

Part 3

Karl Barth's
Theological Ontology

7

Grace and Being

The Role of God's Gracious Election in Karl Barth's Theological Ontology

Introduction: On the Christocentricity of Barth's Doctrine of Election

When the history of theology in this century is written from the vantage point of, let us say, one hundred years from now, I am confident that the greatest contribution of Karl Barth to the development of church doctrine will be located in his doctrine of election. It was here that he provided his most valuable corrective to classical teaching; here, too, that his dogmatics found both its ground and its capstone. Nothing in this claim will seem surprising to those who are acquainted with Barth's teaching on this theme. But a more penetrating analysis will also, I think, yield the observation that it was in Barth's doctrine of election that the historicizing tendencies of well over a century of theology prior to him found, at one and the same time, both their relative justification and their proper limit. What Barth accomplished with his doctrine of election was to establish a hermeneutical rule which would allow the church to speak authoritatively about what God was doing—and, indeed, who and what God was/is—"before the foundation of the world" *without engaging in speculation.*

The latter point especially has rarely been appreciated. Emil Brunner, who was happy enough with Barth's attempt to locate the *noetic* ground of election in the revelation which took place in Jesus Christ and even more pleased

This essay was originally published in a slightly different form under the title "Grace and Being: The Role of God's Gracious Election in Karl Barth's Theological Ontology," in *The Cambridge Companion to Karl Barth*, ed. John Webster (Cambridge: Cambridge University Press, 2000), 92–110. Reprinted by permission.

with the corrective Barth offered to Calvin's teaching, blanched at the point at which Barth made Jesus Christ the eternal, *ontic* ground of election. According to Brunner, to speak, as Barth did, of "Jesus Christ" as the Subject of election was to posit the eternal preexistence of the God-human, with the consequence that the incarnation is no longer a historical event.[1] Brunner's criticism need not detain us long in this essay, resting as it did on a fairly drastic misunderstanding, but it did perform the helpful service of pointing to the truly novel element in Barth's teaching, namely, that at the beginning of all the ways of God with the world stood not a *Logos asarkos* (in Brunner's abstract and absolute sense) but the God-human, Jesus Christ. Now that is Barthian "historicizing"! Whether it is ultimately judged to be speculation will depend on the success of Barth's Christology. For it is in his Christology that Barth grounds the whole of his dogmatic edifice.[2]

This essay will seek to accomplish two goals: first, to introduce Barth's doctrine of election to those unacquainted with it and, second, to offer a critical correction to the doctrine of the Trinity in its light. The exposition will unfold in two major sections, corresponding to the twofold thesis which governs Barth's doctrine of election, namely, that Jesus Christ is the electing God and the elect human. The essay will conclude by drawing some implications from Barth's theological ontology for Protestant dialogue with the Roman Catholics.

Jesus Christ: The Subject of Election

The Logos asarkos *Not to Be Identified with the Hidden God of the* decretum absolutum

Taken on the most superficial level, the revolution which Barth effected in the Reformed understanding of predestination was to replace Calvin's version

1. Emil Brunner, *This Christian Doctrine of God*, trans. Olive Wyon (Philadelphia: Westminster, 1949), 347. For a similar criticism, see Gerhard Gloege, "Zur Prädestinationslehre Karl Barths," *Kerygma und Dogma* 2 (1956): 23–41. For a more than adequate response to these criticisms, see Walter Kreck, *Grundentscheidungen in Karl Barths Dogmatik* (Neukirchen: Neukirchener Verlag, 1978), 215–18, 222–29. It should be noted that the language of "noetic" and "ontic ground" is Kreck's (188).

2. I will not be able to enter into the details of Barth's Christology in this essay. Suffice it here to say that when I speak of Barth's Christology as the foundation of his doctrine of election and apply the term "historicizing" to his procedure, I am referring to the fact that he takes his methodological starting-point in the historically primitive Christian confession "Jesus is Lord" and then seeks to inquire into the eternal ontological conditions in God which would allow such a confession to be true. See, e.g., Karl Barth, *The Göttingen Dogmatics: Instruction in the Christian Religion*, trans. Geoffrey Bromiley (Grand Rapids: Eerdmans, 1991), 1:103–30. Obviously, this is "historicizing" of a quite different character from that found in theologians who would like to base everything that is said about God on a reconstruction of the so-called historical Jesus.

of double predestination with a universal election. Certainly, this is the most conspicuous consequence of Barth's teaching in this area, and those who have been weaned on Reformed understandings of predestination will likely focus their attention on this aspect. But the question "To whom does election apply?" is, from Barth's point of view, a secondary question. What is primary is the question "Who is the God who elects? And what does a knowledge of this God tell us about the nature of election?" Barth's revolution is finally a revolution in the doctrine of God—which means, among other things, that he is working with a very different divine ontology than did his forebears in the Reformed tradition.

Jesus Christ is both the Subject of election and its object, the electing God and the elect human. This is the fundamental thesis which shapes the whole of Barth's doctrine of election. The latter half of the thesis occasions no great surprise. Through the centuries, Reformed theologians have frequently spoken of the election of Jesus Christ to be the Mediator between God and human beings as the "foundation" of the election of others.[3] The scriptural basis for such a judgment may be found in Ephesians 1:3–4: "Blessed be the God and Father of our Lord Jesus Christ, who has blessed us in Christ with every spiritual blessing in the heavenly places, just as he chose us in Christ before the foundation of the world to be holy and blameless before him in love." It is the first half of the thesis, however, which has proven startling to many readers of Barth.

That Jesus Christ, the God-human in his divine-human unity, should be conceived of as the Subject of election is a claim which finds no *direct* confirmation in the New Testament. Barth defends it through a close exegesis of the prologue to John's Gospel, a passage which identifies the Logos who was "in the beginning" with God and was in fact God as the One who also "became flesh" (John 1:14) so that his "glory" might even be observable to human eyewitnesses.[4] Now, taken on one level, the claim which is established through this exegesis is unimpeachable, and its truth has been indirectly acknowledged by seventeenth-century Reformed theologians. The Logos "became flesh"; it is one and the same Logos (a self-identical Subject) who was "without the flesh" (*asarkos*) and who now, through the incarnation in time, is "within the flesh" (*ensarkos*). Orthodox Reformed theologians expressed this thought through a distinction between the *Logos incarnandus* (the Logos "to be incarnate") and the *Logos incarnatus* (the Logos "incarnate"). The distinction for them was one between the Logos as he appears in the eternal plan, or *consilium*, of God (predestination) and the Logos as he appears in the actual execution of this plan in time.[5] So, if precedent means

3. See Heinrich Heppe, *Reformed Dogmatics* (Grand Rapids: Baker Academic, 1978), 168.

4. See Kreck, *Grundentscheidungen*, 222–29.

5. See Heppe, *Reformed Dogmatics*, 452. It should be noted that the early Reformed made this distinction for soteriological reasons, namely, to affirm that Christ's mediatorial activity

anything at all, seventeenth-century terminology would allow Barth to speak of the *Logos incarnandus* (prior to historical "enfleshment") as One whose being was "determined" by the eternal divine decision for incarnation in time. And yet there remains an important difference between this traditional usage and Barth's claim. For seventeenth-century theologians, the Logos appeared in the eternal *consilium* of God as *incarnandus* only insofar as he was the *object* of election. In this view, the Logos is determined to be *incarnandus* in the eternal plan of God as a consequence of a prior decision made by the Triune God. Granted, any decision made by the Trinity is also made by the Logos. But the Logos appears in the actual decision-making process as One whose identity is *not yet* determined by the decision for incarnation. He is *incarnandus* only as a result of that decision; in making it (and prior to making it?), his being and existence are *undetermined*. If now Barth wishes to speak of "Jesus Christ" as the *Subject* of election, he must deny to the Logos a mode or state of being above and prior to the eternal decision to be incarnate in time. He must, to employ the traditional terminology, say that there is no Logos in and for himself in distinction from God's act of turning towards the world and humanity in predestination; the Logos is *incarnandus* in and for himself, in eternity. For that move alone would make it clear that it is "Jesus Christ" who is the Subject of election and not an indeterminate (or "absolute") *Logos asarkos*.

In part at least, Barth's claim that Jesus Christ is the Subject of election was motivated by worries over speculation. If we were to posit the existence of a *Logos asarkos* above and prior to the eternal decision to become incarnate in time, Barth feared that we would be inviting speculation about the being and existence of the Logos in such a state or mode of being. After all, any putative knowledge of the Logos under these conditions would have to look away from the incarnation and seek other sources, other epistemic grounds. And it is precisely this worry that comes to expression in his critique of John Calvin's treatment of the so-called *extra Calvinisticum*.

Excursus: Barth's Critique of the *extra Calvinisticum*

In the history of theology, the technical term *extra Calvinisticum* was coined by Lutheran polemicists to refer to the claim made by Reformed theologians that even *after* the hypostatic union of the Logos with a human nature in the womb of the Virgin Mary, the Logos continued to fill heaven and earth but (and this was the controverted point) did so as *Logos asarkos*—that is, without requiring that the human nature he had assumed was also omnipresent. To put it another way, the Second Person of the Trinity was, at one and the same time, completely within the flesh of Jesus (spatially circumscribed) and

---

was already being exercised prior to his incarnation in time. But they never, to my knowledge, explored the potential of this distinction for the doctrine of the Trinity. It was left to Barth to undertake that work.

completely without the flesh of Jesus (not limited by space). The Lutherans rejected this claim because they thought that they saw in it a fatal "Nestorian" separation of the two natures in Christ. In their view, if the hypostatic union meant anything at all, it meant that once the union of natures has occurred, the Logos cannot be anywhere in heaven and earth in the absence of the human nature which he assumed. It should be noted that what lay beyond dispute in these early Protestant debates was that there was a valid distinction to be made between the *Logos asarkos* and the *Logos ensarkos* prior to the event in which the Second Person of the Trinity became enfleshed. The dispute had to do strictly and solely with the state of affairs which pertained *after* the hypostatic union, *after* the entrance of the eternal Son of God into time.

As the defender of a Logos Christology, Karl Barth quite naturally took an interest in this old debate. Barth had no wish to deny the propriety of the distinction between the *Logos asarkos* and the *Logos ensarkos* altogether. After all, the human nature (body and soul) of Jesus only came into existence at a particular point in time, in history. It was not eternal; the Logos did not bring it with him, so to speak, in entering history. Hence there could be no denying the reality of a *Logos asarkos* prior to the incarnation (and, Barth would add, in agreement with his Reformed forebears, after the incarnation as well). And yet there was something about the Calvinist rendition of this doctrine which made Barth uneasy:

> There is something regrettable about that theory insofar as it could lead, as it has to the present day, to disastrous speculation about a being and activity of a *Logos asarkos* and, therefore, about a God who could be known and whose divine essence could be defined on some other basis than in and from the perception of His presence and action as incarnate Word. And it cannot be denied that Calvin himself (with especially serious consequences in his doctrine of predestination) went a long way in falling prey to the temptation of reckoning with such an "other God."[6]

Barth's concerns, however, cut much deeper than this passage might seem to suggest at first glance. His concern was not just epistemological; it was not just to exclude the attempt to know God on any other basis than that of the Word incarnate in history (though his desire to forestall any form of natural theology clearly played an important role). Barring the door to speculation was not an end in itself. What was really at stake—as the immediate context in which this passage appears in CD IV/1 clearly demonstrates—was divine ontology. How is it possible for God to *become*, to enter fully into time as One who is subjected to the limitations of human life in this world, without undergoing any *essential* (i.e., ontological) change? The answer to this question had already been provided for in Barth's doctrine of election (as we shall

6. CD IV/1:181.

see momentarily). Here, in the context of his doctrine of reconciliation, he merely set forth the implications of his earlier teaching. The incarnation of the Word, he says, does not give rise on the ontic level to a rift in God "between His being and essence in Himself and His activity and work as Reconciler of the world created by Him."[7] Now, the crucial interpretive question to be raised here is: How does Barth intend us to take this claim? Does he merely wish to say that the activity of God the Reconciler is the perfect expression of the divine essence (so that essence precedes act as the ground of the latter)? Or is he suggesting that the activity of God the Reconciler is in some sense (yet to be specified) *constitutive* of the divine essence (so that which God is essentially is itself constituted by an eternal act of Self-determination for becoming incarnate in time—in which case eternal divine action would ground divine essence)? Either reading would make sense of the claim that God undergoes no change on the ontic level in becoming incarnate in time. So which of them is correct? I will return to this question in concluding this subsection. It is sufficient here to observe that Barth's fundamental thesis—in accordance with which "Jesus Christ" is made to be the Subject of election—would certainly seem to require the latter reading. But however this turns out, what is clear is that Calvin's version of the *extra Calvinisticum* leaves Barth worried about the supposition of an indeterminate state of being in the life of the Logos above and prior to the determination to enter time and become human. As we shall now see, Barth's worries here were well founded and led to his departure from Calvin's doctrine of predestination.

Barth's claim that Jesus Christ is the Subject of election carried with it a massive correction of the classical Reformed doctrine of predestination. For classical Reformed theology, the decree to elect some human beings and to reject others (i.e., election and reprobation) *precedes* the decree to effect election through the provision of a Mediator (viz., Jesus Christ). But if this logic holds, then what it means is that who or what the Logos is in and for himself (as the Subject of election) is *not* controlled by the decision to become Mediator in time, that the identity of this Logos is, in fact, *already established* prior to the eternal act of Self-determination by means of which the Logos *became* the *Logos incarnandus*. And if all this were true, then the decision to assume flesh in time could result only in something being added to that already complete identity—an addition which has no effect upon what he is essentially. Being the Redeemer, in this view, tells us nothing about who or what the Logos is in and for himself. It is merely a role which he plays, something that he does; but what he does in time has no significance for his eternal being. The question which such a view raises in dramatic form is this: How coherent can one's affirmation of the deity of Jesus Christ be if his being as Mediator is only accidentally related to what he is as Logos in and for himself? Is Jesus Christ "fully God" or not?

7. *CD* IV/1:184.

188

Calvin's mistake was not simply that he understood predestination to entail a pretemporal division of the human race into two camps. This is only his most conspicuous error. But the root of the difference between Calvin and Barth lies at a much deeper level—at the level of divine ontology. The electing God, Barth argues, is not an unknown *x*. He is a God whose very being—already in eternity—is determined, defined, by what God reveals himself to be in Jesus Christ, namely, a God of love and mercy towards the whole human race. This is what Barth means for us to understand when he says that Jesus Christ is the Subject of election.

We are now in a position to grasp the significance of the material content of Barth's doctrine of election. The content of God's gracious election is the covenant of grace. The eternal act of establishing a covenant of grace is an act of Self-determination by means of which God determines to be God, from everlasting to everlasting, in a covenantal relationship with human beings and to be God in no other way. This is not a decision for mere role-play; it is a decision which has ontological significance. What Barth is suggesting is that election is the event in God's life in which God assigns to himself the being he will have for all eternity. It is an act of Self-determination by means of which God chooses in Jesus Christ love and mercy for the human race and judgment (reprobation) for himself. Choosing reprobation for himself in Jesus Christ means subjecting himself as the incarnate God to the human experience of death—and not just to any death but to spiritual death in God-abandonment. "The meaning of the incarnation is plainly revealed in the question of Jesus on the cross: 'My God, my God, why hast thou forsaken me?'"[8] Thus, ultimately, the reason ontology is very much to the fore in Barth's thinking is that *the death of Jesus Christ in God-abandonment, precisely as a human experience, is understood by Barth to be an event in God's own life.* And yet Barth also wants to insist that when God gives himself over in this way to our contradiction of God and the judgment which falls upon it, God does not give himself away. God does not cease to be God in becoming incarnate and dying in this way. God takes this human experience into his own life and extinguishes its power over us. But God is not changed on an ontological level by this experience for the simple reason that God's being, from eternity, is determined as a being-for this event.

What we see in the collision between Calvin and Barth, then, is not simply a clash between two views of the *extent* of election. At the most fundamental level, it is a clash between a theologian working with what we might call an "essentialist ontology" and a theologian working with an "actualistic ontology." Calvin knows a mode of being or existence on the part of the *Logos asarkos* which is independent of his being/existence as Redeemer. Such a view presupposes an essentialist ontology in accordance with which the "essence"

8. *CD* IV/1:185.

of the Logos (or, as we might prefer, the "self-identical element" which makes the Logos to be the Subject that it is) is understood to be complete in itself apart from and prior to all actions and relations of that Subject. And the essence, in this view, is something hidden to human perception and, finally, unknowable.

Barth, too, knows of an "essence" (a self-identical element) in God, but for him "essence" is given in the act of electing and is, in fact, constituted by that eternal act. It is not an independent "something" that stands in back of all God's acts and relations. God's being, for Barth, is a being-in-act—first as a being-in-act in eternity and then, corresponding to that, as a being-in-act in time. Philosophically expressed, Barth's ontology is thus "actualistic" (i.e., being is actualized in the decision for activity in time). It would be even more accurate, however, to express Barth's ontology *theologically* as a "covenant ontology," since it is not in "relationality" in general that God's being is constituted but in a most concrete, particular relation. Most important, if the eternal being of God is constituted by his eternal act of turning towards the human race—if this is what God is "essentially"—then God's essence is not hidden to human perception. It is knowable because it is constituted by the act of turning towards us. God in himself *is* God "for us." Knowing God in this way, we can trust that the love and mercy towards the whole human race demonstrated in Jesus' subjection of himself to death on a cross is "essential" to God and that election is therefore universal in scope.

Is it Barth's view, then, that the incarnation of the "Son" (and the outpouring of the Holy Spirit) are *constitutive* of the being of God in eternity? We must be cautious in giving an answer. What is beyond question is that if we employ the word "constitutive" in interpreting Barth's position, we must take care not to confuse his position with Hegel's. Barth's critique of Hegel is well known.[9] First, the divine act of Self-differentiation, of positing an Other over against himself and then reconciling that Other to himself, is, for Hegel, a necessary rather than a free act. And this means that creation and reconciliation are both necessary for God—which completely undermines the graciousness of those activities. Second, ultimately, the process by means of which God comes to full consciousness of himself (becomes, i.e., Absolute Spirit) is indistinguishable from the process by means of which human beings come to consciousness of God. God comes to consciousness of himself in and through human consciousness of God. And this can mean only that God's being *becomes* (develops, unfolds) in and through the historical process. It also means—to apply this thought to the doctrine of the Trinity—that the act of Self-differentiation which "constitutes" the Trinity is a historical, "economic" act. The "immanent Trinity" is, in this view, a purely eschatological reality; it is the consequence of the

9. See Karl Barth, *Protestant Theology in the Nineteenth Century* (Valley Forge, PA: Judson, 1973), 384–421, esp. 418.

economy of God. Incarnation is constitutive of the divine being in a very bold sense indeed. The historicization of God here knows no limits.

Barth's view differs from Hegel's on all of these points. First, Barth holds that the incarnation (and with it creation and reconciliation) is a free act of God. Second (and as a consequence of the first decision), Barth maintains a very strict Creator/creature distinction. God does not need to "become" conscious of himself through the historical process; God is, prior to the creation, fully Self-conscious, perfectly fulfilled being. Third, and most important, the act of Self-differentiation by means of which the triune being of God is constituted is an eternal act which may not be collapsed into the historical act of incarnation. The immanent Trinity is complete, for Barth, in protology. It is not the consequence of the historical process. And here historicization finds its limit.

In what sense, then, is the incarnation of the "Son" and the outpouring of the Holy Spirit "constitutive" of the eternal being of God? In this sense only: as a consequence of the primal decision in which God assigned to himself the being he would have throughout eternity (a being-for the human race), God is already in pretemporal eternity—*by way of anticipation*—that which God would become in time. This is not to say that the incarnation is an eternal rather than a historical event. It is not to evacuate the incarnation of its historicity. It is to say, rather, that the being of God in eternity, as a consequence of the primal decision of election, is a being which looks forward. It is a being in the mode of anticipation. Herein we find the relative justification for the historicization which the doctrine of God underwent in the nineteenth century. History is significant for the being of God in eternity. But it is significant only because God freely chooses that it should be so. The limits of historicizing are located finally by Barth in the divine freedom.

In sum, to say that "Jesus Christ" is the Subject of election is to say that there is no *Logos asarkos* in the absolute sense of a mode of existence in the Second Person of the Trinity which is independent of the determination for incarnation, no "eternal Son" if this Son is seen in abstraction from the gracious election in which God determined and determines never to be God apart from the human race. The Second Person of the Trinity has a name and his name is Jesus Christ. Perhaps the most significant consequence of this move is that the immanent Trinity is made to be wholly identical in content with the economic Trinity. As Barth puts it: "We have consistently followed the rule, which we regard as basic, that statements about the divine modes of being antecedently in themselves cannot be different in content from those that are to be made about their reality in revelation. . . . The reality of God in His revelation cannot be bracketed by an 'only,' as though somewhere behind His revelation there stood another reality of God; the reality of God which encounters us in His revelation is His reality in all the depths of eternity."[10]

10. *CD* I/1:479.

And yet the distinction between the immanent and economic Trinities has also been shown to be a necessary one (it is the distinction between eternity and time which may not be eradicated).

Implications for the Doctrine of the Trinity: A Critical Correction

Throughout the exposition provided above, an unarticulated question hovered in the immediate background. We may now bring it more clearly to the light of day: what is the *logical* relation of God's gracious election to the triunity of God? We are not asking here about a chronological relation. Election is an eternal decision and, as such, resists our attempts to temporalize it, that is, to think of it in such a way that a "before" and an "after" are introduced into the being of God in pretemporal eternity. If election is an eternal decision, then it has never not taken place. No, we ask here about the logical relation of election and triunity. Which comes first logically? Which precedes and which follows? To pose this question is not simply to ask about the necessary order of human thinking about these states of affairs, since, for Barth, human thought must be conformed to the "actual order of things."[11] It is to ask about the relation of act and being in God, of will and "essence."

It should be noted that Barth never put the question to himself in this precise form—act and being, yes, but never with the specific content of election and Trinity. He should have but he did not. It is tempting to suggest that he did not do so because of the way in which his thought developed and changed. Barth's mature doctrine of election only began to unfold from 1936 on—which means, *after* he had completed his doctrine of the Trinity.[12] Logically, his mature view of election would have required the retraction of certain of his earlier claims about the relation of revelation and triunity, finding in them a far too open door to the kind of speculation his mature doctrine of election sought to eliminate. As an example of such claims, consider the following: "We are not saying . . . that revelation is the basis of the Trinity, as though God were the triune God only in His revelation and only for the sake of His revelation."[13] Of course, it would always remain true for Barth that God is triune in himself (in pretemporal eternity) and not just in his historical revelation. Were God

11. *CD* IV/1:45.

12. Space limitations will not allow me to enter here into the question of how Barth subjected his doctrine of election to a fairly massive material correction after hearing Pierre Maury's lecture on the subject at a meeting of the International Calvin Congress in 1936. It is, however, worth pointing out here that his earlier version—in accordance with which "election" and "reprobation" are descriptions of the faith or unbelief and every fresh event of revelation is greeted by individual human beings—represents an even more drastic "historicization" of the doctrine than his later version. For more on Barth's development in this area of doctrine, see Bruce L. McCormack, *Karl Barth's Critically Realistic Dialectical Theology: Its Genesis and Development, 1909–1936* (Oxford: Clarendon, 1995), 371–74, 455–63.

13. *CD* I/1:312.

triune *only* in his revelation, the immanent Trinity would collapse into the economic Trinity. But that God is triune *for the sake of his revelation*? How could Barth deny this without positing a mode of existence in God above and prior to God's gracious election—the very thing he accused Calvin of having done? How can he (or anyone else) *know* that God is triune in and for himself, in independence of his eternal will to be revealed? But Barth never, so far as I have been able to discover, corrected such statements. No retractions were ever offered.

The greatest obstacle, however, to putting Barth's failure to reconsider his ordering of Trinity and election down to his own development is that even after his mature doctrine of election was in place, he continued to make statements which created the space for an independent doctrine of the Trinity, a triune being of God which was seen as independent of the covenant of grace. For example, in the context of his treatment of the covenant of grace, Barth wrote,

> In this context we must not refer to the second "person" of the Trinity as such, to the eternal Son or the eternal Word of God *in abstracto*, and therefore, to the so-called *Logos asarkos*. What is the point of a regress to Him as the supposed basis of the being and knowledge of all things? In any case, how can we make such a regress? The second "person" of the Godhead in Himself and as such is not God the Reconciler. In Himself and as such He is not revealed to us. In Himself and as such He is not *Deus pro nobis*, either ontologically or epistemologically.[14]

Why is it "in *this* context" that we must not refer to the Second Person of the Trinity *in and for himself and as such*? What context could there possibly be which would justify speaking in this way? If Barth had stopped there, we might well think that the note of "in this context" had just been the result of a lapse in concentration. But unfortunately, the passage continues: "He [the second 'person' of the Godhead in Himself and as such] *is* the content of a necessary and important concept in trinitarian doctrine when we have to understand the revelation and dealings of God in the light of their free basis in the inner being and essence of God" (emphasis mine). The only conclusion I have been able to come to is that either Barth did not fully realize the profound implications of his doctrine of election for the doctrine of the Trinity or he shied away from drawing them for reasons known only to himself. Either way, in what follows I am going to register a critical correction against Barth, the goal of which will be to remove what I view as an inconsistency in Barth's thought.

The denial of the existence of a *Logos asarkos* in any other sense than the concrete one of a being of the Logos as *incarnandus*, the affirmation that Jesus Christ is the Second Person of the Trinity and the concomitant rejection of

14. *CD* IV/1:52.

free-floating talk of the "eternal Son" as a mythological abstraction—these commitments require that we see the triunity of God, logically, as a function of divine election. Expressed more exactly: the eternal act of Self-differentiation in which God is God "a second time in a very different way"[15] and a third time as well is *given in* the eternal act in which God elects himself for the human race. The *decision* for the covenant of grace is the ground of God's triunity and therefore of the eternal generation of the Son and the eternal procession of the Holy Spirit from Father and Son. In other words, the works of God *ad intra* (the trinitarian processions) find their ground in the *first* of the works of God *ad extra* (viz., election).[16] And this also means that eternal generation and eternal procession are willed by God; they are not natural to God if "natural" is taken to mean a determination of being which is fixed in advance of all actions and relations.[17]

Such a view of the relationship of God's election and his triunity is wholly compatible with Barth's understanding of the doctrine of the Trinity along the lines of a single Subject in three modes of being. God is God three times, in three different forms, in an eternal repetition of himself. But if I am right, then the doctrine of the Trinity might well have been subordinated, in the order of treatment, to the doctrine of election. Barth takes up the Trinity as the first part of his doctrine of revelation, as an answer to the question "Who is the God who reveals himself?" But as we have seen, the answer to this question must take election into consideration.[18] Election must not be postponed until after the Trinity and even after God's existence, nature, and

---

15. *CD* I/1:316, 324; *KD* I/1:334, 342.

16. Barth's position is the opposite: "Ontologically . . . the covenant of grace is already included and grounded in Jesus Christ, in the human form and human content which God willed to give His Word from all eternity" (*CD* IV/1:45). But what sense does it make to speak of the second "person" of the Trinity as "Jesus Christ" without respect to the covenant of grace? Has not Barth here opened the door wide to a *Logos asarkos* in the absolute sense?

17. This much finds some warrant in Barth's treatment of the eternal generation of the Son of God. He rejected John of Damascus's way of distinguishing eternal generation (as an act of nature) and creation (as an act of will), preferring instead the more nuanced reflections of Thomas Aquinas. "Thomas . . . explains that the begetting of the Son is certainly to be understood as an act of will in which God, in freedom of course, wills Himself and in virtue of this will of His is Himself. In this sense, identically indeed with God's being Himself, the begetting of the Son is also an act of will for here will and nature are one and the same" (*CD* IV/1:434). This formulation is excellent—though it has to be conceded that it takes its rise in Thomas on the basis of a very different ontology than the actualistic one called for by Barth's doctrine of election.

18. Hans Theodore Goebel rightly speaks of a "demand," arising out of Barth's claim that the doctrine of election addresses the question of who the Subject of revelation is, that the doctrine of the Trinity be "determined" by the doctrine of predestination ("Trinitätslehre und Erwählungslehre bei Karl Barth: Eine Problemanzeige," in *Wahrheit und Versöhnung: Theologische und philosophische Beiträge zur Gotteslehre*, ed. Dietrich Korsch and Hartmut Ruddies [Gütersloh: Gerd Mohn, 1989], 154). Though Goebel does not draw the conclusions which I have drawn here (especially as they touch upon the eternal processions), his reflections on the

194

attributes have been treated.[19] It may well be that the necessity of reordering his treatment was precisely what prevented Barth from raising the question in the form in which we are pushing it here. To acknowledge the question and its importance might well have forced upon him the necessity of "beginning again at the beginning" in a quite literal sense—which by this point in time was utterly unthinkable.

In stressing the material compatibility of Barth's doctrine of the Trinity with his mature view of election, we are faced with a final critical question, and in raising it we come full circle back to our starting-point in this essay. What sense does it make to speak of "Jesus Christ" as the Subject of election if in God there are not three individuals but one personality (one self-consciousness, one knowledge, one will)? What is clearly ruled out of court by Barth's doctrine of the Trinity is the seventeenth-century idea of a "covenant of redemption." "The conception of this inter-trinitarian pact as a contract between the persons of the Father and the Son is . . . open to criticism. Can we really think of the first and the second persons of the triune Godhead as two divine Subjects and therefore as two legal Subjects who can have dealings and enter into obligations with one another? This is mythology, for which there is no place in a right understanding of the doctrine of the Trinity as the doctrine of the three modes of being of the one God."[20] The Second Person of the Trinity is the "one divine I" a second time, in a different form—a form which is constituted by the anticipation of union with the humanity of Christ. If, then, this second form of the divine I is—again, logically—the function of God's gracious election of human beings, our problem might seem to be exacerbated all the more. How can the Second Person of the Trinity, understood in this way, participate in the decision which gives him his own distinctive mode of origination with its own distinctive *telos* in the historical incarnation (life, death, and resurrection of Jesus)?

In part, the conceptual difficulty we encounter here is the consequence of our inability as humans to comprehend the meaning of an eternal decision. We think of decisions as involving deliberation and therefore as involving a before and an after. First, there must be a subject; without a subject there can be no act. But this is to think all too anthropomorphically. This is to understand "decision" under the conditions of our own finite experience, which is structured by time as we know it. But God's gracious decision is an eternal one, and this means that the triunity of God cannot follow this decision in some kind of temporal sequence of events. The two things belong together because God is a Subject insofar as God gives himself (by an eternal act) his own being. We are only underscoring this point when we add that the "one divine I" is fully himself in

relation of election to Trinity move along the lines which I have suggested and, to that extent, provide important corroboration for the case I am making.

19. *CD* II/1.

20. *CD* IV/1:65; *KD* IV/1:69.

this second form (or "person") and that if he makes a decision in his first form, he (the One Subject) is necessarily making it in his second and third forms as well. Seen in this light, to speak of Jesus Christ as the Subject of election is simply to affirm the oneness of God in his three modes of being.

Jesus Christ: The Object of Election

Jesus Christ is not only the electing God. He is also the elect human. The covenantal relation established by God's eternal act of Self-determination is a relation with the man Jesus and with others only "in Him." Implied in this claim is the further thought that "true humanity" is the humanity realized in the history of Jesus of Nazareth.

The realization of the covenant of grace in time has the character of a history of encounters between God and a people chosen by God, a history which culminates in the relation which Jesus of Nazareth, as the Representative of all women and men, has with God. And what is the nature of this human relation to God as it is disclosed in Jesus of Nazareth? "Not My will, but Thine, be done." Jesus' relation to his Father finds its most characteristic expression in prayer. And it consists in following, obeying.[21] That this basic posture or attitude finds its corollary in the lordship of God is obvious. But God's rule as it is disclosed in Jesus Christ betrays no "autocratic Self-seeking." It is, rather, "a Self-giving to the creature."[22] The election of Jesus, as the election of the humanity which exists in union with the Logos, is an election to a sharing in the suffering of judgment and wrath which God has eternally appointed for himself for the sake of human redemption. We falsify the situation of judgment, however, if we regard God's judgment as having been executed on a mere human being. It is the God-human in his divine-human unity who is subjected to this suffering.

But if Self-giving is the chief characteristic of God's rule, then it is not surprising to find that the rule of God does not exclude a genuine autonomy on the part of the creature. To say that Jesus of Nazareth is subjected by God to the suffering of wrath and judgment is true, but it is not the whole truth. In *free* obedience to the will of his Father, Jesus subjects himself to this suffering. We falsify the situation of judgment if we think of it as an event between "God and God."[23] It is the God-*human* in his divine-human unity who is the Subject of this suffering.

> The man Jesus is not a mere puppet moved this way and that by God. He is not a mere reed used by God as the instrument of His Word. The man Jesus prays.

21. CD II/2:177.
22. CD II/2:178.
23. This is the position of Jürgen Moltmann, *The Crucified God: The Cross of Christ as the Foundation and Criticism of Christian Theology* (New York: Harper & Row, 1974), 241–49.

He speaks and acts. And as He does so He makes an unheard of claim, a claim which makes Him appear the victim of delusion and finally brings down upon Him the charge of blasphemy. He thinks of Himself as the Messiah, the Son of God. He allows Himself to be called *Kyrios*, and, in fact, conducts Himself as such. He speaks of His suffering, not as a necessity laid upon Him from without, but as something He Himself wills.[24]

Seen in the light of God's Self-giving and the freedom of Jesus' obedience unto death, Barth concludes that

the perfection of God's giving of Himself to man in the person of Jesus Christ consists in the fact that far from merely playing with man, far from merely moving or using him, far from dealing with him as an object, this Self-giving sets man up as a subject, awakens him to genuine individuality and autonomy, frees him, makes him a king, so that in his rule the kingly rule of God Himself attains form and revelation. How can there be any possible rivalry here, let alone usurpation? How can there be any conflict between theonomy and autonomy? How can God be jealous or man self-assertive?[25]

Genuine freedom as it is realized in Jesus is not a freedom from God but a freedom for God (and, with that, a freedom for other human beings). "To the creature God determined, therefore, to give an individuality and autonomy, not that these gifts should be possessed outside Him, let alone against Him, but for Him and within His Kingdom; not in rivalry with His sovereignty but for its confirming and glorifying."[26]

Parenthetically, we may observe that Barth's reflections here have enormous consequences for the philosophical conundrum of how to relate divine omnipotence and human freedom. That divine sovereignty and human freedom are compatible realities, that they belong to such different planes of reality that they cannot possibly compete, is not something that can finally be demonstrated philosophically (by philosophical "compatibilism"). The demonstration of the truth of "compatibilism" is strictly theological. It is found in the history of Jesus' free obedience to the will of his Father. "Omnipotence" may not be defined in abstraction from the event in which God gives himself to rejection, judgment, and wrath. By the same token, human "freedom" may not be defined in abstraction from Jesus' freedom for self-surrender to these realities for the sake of redeeming the whole of the human race. The unity of the two is finally christological; it is the unity of the one God-human in his divine-human unity.

If now we take a step back from this consideration of the historical realization of the covenant of grace to inquire into its eternal ground, what we

24. *CD* II/2:178–79.
25. *CD* II/2:179.
26. *CD* II/2:178.

find is that "double predestination" is not eliminated by Barth. It is simply reconfigured. "There are two sides to the will of God in the election of Jesus Christ. And since this will is identical with predestination, from the very first and in itself it is a double predestination."[27] God's eternal will is for fellowship with fallen, sinful human beings. "When God of His own will raised up man to be a covenant-member with Himself, when from all eternity He elected to be one with man in Jesus Christ, He did it with a being which was not merely affected by evil but actually mastered by it."[28] Predestination is "double" because, in choosing himself for the sinful creature, God was choosing reprobation, perdition, and death for himself and mercy, grace, and life for human beings. God, as Barth puts it, "decreed His own abandonment."[29] He "declared Himself guilty of the contradiction against Him in which man was involved; . . . He took upon Himself the rejection which man deserved; . . . He tasted Himself the damnation, death and hell which ought to have been the portion of fallen man."[30] That God ordained himself for this in pretemporal eternity means that Jesus Christ "is the Lamb slain from the foundation of the world. . . . The *crucified* Jesus is the 'image of the invisible God.'"[31] Equally important, however, is what this "double predestination" means for "true humanity." To *exist* in covenantal relationship to God means the exaltation of the human. "The portion which God willed and chose for him [i.e., for humankind] was an ordination to blessedness"—blessedness which consists in the *free* attestation to the overflowing of God's glory in which humanity is given a share.[32] Here again, this is a christologically grounded claim. *The* "royal" human is Jesus Christ.[33] In his human life, the realization of what God has ordained for all occurred.

The election of Jesus Christ to be the "royal" human, to inaugurate a new humanity under the conditions of the old, carries with it an implied human ontology which corresponds to what we saw before in relation to divine ontology. For Barth, human ontology, too, is "covenantal ontology." To the act of self-determination in which God chose himself for us there corresponds an act of human self-determination in which Jesus chose himself for God and other humans and then, and on this basis, we too choose ourselves for God and others. True humanity is realized in us where and when we live in the posture of prayer. Where this occurs, that which we "are" corresponds to that which we have been chosen to be. There true humanity is actualized by faith and in obedience.

27. CD II/2:162.
28. CD II/2:163.
29. CD II/2:168.
30. CD II/2:164.
31. CD II/2:123.
32. CD II/2:168–69.
33. See CD IV/2:154–264.

Of course, it should be added that the *freedom* which is proper to the act of human self-determination in and through which true humanity is actualized means that we may also choose against God's ordination and thereby against our true selves. We may, in fact, continue—even after having been granted a share in revelation—to live in disobedience, to live as those who are reprobate. But to the extent that we do this, we falsify the true meaning of our being and existence. We attempt to do that which is objectively impossible, to expose ourselves to a threat which has "already been executed and consequently removed."[34]

To conclude, insofar as true humanity is realized only in the *act* of faith and obedience, "covenantal ontology" is actualistic on the human side as well. Here too a certain "historicization" has occurred—a Barthian version, to be sure, but historicization nevertheless. Barth has employed historical categories (categories of lived existence) to overcome the essentialistic treatment of classical theological anthropology.

Conclusion

In his famous 1951 book on Barth's theology, Hans Urs von Balthasar concluded that Barth had not been able to eliminate the "analogy of being" after all; indeed, the "analogy of faith" as taught by him required an "analogy of being" to complete it.

> If revelation is centered in Jesus Christ, there must be by definition a periphery to this center. Thus, as we [Roman Catholics] say, the order of the Incarnation presupposes the order of creation, which is not identical with it. And, because the order of creation is oriented to the order of the Incarnation, it is structured in view of the Incarnation; it contains images, analogies, as it were, dispositions, which in a true sense are the presuppositions for the Incarnation. For example, interhuman relationships—between man and woman or between friends—are a true presupposition for the fact that Jesus can become our brother. It is *because* man is a social being that he is capable in the first place of entering into a covenant with God, as God intended. And *this* natural order is for its part only possible on the basis of God's interpersonal nature, his triune nature, of which the human being is a true image.[35]

Von Balthasar is right to find an "analogy of being" in Barth, but he is right for all the wrong reasons. That the order of the incarnation presupposes the order of creation, that Jesus can become our brother because human being is

---

34. CD II/2:346.

35. Hans Urs von Balthasar, *The Theology of Karl Barth*, trans. Edward T. Oakes (San Francisco: Ignatius, 1992), 163.

199

by nature (i.e., as created) interpersonal, and that humans are able to enter into a covenant with God only because of their (inherent?) sociality—all of these claims give expression to an "analogy of being" which remained throughout Barth's life utterly foreign to his thinking. But there is a true "analogy of being" in Barth's thought which was first adumbrated as the predicate of the divine *act* of relating to the human creature[36] and which was then given concreteness in the doctrine of election set forth in *CD* II/2. "Analogy of being," understood in Barthian terms, is an analogy between an eternal divine act of Self-determination and a historical human act of self-determination and the "being" (divine and human) which is given in each. Human being in the act of faith and obedience in response to the covenant of grace corresponds to the being of the gracious God; this is the shape of the analogy. Barth's conflict with the Roman Catholic version was and always remained a conflict between his own covenant ontology and the essentialist ontology presupposed by the Catholic tradition, which von Balthasar's thought continued to embody. To that extent, it was also a conflict between a modern and, in its way, "historicized" mode of reflection on the being-in-act of God, on the one hand, and traditional theism, on the other. Were this basic difference to be grasped, ecumenical dialogue might well find a new ground for its future.

---

36. Karl Barth, *The Holy Spirit and the Christian Life: The Theological Basis of Ethics* (1929), trans. R. Birch Hoyle with a foreword by Robin W. Lovin (Louisville: Westminster/John Knox, 1993), 5: "If creature is to be strictly understood as a reality willed and placed by God in distinction from God's own reality, that is to say, as the wonder of a reality which by the power of God's love, has a place and a persistence alongside God's own reality, then the continuity between God and it (the true *analogia entis*, by virtue of which he, the uncreated Spirit, can be revealed to the created spirit)—this continuity cannot belong to the creature itself but only to the Creator *in his relation* to the creature."

8

Karl Barth's Historicized Christology

Just How "Chalcedonian" Is It?

It has become common in recent English-language Barth scholarship to describe Barth's Christology as "Chalcedonian."[1] It is my intention in this essay to subject this characterization to critical scrutiny. My thesis is that such a characterization has far more validity for the christological material found in CD I/2 than it does for the material found in the later doctrine of reconciliation. The reason for this development has everything to do with the

---

This essay was originally published in a slightly different form under the title "Barths Grundsätzlicher Chalcedonismus?" in *Zeitschrift für dialektische Theologie* 18 (2002): 138–73. Reprinted by permission. In winter semester 2002–2003, Eberhard Jüngel brought to a close his ordinary professorship in systematic theology and philosophy of religion at the University of Tübingen, a position which he had held with great distinction since 1969. In honor of his many great contributions to theology "after Barth," I gladly dedicate this essay to him.

1. Most unguardedly, Thomas F. Torrance, *Karl Barth: Biblical and Evangelical Theologian* (Edinburgh: T&T Clark, 1990), 169 and esp. 198–201; more critically, George Hunsinger, "Karl Barth's Christology: Its Basic Chalcedonian Character," in *Disruptive Grace: Studies in the Theology of Karl Barth* (Grand Rapids: Eerdmans, 2000), 131–47. I, too, have been found on this path—most recently in an essay I completed in autumn 2001; see Bruce L. McCormack, "The Ontological Presuppositions of Barth's Doctrine of the Atonement," in *The Glory of the Atonement: Biblical, Historical and Practical Perspectives*, ed. Frank A. James III and Charles E. Hill (Downers Grove, IL: InterVarsity, 2004), 346–66. In that essay I spoke of Barth's "historicized Chalcedonianism" (356). By this I meant that Barth's later Christology preserves all the theological values resident in the Chalcedonian formula and is, to this extent, faithful to the witness of that formula. That much I can certainly still say. But the question I wish to pose here (as much to myself as to anyone else) is whether Barth's later Christology does not so much constitute a revision of the meaning of the terms employed in the formula as it does the substitution of an altogether different ontology which makes continued use of the term "Chalcedonian" misleading as applied to him.

change which took place in Barth's doctrine of election in *CD* II/2. Prior to that change, where Barth took up and affirmed the Chalcedonian formula, he all too easily lapsed into thinking, for long stretches, in terms of the largely Platonic ontology which undergirded the formula—a move which was not easily reconciled with the antimetaphysical character of his actualistic construal of all divine-human relations elsewhere. After the change, Barth began to develop the outlines of a more thoroughly actualistic ontology which supplanted the traditional categories of "person," "natures," Godhead, and so on.[2] That there is considerable continuity on the level of interests and concerns in Barth's construction of Christology before and after this shift is not, of course, to be denied. But the development is sufficiently significant on the level of the precision of his ontological commitments that it would be a mistake to simply draw now from *CD* I/2 and now from the doctrine of reconciliation in *CD* IV/1–3 in elaborating a unified, synthetic picture of Barth's doctrine of the "person" of Christ without considerable qualification. It is therefore not without justification that Eberhard Jüngel has suggested that Barth's doctrine of reconciliation constitutes "at one and the same time a great recapitulation and a revision of Barth's entire theology."[3]

A close analysis of this development and the reasons for it will also make clearer the motives lying behind the architectonic of the doctrine of reconciliation. It is well known that the later Barth eliminates the classical distinction of loci on the "person" and the "work" of Christ, that he integrates the "two natures" doctrine with that of the "two states," and that he uses the "threefold office" of Christ to order the material which would classically have been treated under the headings of "divine nature," "human nature," and the "unity" of the two, respectively. One of my goals, then, is to make clear the reasons for this architecture and the effect which it had on Barth's relationship to early-church Christology.

In what follows, I will begin with the Chalcedonian definition. The second section will treat the Christology of *CD* I/2 in conversation with Chalcedonian orthodoxy. The next section will assess the impact of Barth's revision of the

---

2. *CD* IV/1:127; cf. *KD* IV/1:139: "The Christ of Nicaea and Chalcedon in itself and as such would be and is quite naturally a being which—even if we should succeed in explaining its peculiar structure conceptually in a more or less consistent and illuminating fashion—could not possibly be proclaimed and believed as the One who acts historically, as the One whom the Christian Church has in fact everywhere and in all times proclaimed and believed under the name Jesus Christ, because the concepts employed were necessarily timeless and removed from history (person, nature, Godhead, humanity, etc.). . . . However important it might seem when taken by itself, an abstract doctrine of the person of Christ is an empty form in which that which is to be said of Jesus Christ cannot possibly be said" (the translation is, in this case, my own).

3. Eberhard Jüngel, "Einführung in Leben und Werk Karl Barths," in *Barth-Studien* (Zurich and Cologne: Benziger; Gütersloh: Gerd Mohn, 1982), 53. Jüngel does not himself offer an explanation for this comment, and yet, for reasons that will be made clear, it must be regarded as resting on sound insight.

doctrine of election on the evolution of his Christology. And the final section will treat the later, mature Christology of *CD* IV/1–2; it will also provide a final answer to the question of the extent to which Barth's Christology may rightly be described as "Chalcedonian."

The Chalcedonian Formula

It is sometimes said that the bishops at Chalcedon did not give a decisive victory to either the party of Cyril of Alexandria or the party of Nestorius of Constantinople, whose controversy led to the calling of that great council. While there is *some* truth in this claim, it also has to be said that although the formula which the council advanced qualified Cyril's position in some significant ways, it did grant him the ultimate victory where the truly decisive issues were concerned. That this is so on the level of intention is seen in the council's readiness to uphold the orthodoxy of the council of Ephesus (AD 431), "whose leaders of most holy memory were Celestine of Rome and Cyril of Alexandria";[4] its condemnation of those who would deny that Mary is *theotokos* (the "God-bearer");[5] and its acceptance of "the synodical letters of the blessed Cyril, pastor of the church in Alexandria, to Nestorius and to the Orientals, as being well-suited to refuting Nestorius' mad folly."[6] Even more important, however, it is seen on a substantive level in the wording of the decree on Christology itself.

The council affirmed "one and the same Christ, Son, Lord, only-begotten, acknowledged in two natures [ἐν δύο φύσειν] which undergo no confusion, no change, no division, no separation; at no point was the difference between the natures taken away through the union, but rather the property of both natures is preserved and comes together into a single person and a single subsistent being [εἰς ἓν πρόσωπον καὶ μίαν ὑπόστασιν συντρεχούσης]."[7] What is decisive in this formulation, where the controversy which initiated it is concerned, is not so much the "two natures" (which did succeed in qualifying Cyril's position) as it is the attempt to find the unity of the two natures in the singularity of the "person" or *hypostasis* in whom the being and existence of both is grounded, a "person" who is immediately identified as "one and the same

---

4. Norman P. Tanner, *Decrees of the Ecumenical Councils* (Washington, DC: Georgetown University Press, 1990), 1:84.

5. Ibid. The Council also condemns those who "mindlessly" imagine "that there is a single nature of the flesh and the divinity"—language that can be found in closely related forms in the writings of Cyril. But given that the council regularly refers to Cyril as "blessed," it is clear that they did not find in his formulations sufficient evidence to link him to the errors of Eutyches—who was condemned by name (ibid., 1:85)—as one might easily have expected.

6. Ibid., 1:85.

7. Ibid., 1:86.

only-begotten Son, God, Word, Lord Jesus Christ."[8] In other words, the unity of divine and human in Jesus Christ is wrongly conceived where it is thought of along the lines of the union of two distinct persons. The unity is, rather, explained in terms of the singularity of the "person" (or as we might say today, "subject") in whom are grounded two distinct "natures." It is the affirmation of a singularity of "person," and its identification with the divine Word, above all, which grants the victory to Cyril's party.

I should add that the language employed here was ill-suited to the purposes of the writers in one respect. The council did not really intend to speak of a union of two "natures" as its language suggests; it was not the divine "nature" which was incarnated but the Logos, the Second Person of the Trinity. So what is brought together is actually, in the strictest sense, the Logos and a human "nature." The divine "nature" was thought to be proper to the Logos as such, of course. But since, in this understanding, it is something he shares with the Father and the Holy Spirit (who are not incarnated), one cannot rightly say that it is the divine "nature" that is incarnated.[9]

Finally, it is not altogether clear what was intended by "human nature." Although the creed had already affirmed, at an earlier point, that the *result* of the incarnation was "one and the same Son, our Lord Jesus Christ . . . the same truly God and truly man, of a rational soul and a body," thereby affirming that Jesus Christ was an individual man, here, where the focus is the *act* of incarnation, the *becoming* of the incarnate One, the language employed is the ambiguous phrase "human nature." The language could be taken in a generalizing direction, in which case it would mean something like "manhood." The intent would in this case be to underscore the universal significance of the reconciling work of Christ. Or it could be taken in an individualized sense: a man.[10] Given that the latter sense might well have seemed, in the eyes of many, to entail adoptionism, it seems likely that it was the former sense that was intended—which would mean that here, too, it is the Alexandrian reading of the formula which is to be preferred.

We may depict the results of the Chalcedonian formula diagrammatically in the following way:[11]

should'nt this be flipped

DN   HN

P (Logos)

8. Ibid.

9. Christopher Stead, *Philosophy in Christian Antiquity* (Cambridge: Cambridge University Press, 1994), 210.

10. The analysis of possible meanings along the lines of "generalizing" and "individualizing" tendencies is taken from Stead; see ibid., 203–4. Seen in context, however, he is reflecting on the meaning of ἄνθρωπος whereas I am reflecting here on the meaning of "human nature."

11. In this diagram, P = person, DN = divine nature, HN = human nature.

Before departing from the Chalcedonian formula, it should be noted that it left two rather important issues unresolved. The first is that of the *communicatio idiomatum*. Had the council chosen to speak to this issue, it would undoubtedly have done so along the lines suggested by the reigning soteriological paradigm of the time. The reigning paradigm was that of *theōsis*, or "divinization." The fundamental problem confronting the human race was not conceived of in this soteriology as primarily moral (i.e., the need for forgiveness) but as ontic (i.e., the need to overcome the corruption of being which leads to death). The solution to this problem was explained in terms of the Logos infusing life into human "nature," restoring and re-creating it, and thereby overcoming the threat of nonbeing. But such a soteriology would logically require that the Logos be understood as a subject who acts upon his human "nature" as his object. And this leads us to the second issue. If we were to ask who is the Subject who performs the work of redemption, the answer given in the soteriology of the bishops is the Logos *simpliciter*—that is, two natures *in* one person (identified as the Logos). Logically, the basic idea that the divine Word is hypostatically united with a full and complete human nature could also suggest that the subject is the *God-human* in his divine-human unity, but this answer could be consistently maintained only where two values were protected. First, any formulation of it would have to be constructed in such a way as to allow the full and free cooperation of the human element in the work of the divine. Second, it would have to uphold the first value without dissolving the unity of the person. But in the historical context in which the Chalcedonian dogma was elaborated, there were two obstacles standing in the way of any formulation which would accomplish these twin aims. The first, as we have already seen, is the soteriology presupposed. There is something residually Apollinarian even in Cyril, in his tendency to make the Logos the directive principle in the human nature. The other obstacle was the abstract metaphysical understanding of divine immutability presupposed. For most, it was unthinkable that God should suffer and die. Suffering and death entail "change" and God cannot change. So there was a perceived need to assign suffering and death to the human "nature" alone.[12] Though such a move was well motivated (given that *some* understanding of divine immutability is mandated by the Christian doctrine of God), it was nonetheless deeply problematic. Certainly, suffering and death are deeply *human* experiences. But if these human experiences are not also the experiences of the divine Word, then the unity referred to in speaking of the subject who performs the work of redemption

---

12. Stead points out that so long as divine immutability is understood in absolute metaphysical terms, immutability can be secured only by understanding "all God's actions as new relationships which result from changes in other beings; to use Plato's illustration (*Theaet.* 155c), Socrates can remain unchanged and yet become smaller than Theaetetus because the young man outgrows him. . . . But this analogy deprives God's action of any personal character" (*Philosophy in Christian Antiquity*, 203).

(handwritten margin note: not if you grasp Cyril's conception of single subject)

as the "God-human in His divine-human *unity*" has been surrendered. The human "nature" is being made a subject in its own right, and a swing has occurred in the direction of the Nestorian "double Christ."

Ironically perhaps, both the Apollinarian and the Nestorian tendencies, however contrary their results, arise from the same source. Their source is a process of thought which "abstracts" the Logos from his human "nature" in order, by turns, now to make the human "nature" something to be acted upon by the Logos and now to make of that "nature" a subject in its own right in order to seal the Logos off hermetically from human experiences such as death. In both cases, the Logos has been "abstracted" from the human "nature" and made into an abstract metaphysical subject (the Logos *simpliciter*).

The solution to these problems would be found by Barth in the rejection of the abstract metaphysical subject of Chalcedon and in its replacement with an understanding of the Redeemer as a subject whose reality is constituted by a twofold *history* (the humiliation of God and the exaltation of the human). But he did not arrive at this solution all at once. He had to spend a long period of time in the school of the Chalcedonian fathers before he was able to find his way through to a new and different theological ontology (of the divine, of the human, and of the God-human). It was only in the doctrine of reconciliation that all of this finally came together. It is to the history of this development that I now turn.

Church Dogmatics I/2, §15

Barth's first foray into the problem of Christology within the bounds of the *Church Dogmatics* is found in the prolegomena under the general heading of the incarnation of the Word. Given that everything that is said about Christology here is said from the standpoint of the "objective reality of revelation," it might initially seem understandable that his focus should be on the incarnation of the Word of God rather than the life, death, and resurrection of Jesus Christ.[13] But here already, at the very outset of §15, an important difference between how Christology is handled here and how it would be handled in the later doctrine of reconciliation makes its presence felt. For here Barth tells us that there *has to be* a "special Christology," a special doctrine of "the Person of Jesus Christ," if Christology is to provide the controlling presuppositions of a church dogmatics (as ought to be the case, in his view).[14] Later, however, he would reject the effort to construct a "special Christology": "In the New Testament there are many christological statements both direct and indirect. But where do we find a special Christology?—a Christ in Himself, abstracted from

13. *CD* I/2:122.
14. *CD* I/2:122–23.

206

what He is amongst the men of Israel and His disciples and the world, from what He is on their behalf? Does He ever exist except in this relationship?"[15] Barth's answer to his rhetorical question is that the New Testament knows nothing of a *Christus an sich*. And the reason for this, ultimately, is that

> the being of Jesus Christ, the unity of being of the living God and this living man, takes place in the *event* of the concrete existence of this man. It is a being, but a being in a *history*. The gracious God is in this history, so is reconciled man, so are both in their *unity*. And what takes place in this history, and therefore in the being of Jesus Christ as such, is reconciliation. Jesus Christ is not what He is—very God, very man, very God-man—in order as such to mean and do and accomplish something else which is reconciliation. Rather His being as God, as man, and as God-man consists in the completed act of the reconciliation of man with God.[16]

The being of Jesus Christ, in other words, is his work. It is his history. Because this is so, the "person of Christ" must not be taken up and considered in isolation from the "work of Christ" as was customary in the dogmatics of the older Protestant orthodoxy. The two must be thoroughly integrated.

I would suggest that the reason Barth could still hold out for a "special Christology" in *CD* I/2 is that the ontology which comes to expression in his treatment of the incarnation is, for the most part, the abstract metaphysical ontology which underwrote the Christology of the Chalcedonian Council. Granted, this lapse into metaphysical thinking is exceptional in Barth's theology even at this time. Already there were strong indications that he would like to revise this ontology.[17] But he was not yet in a position to do so in a consistent

---

15. *CD* IV/1:124.

16. *CD* IV/1:126–27. (Bromiley's translation has here been lightly revised, and the original italics restored to Barth's text.)

17. Already in his *Göttingen Dogmatics*, Barth could say, "The problem dealt with in a doctrine of the Reconciler and reconciliation is the problem of the antithesis of *God* and *man*. We were brought up against this problem not on the way of metaphysical speculation, but rather as we tried to think through the concepts of God and man under the presupposition of revelation. Can this relationship of God to man really be dealt with metaphysically, even if one substitutes for it the abstract formula 'divinity-humanity'? Can there be a more existential relation than this one, when one takes it seriously?" (Karl Barth, *Unterricht in der christlichen Religion*, vol. 3, *Die Lehre von der Versöhnung/Die Lehre von der Erlösung, 1925/1926*, ed. Hinrich Stoevesandt [Zurich: Theologischer Verlag, 2003], 31). In spite of the clear intention signaled in this passage, Barth was as yet unable to completely free himself from the absolute metaphysical subject of Chalcedon. This already announced itself in the priority assigned to the "person" of Christ over the "work" of Christ. "There would be no sense in speaking of the *munus triplex* if we had not already spoken of the hypostatic union. The One who would reestablish peace between *God* and *us*, who would secure *eternal life* for *us*, must be the same as God and the same as us, must be *true* God and *true* man" (ibid., 34). But the real problem lay in the fact that Barth's actualism reached only as far as the "natures" of Christ. He was not able as yet to push the antimetaphysical logic of his actualism back into the "person" of the Logos. And thus the

and thoroughgoing fashion—and would not be until he had carried through his massive revision of the doctrine of election in *CD* II/2.[18]

Barth organizes his presentation in three movements, corresponding to the three elements found in the central affirmation of John 1:14, "The Word became flesh." He begins with the Word ("very God") as the acting subject who unites himself to humanity. He then turns to a consideration of that which is united to the Word ("very man"). And he concludes with reflection on the action, the "becoming" of their union. Thus what we have before us is an account of the two "natures" in Christ which makes the unity of the two the problem to be resolved or, much rather, the mystery to be adored.

In the first place, the one who becomes man is "very God." "It is not the Godhead in itself and as such that was made flesh. For the Godhead does not exist at all in itself and as such, but only in the modes of being of the Father, the Son and the Holy Spirit. It is the Son or Word of God that was made flesh."[19] Moreover, it is the Word who is the active Subject of this "becoming." It is not a fate which befell him; the incarnation does not belong to the evolutionary possibilities resident in the world process. It is not the consequence of an

---

acting subject who accomplishes reconciliation is equated directly with the Logos, understood along the lines of an abstract metaphysical subject. "In this matter . . . only *God* can act, even if in human nature. . . . Therefore *unio personalis* or *hypostatica*, whereby under *persona* or *hypostasis* is to be understood exclusively: the Person of the Logos" (38). The "antithesis" in the relation between God and the human of which Barth wished to speak at this time came to expression only in the relation of the natures. The "overcoming" of the antithesis in which reconciliation between God and the human would consist takes place not in the relating of the natures but in the person of the Logos himself. "The *unio personalis* in the God-man stands *above*, not in, the dialectic of God and man" (52–53).

18. In the aftermath of the publication of Barth's *Die christliche Dogmatik* in 1927, Rudolf Bultmann wrote him a letter in which he offered an explanation for this vestigial attachment: "It seems to me that you are guided by a concern that theology should achieve emancipation from philosophy. You try to achieve this by ignoring philosophy. The price you pay for this is that of falling prey to an outdated philosophy. . . . Now if the critical work of philosophy . . . is ignored, the result is that dogmatics works with the uncritically adopted concepts of an older ontology. This is what happens in your case" (Rudolf Bultmann to Karl Barth, June 8, 1928, in *Karl Barth–Rudolf Bultmann Letters, 1922–1966*, ed. Bernd Jaspert, trans. Geoffrey W. Bromiley [Grand Rapids: Eerdmans, 1981], 39). In response, Barth insisted that he would never defend ignoring the work of philosophy as a matter of principle. But he noted, "It is also a fact that the defect of older theology was never clear to me at the point where Harnack's *Dogmengeschichte* lays its finger, that the Platonism or Aristotelianism of the orthodox was not a hindrance to my (shall we say apparently) perceiving what was at issue and therefore to adopting the older terminology into my own vocabulary without identifying myself with the underlying philosophy of the schools" (Karl Barth to Rudolf Bultmann, June 12, 1928, ibid., 41). Whether Barth could be completely successful in not identifying himself with the philosophy standing in back of ancient creedal formulas such as the Chalcedonian *at this stage of his development* is the question I wish to pose here. But his comment does tell us a great deal about his *intentions*.

19. *CD* I/2:132–33. (The standard English translation is here lightly revised.)

"inner necessity of human history or of a necessity belonging to the divine being or to the relationship of the Father, Son and Holy Spirit."[20] It is a free and sovereign act of the Word.

Thus far Barth has said nothing that he would not still have to say in his doctrine of reconciliation. But at this point he draws a conclusion which would later be rendered questionable. He says that God's "Word would still be his Word apart from this becoming, just as Father, Son and Holy Spirit would be none the less eternal God, if no world had been created."[21] Clearly, one of Barth's concerns in making this claim is that of insisting that the Word is not changed or transformed into a creature in his "becoming." Nor is the product of this "becoming" a third something between God and the human. Hence the immutability of the Word is a leading concern. His other concern here is to underscore the fact that there are an asymmetry and irreversibility in the relation of the Word to the flesh assumed. "The statement 'very God and very man' signifies an *equation*. But strictly speaking, this equation is *irreversible*. If it is reversed and Jesus is called not only very God who is very man, but also very man who is very God, in the second statement we must not neglect to add that it is so because it has pleased very God to be very man. The *Word* became flesh, and it is only in virtue of this becoming of His, which was quite freely and exclusively *His* becoming, that the *flesh* became Word."[22] Both of these concerns would be preserved in Barth's later treatments of the incarnation in *CD* IV/1–2. But there is something problematic, nevertheless, about the formulation which Barth has advanced here: the Word of God would still be the Word of God without the "becoming" that takes place in the incarnation. What this affirmation would seem to imply is that the being of the Word is something complete in itself without respect to the "becoming" which he would undergo in entering time. And the problem which this understanding poses very directly is that of *how* the Word could then "become" without undergoing change? That this was a major problem for Barth had to do, from his *Romans* period on, with his overwhelming preoccupation with the Godness of God in his Self-revelation: how can God reveal himself without ceasing to be God? We shall see in a moment that Barth has an answer to this question and that it is *not* the answer he would give in his doctrine of reconciliation.

Before departing from the "truly God" side of the equation, it should be noted that Barth sides with Cyril of Alexandria in the ancient controversy over Mary as *theotokos*—"God-bearer." He finds this affirmation to be necessary on the grounds that "He whom Mary bore was not something else, some second thing, in addition to His being God's Son. He who was born in time

20. *CD* I/2:135.
21. Ibid. (The standard English translation is here lightly revised.)
22. *CD* I/2:136. (The standard English translation is here lightly revised, and the original italics restored.)

is the very same who in eternity is born of the Father."[23] In taking this position, Barth's Christology was moving more visibly into the sphere of ideas advanced by the councils of Ephesus (431) and Chalcedon (451). The logic of this trend of thought lies in the direction of making the unity of the divine and human elements in Jesus Christ consist in the singularity of the person in whom each has its being and existence.[24] This trend is further strengthened as Barth turns to the *vere homo* side of the equation.

Barth begins his treatment of the *vere homo* with the assertion that in becoming man, the Word acquired a share in our human essence and existence. And this means that "everything ascribable to man, his creaturely existence as an individually unique unity of body and soul in the time between birth and death, can now be predicated of God's eternal Son as well."[25] The predication of all that is proper to the human Jesus to the eternal Son would, logically, make the Word subject to human experiences—including suffering. Whether Barth can say this with any real consistency at this stage of his thinking is a question to which we will return.

Barth comes closest to Cyril and to the Alexandrian contribution to the Chalcedonian formula in what he says next. That the Word became "flesh" does not mean, in the first instance, that he became *a* man, a concrete individual. He became this, too, but this is not the primary significance of the word "flesh" according to Barth.[26] That the Word became "flesh" means that what stood over against the Word in the event of his becoming was the sheer potentiality of human being and existence, a possibility to which he gave reality in the act of becoming human.[27] Thus what the Word took up was humanity as a universal possibility, thereby actualizing this possibility in a concrete individual—a very Alexandrian way of reading the Chalcedonian formula.

It follows quite naturally from all of this that Barth would also affirm the ancient doctrine of the *anhypostasia* and *enhypostasia* of the human "nature" of Jesus Christ. "In that the Son of God made His own this one definite possibility of human essence and existence and gave it reality, *this* man *became* and he, the Son of God, became *this* man. This man was therefore never real in and for himself and therefore too, in that the Son of God became this man, no other, no second, in Jesus Christ next to the

---

23. CD I/2:138. So necessary is this affirmation that Barth makes the affirmation of the *theotokos* a test of whether one has properly understood the incarnation of the Word (ibid).

24. CD I/2:139. Barth explicitly joins Cyril in anathematizing the Nestorian distinction of a "double Christ."

25. CD I/2:147.

26. CD I/2:149: "If we allow ourselves to say that He became flesh, we must note that primarily and of itself 'flesh' does not imply a man, but human essence and existence, human kind and nature, humanity, *humanitas*, that which makes a man man as opposed to God, angel or animal."

27. Ibid.

Son of God."[28] *Anhypostasis* and *enhypostasis* are, as Barth understands it, complementary terms. *Anhypostasis* makes the negative, antiadoptionistic point that this human "nature" had no independent existence alongside the Word. *Enhypostasis* is the positive corollary. It says that this human nature acquired its existence in the existence of God, in the mode of being of the eternal Son.[29] The being of this human "nature" is ontologically *localized*, its existence is an "in-existence" (*en-hypostasis*) *in* the Word. Thus, the "Person of the union," the *hypostasis* in which both divine "nature" and human "nature" have their being and existence, is the person of the Logos, the divine Word. And if the "Person of the union" is identified directly with the divine Word, then it follows that whatever is done in and through the human nature must be done by the divine Word as the Subject of those acts. And this is precisely what Barth says: "God Himself in person is the Subject of a real human being and acting."[30]

It is here that Barth slips most visibly into the substantialist form of ancient metaphysics where his Christology is concerned. What is common to substantialist forms of ancient metaphysics as applied to the problem of an ontology of the person is the thought that what a person "is" is something that is complete in and for itself, apart from and prior to all the decisions, acts, and relations that make up the sum total of the lived existence of the person in question. In other words, a wedge is driven between "essence" and "existence" in such a way that whatever happens on the level of existence has no effect on that which a person is essentially. Applied to the christological problem as envisioned by the ancients, this trend of thought has the consequence of making it impossible to understand anything that happens in and through the human "nature" as having any consequences for that which the "Person of the union" (viz., the Logos) is essentially. "Movement" or "change" is located on the level of existence, where it can have no significance for that which the divine Word "is."

We are not surprised, then, when, under the third heading of John 1:14 (the "becoming" of the Word), Barth should be more concerned to *distinguish* the becoming of the Word from all "becoming" known to us than to understand the becoming of the Word in terms of the "becoming" (and existence) of the human Jesus. "In the sense of the concept familiar to us, we can therefore assert 'becoming' only of the human being in order by that very means to give expression to the inconceivable becoming of the divine Word."[31] So concerned is he at this time to uphold the Godness of God in his Self-revelation that Barth prefers to paraphrase John 1:14, "The Word became flesh," with "the Word assumed flesh."

28. *CD* I/2:150. (The standard English translation is here lightly revised, and the original italics restored.)
29. *CD* I/2:163.
30. *CD* I/2:165.
31. *CD* I/2:160.

Looking back at the problem caused by the incarnation for the concept of divine immutability (a problem which we left unresolved earlier), we now see that Barth has resolved the problem by maintaining an ontological distinction between the divine and the human, such that what takes place in the human nature has no clear ontological significance for the divine Word. Against his earlier claim that God is the Subject of a *real* human being and acting, he has virtually rendered this claim null and void through his distinction between a becoming of the human nature and the becoming of the Word. The most that he can say is that the Word unites himself with this human "becoming" in an ineffable way. But, of course, this hesitation to ascribe "becoming" to the Word in a realistic sense comes at a high price, for it calls into question Barth's entire christological edifice (i.e., the insistence upon two natures whose unity consists in the *singularity* of Subject in whom both natures find their ontological ground). In spite of his explicit rejection of Nestorianism, Barth drifts unintentionally in that direction by making the human nature be a subject in its own right, a subject of its own becoming, thus setting up a "double Christ."

Now if we were to seek for the root of this inconsistency, we would immediately be taken back to the trinitarian background of the event of the incarnation, where the problem of substantialistic thinking first reared its head. God's Word would still be his Word even if the incarnation had never happened. Once Barth has committed himself to this thought, then the only possible way to handle the problem of divine immutability is the way he finally handled it, namely, by driving a wedge between what the divine Word truly is (in and for himself) and what he might seem to be (but is not!) through the verbal ascription to him of acts and experiences which are not really his own.

Now, for the sake of accuracy, it has to be said that this metaphysical moment in Barth's thinking was just that—a *moment* in what was otherwise an antimetaphysical mode of reflection. And it also has to be candidly admitted that such moments would not entirely disappear from his theology even after the change, which we shall discuss, in his doctrine of election. But later, in his doctrine of reconciliation, such moments function as a kind of limit-concept whose purpose is to point to the importance of the divine freedom. Here the metaphysical moment in question is functioning to provide an answer to the problem of divine immutability—and is doing so in terms of the logic of the abstract metaphysical subject.

In sum, in this section, I have tried to demonstrate two things. First, within the bounds of the *Church Dogmatics*, Barth's Christology was never more "Chalcedonian" than it is here in *CD* I/2. Barth holds to the basic formulation "two natures in one person," and he does so without offering any serious qualification to the philosophical ideas which generated this formula in the first place. The realistic-sounding claim that all that is proper to the human as human is rightly predicated of the eternal Son of God held forth the promise of a serious qualification of the Chalcedonian ontology in the direction of a more actualistic ontology.[32] But this was not a promise Barth was able to deliver on. At the end of the day, the predication is rendered merely verbal. And this does create problems for him—not least of which is the drift in the direction of Nestorianism. Second, the real source of all of these difficulties is tied up with the trinitarian claim that the identity of the divine Word would have been no different had he never been incarnated. The relation between the eternal Word and the incarnate Word has been rendered a theological problem of the highest order. What is at stake in the resolution of this problem is finally the deity of Word incarnate.

In concluding this section, it should be pointed out that the actualism which everywhere governed Barth's doctrine of revelation from the earliest years of the emergence of his dialectical theology might have forced him to a more thorough and consistently actualistic ontology if he had had the resources to think through the grounds of such an ontology. At this stage of his development, actualism is certainly present in all of Barth's descriptions of the divine-human *relation* established in revelation. But it has not yet been pushed back into the eternal being of God. It has not been integrated into the concept of the being of the Self-determining God. All of this would change when the ramifications of Barth's shift in the doctrine of election made themselves felt in *CD* II/2.

Christology in the Light of Election (*CD* II/2)

The differences between the Christology of *CD* I/2 and *CD* IV/1–2 are a function of a fairly dramatic change which his doctrine of election experienced in the period 1936–1942. To understand this change is also to understand the theological ontology which was presupposed by his later doctrine of reconciliation—as well as the distancing which then *had to occur* from the terms employed by the Chalcedonian formula.

The first stimulus to the elaboration of Barth's new understanding of election was provided by a lecture given by Pierre Maury at an International Calvin Congress meeting in Geneva in 1936.[33] But it should be noted that this lecture was only a stimulus. Maury did not simply hand Barth's later doctrine to him on a platter, so to speak, complete in all of its details. In the immediate aftermath of hearing Maury, Barth made a first attempt at a revision of his earlier doctrine of election and published it under the title *Gottes Gnaden-*

32. See above, n. 17.
33. See Bruce L. McCormack, *Karl Barth's Critically Realistic Dialectical Theology: Its Genesis and Development, 1909–1936* (Oxford: Clarendon, 1995), 455–58.

wahl.[34] This essay certainly constitutes a significant relocating and reordering of the doctrine. And yet, in one decisive respect, it too fell short of the fully developed doctrine which then emerged in *CD* II/2.[35]

In the *Göttingen Dogmatics*, Barth had correlated election and reprobation with the event in which a human individual is confronted by revelation. Revelation was at that time (and would continue to be) understood as indirect in nature; that is, God as the Subject of revelation conceals himself in a creaturely veil (the flesh of Jesus, the witness of Scripture, and proclamation based upon exegesis of the witness of Scripture). God's revelation takes place in hiddenness because God does not make himself to be directly identical with any medium of revelation. Thus, when an individual is confronted by such a revelation in concealment, a third factor must enter in if he or she is to "see" what is there to be "seen," and to "hear" what is there to be "heard." The Holy Spirit is this third factor.[36] The Holy Spirit must give to the would-be recipient of revelation the "eyes" and "ears" that are needed for revelation to reach its goal. Expressed less metaphorically, the Holy Spirit must grant to the would-be recipient of revelation faith and obedience. Where this happens, "election" takes place. Where it does not, where the flesh of Christ, Scripture, and proclamation remain utterly opaque and revelation does not reach its goal in the human individual, there "reprobation" takes place.[37] Such a view

34. This monograph first saw life as two lectures held in Debrecen and Klausenburg at the end of September and the beginning of October 1936. See Karl Barth, *Gottes Gnadenwahl*, Theologische Existenz heute 47 (Munich: Kaiser, 1936).

35. For the picture of the development of Barth's doctrine of election in the period 1936–1942 which I will here sketch in brief outline, I am indebted to the fine work of Matthias Gockel, "One Word and All Is Saved: Barth and Schleiermacher on Election" (PhD diss., Princeton Theological Seminary, 2002); published as *Barth and Schleiermacher on the Doctrine of Election* (Oxford: Oxford University Press, 2006).

36. Barth treats this problem at some length in his *Göttingen Dogmatics* in §7, "Der Glaube und der Gehorsam." Here he describes the work of the Holy Spirit as constituting the "subjective possibility of revelation" (Karl Barth, *The Göttingen Dogmatics: Instruction in the Christian Religion*, trans. Geoffrey W. Bromiley [Grand Rapids: Eerdmans, 1991], 1:168).

37. This is already made clear in the *Leitsatz* with which Barth opens §18, "Die Gnadenwahl":

If *veiling* is the content of God's unveiling and *unveiling* the meaning of His veiling, then the human is clearly placed under a twofold possibility which finds its ground in God. The *hiddenness* of God in His revelation might mean that with hearing ears we hear only offense or foolishness or nothing at all and therefore do not know God. In this case nothing special happens to us; without being aware of what it means we remain in contradiction, in guilt and need, and finally in the eternal damnation to which we have hopelessly fallen victim. Or else God's *revelation* in His hiddenness becomes, through the Holy Spirit, the basis of faith and obedience and therefore of the knowledge of God. Something special then happens to us, for the darkness in which we find ourselves becomes the judgment of *God*, but we also participate therewith in the *grace* of God and the hope of eternal salvation. In the first case we are passed by or rejected by God; in the second case we are elected or accepted by God." (Barth, *The Göttingen Dogmatics*, 1:440; Bromiley's translation is here lightly revised and the original italics restored)

of the revelation event is quite actualistic—and this is an element of Barth's thought that would not be changed. But in associating election with the revelation event, Barth had advanced a doctrine of election which was more nearly "pneumatocentric" than christocentric, historical rather than eternal, this-worldly rather than otherworldly. What changed as a consequence of Maury's lecture is that Barth now began the process of elaborating the doctrine on a new, christological foundation—thereby dissociating election from the event in which revelation is subjectively acknowledged.

Barth's initial step towards his new, christological foundation took place in *Gottes Gnadenwahl* and consisted in the correlation of election and reprobation with the crucifixion of Jesus.[38] Certainly, this step already meant a relocation of the doctrine, and it initiated a process of reordering its relationship to other doctrines. And yet the truly decisive move had not yet been made. At this point in time, Barth treated Jesus Christ only as the *object* of election and reprobation. Jesus Christ is made the reprobate human so that all others might be elect in him. In accepting God's judgment on sin in the event of the cross, Jesus Christ takes reprobation into his own life and, in doing so, makes it an impossibility for all others. This is what it means to say that Jesus Christ is the *object* of election and reprobation. What Barth was not yet in a position to say is that Jesus Christ is also the *subject* of election. This he did not learn from Maury; it was, as Gockel says, his own contribution.[39] At the time of giving the lectures which became *Gottes Gnadenwahl*, Barth could still speak of the eternal Son of God as the subject of election and the human nature as its object.[40] In *CD* II/2 he would integrate election and Christology in such a way that Jesus Christ (the God-human in his divine-human unity) would henceforth be understood as *both* the electing God and the elect human.

This is not the place for an extended discussion of Barth's new doctrine of election.[41] It will suffice for our purposes to highlight two aspects of this doctrine which are of relevance to a proper understanding of Barth's later Christology.

38. See Gockel, "One Word and All Is Saved," 201–2, 237; cf. idem, *Barth and Schleiermacher on the Doctrine of Election*, 160–61, 196.
39. Gockel, "One Word and All Is Saved," 202n28.
40. Ibid., 200n9. Gockel here cites in support of this contention the following statement (given in response to a question posed in Debrecen): "The logical relationship between the election of the man Jesus as the Son of God and the eternally divine Jesus Christ is this: the eternal Son of God is the *subject* of this election, the object is the *natura humana*." For the source of this statement, see Barth, *Gottes Gnadenwahl*, 46. The logic of this affirmation is, as Gockel rightly observes, supplanted in *CD* II/2, where Barth makes the person of Jesus Christ be the subject and the object of election.
41. For a more complete understanding of the interpretation of Barth's doctrine of election upon which the following observations depend, see ch. 7, "Grace and Being: The Role of God's Gracious Election in Karl Barth's Theological Ontology," in this volume.

First, the doctrine of election belongs to the doctrine of God because it is only in election that the divine Subject that is known, worshiped, and proclaimed in the church is fully defined. The eternal act of establishing a covenant of grace with humanity (which is the content of election) is an act of Self-determination by virtue of which God has elected to be God in the covenant of grace and to be God in no other way. This is not a decision for mere role-play; it is a decision with ontological significance. It is a free act in which God assigned to himself the being God would have for all eternity. It is thus an act of *Self*-determination. But it is also an act of Self-*limitation*. What takes place in election is that God chooses grace and mercy for the human race and reprobation (judgment, perdition, and death) for himself.[42] To choose reprobation for himself is an act of Self-limitation because it sets God on a path in which God's being will be concretely actualized in *humiliation*. We will return to a closer explication of this theme in the next section. For the moment it suffices to point out that one of the most significant consequences of Barth's new doctrine of election is that it makes God so much the Lord that he is even the Lord over his own "essence." For this reason, Barth would later assert that God is not by accident a suffering God but is so "essentially."[43] For the way of humiliation is the way of obedience which leads to a cross.

But we have yet to touch upon that which is most truly revolutionary in Barth's doctrine of election. All that we have said so far could be said abstractly of God and, if said abstractly, would fail to communicate the truth that Barth here thought himself to see. What is truly revolutionary—and this is my second point—is to be found in the assertion that *Jesus Christ* is the subject of election; *Jesus Christ* is the electing God. Why is this so revolutionary? If Barth had simply said that Jesus Christ is the *object* of election, it would have occasioned no great surprise. It is easy to understand how Jesus Christ, the God-human in his divine-human unity, could be the object of an eternal decision made by a Triune God composed of Father, Son, and Holy Spirit. To put it like this is to follow the logic of classical theology, in which the eternal decision that led to the incarnation of the Second Person of the Trinity was a decision in which the eternal Son participated, thereby giving to himself a role to play in the economy of God which would lead to his historical

42. CD II/2:161–75.
43. CD IV/1:164: "The true *God*—if the man Jesus is the true God—is *obedient*. . . . The New Testament describes the Son of God . . . not only as the servant, but rather as the *suffering* servant of God. Not accidentally and provisionally does He *also* suffer—perhaps to the end of testing and preserving His basic conviction, perhaps for the attainment of a concrete goal through struggle, perhaps as a foil for emphasizing His glory in another way, but necessarily and to a certain extent, essentially." (Bromiley's translation is here lightly revised and the original italics restored.) Cf. Bertold Klappert, "Gott in Christus—Versöhner der Welt: Die Christologie Karl Barths als Anfrage an die Christologie der Gegenwart," in *Versöhnung und Befreiung: Versuche, Karl Barth kontextuell zu verstehen* (Neukirchen-Vluyn: Neukirchener Verlag, 1994), 150.

enfleshment.[44] But to just this extent, an ontological gap is opened up between that which the eternal Son is in and for himself and that which he becomes by virtue of this decision—which also leads to a differentiation between the immanent and economic Trinities. One can try to rescue the situation by insisting that the eternal Word and the incarnate Word are one and the same Subject, differing only in modes of being—though how one could possibly know this to be the case is a question for itself. For this would also have to mean that what the Word is *as incarnate* is only accidentally related to what the eternal Word is in and for himself. What the Word is as incarnate would therefore have no ontological significance for the *true* being of the Word in his eternal mode of being.

In saying, however, that it is *Jesus Christ*, the God-human in his divine-human unity, who is the Subject of election, Barth is sweeping aside this classical logic which governed talk of the divine Subject of the work of reconciliation. To make Jesus Christ the subject of election—if carried out consistently[45]—is to bid farewell to the distinction between the eternal Word and the incarnate Word. An eternal Word or eternal Son which had no regard for the humanity to be assumed on the most basic level of personal identity would, in this view, have to be regarded as a metaphysical abstraction with no reality attached to

---

44. *CD* IV/1:65: "The conception of this inter-trinitarian pact as a contract between the persons of the *Father* and the *Son* is also problematic. Can we really think of the first and second persons of the triune Godhead as two divine subjects and therefore as two legal subjects who can have dealings one with another? This is mythology, for which there is no place in a right understanding of the doctrine of the Trinity as the doctrine of the three modes of being of the one God, which is how it was understood and presented in Reformed orthodoxy itself." (Bromiley's translation has been lightly revised and the original italics restored.)

45. Barth was not always consistent—even in *CD* II/2—in carrying through the logic of his basic claim that *Jesus Christ* is the electing God. And so he could also express himself in *CD* II/2:94 in the following manner: "He [Jesus Christ] is the beginning of God before which there is no other beginning apart from that of God with Himself. Except, then, for God Himself, nothing can derive from any other source or look back to any other starting-point." The distinction registered here between the beginning of God in himself and the beginning of God's ways with the human race (his "decree," the covenant of grace) would certainly make sense of the claim that Jesus Christ is the object of election—but the *Subject*? A beginning of God in himself that is not synonymous with the beginning of God's ways with the human race would surely open the door to turning Barth's later criticism of Calvin's God of the absolute decree back upon himself. That is to say, a God who enjoys a higher mode of being than that which he gives to himself in the covenant of grace is the Absolute God of natural theology. Once the distinction between a being of God in himself and a being of God in the covenant of grace has been established, it matters not whether the covenant is established in Jesus Christ with all men and women or only with a select number (Calvin's "elect"). The damage would already have been done. Now, obviously, such statements are not easily reconciled with the claim that *Jesus Christ* is the electing God. The reason for this inconsistency, I would suggest, is that Barth knew of no other way to secure the freedom of God in election than to give a place to what I called earlier "metaphysical moments" in his otherwise antimetaphysical theology. But such moments are exceptional and function as limit-concepts which do not define the overall cast of his thought.

it. Here the antimetaphysical tendencies which had governed Barth's theology from very early on have reached their zenith. What has happened is that the actualism which had always governed Barth's talk of the divine act of relating to the human had now been pressed back into the very being of God. To put the matter as sharply as possible: God *is* in himself, in eternity, the mode of his Self-revelation in time—God as Jesus Christ in eternity and God as Jesus Christ in time—thus guaranteeing that the immanent Trinity and the economic Trinity will be identical in content. Now we can see how the intention expressed in the first point above is concretely realized in terms of the second point. On Barthian soil, the statement that God is "essentially" a suffering God is not an abstract metaphysical assertion. It is a concrete affirmation of a concrete reality—Jesus Christ as the One who suffers in time is what God is "essentially."

No doubt, critics of this assertion would want to ask how Jesus Christ can possibly be the Subject of a decision which gives to him his being as Jesus Christ. Expressed alternatively: How can God, as the Subject of election, already "be" the incarnate Lord *even if only by way of anticipation*, if being the incarnate Lord is the *consequence* of the decision? Surely God must be, in the moment of deciding, something other than what God becomes as a consequence of that decision? Such a line of questioning all too easily snaps back into metaphysical thinking, but I will try to give a reasoned answer to it. To understand Barth's claim that "Jesus Christ is the electing God" requires close attention to his doctrine of the Trinity. For Barth, the triunity of God consists in the fact that God is one Subject in three modes of being. One Subject! To say then that "Jesus Christ is the electing God" is to say, "God determined to be God in a second mode of being." It lies close to hand to recognize that it is precisely the primal decision of God in election which constitutes the event in which God differentiates himself into three modes of being. Election thus has a certain logical priority even over the triunity of God. "'*Jesus Christ is the electing God*.' In that here one of the three modes of being is *determined* to be the God who elects, we have to understand God's primal decision as an *event* in the being of God which *differentiates* the modes of God's being [werden wir die Urentscheidung Gottes auch als ein die Seinsweisen Gottes *unterscheidendes Ereignis* im Sein Gottes zu verstehen haben]."[46] So the event in which God constitutes himself as triune is identical with the event in which he chooses to be God for the human race. Thus the "gap" between the "eternal Son" and "Jesus Christ" is overcome, the distinction between them eliminated. It should be added, finally, that the primal decision in which God determines to be the electing God in a second mode of being is a decision which has

---

46. Eberhard Jüngel, *God's Being Is in Becoming: The Trinitarian Being of God in the Theology of Karl Barth*, trans. John Webster (Grand Rapids: Eerdmans, 2001), 86; cf. idem, *Gottes Sein ist im Werden: Verantwortliche Rede vom Sein Gottes bei Karl Barth, eine Paraphrase* (Tübingen: Mohr Siebeck, 1986), 85.

never *not* already taken place. So there is no "eternal Son" if by that is meant a mode of being in God which is not identical with Jesus Christ. Therefore Jesus Christ is the electing God.

The Christology of the Doctrine of Reconciliation

Karl Barth's doctrine of reconciliation is truly a dogmatics within a dogmatics. Though it stands in profound continuity with material decisions made earlier (above all in the doctrine of election), it could also stand on its own. Here, if anywhere, Barth took his own advice "to begin again with the *beginning*" with strict seriousness.[47] For in the doctrine of reconciliation, Barth, in a very real sense, started over. He said what he had been trying to say before, but he said it in new and sometimes surprising ways.

The bridge from the doctrine of election to the doctrine of reconciliation is provided by §57, "Das Werk Gottes des Versöhners"—a treatment of the covenant of grace. This material is significant for the treatment of the doctrine of the incarnation which will follow in §59.1 in that the door is closed firmly on the thought of the incarnation of a Logos understood along the lines of an abstract metaphysical subject. If God is who and what God is in the act in which God is "with us," then we may not abstract from this act to seek a being of God above and behind this act. And because this is so, "one may not retreat here to the second 'Person' as such, to the eternal Son or the eternal Word of God *in abstracto* and, therefore, to the so-called λόγος ἄσαρκος. What is the meaning of the regress to Him as the alleged ground of the being and knowledge of all things? How should this regress even be accomplished? How is it supposed to get off the ground and where should it lead? The second 'Person' of the Godhead in Himself and as such is not God the Reconciler. In Himself and as such, He is not revealed to us. In Himself and as such, He is precisely not *Deus pro nobis*—neither ontologically nor epistemologically."[48] Barth concedes that the Second Person of the Trinity in and for itself is a "necessary and important concept" in the doctrine of the Trinity—where it is a question of understanding the revelation and activity of God on the basis of its free ground in the "inner

---

47. Karl Barth, *Evangelical Theology: An Introduction*, trans. Grover Foley (Grand Rapids: Eerdmans, 1963), 165: "Theological work is distinguished from other kinds of work by the fact that anyone who desires to do this work cannot proceed by building with complete confidence on the foundation of questions that are already settled, results that have already been achieved, or conclusions that have already been arrived at. He cannot continue to build today in any way on foundations that were laid yesterday by himself, and he cannot live today in any way on the interest from a capital amassed yesterday. His only possible procedure every day, in fact every hour, is to begin anew at the beginning." With considerable justification, Eberhard Jüngel has seen in Barth's fidelity to his theological axiom an explanation for the great length of *Die kirchliche Dogmatik*. See Jüngel, "Karl Barth," in *Barth-Studien*, 17.

48. *CD* IV/1:52.

being and essence of God." But one is probably not wrong to sense that there is something improper about this move.[49] For when has God ever been anything other than God the Reconciler? And so Barth concludes,

49. Where this move is not seen as having a certain impropriety about it, the temptation will be great to see Barth's integration of being and becoming in God as applying *only* to an eternal Self-relating on the part of Father, Son, and Holy Spirit—i.e., as affirming only a "non-temporal" becoming which stands in no ontic connection to the becoming of God in history. Alan Torrance provides a good example of this tendency: "God's being is inseparable from God's relating to himself, thus from that non-temporal 'becoming,' namely, that begetting and issuing constitutive of the 'being' of God. God's being requires to be interpreted in the light of—and not in advance of—the relational structuring of God's being" ("The Trinity," in *The Cambridge Companion to Barth*, ed. John Webster [Cambridge: Cambridge University Press, 2000], 85). What is constitutive of the being of God for Torrance is a "non-temporal" becoming, an essential act of Self-relatedness that is complete in itself without regard for God's Self-communication in history.

What we have before us in this passage is an attempt to overcome a metaphysical account of the unity of the divine "being" by means of an equally metaphysical account of the relationality of the Triune God. That Torrance should appeal to Eberhard Jüngel's classic text *Gottes Sein ist im Werden* in support of his interpretation of Barth's doctrine of the Trinity demonstrates a surprising failure to understand what that book was about at the decisive point. Indeed, Torrance stands in very close proximity to the views of Helmut Gollwitzer, against whom the entire book is directed. Contrary to Gollwitzer's claim that God "in the mode of being of a subject within history" has its ground only in the will of God but not in the essence of God, Jüngel observed, "Gollwitzer (following Karl Barth as the context makes clear) wants to avoid an '*analogia entis*' in favor of an '*analogia relationis*.' It must be asked, however, whether that goal can be attained in this way. Does not this very distinction which Gollwitzer draws between the essence and the will of God (in distinguishing between the 'essence of God in the sense of how God is constituted' from the 'essence of His will') leave a gap in a metaphysical background to the being of God which is indifferent to God's historical acts of revelation? . . . Is God's essence not *decided* precisely in His will?" (Jüngel, *God's Being Is in Becoming*, 5–6; Webster's translation is here lightly revised).

John Webster has more accurately captured in the following passage what is at stake in Jüngel's understanding of the relation of the immanent Trinity to the economic Trinity: "Perichoresis stresses the unity of God as an event of the mutual interpenetration of the divine modes of being—though this unity is not to be thought of as some 'essence' behind the work of God, as if the perichoretic oneness of God were anterior to the differentiated reality of God encountered in his work in the world" ("Translator's Introduction," ibid., xv). The problem with Torrance's interpretation of Barth, as against Jüngel's, is that he makes the perichoretic unity of God be an event that is indeed *anterior* to the differentiated reality of God encountered in his work in the world. Given this mistake, it is not surprising that Torrance ("The Trinity," 90n28) can also say, "The identification of being and act in God has led Barth to be described widely as a 'theological actualist' (to be distinguished from philosophical actualism). The case is not convincing, however, and does not sit easily with Barth's statement, 'God is who He is in His works. He is the same even in Himself, even before and after and over His works, and without them. They are bound to Him, but He is not bound to them. They are nothing without Him. But He is who He is without them. He is not, therefore, who He is only in His works (*CD* II/1, 260).'" Such passages as the one appealed to here by Torrance occur with greater consistency before the writing of *CD* II/2, with less consistency on Barth's part after that point in time. But I have already acknowledged that they do exist even after the doctrine of election; see above, n. 45. But an appeal to a single one of them can hardly be sufficient to explain away the problem created by statements such

But since we are now concerned with the revelation and the acting of God and particularly with reconciliation, with the Person and work of the Reconciler, there is no point—it is in fact not permitted—to return once again to the inner being and essence of God and in particular to the second Person of the Trinity as such out of a desire to ascribe to this Person another form than the one which He has given Himself in that God has willed to reveal Himself and to act outwards. . . . According to the free and gracious will of God, the eternal Son of God is *Jesus Christ* as He lived and died and rose again in time and He alone . . . with the result that we are barred from ignoring it and dreaming of a "Logos in and for itself" which did *not yet* have this content and form, which would be the eternal Word of God *without* this content and form.[50]

Bertold Klappert's striking claim that "Barth does not think incarnationally in the neoorthodox sense"[51] will surely sound jarring even at this late date to English-language students of Barth. But seen in context, the judgment is correct. Klappert is not saying that the Barth of *CD* IV/1–2 lacks a doctrine of the incarnation. He is pointing instead to the equation which Barth advances

---

as the following, wherein Barth describes "the Word" of John 1:1 as "a provisional description of the place where later something wholly other or a Wholly Other will be made visible." The concept of the Logos, Barth goes on to say, stands in John 1:1 representatively, as a provisional veil for the other, the "proper concept": "ὁ λόγος is unmistakeably substituted for: Jesus. It is *His* place which, by means of the predicates given to the Logos, is simultaneously marked off, cleared away and secured. He, Jesus, in the beginning, is with God, is by nature God. That is what is being secured in John 1:1" (*CD* II/2:96; Bromiley's translation has been revised). What Barth says here is breathtaking in its significance. It is the Logos who appears in the text as a placeholder for Jesus, not the other way around. It is Jesus to whom all of the predicates assigned to the Logos belong. See Jüngel, *God's Being Is in Becoming*, 95.

This is perhaps the appropriate place to note—with gratitude—the impact which Jüngel's little book has had on my thinking (both as a reader of Barth and with regard to the systematic issues involved). I first read it as a graduate student nearly twenty years ago. Since then I have returned to it again and again, and each time I have been able to learn something new—ways in which my own patterns of thought or speech needed to be corrected, and even the opening up here and there of new horizons of thought which previously had eluded me. Truly, this book deserves much greater attention than it has received. Many of the mistakes found in contemporary English-language Barth scholarship might have been avoided if those working in the field had absorbed its lessons.

50. *CD* IV/1:52. (Bromiley's translation has here been revised.)

51. Klappert, "Gott in Christus—Versöhner der Welt," 144. Cf. 143: "Karl Barth's cross-centered Christology is, therefore, not—as in classical Christology—an explication of a two-natures doctrine oriented to the incarnation but just the reverse: the two-natures doctrine is an explication of a doctrine of reconciliation oriented to the cross." This also means that the nineteenth-century distinction between Christologies "from above" and "from below" has been effectively set aside—*not* overcome by mediating between them but set aside as irrelevant to what the New Testament witness has to say about Jesus Christ (ibid., 150). Ironically, the "from below" methodology of nineteenth-century liberalism, by constructing its Christology in direct response to the "from above" approach to interpreting the incarnation of the absolute metaphysical subject, remained tied to it. Neither was found acceptable by the Barth of *CD* IV/1.

between the "eternal Son" and "Jesus Christ." The eternal Son of God is Jesus Christ as he lived, died, and rose again in time *and he alone*.

But if the incarnation is not to be construed along the lines of the incarnation of an absolute metaphysical subject, then the fundamental problem addressed by Chalcedon—that of the unity of the divine and the human in Jesus Christ—is now being addressed under the impress of ontological commitments which are other than those of the fathers at Chalcedon. The problem is no longer that of explaining the union of an abstract metaphysical subject that is complete in itself with a historically constituted human "nature" (along with the attendant problem which this creates for the concept of a divine immutability which is embedded in the idea of an abstract metaphysical subject); the problem is, rather, that of reflecting upon the unity of a Subject whose being is constituted both in time and in eternity by a twofold history.

The thesis I will argue in this section is that although Barth certainly preserves in his doctrine of reconciliation the theological values registered in the Chalcedonian formula, he does so only by replacing the category of "nature" with the category of "history" and by then integrating "history" into his concept of "person." The result is a theological ontology that can be compared to that presupposed in Chalcedon only on the formal level of affirming the "true divinity" and "true humanity" of Jesus Christ. Materially, the two Christologies are sufficiently different, however, that we mislead ourselves and others where we speak simply of Barth's "Chalcedonian" Christology or even only of Barth's "*basically* Chalcedonian" Christology.[52]

52. Hunsinger, "Karl Barth's Christology: Its Basic Chalcedonian Character," is governed by two contentions—one historical and the other systematic. The historical contention is that the "Chalcedonian Christology" constitutes a third distinguishable *type* of early-church Christology, over against the "Alexandrian" and the "Antiochian." Whether such a reading of early-church doctrinal development can be sustained is doubtful, given the degree of Alexandrian influence on the Chalcedonian formula (as argued above) and given the fact that Hunsinger himself is able to make it work only by taking the most extreme examples of the "Alexandrian" (Apollinaris of Laodicea) and the "Antiochian" (Nestorius) and allowing them to define the type in question. The problem with this procedure is that "Alexandrian" and "Antiochian"—if the terms are to be retained at all!—are best understood as descriptive of *traditions*, not of arbitrarily selected individuals whose theology can then be used to generate a type. More interesting, however, is the systematic contention. Hunsinger holds that "any Chalcedonian Christology that is true to type will display certain basic features. It will see Jesus Christ as 'one person in two natures.' It will regard him as at once 'complete in deity' and 'complete in humanity.' And it will hold that when these two natures met in Christ, they did so 'without separation or division' and yet also 'without confusion or change'" (ibid., 133). Now, what is interesting about this is that in the argument that follows, Hunsinger effectively departs from the definition of "any Chalcedonian Christology that is true to type" that he has been at pains to elaborate and leaves it out of account. His argument is that Barth elaborates his basically Chalcedonian Christology by means of a "method of juxtaposition": "Barth is probably the first theologian in the history of Christian doctrine who alternates back and forth, deliberately, between an 'Alexandrian' and an 'Antiochian' idiom. The proper way to be Chalcedonian in Christology, Barth believed, was to follow the lead of the New Testament itself by employing a definite diversity of idioms" (135).

The root of Barth's Christology is to be found in his doctrine of election. Divine election, as we have seen, is the event in which God determines never to be God apart from humanity—in which God determines himself to be, in a very real sense, a "human" God. Thus divine election means the taking up of humanity into the *event* of God's being[53]—the event, that is to say, in which God's own being receives its own most essential determination. At the same time, humanity is given its most essential determination (that which makes humanity to be what it is). But there is an asymmetry in the ontological relation here established which is rooted in the fact that God alone is the active Subject of the decision in which God gives to divine and to human being their most essential determinations. And the result of this asymmetry is that humanity does not "participate" in God's being and life in the same way that God "participates" in human being and life. The modes of participation differ in each case. To explore these modes of participation will help us in teasing out the theological ontology which comes to expression in Barth's doctrine of reconciliation. We will consider each of the modes of participation in turn.

How does God participate in human being and life? The brief answer is that God enters time *as a human being*. The history which constitutes the being and existence of the human Jesus belongs to the history of God in the second of God's modes of being (as "Son"). If, in Jesus Christ, God has elected to become human, then the human history of Jesus Christ is constitutive of the being and existence of God in the second of God's modes to the extent that the being and existence of the Second Person of the Trinity cannot be rightly thought of in the absence of this human history.[54] The Second Person of the

---

Now, there is little doubt that Barth does indeed affirm a dialectical procedure in adjudicating between the Christologies of Alexandria and Antioch in *CD* I/2—though it has to be added that his procedure at this point simply reflects earlier commitments found first in the Christology of the *Göttingen Dogmatics* and may not be assumed, without further ado, to be the procedure followed in the later doctrine of reconciliation. But the major problem with Hunsinger's argument has yet to be touched upon. To the extent that Hunsinger is right in alleging a "method of juxtaposition" which allowed Barth to speak now in an "Alexandrian" idiom and now in an "Antiochian" idiom, *Barth could not be judged "Chalcedonian" by the measure of Hunsinger's three-point definition of "any Chalcedonian Christology that is true to type."* The method of juxtaposing "Alexandrian" and "Antiochian" idioms could bear witness to the desire to say that Jesus Christ is "complete in deity" and "complete in humanity." It might even, if sufficiently finessed, bear witness to the third of Hunsinger's three points. What it could never do, taken by itself, is to yield up the first of the requisite elements: the "two natures in one person." Hunsinger effectively leaves to one side the first element in his definition because he never treats the problem of the ontology of the *subject* of the twofold history of humiliation and exaltation. But if Barth were really "Chalcedonian," it would surely be incumbent upon Hunsinger to have done this.

53. Jüngel, *Gottes Sein ist im Werden*, 75.

54. *CD* IV/2:43: "The older dogmatics was quite right when it described the incarnation as the work of the entire Holy Trinity. None of the three modes of God in God either is or works without the other two: *opera trinitatis ad extra sunt indivisa*. But if the essence of God existing in these three modes of being is one, it is that of the one personal God, and not of the three 'persons' in our sense of that term. As such, He is also the Subject of the incarnation, of the

Trinity has a name, and his name is "Jesus Christ." To put it this way is to suggest that we cannot think about the Second Person of the Trinity in isolation from his history, for it is in his history that he is constituted the "person" that he is. The mode of participation in this case is direct and immediate. God the Son participates in the human being and existence of Jesus of Nazareth in the sense that all that occurs in and through and to this human is taken up into the divine life and made to be God's own. How this takes place is the mystery of the incarnation.[55]

But now we have to take a further step. "The fulfillment in time of God's eternal resolve is God's existence as man in Jesus Christ. God's existence as man is not only God's existence as creature, but equally God's handing of Himself over to the opposition to God which characterizes human existence. The consequence of God's self-surrender is his *suffering* of the opposition to God which afflicts human existence in opposition to God—even to *death* on

---

assumption of human being into unity with Himself and therefore with His essence. He is this, however, in the mode of being of the Son, not of the Father, not of the Holy Spirit." (Bromiley's translation is here lightly revised.)

55. In reflecting on this problem, Barth again leans in the direction of "Alexandrianism" but this time without so much as a provisional acceptance of the ancient Greek ontology that underlay that christological tradition. In treating the question of the "object" of the divine act that is the incarnation, Barth says,

Our present question—with reference always to the act of God as such—concerns the nature of this object. We have again described it as *human being*. We might also use the term human "nature"—with the older dogmatics—but only with the proviso that if the concept should be serviceable as a description of the humanity of Jesus Christ, then it would have to be made free of the representation of a generally-known humanity. . . . That which the Son of God assumed into unity with Himself and His divine being was and is—in a concrete individual form, elected and prepared for this purpose—not "a man" but rather the *human*: that being and essence, that kind and nature, which is that of all men and women, that which characterizes them all as human and distinguishes them from other creatures. It is not the idea of the human, in which *per definitionem* this [One] could exist never and nowhere or only always and everywhere. It is the concrete possibility of the existence of one man in a definite form—a man elected and prepared for this purpose, not by Himself but by God (here the election and calling of Israel and of Mary is relevant). But in this form, it is that which is human in all men and women. It is the concrete possibility of the existence of a man which will be *identical* with the concrete possibility of all men and women. (*CD* IV/2:47–48; Bromiley's translation is here lightly revised.)

Here Barth clearly breaks through the Platonic idealism that influenced the Alexandrians so deeply. The "possibility" of the human that is actualized in the incarnation is not the abstract universal possibility of the Platonic ideal humanity but the concrete possibility of a Jewish existence that has been elected by God from eternity. On the basis of these ontological conditions, one would have to say that what gives to the "human nature" assumed by the Son of God its universality is not its participation in an abstract universal. What gives to it its universality is its election by God to be the universal, the true human, in whom all others will participate. The "human nature" of Christ does not participate in a universal; it *is* the universal—precisely in its concreteness.

224

for Barth,
history –
for Balthasar,
mission –
constitutive
of "person"

the cross."[56] If all that is done by and happens to Jesus of Nazareth is done by and happens to Jesus Christ, the God-human, the Second Person of the Trinity, then it necessarily follows that the passion and death of Jesus is an event in God's own life. It follows too that the history which leads to this as its appointed result is a history of divine Self-humiliation.[57] It is "the way of the Son of God into the far country."[58]

Barth's primary concern in this remarkable section of *Die kirchliche Dogmatik* is to show that God is God in the history of his Self-humiliation. That is to say, God does not cease to be God in that, in Jesus Christ, as creature and as sinner, God places himself under his own wrath, accusation, sentence, and judgment[59] and, having done all of that, gives himself over to the experience of death. But how can God give himself over to judgment and wrath, suffering and death, without giving himself over to that which negates his being? How can it be true that "the Almighty exists, speaks and acts here in the form of One who is weak and without power, the eternal as One who is temporal and perishing, the Most High in the deepest humility"[60]? The answer again is to be found in the doctrine of election. In that God gives himself over to judgment and wrath, suffering and death, God does so in fulfillment of that for which God has eternally determined himself. He gives himself over to that in and through which his true being is realized. Thus God is never seen more clearly as the God that he truly is than when he suffers death on a cross. Here is where his true being is disclosed. Contrary to the idea that in the incarnation, passion, and death of Jesus Christ we have to do "with what noetically and logically is an absolute paradox, a pure antinomy, with what ontically is the fact of a cleft or rift or abyss in God Himself, between His being and essence in itself and His activity and work as Reconciler of the world created by Him,"[61] Barth insists that "in Him there is no paradox, no antinomy, no division, no unfaithfulness to Himself. . . . What He is and does, He is and does in full unity with Himself. . . . Who God is and what it means to be divine is something we have to learn there where God has revealed Himself and, thereby, also His nature, the essence of the divine."[62] "God gives Himself, but

56. Jüngel, *God's Being Is in Becoming*, 98.

57. Though it is quite unpopular today to say so, Barth is quite insistent that the passion of Christ was no catastrophe which befell him but the appointed end of his life and the purpose for which He came into this world. See his stinging criticism of J. S. Bach's *Matthäuspassion*, where he says, "When is the Church going to realise, and to make clear to the thousands and thousands who may have direct knowledge of the evangelical passion-story only in this form, that what we have here is only an abstraction and *not* the real passion of *Jesus Christ*?" The death of Jesus Christ is not the death of a tragic hero; it is not the death of a victim (*CD* IV/2:252–53).

58. *CD* IV/1, §59.1.

59. *KD* IV/1:189.

60. *CD* IV/1:176. (Bromiley's translation is here lightly revised.)

61. *CD* IV/1:184. (Bromiley's translation is here lightly revised.)

62. *CD* IV/1:186. (Bromiley's translation is here lightly revised.)

He does not give Himself away, in that He becomes man. He does not cease to be God in doing so."[63]

But we have not fully described the Reconciling Subject when we have spoken only of the participation of God in the history of Jesus of Nazareth. We must also speak of the other aspect, the "participation" of the human Jesus in the being and existence of God. What sort of participation is this? The brief answer here is: the mode of participation of the human Jesus in the being and existence of God is that of "sharing" *in God's history* through active obedience to the will of his Father. A "sharing" in God's history: in no way does this entail the elimination of the distinction between the being of God and the being of the human. It is a sharing in the sense that the history of the human Jesus is a history of obedience to the will of the Father, which brings his history into complete conformity or correspondence to the history of God's Self-humiliation.[64] The "exaltation" of the human Jesus consists in this: that he actively conforms himself to the history of God's Self-humiliation and, in doing so, *is made the vehicle of it*. That true humanity should consist in this action will be understood where it is remembered that the "primal decision" which determines the essential being of the human is God's alone to make; the human can only receive and acknowledge it.[65] In that the human Jesus does receive and acknowledge this primal determination, in that he lives in conformity to it, he is "exalted." His history is a history of exaltation. It is "The Homecoming of the Son of Man."[66]

Two implications follow immediately from this understanding. First, Barth retains the distinction between the *anhypostasia* and the *enhypostasia* of Jesus Christ as a witness to the fact that the human Jesus has no *independent* existence—no existence, that is, in independence of the event of his assumption into unity with the Word.[67] But the ontological frame of reference in which this *theologoumenon* does its work is no longer that which gave rise to it in the first place. No longer is it a question of subsistence in an abstract metaphysical subject. Here it is a question of living from the gracious decision of election.

> The existence of the man Jesus Christ is an event by and in the existence of the Son of God, i.e., by and in the event of the divine act of reconciliation, by and in the electing grace of God. He comes *entirely* from thence. . . . The grace of God is not addressed to Him in the sense that He is first without it and subject to

63. *CD* IV/1:185. (Bromiley's translation is here lightly revised.)
64. *CD* IV/2:166–92. The whole of section II of §64.3, "Der königliche Mensch," consists in a discussion of the fact that "the royal man . . . exists analogously to the mode of existence of God. In what He thinks and wills and does, in His attitude, there is a correspondence, a parallel in the creaturely world, to the plan and purpose and work and attitude of God" (IV/2:185).
65. *CD* IV/2:88.
66. *CD* IV/2, §64.2.
67. *CD* IV/2:49–50.

[Handwritten margin note: If McCormack's right, then how can Barth have such a sense of participation, if he were so worried about deification at the same time.]

other determinations but then receives it. . . . The grace of God and it alone is His origin; it alone is His determination. He *is* by it and in it and *only* in this way: not abstracted, not cut loose from its demonstration, from its occurrence. He is not in and for Himself. He derives entirely from His divine origin. In all of this we are again describing the *enhypostasia* or *anhypostasia* of the human nature."[68]

The human Jesus has his being and existence from and in the event of the electing and reconciling grace of God. To speak of this as an actualization of the *anhypostasia* and *enhypostasia* would be accurate as far as it goes. But it is a paltry way to describe what, in fact, is a shift in ontological frames of reference.

The second implication is that "divinization" of the human Jesus in the classical sense of the word has been rendered an impossibility. That Barth consistently rejected this soteriological concept throughout his dogmatics is well known. What is not fully appreciated, however, is that he had to reject it because the theological ontology he developed in the light of his newly revised doctrine of election rendered it impossible.[69] Where it is said that the human Jesus "participates" in the being and life of God by means of a willed correspondence of his thinking and willing, his doing and attitude, to the work and attitude of God, where, further, it is said that such human thinking and willing, and so on, stands in *analogy* to the mode of existence of God, constituting a *parallel* in the creaturely world to God's plan and intention, his work and attitude,[70] there one can rightly speak of the "exaltation" of the human

68. *CD* IV/2:90–91. (Bromiley's translation is here lightly revised and the original italics restored.)

69. From the beginnings of his dogmatic theology, what Barth feared in the idea of "divinization" was the Lutheran *genus majestaticum*—a version of the ancient doctrine of the *communicatio idiomatum* in accordance with which the attributes of the divine majesty (omnipotence, omniscience, and omnipresence, inter alia) are communicated to the human nature of Jesus Christ as a consequence of the hypostatic union. As Barth expressed it (*CD* I/2:166), Lutheran orthodoxy developed the notion of "a perichoresis between the Word of God and the human being of Christ" which allowed for "a reversal of the statement about the *enhypostasia* of the human nature of Christ to the effect that as the humanity has reality only through and in the Word, so too the Word has reality only through and in the humanity." In his later Christology, Barth was able to soften his objection to the Lutheran Christology just a bit, as he gradually found a way to say that the Word has reality only in and through the humanity and to say it *without* (1) giving the impression that the human Jesus cooperates in the decision for the "becoming" of the Word and (2) giving rise to a "perichoresis" of divine and human "natures" substantially conceived (which would have to result in the attribution of divine predicates to the human Jesus). Both of these conditions are met in the way Barth was able to affirm the "intention" of the Lutheran Christology but to execute it within the framework of a nonmetaphysical, "historicized" understanding of the being of the human Jesus. See *CD* IV/2:78–80. But, of course, this also meant that his opposition to the idea of "divinization" remained steadfast and pronounced. On Barth's rejection of "divinization," see (among the many passages devoted to this theme) IV/2:72, 79–82, 88–89.

70. See above, n. 64.

but not of "divinization." And so Barth can say of all those who are elected in Christ, "Created being as such needs salvation, but does not have it: it can only look forward to it. To that extent, salvation is its 'eschaton.' Salvation, fulfilment, perfect being means—and this is what created being does not have in itself—a being which *participates* in the being of God, a being which comes from it and proceeds towards it; not a divinized being but a being which is hidden in God and in that sense (distinct from God and secondary) an *eternal being*."[71] But this is precisely what is true of the human Jesus in advance of all of the rest of us: he has a "share" in the being of God in the specific sense that he is granted an eternal being which is analogically related to God's own, one which maintains a definite ontological "distance" from God's being but which is an eternal being nonetheless. In this is his exaltation as the kingly man.

There remains but one major question to be addressed. We have seen that God "participates" in the being and existence of the human Jesus. We have seen that the human Jesus "participates" in the being and existence of God. We have also seen that the mode of participation is different in each case: that the human Jesus participates in the being and existence of God indirectly, by freely willing to live in correspondence to the history of God inaugurated in the covenant of grace and that God participates in the being and existence of the human Jesus directly, by freely making the history of the human Jesus be the vehicle of God's own history of Self-humiliation. But why should the history of God and the history of the human Jesus not be regarded as *two* histories? Why should they be regarded as two aspects of a single history (as Barth most certainly does)? The problem before us is that of the unity of the subject we call "Jesus Christ." What we have said thus far is sufficient to guarantee that Jesus Christ is "complete in deity" and "complete in humanity." What we must now address is the question of the unity of "person."

The unity of what might seem to be two distinct histories finds its ground in the "primal decision" of God in election. The unity here is not the unity provided by an abstract metaphysical subject; it is the concrete unity of a decision in which God gives both to himself and to humanity his and their essential being and does so with respect to one and the same figure, Jesus of Nazareth. It is in and through the *one* history of the man Jesus that what is essential to both God and humanity is concretely realized. The problem that appears to be created by this train of thought for the concept of a unity of "person" does not lie on the side of the human but on the side of God. How can the history of the human Jesus, a history which (considered in and for itself) is only analogically related to God's own history, be at the same time the history of God? The answer is that this human history is so taken up into God's

---

71. CD IV/1:8–9. (Bromiley's translation is here lightly revised and the original italics restored.)

own life that it constitutes the fulfillment of the divine Self-determination to be God only in and through it. To say this much does not resolve the mystery of the incarnation, but it does help us to ensure that we are talking about *this* mystery and not some other.

To recapitulate: What I think I have shown here is that Barth preserves the theological values registered in the Chalcedonian formula but that he has done so by fundamentally altering the theological ontology in which those values find their home. He has replaced the language of "natures" with the concept of "history," and he has integrated the concept of "history" into his concept of "person." The result is that Jesus Christ is still seen as truly God, truly human, and is both in a single Subject. But he is seen to be all of this under quite different ontological conditions.

We may present the understanding of the "person" of Christ which we have teased out of Barth's writings diagrammatically this way:[72]

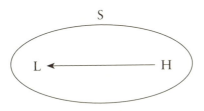

In this view, the Reconciling Subject is no longer the Logos *simpliciter* (the abstract metaphysical subject) but the God-human in his divine-human unity.[73] And he is this not only in time but already in eternity.

Conclusion

It lies close to hand to suspect that the mistakes found in a good deal of English-language reflection on Barth's Christology are bound up with a failure to discern development within the bounds of the *Church Dogmatics*. For an earlier generation, who first encountered Barth's Christology in the form it took in *CD* I/2 and who were led by it to a strong commitment to the patristic doctrine of Christ, the temptation to read the later doctrine of reconciliation through the lens provided by the Christology of *CD* I/2 must have been very strong indeed. And for those today who are strongly influenced by the Barth scholarship of that earlier generation, the tendency to repeat old errors may be difficult to overcome.

72. In this diagram, S = Subject, L = Logos, and H = humanity (or human "nature").
73. *CD* IV/1:126: "We cannot avoid the old formula: very God, very man, very God-man. . . . As this One He is the subject of the act of reconciliation between God and all men."

Unfortunately, such tendencies feed into and are in turn fed by the antimodern mood of much English-language theology. "Modernity" has always been a term of opprobrium for conservatives. But in recent years, it has also become the favorite target of disaffected liberals as well. One of the most powerful movements in English-language theology today is what I will call, for want of a better phrase, the "new orthodoxy." This is not simply an outgrowth of what used to be called "neoorthodoxy" twenty years ago. The older neoorthodoxy was a typically Protestant movement. The new orthodoxy is Orthodox and Catholic in its inspiration. Where the old neoorthodoxy advocated a return to Reformation theology, the new orthodoxy would like to see a return to patristic and medieval theology (or to a Reformation theology which is itself interpreted as Orthodox and Catholic in inspiration). The movement is diverse, ranging from the evangelical Catholicism of Robert Jenson, Carl Braaten, George Lindbeck, and Reinhard Hütter to the "radical orthodoxy" of John Milbank and the communitarian ethics and theology of Stanley Hauerwas. For some in this movement (certainly not all), there is an evident desire to find in Barth a guarantor of their own interests and concerns so far as possible and to fault him where he falls short.[74] And even among those who would not

74. In two of his essays, Reinhard Hütter complains that current studies of Barth's theological development underplay the importance which an engagement with Roman Catholicism had for him from very early on. Current interpretations, he says, see Barth "exclusively in the triangle of his retrieval of classical Reformed theology, his ongoing (albeit mainly negative) connectedness to liberal Protestantism, and his way of broadly presupposing the Kantian epistemological framework." This includes my own, in regard to which he writes, "McCormack does not acknowledge the central importance of Roman Catholicism as the main conversation partner for Barth's theology from the so-called 'Göttingen Dogmatics' on. . . . While McCormack records and interprets Barth's encounter with Roman Catholicism in Münster in detail and very accurately, he fails to understand the systematic importance of this engagement for Barth's own constructive theological project" (Reinhard Hütter, "Barth between McCormack and von Balthasar: A Dialectic," *Pro Ecclesia* 8 [1999]: 108). On what grounds is Hütter able to argue that Roman Catholicism was Barth's "main conversation partner" from the *Göttingen Dogmatics* on? On these grounds only: that Barth could not have studied Reformation sources as intensively as he did without also taking into account Catholic theology "as the decisive counterpart to this engagement." The engagement with Roman Catholicism, he says, was "implicit" in his encounter with Reformation theology, an encounter which "is not intelligible without a parallel engagement with the common Catholic tradition and the Roman Catholic counter-critique of the Reformation tradition" (Reinhard Hütter, "Karl Barth's 'Dialectical Catholicity': Sic et non," *Modern Theology* 16 [2000]: 139, 152n7). This is surely a strained argument. Though Barth did occasionally make reference to Catholic teachings on particular subjects (particularly in his Münster dogmatic cycle), he did so by means of references to Bernhard Bartmann's *Lehrbuch der Dogmatik*, which was his primary access to Catholic theology at this time. This hardly justifies the claim that in the *Göttingen Dogmatics* there was a "theological urgency to engage Roman Catholicism" (Hütter, "Karl Barth's 'Dialectical Catholicity,'" 152n7). So why, when Hütter knows that Barth really began to engage Catholic theology out of its own sources only in the Münster period, is he so insistent upon making Catholicism "the main conversation partner" already in Göttingen? The only answer that I can think of is that Hütter is well aware that many of the most important material decisions which would shape Barth's thought on into

wish to be lumped together with the above-named theologians, the temptation to narrow the distance between their concerns and those of Barth has
proven to be great. Where the interpretation of Barth is concerned, this can
easily lead to the following tendencies, among others: the elevation of the
theme of union with Christ to a place of centrality in Barth's soteriology; a
downplaying of the language of correspondence, where the elaboration of
theological ontology is concerned, in favor of the language of communion;
the suppression of actualism; and the suppression of the judicial element in
his doctrine of reconciliation.[75]

---

the *Church Dogmatics* were already made in Göttingen. If the encounter with Catholicism had
first occurred in Münster, that would be too late—where an argument for the formative influence
of Catholic theology on Barth's development is concerned.

The irony in all of this, however, is that Hütter is not really all that interested in Barth's
development. He uses the seriousness of Barth's engagement with Roman Catholicism to argue
that Barthians today should "go and do likewise." More ironic still, even this much is still only
preparatory to his real interest. What Hütter really wants is that we should understand "church
doctrine" (i.e., dogma) and "church practices" as "concrete embodiments of the Holy Spirit."
Indeed, he holds that church doctrine and church practices "subsist enhypostatically in the
Spirit" (Reinhard Hütter, *Theologie als kirchliche Praktik: Zur Verhältnis von Kirche, Lehre
und Theologie* [Gütersloh: Kaiser, 1997], 181; cf. 189). This is not the place to evaluate Hütter's dogmatic claim. Suffice it to say that it deserves a serious response and simply labeling it
"Catholic" is not that response. The point here, however, is that Hütter wants us to follow Barth
only up to the point where we see that the *Realdialektik* in Barth's concept of revelation will not
allow his understanding of church doctrine to transcend the status of witness nor will it allow
his "catholicity" to be anything other than "dialectical." At that point, we must move beyond
Barth to the "concrete catholicity" which Hütter thinks himself to find in Luther.

75. Easily the best of those who give evidence of these tendencies is George Hunsinger. One
cannot say that Hunsinger's work in this area is simply wrong. With him at least, it is a question
of where the accents are laid. In a thought-provoking essay, Hunsinger argues that, for Barth,
"communion with Christ in the Spirit involves participation in the communion of the Holy Trinity. Those joined to Christ by faith are granted a share through him in that communion where
God is eternally God: the primordial communion of love and knowledge between the Father and
the Son in the Holy Spirit" ("The Mediator of Communion: Karl Barth's Doctrine of the Holy
Spirit," in *Disruptive Grace*, 169). In support of this thesis, he is able to call upon passages from
Barth's writings such as the following: "He takes us up into His fellowship, i.e., the fellowship
which He has and is in Himself" (*CD* II/1:276). Hunsinger is careful to acknowledge that the
union of the Christian with Christ is one in which the "indissoluble" ontological divide between
God and the human is preserved ("The Mediator of Communion," 170). He also shows himself
to be well aware that "the unity effected by the Spirit can only be described as a 'history,' not as
'a datum or a state'" (168). But given that the union of the Christian with Christ is said to have
its prototype in a Christology in which a "mutual indwelling of Christ's two natures" (168) is
said to be effected by the Holy Spirit, it is not clear how the ontological divide can be preserved—
or even whether it needs to be. Hunsinger has a tendency, at the points where we might have
expected closer reflection on the nature of the union in question, to insist upon its ineffability.
The result is that the union of the believer with Christ is made to be a form of mystical union
whose relationship to the hypostatic union of divine and human in Christ is left rather vague.
Now, as I say, it is a question here of where the accents are laid. When Hunsinger says, "The
Holy Spirit 'constitutes and guarantees the unity of the *totus Christus*' (IV/3, p. 760) through
a mediation in union, correspondence, and love" (169), it is hard to avoid the impression that

231

In a different situation, it might not be so important to avoid misleading descriptions of Barth's Christology as "Chalcedonian." But if, as I have suggested here, the doctrine of divinization can make sense only on the soil of Greek metaphysics, then the stakes in getting right the language used to describe Barth's Christology have been significantly raised. Barth's theological ontology constitutes a rejection of Greek metaphysics. His achievement lay in revising what it means to be "orthodox" in the realm of Christology *under the conditions of modernity*.[76]

Karl Barth never held the Chalcedonian dogma to be anything more than a human witness to a subject matter which he too was seeking to express. As the

---

this is rather more than a haphazard ordering of modes of participation; it is more likely that it is intended as a ranking. "Union" has, for Hunsinger, a certain priority over "correspondence" where thinking through Barth's theological ontology is concerned. But is this accent entirely faithful to Barth? Our questions mount when Hunsinger says that it is "through proclamation *and sacrament*" (160, emphasis mine) that the Spirit unites believers to Christ and that "the flesh of the Son, his body and blood, is the indispensable means through which the faithful . . . come to participate indirectly in the life of the Holy Trinity" (185). In light of Barth's dramatic revision of traditional sacramentology (which set aside the understanding of the Eucharist as a means of grace), one has to wonder whether all of this does not, at the decisive points, give better expression to Hunsinger's dogmatic interests than it does to Barth's.

76. The conditions that gave rise to modernity where theology is concerned include the collapse of the old synthesis of biblical material with Aristotelian cosmology where the picture of the world is concerned, the rise of biblical criticism, the turn to the subject in epistemology, and the nearly complete demise of ancient Greek metaphysics. Given that these conditions could and did generate a number of theological options, it is important that we not reduce what it means to be "modern" to a set of characteristics found in a few influential figures. In a recent article, John Yocum has suggested that "we have to be careful about McCormack's characterization of Barth as a 'modern theologian.'" Yocum grants to me that Barth is not "post-modern" and that Barth makes use of Kant in elaborating his own theological epistemology. But, he says, "in another, more important way, Barth is *not* a modern theologian. . . . In what he affirms materially Barth is not modern, neither in the Kantian, nor the Hegelian, nor the Schleiermacherian sense." As evidence for the last assertion, Yocum adds, "He opposes both the *material theological implications* of the notion of the 'disengaged rational agent' or 'detached rationality,' and the pantheism of Hegelian and Schleiermacherian theories of immanence" (John Yocum, "What's Interesting about Karl Barth? Barth as Polemical and Descriptive Theologian," *International Journal of Systematic Theology* 4 [2002]: 42–43). Although I would certainly agree that Barth was no pantheist and that the "disengaged rational agent" has no place in his epistemology, it is not at all clear to me that we have an adequate description of what it means to be materially "modern" in theology when we have these points before us. The problem is twofold: (1) The characteristics mentioned by Yocum cannot be regarded as essential to the definition of "modern" in the realm of theology, since not all "moderns" were pantheists and not all worked with the notion of a "disengaged rational agent." In truth, neither of these characteristics may be fairly ascribed to Schleiermacher. (2) Even if Yocum were right, even if his depiction did touch on elements that were essential to the definition of what it means to be "modern" in the realm of theology, he would still not have provided an exhaustive description by mentioning just these two points. He fails to mention, for example, the death of classical metaphysics as a shared conviction among the vast majority of modern theologians. And certainly, on this front, Barth's antimetaphysical Christology has to be counted as *materially* "modern."

decree of an ecumenical council, it was, granted, a relatively binding human witness, a witness with a stature that exceeded that of other witnesses, but a witness all the same. And a witness is not the thing itself. This is why Barth was able to be so free in his appropriation of its insights and values. This is why his encounter with Chalcedon was not finished in a moment but consisted in a history characterized by growth and change. Here as elsewhere, it is important to remember what Barth said with respect to the dogmas of the church: "Dogmas are not *veritates a Deo formaliter revelatae*. In dogmas it is the Church of the past that speaks. This is venerable. It deserves respect. It is normative. It speaks *non sine Deo*, as is fitting. Yet it is still the Church. In dogmas the Church defines, i.e., limits revealed truth, the Word of God. The Word of God thus becomes the word of man. It is not an insignificant word. Indeed, it is a supremely significant word. Yet it is still the word of man. The Word of God is above all dogmas as the heavens are above the earth."[77]

---

77. CD I/1:266.

9

Participation in God, Yes; Deification, No

Two Modern Protestant Responses to an Ancient Question

Among the Protestant theologians in the Anglo-American world who still care about the Christian tradition and find in it an authoritative guide for the theology which is done today, there is no theme enjoying greater popularity currently than the ancient soteriological theme of "deification."[1] Typically, the elevation of this theme is accompanied by a strong emphasis on the theme of "union with Christ" and a depreciation of legal or juridical images in soteriology. The reasons for this are complex—having to do, no doubt, with the sheer beauty and spiritual profundity of Orthodox theologies but having to do also with fears

---

This essay was originally published in a slightly different form under the title, "Participation in God, Yes, Deification, No: Two Modern Protestant Responses to an Ancient Question," in *Denkwürdiges Geheimnis—Beiträge zur Gotteslehre: Festschrift für Eberhard Jüngel zum 70. Geburtstag*, ed. Ingolf U. Dalferth, Johannes Fischer, and Hans-Peter Grosshans (Tübingen: Mohr Siebeck, 2004), 347–74. Reprinted by permission.

1. The literature is already immense and still growing. Among the leading examples are the following: Dennis Cunningham, *These Three Are One: The Practice of Trinitarian Theology* (Oxford: Blackwell, 1998), 165–95; Robert Jenson, *Systematic Theology*, 2 vols. (New York: Oxford University Press, 1997–1999), 1:71, 83–84, 87, 226–27; 2:296–98, 311–12, 322–23, 340–46; Bruce Marshall, "Justification as Declaration and Deification," *International Journal of Systematic Theology* 4 (2002): 3–28; Thomas F. Torrance, *The Trinitarian Faith* (Edinburgh: T&T Clark, 1988), 138–41, 184, 188–90, 264. It should be noted that Torrance's reading of Karl Barth's doctrine of reconciliation closely parallels what he finds in Athanasius and other early fathers, even though he is careful not to use the word "deification" in his exposition of Barth. See Thomas F. Torrance, *Karl Barth: Biblical and Evangelical Theologian* (Edinburgh: T&T Clark, 1990), 198–212, 227–40.

over declining membership in the Protestant churches, the specter of neopaganism on the left-wing of these churches, and a longing for theologies of human transformation capable of competing with options provided by a surrounding culture that is increasingly religious and therapeutic. What I want to argue here is quite simply that while a human participation in God does indeed belong to any authentically Christian understanding of salvation, an affirmation of the ancient doctrine of "deification" is not the only way to bring this idea to expression. There are other, equally coherent ways of treating the problem of participation which do not lay upon us the obligation to embrace—as a straightforward affirmation of "deification" most certainly would—the metaphysical structure which (historically) made the idea of "deification" possible in the first place. Both Karl Barth and Eberhard Jüngel had a place in their theologies for the theme of "participation," but both treated the theme on the basis of a quite different understanding of divine "being" and human "being" than that found in the Eastern churches. It is in the interest of unfolding their (largely) shared vision of participation in God that this essay has been written.

Participation in God in the Theology of Karl Barth

Those coming to the writings of Karl Barth fresh from an encounter with Eastern Orthodox soteriologies may be forgiven for thinking that Barth is confused—and that his confusion is of a very fundamental sort. On the one hand, Barth can make statements such as the following:

> Jesus Christ . . . does not exist as *the Son of God* without also participating as such in *human* essence [*meschlichen Wesens*]. And He does not exist as *the Son of Man* without participating as such in the essence of the Son of God and therefore in *divine* essence [*göttlichen Wesens*]. On both sides, there is a genuine and real *being-in-participation* [*teilhaftigsein*]. . . . In His divine essence, He shares in *human* essence. So radically and totally does He share in it that He causes His existence to become and to be the existence of the man Jesus of Nazareth as well. And, again, He thereby gives to the human essence of Jesus of Nazareth a share in His own, the *divine* essence of the eternal Son who is equal to the Father and the Holy Spirit.[2]

On the other hand, Barth everywhere rejects the concept of "divinization." He denies that what he calls the "exaltation" of the human is at all the same thing as "divinization."[3] The objection lies immediately to hand: surely, Barth must not have understood the meaning of the word "divinization" as the Orthodox employ it. Had he done so, he would have seen that although his language

---

2. *KD* IV/2:67 (*CD* IV/2:62). All translations in this chapter are my own.
3. *KD* IV/2:72; cf. 60, 68, 71, 77–83, 87–90, 94, 100, 117.

is a bit sloppy—no Orthodox theologian today would make himself guilty of suggesting that the human participates in the divine *essence*—what Barth wants to affirm with his first set of statements is basically what the Orthodox are seeking to bring to expression with their concept of "divinization." How can he, then, with any consistency at all, affirm the one and deny the other? Surely, he must be confused.

As I say, such perplexity is understandable—but the truth is that Barth is not in the least confused. The reader who thinks he is has made two closely related mistakes. First, Barth's use of the word "essence" in relation to the category of "participation" is not the result of sloppy thinking or faulty expression. He means exactly what he says—and what he means lies at the heart of his differences with the Orthodox. In truth, the urge immediately to compare Barth's statements on human participation in God with those of the Orthodox must be curbed, or what is distinctive about Barth's teaching on this subject will inevitably be missed. The second (less serious) mistake is that of not allowing Barth himself to define what he means by "divinization" before deciding that he is in error. Barth's primary conversation-partner in his treatment of the theme of "divinization" is classical Lutheranism. To the extent that Eastern Orthodoxy comes into the picture, it is only as a possible forerunner of certain Lutheran concerns. One might be tempted to suppose—on the basis of such an acknowledgment—that if Barth was not really addressing himself to Orthodoxy, then there might still be room in his thought for a more Orthodox conception of participation. And yet the first mistake would still prevent us from appreciating fully the consequences of his rejection of "divinization."

Barth's treatment of the problem of participation differs from the Orthodox approach, at the end of the day, by being historically oriented rather than metaphysically oriented. The "exaltation" of the human occurs in and through a history—the history of Jesus Christ. It is not the consequence of a metaphysically conceived "indwelling" of the divine on the part of the human; it is the consequence of a human participation in a concrete history in which both the "essence" of God and the "essence" of the human are—in a sense yet to be established—*made real*. Thus the link which "joins" divine "essence" to human "essence" is not an abstract doctrine of being but rather *history*; if human "exaltation" takes place in the same history as that in which the "essence" of God is made real, then one can speak meaningfully of a participation in the divine "essence." But now we will need to spell out in greater detail how Barth arrives at these conclusions.

The Gracious Election of God as the Basis for Humiliation and Exaltation

For Barth, both the humiliation of God and the exaltation of the human have their ontological ground in the divine election of grace. "God's eternal election is concretely the *election of Jesus Christ*, i.e., the decision and action in which God in His Son elected and determined Himself for the human and . . . the human *for Himself*. It is the decision and action of God in which He took upon Himself the reprobation of the sinful human with all of its consequences and . . . elected precisely this human *for participation* in His own holiness and majesty, humiliation for Himself and exaltation for the human."[4] In the gracious election of God, both divine and human being are given their own most essential determination—that which makes God to be God and the human to be human. And given that election consists in an *eternal* decision, there was never a "time" when this decision had not already been made. There is no "essence" of God and no "essence" of the human abstracted from the concrete determination which gives to each its character. For Barth, this means (among other things) that we are forbidden to postulate a mode of being or existence in God above and prior to this eternal decision.[5] "Essence" is to be understood as a function of that original and originating act.

So, when in the history of Jesus Christ there takes place the humiliation of God and the exaltation of the human, what is taking place is the "making real" in time of that which was already real and true of both God and the human in the divine decision.[6] What takes place is, in a real sense, a repetition of that eternal act of determination in time by means of its historical fulfillment.[7]

4. *KD* IV/2:33 (*CD* IV/2:31).
5. See *KD* IV/2:34 (*CD* IV/2:32–33):

God was not alone even in the beginning of all his ways and works and not even effective alone: *not without man*. . . . The man who, by God's grace, is directed towards God's grace and thereby caught up in this homeward movement is not a latecomer on the scene who would later have to withdraw and disappear. He does not exist only secondarily. He is there, precisely there, in the Whence from which all things (including himself as the last created!) derive in the temporal execution of the will of God. He is there in the eternal decision of God with God's Son as the *first*, the primary object and content of the divine primal and foundational will [*Ur- und Grundwillens*]. Certainly not as a second God, certainly not himself eternal like God, certainly as a creature bound by time and limited in other ways, unable in his own strength to rise above the threat posed by nothingness. As this creature, he is, however—because longed for and willed by God before all things, even before the in-breaking of his own time—by, with, and before God, as real in his way as God is in his. In the decree of God which grounds all reality, he is even *foundationally* real [grund*real*]. There are no heights or depths, no one day or at that time, in which we can have anything to do with God without also immediately having to do with him, with this *human*.

In support of this last claim, Barth understands John 1:2 to refer to Jesus Christ, the God-human, and not to an eternal Son abstracted from his humanity. It was Jesus Christ who was in the beginning with God. See *KD* IV/2:35 (*CD* IV/2:33). I have already treated these matters on the basis of a close reading of Barth's doctrine of election in *KD* II/2 and will not revisit here the many passages that could be brought forth in support of the claims I am making (see ch. 7, "Grace and Being: The Role of God's Gracious Election in Karl Barth's Theological Ontology," in this volume).
6. *KD* IV/2:91 (*CD* IV/2:84).
7. *KD* IV/2:38 (*CD* IV/2:36).

The "essence" of God therefore is not something that can be spoken of rightly without reference to the divine humiliation which takes place in the *history* of Jesus Christ. And the "essence" of the human is not something that can be spoken of rightly without reference to the exaltation that takes place in the *history* of Jesus Christ. Thus, for Karl Barth, "essence" is not something that is fixed and immovable in itself, a metaphysical substructure or "substance" that guarantees to God or to the human Jesus identity with himself. To repeat: "essence" exists nowhere—neither in eternity nor in time—in abstraction from the concrete material "determination" which makes it to be what it is. Moreover, both the "essence" of God and the "essence" of the human can be placed "in motion,"[8] for both are actualized in the history of Jesus Christ. And this also means, then, that Barth's oft-discussed *actualism* finds its home not in acts abstracted from an "essence" which is untouched by them but in "essence" understood as a complete description of a being-in-act. God is what God does—and humanity is what Jesus does. "Essence" is thus a description of a person or thing *in its entirety*, in the sum total of its existence, in all of its acts and relations[9]—above all, where the question of that which differentiates the person or entity from others is in view. This is the first thing that needs to be said about the relation of election to exaltation.

But there is also a second thing to be said which already announced itself in the foregoing discussion and now needs to be specified. What is "assumed" by the Word of God in the incarnation is, to be sure, a particular human nature. But precisely in its particularity, it is the humanity of all men and women in all times and places. "That which God received into unity with Himself and His divine being was and is—in a definite, individual form elected and prepared by Him for that purpose—not 'a man' but rather the *human*, the same being and essence, the same species and nature which is that of all men, which distinguishes them as men and differentiates them from other creatures."[10] And so it comes about that in the movement in which this person has his particular humanity, "*humanitas* itself is set in motion."[11] The exaltation of Jesus *is* the exaltation of the humanity of all men and women—and this not merely as potentiality but really and truly. And it can be this because what it means to be human has been decided in eternity by means of our election

8. See, e.g., *KD* IV/2:30 (*CD* IV/2:29), where Barth speaks of "exaltation" in terms of "human essence in its purely creaturely determination as well as its fleshly determination, in its nature as well as its unnature, from its very center being placed in a *movement* through the act of the existing Subject which is here in view [i.e., Jesus of Nazareth]." The movement in question takes place in that human "essence" in its determination as creaturely and as fleshly is subjected to a higher determination, one that overrules both (being more original and fundamental than both) and therefore "exalts" human "essence."

9. *KD* IV/2:65 (*CD* IV/2:60–61). Here Barth says that "divine and human *essence*" is "synonymous with divine and human 'nature' or simply 'divinity' and 'humanity.'"

10. *KD* IV/2:51 (*CD* IV/2:48).

11. *KD* IV/2:30 (*CD* IV/2:29).

in Jesus Christ. We are "chosen in Him"—this is a statement pregnant with ontological significance. We are who we are "in Him." We can decide to live in conformity to our true being in him or not—we are free to do that. But whether we do the one or the other changes nothing with respect to the "in Him" of the divine election by which our true being—our "essence"—has been established.

The Relation of Divine Participation in the Human to Human Participation in the Divine

Because election is, concretely, the election of Jesus Christ and the election of ourselves only "in Him," the problem of participation must be handled christologically. For Barth, this means thinking in the direction pointed out by the "two natures" Christology of Chalcedon. And so he comes to an elaboration of the nature of "exaltation" only after setting the problem in the context of the unity of the Subject in whose act both humiliation and exaltation take place. This leads him to a consideration of the *unio hypostatica* and the *communio naturarum* (in that order). Much of this material need not detain us here. But some mention should be made of the conclusions which impact his discussion of the relation of humiliation to exaltation—and, most particularly, of the different kinds of participation which are in view when we speak of a divine participation in the human, on the one hand, and a human participation in the divine, on the other. As we shall see, although Barth speaks of a "reciprocal" or "two-sided" participation, he is very careful to insist that each differs in character from the other.

The exaltation of the human is made possible by the act of God by means of which God takes up human "essence" and unites it to himself. God alone is the Subject of this uniting action; there is no "point of contact" for it on the human side, no cooperation on the part of the creature. This is a "new creation" (2 Cor. 5:17) which consists in God's act of taking "human being into unity with His own."[12] The result of this uniting action is that "the existence of the Son of God became and is also the existence of a man." This, for Barth, is the most difficult point to comprehend, the truth that beggars all the language we might choose to describe it. There is no analogy to the *unio hypostatica*—not in the heavenly sphere and certainly not in the earthly. The *unio hypostatica* can be understood, to the extent that it is understood at all, only in terms of itself.[13] What we can do is to try to speak correctly of its result. That the existence of the Son of God became and is also the existence of a man does not mean that there are "two existing side by side or even in one another. There is only One—and no one, nothing, next to or in him: *God*

12. *KD* IV/2:49 (*CD* IV/2:46).
13. *KD* IV/2:54–64 (*CD* IV/2:51–60).

the Son, but this One now not only in His divine but also in His human being and essence."[14] And therefore "we have to do with *God Himself* when and as we have to do with this man. *God Himself* speaks when this man speaks in human language. *God Himself* acts and suffers when this man acts and suffers humanly. *God Himself* triumphs when this One triumphs as man. And it is for this reason that the human speaking, acting, suffering, and triumphing of this one man immediately concern us, it is for this reason that His human history is our salvation-history, which alters the whole human situation: because *God Himself* in His Son is its human Subject."[15] God himself is the Subject of a human life, a human death, and so on? How can this be? This is the mystery of the *unio hypostatica*. What we must not do is to seek to explain the fact that God is the Subject of this life in such a way as to overwhelm and finally negate his humanity. On the other hand, we must not say—in an effort to honor the real humanness of all that is said and done and experienced by Jesus of Nazareth—that God the Son is simply a human subject, that the Second Person of the Trinity is a human being without remainder (as occurred, e.g., in Hegel). We can come right up to the very edge of affirming this, but we cannot finally say it. Jesus Christ is the God-human, not a human being only. Without ceasing to be God, he is *also* true man.[16]

In this refusal of Hegel's direct identification of the being of the Son of God with the being of the human Jesus, in Barth's ongoing insistence on an "infinitely qualitative distinction" between that which Jesus Christ has in common with the Father and the Holy Spirit as the Son of God and that which he has in common with all other human beings as the Son of Man,[17] a confessional peculiarity surfaces whose significance becomes more clear as he turns to the subject of a *communio naturarum*. This is a subject on which Reformed and Lutheran theologians were sharply divided in the seventeenth century. Barth makes it clear that if he were forced to choose between them, he would have to side with the Reformed—because of his concern to avoid a direct identification of God with the human Jesus. But he also wants to affirm what he sees to be the valid concern in the Lutheran position.

The valid concern is that there is, indeed, a participation of the human in the divine and not merely a participation of the divine in the human. "There is no moment of the human essence which is untouched or excluded from its existence in and with that of the Son of God and thereby from the union with, and participation in, this divine essence."[18] Certainly, such an affirmation does give place to a Lutheran concern. Participation is two-sided or reciprocal; it is not unidirectional. And yet the Reformed element comes into play at the point

14. *KD* IV/2:53 (*CD* IV/2:50).
15. *KD* IV/2:54 (*CD* IV/2:51).
16. *KD* IV/2:43 (*CD* IV/2:41).
17. *KD* IV/2:65 (*CD* IV/2:61).
18. *KD* IV/2:69 (*CD* IV/2:64).

at which Barth finds it necessary to distinguish the *kind* of participation we are dealing with in each case.

Barth explains the difference this way: "Notwithstanding all their reciprocity, the two moments of this happening are different *in character*. They differ in that the one, as the essence of the Son of God, is wholly the *giving*; the other, exalted to existence and reality only through Him and in Him, is wholly the *receiving*."[19] Thus divine essence is structured by a giving, and human essence is structured by a receiving that finds its basis in the divine giving. All of this sounds very formal; in truth, it is not. The difference is material in nature. "In the Son of God and therefore through the divine Subject, united in His act, each of His two natures receives and has—without being sublated or altered as such—a *determination*. Through and in Him, the divine receives its determination to the human; through and in Him, the human receives its determination from the divine."[20] A determination *to* the human is materially different from a determination *from* the divine. For the determination of the divine essence *to* the human allows Barth to say—in a way that sounds like direct identification—that the Subject who suffers and dies on the cross is God the Son. But the determination of the human essence *from* the divine is realized in and through the willed obedience of the human Jesus to the will of his Father, two wills which remain distinct even as the one is conformed to the other. And so Barth concludes that although the divine humiliation means that "God became man," it is not the case that the exaltation of the human means that "He [Jesus] became God."[21]

Now, admittedly, it is not easy to understand how these two sets of claims can be compatible. I said earlier that Barth locates the mystery on the side of the first statement: that the Subject who suffers and dies is God the Son. Lutheran theologians can make this statement more cleanly—but also, from Barth's point of view, with less regard for the mystery that is involved. I also suggested earlier that Barth comes up to the very edge of the Hegelian identification of the Son of God with a human being. The

---

19. *KD* IV/2:78 (*CD* IV/2:72).

20. *KD* IV/2:75 (*CD* IV/2:70). "Without being altered or sublated"—that is the Reformed element.

21. *KD* IV/2:77 (*CD* IV/2:71). The root of Barth's protest against "divinization" is to be found at this precise point—in his insistence that divine humiliation and human exaltation do not stand in a relation of simple correspondence and that therefore the participation which each entails differs in kind. Divine humiliation and human exaltation do not stand in a relation of simple correspondence because both depend on the assumption of human flesh by the Son of God and on it alone. The Son of God assumed human flesh into unity with himself and thereby became human. But "there was and is . . . no Son of Man who assumed divine essence to his human essence and thus became the Son of God." And *KD* IV/2:78 (*CD* IV/2:72): "Thus, whatever may be the nature of the second moment of that history, the exaltation of the Son of Man, it is not to be sought in a divinization of His human essence corresponding to His becoming human."

second set of statements—involving a conformity of a human will to the will of the Father—would bring Barth very close to saying that all there is on the side of the "Son of God" is the human will. But, of course, that is not what he wants to say. What he wants to say is that there is, in the one Son of God, a human will which conforms to the divine will which he shares with the Father and the Holy Spirit. But the tension which seems to arise here between the two sets of claims is, in part at least, the consequence of our natural tendency to think of "subjects" in substantial terms. Barth does not do this. He is quite explicit in saying that *the Subject Jesus Christ is this history*"[22]—the history in which God takes up human essence into unity with himself, a history which happened at a definite time and place and, because it did happen, continues to happen. "As this history, it is not enclosed, it is not imprisoned in that time."[23] Jesus Christ, the same yesterday, today, and forever. Hence we would do better to think of the hypostatic union in actualistic terms, as a *uniting*, rather than as a completed action, a union. For then we would understand that Barth is *not* trying to think through the relation of a divine Subject (conceived along the lines of an unchanging substance) to a history of human willing and acting. He is saying that the divine Subject (in this case, God the Son, the Second Person of the Trinity) *is* the history in which the human willing of Jesus conforms to the will of his heavenly Father—a history which is anticipated in the subjection of the Son to the Father in election. This does not remove the mystery of the incarnation, certainly; it merely seeks to locate this mystery in the right place. But it does show us that the tension between the two statements has a lot to do with our tendency to revert to substantialist modes of thinking.

Barth has done as much as he can—on Reformed soil—to honor the Lutheran concern. We are now in a position to look more closely at the nature of "exaltation" and the participation in God which it entails.

The Nature of Exaltation

To be "exalted," according to Barth, is to be "placed at God's side . . . in true *fellowship* with Him."[24] Now, how does this come about? It does not come about on the basis of a "penetration" (*Durchdringung*)[25] of the divine nature of Jesus Christ by the human. Earlier in his career, at the time of writing the first edition of his *Romans* commentary, Barth had a fondness for what Herbert

22. *KD* IV/2:118 (*CD* IV/2:107). It should be noted that although Barth placed this entire sentence in italics to give it emphasis, such emphasis is altogether lacking in Geoffrey Bromiley's translation.
23. *KD* IV/2:119 (*CD* IV/2:107).
24. *KD* IV/2:4 (*CD* IV/2:6).
25. *KD* IV/2:84 (*CD* IV/2:77).

Anzinger has called an *organologische Metaphorik*[26]—implying, above all, an "indwelling" of the human by the divine. After turning his back on such imagery in the second edition of his commentary, however, Barth consistently kept his distance from the language of "indwelling" with respect to *both* sides of the christological problem: the relation of the divine to the human as well as the relation of the human to the divine. How, then, does "exaltation" come about if not by a "penetration" of the divine by the human in Jesus Christ?

The first thing to notice is that Barth says our attention should always be focused on the *event* in which the divine "communication" to the human takes place in Jesus Christ. What must not happen is a consideration of the human Jesus as "cut off from the dynamic of the history in which it becomes and is one with the divine."[27] The effect of this decision is to see the communication in the present tense rather than the past tense, as a giving rather than as a giftedness.

The second thing to observe is the nature of the event in which "communication" takes place. On the side of God, it consists in a "turning towards" (*Zuwendung*) the human Jesus in electing grace. On the side of the human Jesus, it consists in a "confrontation" with this electing grace of God.[28] The human Jesus *confronts* the electing grace of God as his "first" and "last," as his "exclusive" and "complete" determination.[29]

And, finally, the third thing which needs to be understood is the nature of this "determination." The word "determination" (*Bestimmung*), which Barth frequently uses to describe the act of God which gives rise to "exaltation," has nothing to do with a determinism which leaves no room for human freedom. Throughout, it is presupposed that the One to whom the electing grace of God comes may act freely in response. We would do better, perhaps, to translate the word "vocation" but then we would need to add that this vocation comes with a sense of "right" (the electing and creating God's "right" to fulfill his covenant with his human creatures). Thus an authoritative "claim" would not be far from the mark.

"Exaltation," then, takes place through a free act which in turn consists in agreement with the divine will, service of the divine act, correspondence to the grace of God, and a posture of gratitude, which is the only possibility on the basis of electing grace.[30] Agreement, service, correspondence, gratitude—all

---

26. Herbert Anzinger, *Glaube und kommunikative Praxis: Eine Studie zur "vordialektischen" Theologie Karl Barths* (Munich: Kaiser, 1991), 246.

27. *KD* IV/2:87 (*CD* IV/2:80). See also *KD* IV/2:86 (*CD* IV/2:79), where Barth says that we are not to look away from "the event of the divine giving and human receiving to that which is *given* to the human essence of Jesus Christ in this event." To look away from this event would presuppose that human "essence" could be abstracted from this history in which it is what it is.

28. *KD* IV/2:96–97 (*CD* IV/2:87–88).

29. *KD* IV/2:97 (*CD* IV/2:88).

30. *KD* IV/2:101 (*CD* IV/2:92).

of these speak of the man Jesus *standing before* God, not of his *indwelling* of God. The ontological distinction between the Creator and the creature is in no way set aside or even qualified. It is an exaltation to true human freedom (a freedom which is to be found only in obedience), to sinlessness, to the "authority" (*exousia*) to be the Mediator between God and humanity, and to a share in the dignity and majesty of the Son of God.[31] Throughout, the otherness of the creature from God, his integrity as creature, is preserved. "God became man in order that man may—not become God but come to God."[32]

Provisional Summary

Barth himself summarized his achievement this way: "We have 'actualized' the doctrine of the incarnation."[33] And he added, "Nothing is left of the static [element] in the broad center of the traditional 'doctrine of the Person of Jesus Christ'—in its unfolding of the concepts *unio, communio,* and *communication.* . . . Thinking and speaking in pure concepts of movement, we have *translated* that entire phenomenology *back* into the report of a *history.* And we have done this because the object of that report . . . is not originally a phenomenon, or a complex of phenomena, but rather a history: the history of *God* in His mode of existence as the Son."[34]

Another way to describe Barth's accomplishment—a way which sets the stage for comparison with Jüngel—is to say that he took up the ancient doctrine of the *anhypostasis* and *enhypostasis* of the human nature of Christ and translated it into relational and historical categories.[35] In *CD* IV/2 the *anhypostasia* becomes an explanation of the lived (historical) relation of the human Jesus in his historical existence to the divine Logos. Its meaning is that the human Jesus lives from his confrontation with the electing grace of God. This, as we have seen, was his first and last, his exclusive and complete determination. He had no existence independent of this confrontation and the determination given in and with it. His being is a being *in the act* of confronting the electing grace of God. And insofar as the electing grace of God encounters him in the ongoing act by means of which the Logos unites himself with the human Jesus, the being of the man Jesus—precisely as a being in the act of confronting the electing grace of God—is a being in the Word. On the other hand, the *enhypostasia* becomes an explanation of the lived (eternal) relation of the Logos to Jesus. The being of the human Jesus in the act of confronting the electing grace

31. *KD* IV/2:101, 106, 110 (*CD* IV/2:92, 96, 100).

32. *KD* IV/2:118.

33. *KD* IV/2:116 (*CD* IV/2:105).

34. *KD* IV/2:117–18 (*CD* IV/2:106).

35. On what follows, see esp. *KD* IV/2:99–100 (*CD* IV/2:90–91). For Jüngel's relatively independent elaboration of this theme, see below, pp. 248–51.

of God as a being in the Logos finds its ontological ground in the turning of the Logos towards him in grace from all eternity. And this in turn tells us something very important about the Logos. The Logos is not what it is apart from this turning in grace towards the human Jesus. This revised understanding of the *enhypostasia* is therefore the key to understanding what Barth meant by the "humanity of God."[36] That Jesus has his being in the Logos *eternally* can mean only that the Logos is never without Jesus and that therefore God is a human God.

Barth was fully aware that he would be criticized for this actualistic ontology.[37] And so he posed to himself the rhetorical question "How can a being be interpreted as an *act*, an act as a *being*? How can God, how can man, how can both in their unity in Jesus Christ be interpreted as *history*?" His answer was that, however incomprehensible it may be to think in this way, so long as there is a genuine necessity for it, then even doubts about its possibility cannot finally be made decisive.[38] And he found this necessity in the demand which Jesus Christ, as the divine-human reality that he is, lays upon us.

The entire metaphysical apparatus by means of which the ancient idea of "divinization" was first elaborated (and continues to be so today) has been set aside and replaced by an actualistic understanding of the history of God in God's mode of existence as Son. In this history, the human too participates. But as stated at the outset, the link which joins the two together is not an abstract doctrine of being but a common history. Both true divinity and true humanity are—on the basis of a free, eternal decision—constituted in and through the same history. It is the singularity of this history which constitutes the unity of the "person" of Christ.

And yet! On the basis of his actualistic Christology, Barth is able to say everything that the Orthodox would like to say with their concept of "divinization"—and this is a point of no little ecumenical significance. "Exaltation" is, in the final analysis, "the movement of man from below *to above*, from the earth as his own proper realm—a realm made good by God's creation and made ever so dark by himself—*into* heaven as the proper realm of God."[39] Or again, "He . . . *raised up* human essence into essence in Himself."[40] What more could the Orthodox want?

36. Karl Barth, *Die Menschlichkeit Gottes*, Theologische Studien 48 (Zollikon-Zurich: Evangelischer Verlag, 1956).

37. *KD* IV/2:117 (*CD* IV/2:106). Speaking of his unwillingness even to attach himself to the Reformed version of the timeless and nonactual treatment of the divine and human in Jesus Christ, Barth observed, "There can be no doubt we have left it behind us as well, along with the entire conception. From no side may we expect to be praised for our 'orthodoxy.'"

38. *KD* IV/2:120 (*CD* IV/2:108).

39. *KD* IV/2:30 (*CD* IV/2:29).

40. *KD* IV/2:47 (*CD* IV/2:44).

The Participation of the Believer in God

As a consequence of the divine election, the particular humanity of Jesus is "humanity as such, to which every man is determined."[41] As we have already seen, he is the true, exalted human; in him human essence was "set in motion" and lifted above its creaturely and fleshly limitations. In him human essence was granted a place alongside God, as the loyal covenant-partner in God. No one other than Jesus himself participates in God in this unbroken way where their lived "existence" in this world is concerned. Only in him is essence *already* existence and existence *already* essence. For those who live "in the flesh," essence and existence fall apart. Our "essence"—our true humanity—stands behind us in the "there and then" of Jesus of Nazareth as the reality which sets a limit to our being in sin. And it stands before us as the eschatological goal of our lives, a goal which will mean a complete overcoming of the division between our true essence and our lived existence. But this then also means that participation in God belongs to our eschatological future, a future whose arrival will mean the end of history.

It is not surprising, then, that Barth never speaks directly of a participation in God *in this world* with respect to anyone other than Jesus. He does not do so even in the case of the believer. He does indeed speak of a *participatio Christi*—a participation in the holiness of the *human* Jesus.[42] But such conscious and willed participation in the humanity of Jesus never succeeds in bringing an end to our existence in the flesh. In that we hear his call, in that it is given to us to share in an event of Self-interpretation in and through which Jesus Christ corresponds here and now to the event of his existence there and then,[43] we are given a share in his sanctity—and to just this extent, we anticipate our future participation in God. We do not cease to be sinners—but we are now "disturbed sinners."[44] Without ceasing to live "below" and therefore "in the flesh," we are enabled to look away from ourselves, to lift up our heads to the One who is exalted above.[45] Our positive sanctification consists in this act of looking to him, of bearing witness to *his* sanctity—a sanctity which we never possess in ourselves but is always "alien" to us.[46] But such "looking to Him" does indeed mean real change, a "positive alteration of our being below."[47] For in those moments in which we do look to him, our existence is brought into a relation of correspondence to our true essence in him and the split between them overcome—even if only actualistically.

41. *KD* IV/2:587 (*CD* IV/2:519).
42. *KD* IV/2:586 (*CD* IV/2:518).
43. *KD* IV/2:42 (*CD* IV/2:39).
44. *KD* IV/2:593–95 (*CD* IV/2:524–26).
45. *KD* IV/2:596 (*CD* IV/2:527).
46. *KD* IV/2:586 (*CD* IV/2:518).
47. *KD* IV/2:596 (*CD* IV/2:527).

Participation in God in the Theology of Eberhard Jüngel

Virtually all of the themes which we have just traced in Barth can be found in the various writings of Eberhard Jüngel—above all, in his masterpiece, *Gott als Geheimnis der Welt*.[48] But there are differences in the way these themes are handled—differences which reflect differing attitudes towards the dogmatic value of research into the life of Jesus, differing attitudes towards hermeneutics, differing confessional orientations, and, above all, differing assessments of the situation in which theology is to be done. The subtitle of Jüngel's great work— "On the Grounding of the Theology of the Crucified One in the Controversy between Theism and Atheism"[49]—is disclosive of the primary concern which runs like a red thread through the whole of his theological work, namely, to address the challenge posed to Christian theology in modern times by atheism. This gives to his work an apologetic edge not found in Barth.

Jüngel's Early Reception of the anhypostasia and enhypostasia Doctrine

The christological foundation for Jüngel's highly suggestive treatment of the problem which interests us here was already laid in an early essay, written on the occasion of Karl Barth's eightieth birthday in 1966.[50] In "Jesu Wort und Jesus als Wort Gottes," Jüngel seeks to elaborate the christological problem as the problem of the relation of the "earthly Jesus" to the risen Lord of the church's kerygma. And he seeks to address this problem along the lines of a modified understanding of the *anhypostasia-enhypostasia* doctrine of the ancient church—which invites comparison with Barth.

Jüngel self-consciously follows Barth in translating the concepts of *hypostasis, enhypostasis*, and *anhypostasis* into relational and historical concepts. But there are differences between them.

First, the anhypostatic element. "Jesus proclaimed the lordship of God. Jesus' behavior corresponded to His proclamation. Jesus' earthly existence was therefore, as such and in its entirety, determined by its relation to the lordship of God. What was decisive was the fact that Jesus *proclaimed* the

---

48. Eberhard Jüngel, *Gott als Geheimnis der Welt*, 6th ed. (Tübingen: Mohr Siebeck, 1992); translated from the 3rd rev. ed. as *God as the Mystery of the World*, trans. Darrell L. Guder (Grand Rapids: Eerdmans, 1983).

49. My translation.

50. Eberhard Jüngel, "Jesu Wort und Jesus als Wort Gottes: Ein hermeneutischer Beitrag zum christologischen Problem," in *Parrhesia (Karl Barth zum 80. Geburtstag)*, ed. Eberhard Busch, Jürgen Fangmeier, and Max Geiger (Zurich: Evangelischer Verlag, 1966), 82–100; repr. in Jüngel, *Unterwegs zur Sache: Theologische Bemerkungen* (Munich: Kaiser, 1972), 126–44. (It is the latter edition which I will cite from here.) It should be noted that Karl Barth greeted this essay with interest and told its author that he would "gladly" hear more along the lines developed in it. See Karl Barth to Eberhard Jüngel, September 9, 1967, in Karl Barth, *Briefe, 1961–1968*, ed. Jürgen Fangmeier and Hinrich Stoevesandt (Zurich: Theologischer Verlag, 1975), 424.

lordship of God. Jesus' deeds, His behavior, His entire earthly existence was constituted by the fact that this man was the Proclaimer of the lordship of God. . . . The event of proclamation constitutes the existence of the man Jesus. It is in this sense that the being of the man Jesus is essentially *a being in the act of the word*"[51]—and not just any word but the word which proclaims the divine lordship. Whereas Barth laid almost the whole of his emphasis upon Jesus' confrontation with the electing grace of God, Jüngel holds that a more responsible appropriation of (then) recent research into the life of the earthly Jesus would see him as the Proclaimer of the lordship of God. Although these two things—election and the lordship of God—are obviously closely related (what is election if not an exercise in lordship, dominion, sovereignty?), there is a subtle shift of emphasis which occurs here and has to do with more than developments in New Testament studies. It also has something to do with confessional differences. Barth, the Reformed theologian, is preoccupied with election; Jüngel, as a Lutheran theologian, is preoccupied with the word preached and heard. In any event, Jüngel's understanding of the being of the earthly Jesus as a being in the act of the word of divine lordship leads directly to his recasting of the *anhypostasia*. The meaning of the *anhypostasia* is that Jesus wanted to be, and was, "nothing for Himself." He did not exist "out of Himself" and therefore had no independent existence. Without the lordship of God which he proclaims, he would not only not be who he was; he would in fact be nothing at all.[52] Jesus was who he was in his relation to the divine lordship in and through his historical existence; this is the modified meaning of the *anhypostasia*.

The meaning of the *enhypostasia* is tied to the fact that Jesus' being in the act of the word of proclamation is, in truth, a being in the Word of God. Jesus' uniqueness as the man who exists anhypostatically finds its explanation theologically in the fact that God turned towards him in grace; it finds its explanation ontologically in the grounding of his human being in the mode of being of the Logos. Jesus' relationship to his Father is "possible only because the eternal Son, for His part, is obedient to the Father" and, in this obedience, "turns Himself preveniently to the man Jesus as the One *who makes possible* personal unity with Him."[53]

That any of this is known at all is the consequence of the resurrection of Jesus. "In the light of the Resurrected One . . . the *becoming* of the eternal Word as a prevenient turning of God to this man and therefore the relationship of the Logos to Jesus as that which makes possible the relationship of Jesus to the Father are revealed. The identification of the Word of God with Jesus of Nazareth that took place on Easter makes it clear that Jesus 'lived

51. Jüngel, "Jesu Wort und Jesus als Wort Gottes," 128–29.
52. Ibid., 136.
53. Ibid., 141.

249

towards the Father and from the Father' only insofar as the eternal Word of God lived from the Father and towards Jesus."[54] Thus the being human of Jesus is enhypostasized in the becoming of the eternal Word—a becoming which reaches its climax in death.[55]

Put this way, it is clear that the *enhypostasia* has more to do with the relation of the eternal Word to Jesus than it does Jesus' relation to God. The theological significance of the *enhypostasia* is missed where it is simply made to be the positive form of the negative term *anhypostasia*. The significance of the *enhypostasia* lies in the humanity of God, the participation of the Logos in the being human of Jesus. If it is the relation of the Word to Jesus which makes possible Jesus' relation to his Father, then the relation of the Word to Jesus is a relation with a history, a history in which the Word himself becomes what he is.

But now we come to a final question. What we are dealing with here is two relations: the relation of Jesus to the Father and the relation of the Word of God to Jesus. The former, we have said, finds its ground in the latter. But can anything more be said about the relation of these two relations to each other? Jüngel's answer to this question constitutes a final departure from Barth.

Barth made much of the simultaneity of divine humiliation and human exaltation in Jesus. These were not, for him, two different and successive states but a description of two basic moments of a single history which are strictly related even as they are placed over against each other, which are simultaneously effective and mutually interpreting.[56] Jüngel can accept the note of simultaneity only in a qualified form. While it is true that the anhypostatic existence of the man Jesus would not have been possible, at any point in his history, apart from the becoming (i.e., the Self-emptying and humiliation) of the eternal Word, this is something that is revealed only in the resurrection. What this means for Jüngel at this point in the development of his thinking is that the relations depicted by the *anhypostasia* and the *enhypostasia* have their own special times.[57] The *anhypostasia* alone is revealed in and through the life of the earthly Jesus. The *enhypostasia*, which is revealed in the resurrection, remained hidden during his life.

The question then becomes this: Is this a matter of revelation alone? Is it a merely epistemological state of affairs? Or does it have ontic—if not ontological—significance? Jüngel sets the stage for his later development of the theme of the humanity of God in *Gott als Geheimnis der Welt* when he says, "As relations between time and eternity which take place in time, they are, however, to be distinguished historically, insofar as each of the relations which determine the *whole* being of Jesus Christ has its *special* time. . . . He

54. Ibid., 141–42.
55. Ibid., 142n41.
56. See ibid., 139n34. Jüngel is here citing from *KD* IV/2:118 (*CD* IV/2:106).
57. Jüngel, "Jesu Wort und Jesus als Wort Gottes," 139.

exists thereby in each time in the same being but exists in each time in the same being *differently*. Therefore the existence of Jesus Christ is an existence in the difference of the times."[58] Jüngel is able to affirm a simultaneity of humiliation and exaltation only in the restricted sense that both of these moments in the history of the being of Jesus Christ participate in the eternity of God. In history, however, there is a succession made possible by a turning point with ontic significance.

Gott als Geheimnis der Welt: *The Logic of Love*

The being of God as the event in which God *comes* to the world in his Self-identification with the crucified man Jesus is expressed *ontologically* by the Johannine statement "God is love"; *theologically*, it is expressed by the doctrine of the Trinity.

"God is love" (1 John 4:8). The task of theology in the ontological sphere is "to think God as love. . . . In doing so, it must accomplish two things. On the one hand, it must do justice to the essence of love, which, as a predicate of God also, may not contradict what humans experience as love. And on the other hand, it must do justice to the being of God, which remains so distinctive from the event of *human* love that 'God' does not become a superfluous word."[59] It is Feuerbach's reduction of "God" to human love which Jüngel has in view in his insistence on maintaining the distinction between God and the human. But the effort to keep God and the human distinct must not result in a construal of God as love which would contradict what humans know as love. For if the meaning of the word "love" as applied to God were completely other than what humans normally understand as "love," then any word could be used to describe the being-in-act of God, and the use of "love" or any other word would be equally arbitrary. Jüngel is right, I think, to call this "hermeneutical nonsense."[60] But our customary "preunderstanding" of love will have to undergo correction and elaboration in directions not anticipated in what is experienced on the human plane.[61] And it is important to keep in mind that "the being of the Triune God should not and may not be deduced from the logic of the essence of love. Rather, the full understanding of the statement 'God is love' first becomes discernible on the basis of the history

58. Ibid., 139–40 (emphasis mine).

59. Jüngel, *Gott als Geheimnis der Welt*, 430–31 (*God as the Mystery of the World*, 315). Translations from this work are my own.

60. Ibid., 434 (*God as the Mystery of the World*, 317).

61. A critic coming to Jüngel's work directly from Barth might well be tempted to regard his procedure here as an exercise in speculation. But such a judgment must not be made too quickly. In carrying out his corrections, Jüngel never loses sight of the concrete event in which God identified himself with the crucified Jesus. And it is, after all, the First Epistle of John which makes "God is love" to be the ontological explanation for the incarnation.

of the being of God, in which and as which He realizes His being as Subject in a trinitarian way."[62]

Thus Jüngel begins his exposition of "love" with an account of the "phenomenal situation"[63] in which human love realizes itself in its most complete form—that is, when the love of the loving I is reciprocated by the beloved thou. What happens in this situation is this: "In love, the I gives itself to the beloved thou in such a way that it no longer wants to be I without this thou. . . . The relation of the I to itself which has characterized its existence to this point in time is profoundly disturbed."[64] There is something akin to death in this. From a being that is structured by self-possession or self-having, the loving I steps out of itself, risking the loss of self in its desire to be had by its beloved thou. The loving I surrenders itself to its beloved thou—with no conditions or demands or expectations. In that such love is reciprocated by the beloved thou, an ontological transformation occurs. The loving I receives a "new being." "In the place of self-possession, of self-having, there enters in a becoming possessed and, in a certain sense, a being possessed."[65] The surrender in question is not an act of *absolute* selflessness. I have, after all, set my affections on only one out of many. I have made a selection. And to this extent, my act of surrender to my beloved thou is still an act of self-relating. But the character of this act is such that I only have myself now in the form of being had by another. And thus genuine love, formally considered, is "the event of a still greater selflessness in the midst of a great and justifiably very great self-relatedness." Materially, it is "the event of the unity of life and death in favor of life."[66]

But the selflessness which emerges in the event of love is not only transformative of the loving I's relation to itself (its self-relatedness); it is also transformative of all of its relations. Where selflessness enters in, there an element emerges—again, a "new being"—which has a tendency to reach out to others. "The I-thou relationship which [exists in the event of] love leads beyond itself. Love wants to radiate. For this reason, love does not lead into an idyllic retreat. It does not lead into a realm which stands over against lovelessness, hate, or even only inattentiveness and boredom. Rather, it leads into all of these, engaging them, penetrating ever more deeply into them. True love is lavish in view of itself. It wants to radiate into lovelessness."[67]

In doing all of this, love makes itself vulnerable in the extreme. It cannot destroy that which opposes it; it would destroy itself if it were anything but love. And so it must remain in its sphere, not transgressing the chasm which separates love and lovelessness, for to do so would mean its death. It can only seek to

---

62. Ibid., 432 (*God as the Mystery of the World*, 316).
63. Ibid., 450 (*God as the Mystery of the World*, 329).
64. Ibid., 434 (*God as the Mystery of the World*, 318).
65. Ibid., 439 (*God as the Mystery of the World*, 321).
66. Ibid., 434 (*God as the Mystery of the World*, 317).
67. Ibid., 445 (*God as the Mystery of the World*, 325).

transform lovelessness by remaining what it is. And thus its greatest strength lies in its weakness. Here again love unites life and death in favor of life.

Taken together, these reflections on the essence of love constitute the "pre-understanding" which Jüngel will call upon as an aid in understanding the statement "God is love" as an exposition of the Self-identification of God with the crucified man Jesus. But, of course, these reflections can perform this function only to the extent that they undergo correction. God *is* love; love is essential to his being. God does not need to be loved by human beings, for example, in order to *be* love. We make a first approach to understanding the statement that "God is love" when we recognize that God's love differs from human love in that God is lover and beloved at the same time. "God *differentiates* Himself in that He loves Himself. . . . In John's language, He is God the Father *and God the Son.*"[68] God's love for himself is not the self-love of an I who remains only I. But even now, we have not arrived at a complete explanation of the statement "God is love." God is not yet love itself in the relation of loving Father and the beloved Son who stands over against him. "God is . . . the radiant event of love itself"—the love of the Father for the Son spills over to the world of human beings. They, too, must participate in the relation of love which joins Father to Son and Son to Father.

But here an obstacle arises—which leads to a final clarification of the difference between divine love and human love. The humans who would be drawn into the love relationship between Father and Son exist in lovelessness. Unlike human love, which cannot enter into the sphere of lovelessness without ceasing to be what it is, divine love passes into the sphere of lovelessness itself in order that it may be what it truly is. And so the Father "sends" his beloved—"who is closer to Him than He is to Himself!"—into a situation which means certain death.[69] God can do this—without ceasing to be who he is and what he is as love—because the separation between Father and Son which is created by death is bridged by God as Spirit. "We are . . . speaking of *God as Spirit* when we have to interpret the separation of lover and beloved leading to death in such a way that God does not cease to be the *one* and the *living* God in the midst of this most painful separation but rather is supremely God in this situation."[70] But if God as Holy Spirit is the link between Father and Son in their separation, God is also as Holy Spirit the power which draws human beings into their relation of love. "We speak of *God as Spirit* when we have to interpret the separation of lover and beloved leading to death in such a way that lover and beloved grant a share in their mutual love to others."[71]

It is important to remember that Jüngel has explicitly told us that he is not seeking to deduce the doctrine of the Trinity from the logic of love. Ultimately,

68. Ibid., 448 (*God as the Mystery of the World*, 327).
69. Ibid.
70. Ibid., 449 (*God as the Mystery of the World*, 328).
71. Ibid.

it is only God's "identification" with the crucified man Jesus which requires that God be differentiated as Father, Son, and Spirit. But the logic of love does help us to understand what is happening in this differentiation—and why!—when once we come to know of it.

Gott als Geheimnis der Welt: *Christology and Trinity*

If the doctrine of the Trinity is not to be speculative, it must find its root in the human life and death of Jesus.[72] The earthly existence of Jesus as reported by the Gospels is not that of a superhuman or even a "divine man."[73] It is the existence of one who is strangely human, uniquely human, human in a way that no other has ever been human. Jüngel's explanation of this follows along the lines laid down in the earlier essay considered above, but is much more expansive. Jesus has his being in the act of proclaiming the lordship of God. But the lordship of God "is an expression for God Himself or, more precisely, for the active being of God in the horizon of this world, transforming it from the ground up."[74] In that Jesus is nothing for himself but has his being only in the act of proclaiming this lordship, his is a being in the active being of God in this world. What characterized Jesus' self-relationship in this world was his "unique *openness* for this divine activity in the performance of His existence, which corresponds to the [saying] 'God is closer to me than I am to myself.' . . . The *being* of this man was . . . the *event* of a selflessness which surpasses all self-relatedness." As such, the being of Jesus is the "human parable of the God who is love."[75]

Why did Jesus die as he did? The human existence of Jesus was a perfect fulfillment of the law of love—love of God and the neighbor. But this fulfillment did not come about through moral exertion; it was not the result of obedience to the law. Jesus did not even need the law to fulfill it because, living entirely out of himself and his love for God and the neighbor, he preceded the law. He anticipated it in fulfilling it. And this led to opposition, for the "royal freedom" by means of which he fulfilled the law without moral exertion brought the law into conflict with itself. For those "under the law," fulfillment of it is a demand, a compulsion. That Jesus should do what he does without respect to it, that he should be free of it in this sense, must have seemed to many to

---

72. Jüngel faults Barth's presentation of the foundation of the doctrine of the Trinity in *KD* I/1 in that it gave the impression of deducing the doctrine from the axiomatically held proposition "God reveals Himself as Lord" with the help of the formal logic of subject, predicate, and object. He congratulates Barth for overcoming this tendency in IV/2 by founding the doctrine in the humanity of Jesus. See Jüngel, *Gott als Geheimnis der Welt*, 481n22 (*God as the Mystery of the World*, 351n22).

73. Ibid., 489 (*God as the Mystery of the World*, 357).

74. Ibid., 484 (*God as the Mystery of the World*, 353).

75. Ibid., 490 (*God as the Mystery of the World*, 358).

constitute a destruction of the law and of the ordering of the community's life which it was intended to provide. In any event, it was this conflict which led to the death of Jesus as a criminal. According to the law itself, "the crucifixion of a criminal is the event of total God-abandonment."[76] By internalizing the conflict into which Jesus had brought the law with itself, he embraced death in God-abandonment. He whose entire existence was determined by the intimacy of its relation to God dies in God-abandonment.

The question now becomes, How do we get from the intimacy of Jesus' relation to God to the notion—decisive for the whole of Jüngel's theology—of God's Self-identification with the crucified man Jesus? The answer given here, as before, is by means of the resurrection. The meaning of the resurrection is that the human life of Jesus did not simply come to an end. Something took place in and through his death. And given that this something cannot be done by the dead Jesus (humanly speaking, death is a nonevent, the cessation of all activity), it can have been done only by God. "In this death, God Himself happened. . . . The resurrection of Jesus from the dead says that God identified Himself with this dead man. And this, then, also means that God identified Himself with Jesus in His God-abandonment. And this means further that God identified Himself with the life lived by this dead man."[77]

Where Jüngel's Christology is concerned, it is clear that the concept of "identification" is being asked to do all the work which the traditional language of incarnation, hypostatic union, and so on, was asked to perform. The unity of God with Jesus takes place in the event of identification, which Jüngel locates at the end of Jesus' life rather than at its beginning. What kind of "unity" is it that is produced in this way? Certainly, it is not a hypostatic unity. It is not even the unity of a single Subject—as Barth would have it. So what precisely is it? Jüngel is not altogether clear at this point, but I will risk the following interpretation.

The "identification" in question is an act of *love*. Love means surrender, the giving of oneself to another so completely and unreservedly that one's very being is determined from without. What happens in the event of God's identification with the dead Jesus is that "the being of this dead man determines God's being in such a way that one must speak of a differentiation of God and God."[78] For God to be determined in this way by Jesus is to allow Jesus to participate in God's own being. Hence Jesus *is* God but God *as Self-differentiated*. It is not necessary, on the soil of Jüngel's reflections, to think further about the relation of a preexisting Son of God to the man Jesus. The man Jesus *is* God. Earlier I noted that Barth comes up to the very edge of identifying the Second Person of the Trinity ("God the Son") with a human

76. Ibid., 495 (*God as the Mystery of the World*, 361).
77. Ibid., 497 (*God as the Mystery of the World*, 363).
78. Ibid., 498 (*God as the Mystery of the World*, 363).

being, only then to pull back. Jüngel does not pull back. The "identification" of God with the human Jesus is direct and immediate. Given that the Second Person of the Trinity is a human being, it follows quite naturally that Jüngel's view allows for a *kind* and degree of sociality that Barth's does not. Though united in love, the "Son" remains other than the "Father"—not an autonomous subject, certainly, but a distinct subject. It is not surprising, then, that Jüngel should warn against an overuse of the trinitarian axiom so loved by Barth, namely, *Opera Trinitatis ad extra sunt indivisa.*[79]

Of course, we do not have a complete doctrine of the Trinity before us when we have spoken only of the differentiation of God *and* God which occurs in God's identification with Jesus. The Self-differentiation which occurs in this act of identification does not stop with the differentiation of "Father" and "Son." For God identifies himself with the *dead* Jesus. How can God give himself over to death—and specifically to death in God-abandonment—and remain who and what he is? The answer to this question is provided by Jüngel's pneumatology. The Holy Spirit is the "bond of love" which joins together Father and Son even in their utter separation, thereby assuring that God remains God even as he "bears"[80] in his own being the death of his Son in God-abandonment. Thus talk of the Self-differentiation of God is incomplete without the further differentiation of the Spirit. Only with this further differentiation in God does it become possible to speak of a greater selflessness in the midst of ongoing self-relatedness. In giving himself (as "Son") away, God has himself.

The description of the event of the divine Self-differentiation which has here been set forth belongs entirely to the so-called economy of God. "The death of Jesus Christ . . . *forced* a differentiation between God and God."[81] Thus the differentiation in question is an event which occurred in time, as a historical event. Is it still possible to speak meaningfully of an "immanent Trinity" in distinction from this "economic Trinity"? Jüngel's answer is affirmative, but only insofar as the "immanent Trinity" is regarded (in Hegelian fashion) as a "summarizing concept." "If the economic Trinity speaks of God's *history* with man, then the immanent Trinity speaks of God's *historicity*. God's history is His coming to man. God's historicity is God's being in coming."[82] The immanent Trinity thus addresses the capacity of God to undertake that which occurs economically—a capacity rooted in the freedom of God's love. The traditional use of the language to distinguish between a being of God in and for himself without regard for his relationship with man (immanent Trinity) and a being of God in its relationship to man (economic Trinity) concedes too much to the Arian preoccupation with a static concept of immutability and surrenders the coherence of its claim that when God comes to

---

79. Ibid., 507 (*God as the Mystery of the World*, 370).
80. Ibid., 471 (*God as the Mystery of the World*, 344).
81. Ibid., 513 (*God as the Mystery of the World*, 374).
82. Ibid., 475 (*God as the Mystery of the World*, 346–47).

this world, he comes *as God*.[83] Still, the distinction is a necessary one because the "being in coming" of God is not just a being in time but an *eternal* being in time, a coming into this world. That this is so is demonstrated once again by the resurrection—which is not itself a historical event but an eternal event in history. The resurrection is an eternal event in that the relation which the Holy Spirit creates between the Father and the Son, who had been separated in the death of the Son, is not simply a restoration of an old relation. It is, rather, the emergence of a new relation between those whose being has been transformed through their separation, a new relation at which the being in coming of God had aimed eternally. As such, it was the fulfillment of God's eternal being *as love*. "The concept of the trinitarian God who is love implies therefore the eternal newness according to which the eternal God is Himself the future."[84]

Consistent with these insights, Jüngel elaborates the doctrine of the immanent Trinity by means of an exposition of the statement "The being of God is a being in coming." God comes *from God*.[85] As "Father," God is the origin of himself. God comes *to God*.[86] It is not only the resurrection which is an eternal event in time. If the newness of relation between Father and Son was the goal towards which the love of God was directed eternally, then the differentiation of Father and Son in the death of the Son must have been aimed at eternally by God as well—which means that we must also speak of this event in time in terms of an "eternal begetting." And finally, God comes *as God*.[87] If God is "indestructibly his own origin," then God is also "irrevocably His own goal." The guarantor of this final outcome is God's mode of being as "Spirit."

Human Participation in God

As we have seen, the Holy Spirit is the bond of love between the Father and the Son. Indeed, in the hour of their separation, the Holy Spirit is the "relationship between the relationships" of Son to Father and Father to Son, which would otherwise have been simply torn asunder. But the Spirit is not only "the relationship between Father and Son which constitutes the life of God"; the Spirit is also "their powerful turning to man, who will be drawn in this way into the relation of the Son to the Father."[88] The language used here is exact—and delimiting. Participation in God is, for Jüngel, participation in the relation of the Son to the Father. It is not a participation in the relation of the Father to the Son which constitutes the life of God. Such a delimitation

83. Ibid., 526 (*God as the Mystery of the World*, 384).
84. Ibid., 513 (*God as the Mystery of the World*, 375).
85. Ibid., 522 (*God as the Mystery of the World*, 381); emphasis mine.
86. Ibid., 524 (*God as the Mystery of the World*, 382); emphasis mine.
87. Ibid., 531 (*God as the Mystery of the World*, 387); emphasis mine.
88. Ibid., 520 (*God as the Mystery of the World*, 379).

means that the "union" of God with the human and the human with God never abolishes the ontological difference between the two—a difference which, like the early Barth, Jüngel can call "qualitatively infinite."[89] For this reason, he thinks it best that we do not call this union a "mystical union."[90]

What does happen, in that the love of God for the human Jesus overflows to other humans, is that the latter are brought into a relationship of "correspondence" to the Son. They become analogous to him in that the Spirit draws them into the Son's relation to the Father. In that this happens, they too are made to be nothing for themselves. They too are enabled to offer themselves up to God in such a way that their entire humanity is drawn out of itself. They cease to be the isolated I, in possession of itself. For they too know of a love that socializes their being in this world, that radiates beyond God as the object of their love to include other humans as well.[91] Like Barth, Jüngel makes the category of "correspondence" to be central to his soteriology. And like Barth as well, Jüngel understands such events of correspondence to constitute anticipation of an eschatological future.

In Jüngel, as in Barth, a concept of participation in God is elaborated whose meaningfulness is made to rest on a relational and historical ontology. The older metaphysics have been set aside. But the ontology that is employed is able to do justice to all of the theological values which the older conception sought to uphold—an intimacy of fellowship with God which transforms the human in the very depths of his or her being.

Final Comparison of Barth and Jüngel

God's being is in becoming—God's being is in coming.[92] These two formulas signal a decisive difference between Barth and Jüngel. The first—which describes Barth's theological ontology—suggests that the being of God is already in protology what it will become in time in the incarnation of the Son and the outpouring of the Spirit. In God's electing grace, God gives to himself the being which God will have for all eternity. And when the being which God has assigned to himself in an eternal and free decision is realized in time, the result is that no change occurs in God. Divine immutability is as important to Barth as it was to the ancients—even though Barth has defined it on the basis of the concrete being of God in God's history with humanity. To say,

---

89. Ibid., 523 (*God as the Mystery of the World*, 381).
90. Ibid., 469 (*God as the Mystery of the World*, 342).
91. Ibid., 529–31 (*God as the Mystery of the World*, 386–87).
92. The first formula was made famous by Jüngel himself, as a way of capturing the decisive feature of Barth's theological ontology. See Eberhard Jüngel, *Gottes Sein ist im Werden: Verantwortliche Rede vom Sein Gottes bei Karl Barth, eine Paraphrase* (Tübingen: Mohr Siebeck, 1964). The second formula, as we have seen, is Jüngel's preferred way of speaking of his own theological ontology.

then, that God has his being "in becoming" is to say that God's being does not "become." It undergoes no change, no modification, in that it is what it is *in a history* with the human race. The second formula—which describes Jüngel's theological ontology—does allow that God's being *becomes*. The "coming" of God is a coming in which the being of God undergoes real change. To be sure, in his insistence that the origin is not left behind, Jüngel is making it clear that the being of God is the same being both before and after the death/ resurrection of Jesus Christ but it is the same being *differently*.

It would be a mistake to try to explain this difference by reference to the influence of Hegel alone. Certainly, Jüngel's theology stands more directly under the influence of Hegel than does Barth's. The "Hegeling"[93] which the later Barth of *CD* IV professed to be fond of found its limit in his un-willingness to allow for change in God.[94] But the difference which emerges at this point is not simply a function of Jüngel's "Hegelianism." After all, the same difference was already at play in "Jesu Wort und Jesus als Wort Gottes," although there it was elaborated in terms of the confessional dif-ference between a Reformed and a Lutheran rendition of the humiliation/ exaltation scheme. It would be more accurate to say that Jüngel's Lutheran-ism has made him more sympathetic to Hegel than Barth could finally be as a Reformed theologian, than to speak simply of Jüngel's "Hegelianism."[95] One can best explain the move from "God's being is in becoming" to "God's being is in coming" in terms of a shift in the center of gravity which stamps each theology, from a center in election to a center in the death of God. Along the way, differences in starting-point and method also have their role to play. What was the second thing in Barth's Christology, the exaltation of the human in Jesus of Nazareth, is the first thing in Jüngel's Christology. If

93. From a conversation with pastors and laypeople from the Pfalz, September 1953, cited by Eberhard Busch, *Karl Barths Lebenslauf: Nach seinen Briefen und autobiographischen Texten* (Munich: Kaiser, 1975), 402; translated as *Karl Barth: His Life from Letters and Autobiographical Texts*, trans. John Bowden (London: SCM Press; Philadelphia: Fortress, 1976), 387.

94. Jüngel is certainly right when he suggests that anyone who is able today to ascribe suffering to God in a meaningful way has a debt to Hegel. For it was Hegel who set aside "the axiom of absoluteness, the axiom of apathy, and the axiom of immutability as unsuitable for the Christian concept of God" (Jüngel, *Gott als Geheimnis der Welt*, 511 [*God as the Mystery of the World*, 373]). Certainly, Barth too set aside all three where their axiomatic character was concerned. But he set aside only absoluteness and apathy. He retained immutability in a revised form.

95. There are also differences between Jüngel's doctrine of the Trinity and Hegel's which ought not to be missed. First, the Self-differentiation of God in Jüngel's theology is not, as for Hegel, a necessary step in the evolution of divine Self-*consciousness*; it is an act of love, and as such, it is a wholly *free* act. And second, Jüngel is very critical of Hegel for the latter's loss of concreteness. "Hegel's view, that through the incarnation and death of God there comes about a resurrection of an Absolute Spirit which turns the unity of divine and human nature into a universal, must be opposed by theology because of the danger it poses to the concrete being of Jesus Christ and the proper distinction of God and the human" (ibid., 127 [*God as the Mystery of the World*, 96–97]).

Jüngel can say anything about the incarnation, it is only after treating the life and death of the earthly Jesus.

These differences notwithstanding, Barth and Jüngel have arrived at a very similar conception of participation in God. For both, participation is an eschatological reality whose ground is to be found in Jesus' relation to the Father. For both, participation in God is mediated by participation in the humanity of Jesus—a participation which takes place in this world only actualistically and by way of anticipation of the realization of eschatological humanity. In both cases, the older metaphysics has been set aside in order to achieve a relational and historical understanding.

Conclusion

Traditional Protestant criticism of the idea of "deification" centered on the question of whether such a concept did not set aside a proper ontological distinction between the Creator and the creature. In response, defenders of the idea of "deification" have frequently had recourse to the Palamite distinction between the divine essence and the divine energies, restricting participation only to the latter.[96] In this way, the ontological otherness of God is certainly preserved—but at what cost? If participation is limited to the energies of God and the true being of God belongs to a realm inaccessible to human beings, then it is hard to understand why one would still care to speak of a "deification" of the human. Moreover, the delimitation of participation to the divine energies presupposes that the immanent and economic Trinities will differ in content—an assumption which was certainly widespread in the premodern West but which, in modern times, contributed to the sense that the true being of God was unthinkable and unsayable and, to just that extent, *unreal*.

The relational and historical ontologies of Barth and Jüngel, on the other hand, preserve the ontological distinction between God and the human even as they allow for participation in that history in which the being of God is realized. Thus these ontologies hold forth the promise of a real and genuine participation in the being of God. No doubt, defenders of the older metaphysics will find in the historical and relational account of participation in God offered by Barth and Jüngel too little in the way of present realization. That's as may be. But eschatologically, these Protestant ontologies offer much more than do the metaphysics of the Eastern churches. The word "deification" is not the best way to describe this "much more," since the ontological difference between God and the human will be infinite even then. But the "much more" remains.

96. Duncan Reid, *Energies of the Spirit: Trinitarian Models in Eastern Orthodoxy and Western Theology* (Atlanta: Scholars Press, 1997).

10

Seek God Where He May Be Found

A Response to Edwin Chr. van Driel

As though there were such a thing as God Himself and as such, or any point of seeking Him!

CD IV/1:530

I would like to begin by expressing gratitude to Edwin van Driel for creating the conditions which make possible a genuine debate on the issues raised by my essay in *The Cambridge Companion to Karl Barth*.[1] I have, of course, long been aware of Paul Molnar's—shall we say?—rather vigorous rejection of the position I took in that essay on the question of the logical relation of election to the triunity of God in Barth's "mature" theology—that is, subsequent to publishing his revised doctrine of election in *CD* II/2.[2] If I have kept silent this long, it has not been without good reason. I was unwilling to respond to Molnar for two reasons. First, in his criticisms of my views, Molnar failed to engage the one point which would have been decisive for launching a serious "debate"; that is, he made no attempt to explain the meaning of Barth's thesis that Jesus Christ is the subject of election[3] or to show how his own reading

---

This essay was originally published in a slightly different form under the title "Seek God Where He May Be Found: A Response to Edwin Chr. van Driel," in *Scottish Journal of Theology* 60 (2007): 62–79. Reprinted by permission.

1. Bruce L. McCormack, "Grace and Being: The Role of God's Gracious Election in Karl Barth's Theological Ontology," in *The Cambridge Companion to Karl Barth*, ed. John Webster (Cambridge: Cambridge University Press, 2000), 92–110. The article appears in a slightly different form as chapter 7 of this book.

2. See Paul D. Molnar, *Divine Freedom and the Doctrine of the Immanent Trinity: In Dialogue with Karl Barth and Contemporary Theology* (London: T&T Clark, 2002), 62–64, 81.

3. See *CD* II/2:102.

of Barth is not called into question by that thesis. He simply set it aside as (apparently) unworthy of discussion and chose instead to merely insist on his own reading. It should go without saying that no real debate can take place when the evidence brought forth to support a new proposal is passed over in silence. Less important was the second reason. Molnar had a rather annoying tendency to ascribe to me views which I have explicitly repudiated. It is one thing to say that the position of one's opponent leads logically to certain conclusions and to then suggest—in light of the opponent's explicit rejection of those conclusions—that he is inconsistent. It is an altogether different thing to ascribe the conclusions one has himself drawn to the opponent as if they were his own. But this is what Molnar does when he hints that I have made myself guilty of operating with a "principle of love"—or when he ascribes to me a "thoroughgoing rejection of the *logos asarkos*."[4] With regard to the former, virtually the whole point of making the divine being and essence be contingent upon the divine election of grace in Jesus Christ is to render impossible the use of *any* abstract principles in the construction of a doctrine of God. This fact alone casts doubt on whether Molnar has understood the basic aim of my position at all. With regard to the latter, the argument elaborated in my essay—so far from constituting a rejection of the idea of a *Logos asarkos*—was designed to demonstrate that the critical remarks which Barth directed towards the concept in *CD* IV/1 did *not* have the effect of setting it aside altogether but, rather, of identifying the *Logos asarkos* with the *Logos incarnandus*.[5] It was for these reasons that I decided to simply wait a while and see how things would develop. My gratitude to van Driel has to do with the fact that he has at last taken up my challenge and tried to give an alternative explanation for Barth's thesis concerning the identity of the electing God.

A Modest Correction to My Paradigm for Interpreting Barth's Development

Perhaps the best place to begin a conversation with van Driel is with a clarification of my genetic-historical interpretation of the development of Barth's theology. Ten years ago I located the beginnings of a fourth and final phase in the unfolding of Barth's dialectical theology in the years 1936–1937. The impetus for this shift was the lecture given at the International Calvin Congress in Geneva by Pierre Maury in 1936.[6] In coming to this conclusion, I was led in part by Barth's own retrospective comments on the importance of

---

4. Molnar, *Divine Freedom and the Doctrine of the Immanent Trinity*, 62, 81.

5. See ch. 7 in this volume, "Grace and Being: The Role of God's Gracious Election in Karl Barth's Theological Ontology," pp. 183–200.

6. Maury's lecture was translated by Charlotte von Kirschbaum into German and published by Barth: Pierre Maury, *Erwählung und Glaube*, Theologische Studien 8 (Zurich: Evangelischer Verlag, 1940).

Maury's lecture for his own revision of the doctrine of election. In a foreword to Maury's 1957 collection of essays, Barth wrote the following: "Most of those present at the Calvin Congress were hardly prepared to accept with their hearts, or even to register with their minds, what Pierre Maury was saying to them then. There were but few who realized the implications in the course of the years that followed. . . . But I remember one person who read the text of that address with the greatest attention—myself! . . . One can certainly say that it was he who contributed decisively to giving my thoughts on this point their fundamental direction."[7] What is undoubtedly true in this statement is that it was Maury especially who influenced Barth to carry out a christological recentering of the doctrine. But Maury never quite reached the point of equating divine reprobation with the reprobation of Jesus Christ. In fact, as Matthias Gockel has shown, the German translation of Maury's lecture done by Charlotte von Kirschbaum introduced elements into the text which served to bring it more into line with Barth's emerging doctrine. Gockel's conclusion is that an election to reprobation is Barth's "invention," not Maury's.[8] Even more important for our purposes here, however, is the fact that Gockel also demonstrates that the identification of "Jesus Christ" with the electing God is also Barth's invention—and one that did not appear until *CD* II/2.[9] In his Debrecen lectures on predestination in the autumn of 1936 (and therefore after the congress in Geneva), Barth still spoke of "the eternal Son of God" as the subject of election.[10] Only in *CD* II/2 does Barth shift the logic, so to speak, by means of an identification of the subject of election with Jesus Christ.[11] In other words, the christological recentering of the doctrine took place when I said it did—in 1936. But the full implications of that recentering would not be teased out until Barth began work on *CD* II/2 in the winter semester of 1939–1940.

The importance of this observation lies in the fact that I have been forced to adjust my periodization slightly. The transition to Barth's mature doctrine of election was not as sudden or dramatic as I once thought, but took place gradually. It is anticipated here and there in *CD* II/1 but only just anticipated. The truth is that *CD* II/1 gives testimony at a number of points (especially in Barth's treatment of the "perfections" of God) to the presence of residual elements of classical theism (and the ancient metaphysics which made it possible). It was not until *CD* II/2 that Barth finally became the "postmetaphysical"

7. Karl Barth, foreword to *Predestination and Other Papers*, by Pierre Maury, trans. Edwin Hudson (London: SCM Press, 1960), 15–16.

8. See Matthias Gockel, published as *Barth and Schleiermacher on the Doctrine of Election* (Oxford and New York: Oxford University Press, 2006), 162n14.

9. Ibid., 200n9.

10. Karl Barth, *Gottes Gnadenwahl*, Theologische Existenz heute 47 (Zurich: Evangelischer Verlag, 1936), 46.

11. Gockel, "One Word and All Is Saved," in *Barth and Schleiermacher*, 200n9.

theologian who would write the magnificent doctrine of reconciliation found in volume IV of the *Church Dogmatics*.[12]

The difference which this modification of my periodization of Barth's development makes for my paradigm as a whole (i.e., a continuous development after 1915 through four phases) is virtually nil. I continue to believe that the unfolding of Barth's dialectical theology admits of four distinct phases within a development in which continuity far outweighs discontinuity. I continue to believe that it was material decisions in relation to key dogmatic themes (revelation, Christology, and election) rather than methodological decisions which are decisive for establishing where one phase ends and another begins. And I continue to believe that it was Barth's intention throughout all the phases of his development to elaborate a postmetaphysical understanding of God. This intention belongs to the elements of continuity in Barth's development. But! Barth finally created the material conditions which would necessitate the elimination of remaining vestiges of classical metaphysics from his thinking only at the point at which he made Jesus Christ to be the subject of election—and therefore only in CD II/2. Where my developmental paradigm is concerned, the modification consists only in an adjustment of the *timing* of the inauguration of the fourth and final phase.

But this adjustment does bear in an important way on the debate before us. Van Driel would like to play Barth's understanding of the logical relation of Trinity and election off against my own.[13] In order to do so, he makes almost exclusive use of the early volumes of the *Church Dogmatics*—those written prior to CD II/2. Such an appeal, however, proves nothing where my thesis is concerned. The fact that Barth prior to CD II/2 gave considerable play to the belief of the ancient church that God's triunity was "natural and necessary"[14] and therefore that God's being and essence is complete in itself above and prior to the "eternal" act in which God chose to be God in the covenant of grace is not under dispute. What is disputed is the logical relationship of election to the triunity of God *after* the emergence of Barth's mature doctrine of election in CD II/2. Appeals to earlier volumes are quite obviously irrelevant for addressing that thesis. What is relevant is the meaning and ontological implications (if any) of Barth's claim that Jesus Christ is the subject of election—when seen in the light of the immediate context in which this claim appears in CD II/2

12. Bruce L. McCormack, "The Actuality of God: Karl Barth in Conversation with Open Theism," in *Engaging the Doctrine of God: Contemporary Protestant Perspectives*, ed. Bruce L. McCormack (Grand Rapids: Baker Academic, 2008), 185–242, gives some indications as to the elements in CD II/1 which would pass successfully through the crucible of testing in the light of the doctrine of God entailed in the revised doctrine of election in CD II/2, and elements which would need correction.

13. See Edwin C. van Driel, "Karl Barth on the Eternal Existence of Jesus Christ," *Scottish Journal of Theology* 60 (2007): 45–61.

14. Ibid., 53.

and in the light of the materials relevant to the further elaboration of Barth's theological ontology in the volumes which follow II/2—*and that alone.*

Van Driel's Critique and My Response to It

I should note at the outset that my proposal is not to be taken as an exercise in doing my own theology. The "correction"[15] which I advanced against a class of statements which can be found in the *Church Dogmatics* subsequent to volume II/2 in my *Cambridge Companion* essay was intended as a correction of Barth—*by Barth.* It is to be understood as saying that this is the best way to understand the significance of Barth's doctrine of election for his theology as a whole and therefore the best way to read Barth from *CD* II/2 on. In what follows, then, it is only at the locations where I point out inconsistencies in Barth that I am speaking "in my own voice." At all other locations, the reader may assume that what I say is intended to be taken as my understanding of Barth's view, too.

My proposal is that at least five consequences follow logically from the fact that Barth made *Jesus Christ* (rather than the "eternal Logos") be the electing God, that is, the "subject" of election. First, there is no mode of being or existence in the triune life of God above and prior to the eternal act of Self-determination in which God "constitutes" himself as "God for us," and therefore there is no such thing as an "eternal Logos" in the abstract. The Logos appears already in the immanent Trinity as the *Logos incarnandus.* Put another way, the Father never had regard for the Son apart from the humanity "to be assumed." Second, the eternal act in which God gives to himself his own being as Father, Son, and Holy Spirit and the eternal act in which God chooses to be God in the covenant of grace with human beings are *one and the same act.* These are not two acts but one. Traditionally, of course, it was believed that the works of God *ad intra* precede and make possible the works of God *ad extra*—so that the eternal generation of the Son and the eternal procession of the Holy Spirit constitute an activity that is natural and necessary for God and therefore an activity which precedes and grounds all activity that is willed and contingent (which is what election was understood to be). To the extent that God also wills to be what he is naturally and necessarily, this is an act of Self-affirmation (rather than an act of Self-determination) and, as such, must be kept clearly distinct from any subsequent act of Self-determination. To insist as I do, however, that both the works of God *ad intra* and the first of God's works *ad extra* take place *simultaneously,* in one and the same eternal event, would set aside

---

15. See ch. 7 in this volume, "Grace and Being: The Role of God's Gracious Election in Karl Barth's Theological Ontology," pp. 192–200.

this traditional understanding. What is "natural and necessary" in God is itself the consequence of the one eternal act of Self-determination. God may indeed be said to exist "necessarily," but *how* God exists, how his being is structured, is (I am suggesting) a function of his will and decision. Put another way: God is so much the Lord that he is Lord even over his being and essence. The only thing that is absolutely necessary for God is existence itself, but such a consideration may not be abstracted from the decision in which God gives to himself his own being and then played off against that which is contingently necessary for him. To think in this way is to snap back into the logic of a precritical metaphysics of "pure being." What God cannot do precisely *in* the one eternal event in which God gives to himself his own being (i.e., to decide not to exist) is something that can be thought about only in the light of what God decided, in fact, to do and to be. In this way, the one thing which is absolutely necessary for God will also be brought under the control of that which is only contingently necessary—and therefore under the control of the divine freedom. Third, the triunity of God is a function of the divine election. Granted, neither precedes the other chronologically. But it is God's act of determining himself to be God for us in Jesus Christ which constitutes God as triune. Fourth, although it is true that there is no act (or decision) without a subject, the identity of that subject may not be distinguished from the identity of God as constituted *in* the event in which God chooses to be God "for us"—because the being of the subject may not be distinguished finally from the act in which its being is given. That being the case, we can speak simply of *God's* act of Self-determination to be God "for us," but we would be speaking more accurately if we were to speak of the "Father" as the subject who gives himself his own being in the act of election. Because God's being is a being *in* the act of electing, the identity of the one divine subject as "Father" is something he gives to himself precisely in this decision—and therefore in the one eternal event in which the Son is begotten and the Holy Spirit is spirated.[16] Fifth and finally, there is no difference in content between the immanent Trinity and the economic Trinity. The *Logos incarnandus* is both *asarkos* (because not yet embodied) and *ensarkos* (by way of anticipation, on the basis of God's Self-determination in the act of electing); the *Logos incarnatus* is both *asarkos* (the so-called *extra Calvinisticum*) and *ensarkos* (having become embodied). Thus the identity of both the *Logos incarnandus* and the *Logos incarnatus* is the same. The Second Person of the Trinity has a name, and his name is "Jesus Christ" (the God-human in his divine-human unity).

16. According to one prominent strand of ancient reflection upon the Trinity, the "Father" alone is *autotheos* and, because this is so, he is the *fons deitatis* and the *fons et origo* where the being of the other two "persons" of the Trinity is concerned. I can walk hand in hand with this line of reflection for a considerable stretch. The point of differentiation comes at the point where I say that there is only one eternal event rather than two.

I might add that I took this last position in order to overcome a problem resident in traditional formulations of the *extra Calvinisticum*—namely, the unwanted but unavoidable implication that the identity of the eternal Logos is something more or other than the identity of the Word made flesh. Lutheran theologians have always worried that Calvinist talk of the *extra* would lead to an undermining of the full deity of the God-human. In establishing the complete identity of the *Logos incarnandus* with the *Logos incarnatus*, I have addressed this wholly justified concern, while still leaving room for a reconstructed understanding of the *extra*. Once the identity of the two has been ensured by the grounding of both in the one eternal act of divine Self-determination, it is now possible to speak again in terms of the *extra* without awakening the specter of another unknown being of the Son of God.

This is my proposal thus far on how best to construe Barth's startling thesis. Van Driel rightly notes that I am motivated throughout by two concerns: to safeguard divine immutability in view of Barth's affirmation of divine suffering in *CD* IV/1 and to ensure that "in the incarnation God is not just playing a role"[17]—that is, that Jesus Christ is not merely an accommodation of an as-yet-unknown eternal Son. Van Driel offers no response to the second concern, which is certainly a shortcoming. But he does take up the first. He says that "classical Christology thinks about the incarnation in terms of 'addition': the divine subject adds a second nature, a set of human powers and properties, to the first nature. This does not necessarily imply a 'becoming' or change for the first nature."[18] He is quite right about this where the tradition is concerned. But the net effect of this classical line of thought was to assign suffering to the human nature alone. The classical commitment to interpreting immutability in terms of impassibility always had as its consequence a separation of the natures which could only serve the interests of Nestorianism in the long run. For those, like Barth and myself, who are committed to the proposition that it is the God-human in his divine-human unity who suffers and dies the death of the reprobate, such a strategy for preserving immutability is not a live option.

We may turn then to van Driel's critique of my proposal. Van Driel sees three difficulties. "First, if divine election is an essential act of the divine will, constitutive of the divine being, how can McCormack avoid that *creation* is likewise essential to God and constitutive of the divine being?"[19] The question is rather awkwardly expressed, since the point of making election to be constitutive of the divine being is that no act can be called "essential" in van Driel's completely traditional (abstract) sense of the word. What he should have asked is this: if divine election is constitutive of the divine being, does this

---

17. Van Driel, "Karl Barth on the Eternal Existence of Jesus Christ," 51–53.
18. Ibid., 51n21.
19. Ibid., 54.

not make creation to be essential to God and constitutive of the divine being? My answer to this question is quite simple. Only that is "essential" to God and therefore "constitutive" of the divine being which God has determined *himself* to be, not what God has determined the world to be—as the "space" in which God becomes what he chose to be. Van Driel would no doubt respond, "But a relation of God to the world is contained in the relation to the Incarnate One. If the incarnation is 'essential' to God, then surely creation must be as well." Everything depends, however, on how we understand the word "contained" in the statement "a relation of God to the world is contained in the relation to the Incarnate One."

I can best explain what I mean by reference to Hegel's Christology. Hegel, as is well known, makes Jesus to be the revelation of something that is true of all human beings. The divine-human unity which is characteristic of all human beings is made explicit or manifest in him. In establishing this claim, Hegel works consistently from the general (what is true of all) to the particular (Jesus). It is also well known that Barth worked consistently from the particular to the general. All human beings are, for Barth, elect in Jesus Christ. All human beings are "in" Jesus Christ by virtue of their election. Because they are *already* "in him" *even as* he becomes incarnate, all that takes place in him (as a consequence of the divine humiliation and the exaltation of the royal human) is effective for them in that it takes place: justification, sanctification, vocation. No further work need take place in order to make this work of Christ effective. The work of the Holy Spirit does not make effective a work of Christ that would otherwise be ineffective. The work of the Holy Spirit in awakening human beings to faith and obedience is a work in awakening them to the fact that the work of Christ is already effective for them, thereby enabling them to live in correspondence to their true humanity in him.[20] But!—and here is the crucial bit—living in correspondence to our true humanity (the royal human, Jesus) does not set aside the ontological distinction between Jesus and ourselves. To "participate" in our true humanity, then—given that the ontological distinction is not set aside—means to share in the *kind* of humanity which Jesus instantiated and embodied through his life of sinless obedience. It means to share in the *history* by means of which Jesus' humanity was realized through God's gracious *reiteration of that history* in ourselves. "Participation" is thus a historical/actualistic/ethical concept in Barth's hands rather than a concept of "substantial indwelling" in the historical humanity of Jesus.[21] But if this is

20. See Bruce L. McCormack, "*Justitia aliena*: Karl Barth in Conversation with the Evangelical Doctrine of Imputed Righteousness," in *Justification in Perspective: Historical Developments and Contemporary Challenges*, ed. Bruce L. McCormack (Grand Rapids: Baker Academic, 2006), 167–96.
21. For a more complete elaboration of my views on the subject of "participation" in Barth's theology, see ch. 9, "Participation in God, Yes; Deification, No: Two Modern Protestant Responses to an Ancient Question," in this volume. See also the very fine dissertation by Adam

what being "contained in Jesus" means, if the ontological distinction between Jesus and the rest of us is in no way set aside by Barth's concept of "participation," then what is "essential" to God is only what takes place in Jesus himself and not what takes place in us. It goes without saying that creation generally cannot be viewed as "essential" to God on this basis. Have I come out at the same place as Hegel, as van Driel suggests? Not even remotely. Hegel makes God's relation to Jesus to be a function of God's relation to human beings generally, a relation (mind you) in which the ontological distinction between God and humankind is set aside. I follow Barth in making God's relation to human beings to be a function of God's relation to Jesus, a relation in which the ontological distinction between God and the human is never set aside.

The second "difficulty" can best be addressed after the third has been dealt with. I turn, then, to the third and most significant of van Driel's challenges. It is here that everything happens—or should happen if van Driel's argument against my position is to be sustained. But the truth of the matter is that what follows is an exercise in futility. The heart of van Driel's argument consists in the analysis of a series of propositions derived from statements made in my essay (propositions a through c) in order to show that they lead logically to a fourth, which then becomes the focal point of van Driel's case against me. The problem is that the fourth statement becomes a logical implicate of the preceding three only *if* one begins, as van Driel does, with a strictly formal analysis of the possible meanings of the statement "subject x chooses to be y," a statement which is taken to be equivalent in significance to "Jesus Christ is the subject of election." In other words, van Driel looks away from the *material content* which I assign to the statement "Jesus Christ is the subject of election," in order to carry out a completely formal analysis. And the reason this is problematic is that the material content which I assign to the statement "Jesus Christ is the subject of election" would not allow it to lead logically to the conclusion "Jesus Christ elects to be Jesus Christ"—which means that virtually the whole of this analysis is irrelevant to my position. Only at the very *end* of his third challenge does van Driel finally turn to the material content I assign to the statement "Jesus Christ is the subject of election," but by then his course has already been set, and he is unable to see that my trinitarian resolution really does work.

My position is this: The statement "Jesus Christ is the subject of election" makes sense only against the background of Barth's doctrine of the Trinity. I should emphasize again, before proceeding, that I have never held that the revision of Barth's doctrine of election meant a break with *all* that went before. Some things which Barth held earlier he is still able to say after the revision.

Neder, who traces the fortunes of the concept throughout the *Church Dogmatics* in "'A Differentiated Fellowship of Action': Participation in Christ in Karl Barth's *Church Dogmatics*" (PhD diss., Princeton Theological Seminary, 2005).

Church Dogmatics II/2 is, for me, like the peak of a mountain. The way which led up this mountain involved some side paths which would no longer have any relevance once the peak had been attained. But the way up the mountain did lead eventually to the peak. Alternatively expressed, the building blocks for revising the doctrine of election had been in place for a very long time—though they had been accompanied by material contents which would not survive the revision. The peak having been attained, however, everything that comes after is rather like water rushing in a torrent off the side of that mountain (and gaining momentum as it rushes towards the bottom). There is therefore a greater consistency of thinking on the descent than had been the case on the ascent.[22] My point is this: Barth's basic paradigm for understanding the Trinity in terms of a *single* divine Subject in three modes of being was maintained. What changed was simply the logical relation of this paradigm to election. Where before election had been understood as an altogether this-worldly, historical activity on the part of God, it now became part of the doctrine of God itself—with some very obvious ontological implications.

One subject in three modes of being. This means the *one* divine Subject three times, an eternal repetition in eternity.[23] And if God is the same Subject as "Father" and as "Son," then the Subject who makes the decision to be Jesus

22. The reason for this is quite clear. In the period 1924–1939, Barth's intention to overcome classical metaphysics took a backseat to another intention, namely, that of making contact with the ancient church. I am expressing myself here with as much precision as possible. "Making contact" means that it was never Barth's intention to simply repristinate the ancient trinitarian and christological formulas. But he did wrestle with the ancient formulas in order to identify what the theological values were which came to expression in them, so that he might then take these values up and do justice to them within his own frame of reference. "Within his own frame of reference"—this means, at a minimum, that he would have to be able to show that the desire to overcome classical metaphysics was thoroughly compatible with taking up and preserving these values. But this is something Barth achieved only with the revision of election in *CD* II/2. Until then the two intentions (overcoming metaphysics and listening carefully to the voice of the church in the past) sit alongside each other in a tensive, unresolved relationship. Barth tended in this period, 1924–1939, to simply go as far with the ancient church as he could, even to the point of taking on board a good bit of residual metaphysics. But this was obviously not wholly compatible with his basic intention. And this means that even if Barth had not revised his doctrine of election, he would have had to do something about the uneasy relationship between his two intentions sooner or later. One area in which the resolution of the conflict made an important difference is Christology. In Bruce L. McCormack, "Barths grundsätzlicher Chalcedonismus?" *Zeitschrift für dialektische Theologie* 18 (2002): 138–73, which appears in slightly different form as chapter 8 in the present volume, I tried to trace the development of Barth's Christology from *CD* I/2 to IV/1 in order to show that although Barth was still embracing a fair bit of the ancient metaphysics which made the Chalcedonian formula possible in the first place, by *CD* IV/1 he had left this metaphysics behind and had completely actualized and—in his way—historicized Christology.

23. *CD* I/1:350. The translation at this point is very rough, not only materially but grammatically and syntactically. I have had to modify it a bit to turn Bromiley's English into good English which approximates Barth's German in its sense.

Christ is the same Subject who "becomes" Jesus Christ as a consequence of the decision. As Barth puts it in *CD* IV/1—now with much more consistent emphasis upon the decisive role played by the eternal act of Self-determination—"Christian faith and the Christian confession has one Subject, not three. . . . He is the one God *in self-repetition*, . . . in three different modes of being. . . . He does not exist as such outside or behind or above these modes of being."[24] Or again: "He is the same as the Son, i.e., as the self-posited God (the eternally begotten of the Father as the dogma has it), as He is as the Father, is as the self-positing God (the Father who eternally begets)."[25] What emerges in this striking passage—in the emphasis upon God as a Self-positing reality (*der sich selbst setzende Gott*)—is an instance of the "bit of Hegeling" which, according to Barth himself, he was fond of engaging in precisely in the 1950s when this passage was written.[26] The important thing to say here is that God is the same Subject as positing and as posited. All that the Father is, we might say, he gives to the Son.

But this then means that van Driel's objection to this material elaboration falls to the ground. Van Driel says of my argument that what gets it started "is that God makes this first decision in God's first mode—that is, not in the mode of Jesus Christ, but in the mode of God which precedes Jesus Christ. A mode, not even being the *Logos asarkos*, but more unknown than that."[27] But why should God be unknown in the mode in which God makes the decision as Father? Simply because God in this first mode logically and ontologically precedes the first act of the divine will?[28] But if all that the Father is he gives to the Son, then when we know God in his mode as "Son" (i.e., as the Self-posited God, Jesus Christ), we, of course, also know God as "Father" (as the Self-positing God). For God in both modes of being is one and the same Subject. There is no unknown mode of God here, and no being of God which is not constituted in the eternal act of Self-determination to be God in Jesus Christ.[29] And in any event, this is an *eternal* decision—understood as a single event in which God both constitutes himself as triune and chooses to be God "for us" in Jesus Christ. This does, quite obviously, raise issues with respect to God's freedom (as Molnar has insisted), and I will return to this problem

24. *CD* IV/1:205.

25. *CD* IV/1:209 (*KD* IV/1:229). (I have lightly modified Bromiley's translation here.)

26. From a conversation with pastors and laypeople from the Pfalz, September 1953, cited by Eberhard Busch, *Karl Barth: His Life in Letters and Autobiographical Texts*, trans. John Bowden (London: SCM Press; Philadelphia: Fortress, 1976), 387.

27. Van Driel, "Karl Barth on the Eternal Existence of Jesus Christ," 56.

28. Ibid., 55.

29. The fact that van Driel is unable to see that Barth's basic model of the Trinity (i.e., one Subject in three modes of being) provides the solution to the question he poses to me makes me wonder how far he comprehends its logic and how far, at the end of the day, he is committed to it. But this is a question he and all others involved in this debate will have to answer for themselves.

in a moment. But here it is necessary only to say, in response to van Driel, that the statement "Jesus Christ is the subject of election"—when defined materially as I have defined it, in terms of Barth's doctrine of the Trinity—does *not* lead logically to the statement "Jesus Christ elects to be Jesus Christ." On the contrary, defined as I have defined it, the statement "Jesus Christ is the subject of election" *forbids* the conclusion "Jesus Christ elects to be Jesus Christ." For in the strictest sense, it is the "Father" who is the Subject of election—and because this is so, "Jesus Christ" can be the Subject of election only because the Subject that the "Father" is, is the same Subject that "Jesus Christ" is. "Before" and "after" the decision, there is but one divine Subject, identical with himself, albeit in differing "modes." This is also why I am able to reject any formulation which would open up a gap in material content between the immanent Trinity and the economic Trinity. This is a fully coherent position—and it is not one which leads to the logical difficulties surrounding the proposition "Jesus Christ elects to be Jesus Christ" which van Driel teases out skillfully but to no purpose relevant to my position.

Turning then to the question of the divine freedom. The problems here are real—but certainly not insuperable. The eternal triunity of God is, I have suggested, a being which God gives to himself in the event in which he determines to be God "for us" in Jesus Christ. God is, as Barth says in one of the significant statements in *CD* II/1 which constitute a building block for the later revision, *actus purus et singularis*; that is, God is not *actus purus* in the abstract but concretely, in the singularity of the event of God's Self-revelation in time. "What God is as God . . . the *essentia* or 'essence' of God, is something which we will encounter either at the place where God deals with us as Lord and Savior or not at all."[30] And again: "To its very depths God's Godhead consists in the fact that it is an event—not any event, not events in general, but the event of His action, in which we have a share in God's revelation."[31] And most conclusively for my own reading: "The fact that God's being is event, the event of God's act, necessarily . . . means that it is His own conscious, willed and executed decision. . . . No other being exists absolutely in its act. No other being is absolutely its own, conscious, willed and executed decision."[32] Absolutely! God's being is *absolutely* his willed decision, not additionally, not subsequent to a being above and prior to that decision, but *absolutely* his willed decision. But if God's being and essence are defined by this act, then this has to raise questions among reasonable men and women as to the freedom of the decision which founds this being-in-act. Classically,

---

30. *CD* II/1:261.

31. *CD* II/1:263. Cf. II/2:115: "Jesus Christ is the electing God. We must not ask concerning any other but Him. In no depth of the Godhead shall we encounter any other but Him. There is no such thing as Godhead in itself. Godhead is always the Godhead of the Father, Son and Holy Spirit."

32. *CD* II/1:271.

theologians always secured the freedom of God by means of a concept of on-tological independence which was controlled by the thought of "pure being," an abstract, wholly timeless mode of existence. The doctrine of the Trinity was simply added on to this prior conception—which led to the supposition that God is triune in and for himself, in a timeless realm above all relation to the world (or even to Jesus Christ as the embodied existence of God in the world). On the basis of this conception, securing divine freedom came quite easily. God's freedom, in this account, is a function of God's timeless triunity "in and for itself." When God steps out of this mode of "pure being" and determines to be God in the covenant, this is an utterly free act because God was "already" perfectly realized and fulfilled being. Of course, the price paid for this way of securing the divine freedom was that God was also conceived of as impassible, as removed from suffering, and so forth. What is at stake in this entire question is, quite obviously, the relation of eternity to time. It is Molnar, rather than van Driel, who raises this question most forcefully, and so I will turn to the former briefly before returning to the latter.

In my *Cambridge Companion* essay, I wrote, "If election is an eternal de-cision, then it has never not taken place."[33] To this Molnar has responded, "But if God's election has always taken place, how then can it be construed as a decision; does it not then become a necessity (a logical necessity at that), that is, the very opposite of what Barth intended with his doctrine of the im-manent Trinity?"[34] Molnar's mistake at this point is rather easily cleared up. To say that election "has never not taken place" may logically be the same thing as saying that it has "always taken place." But it is not the same thing materially. The point of my statement was to suggest that the election of the human race (as the internal ground of creation) is, in fact, the act which *founds* time. Because this is the case, we must seek to avoid speaking of the being of God in any way which might suggest that there was a "time" before this act which founds time, a "time" in which the being of God was simply "indeterminate." But this is not at all the same thing as saying that the divine election has "always been"—as though this event of God's primal decision cannot really be described as an event at all since it is timeless in nature. No, the event which founds time is not itself timeless—and time as we know it is not simply alien to it. The event that founds time *comprehends* time, encloses and embraces it and takes it up (ineffably) into itself. We would hardly expect it to be otherwise, given that the event in which God constitutes himself as triune is also the event in which God determines himself for the covenant of grace and therefore for the human experience of suffering and dying *in time*. But if the primal decision has not "always taken place," as Molnar wrongly

33. See ch. 7 in this volume, "Grace and Being: The Role of God's Gracious Election in Karl Barth's Theological Ontology," pp. 183–200.
34. Molnar, *Divine Freedom and the Doctrine of the Immanent Trinity*, 62.

accuses me of saying, then the specter of necessity must evaporate like an early-morning mist with the onset of the heat of a new day.

It seems to me that where the relation of eternity to time is concerned, our options are basically three. Either we stand with the early church fathers and wed the doctrine of the Trinity to an understanding of the being and attributes of God which was generated by means of an attachment to an abstract doctrine of "pure being," *or* we stand with Hegel and his followers in so completely temporalizing the divine being that the immanent Trinity (if it exists at all) can only be the product of the temporal process (world history), *or* we stand with Barth in seeing eternity as defined by the being of a God who freely determined himself for a covenant relation with creatures who exist in time—which makes the relation of eternity to time to be the relation of a founding "moment" to all subsequent temporal moments. It is quite clear which of these options Molnar chooses. He believes it to be Barth's view that "God exists eternally as Father, Son and Holy Spirit *and would so exist even if there had been no creation, reconciliation or redemption.*"[35] To put it that way, it seems to me, has to mean that Molnar has joined himself to the classical belief that God's triunity is *timeless* in nature. I don't see any way around this conclusion. This is not to say, of course, that there is not a grain of truth embedded in Molnar's concerns which must be honored; there is. A statement which took the form "*God* would be God without us" would be a true statement and one whose truth must be upheld at all costs if God's grace is to be truly gracious. But it is also a statement which stands at the very limits of what human beings ought to say about God. If we were to go further and seek to specify precisely what God would be without us—as occurs, for example, when Molnar says that God would still be triune without us—then we would make ourselves guilty of the kind of metaphysical speculation which was the bane of early-church theology. And in truth, such speculation must always have the result of opening up a gap in material content between the immanent and the economic Trinity—as Molnar's own reflections on the relation of Trinity to election amply demonstrate.

As for van Driel, he insists that he has no interest in temporalizing the relation of the being of the divine Subject to his eternal act in establishing the covenant of grace.[36] And yet he also seems to maintain that we are confronted here not with one eternal event but two: first, the event in which God is naturally and necessarily triune (the works of God *ad intra*) and, second, the event in which God chooses to be God "for us" in Jesus Christ (the first of God's works *ad extra*). Two events—not one. Once this two-event structure is in place, the *only* way to avoid temporalizing the relation between them is by making the first to be *timeless*. Applied to Barth, such a timeless understanding

---

35. Ibid., 63 (emphasis mine).
36. Van Driel, "Karl Barth on the Eternal Existence of Jesus Christ," 56.

does Barth really have that strong an emphasis on divine suffering? [handwritten margin note]

of the triunity of God would make Barth's actualistic ontology, his emphasis on divine suffering and so forth, to be impossible.

It remains only to say a brief word in response to van Driel's second challenge. It is because van Driel presupposes a being of the Trinity which is logically and ontologically prior to election that he can also say that there already exist in God both the will (as a capacity?) and the power to do that which is willed prior to any decision taking place. He goes on to suggest that all of the perfections of God are complete in God above and prior to his eternal decision to be God "for us." His conclusion is that "for Barth . . . it is the trinitarian nature of God, and the divine attributes established in and by that trinitarian nature, which makes election and incarnation possible."[37] It is against the background of these commitments that he then asks what makes God's eternal decision "possible" in my reading of Barth. "If election and incarnation logically and ontologically precede the triune nature and God's attributes, then what, on McCormack's proposal, makes it possible for God to elect and to give God to what is not God?"[38]

why can election not be grounded in God's being [handwritten margin note]

In response, let me just say that I have no doubt that statements can be found in *CD* II/1 and in earlier volumes which are difficult to explain on the basis of my position. And I don't even doubt that statements can be found after *CD* II/2 in which—motivated by a desire to think along with the tradition for a while—Barth can still be found to speak in ways similar to this. I do question whether such later statements give adequate expression to Barth's own deepest-lying convictions in relation to the issues at question here. But this is a hermeneutical question to which an adequate answer would require close reading of a great many texts—far more than can be considered here. Suffice it here to say that the net effect of Barth's revision of the doctrine of election in *CD* II/2 is to render impossible every attempt to lay a foundation for election in divine power considered in the abstract. In van Driel's account of the relation of the divine perfections to election, we catch sight of something akin to the fourth of the possible foundations for the doctrine of election which Barth considered—only to reject.[39] Certainly, Barth's question to this putative foundation is pertinent to van Driel: "May it not be that it is as the electing God that He is the Almighty, and not *vice versa*?"[40] As to van Driel's question to me ("What makes it possible for God to elect?"), my answer is that the form of the question makes giving an answer to it impossible on Barthian soil. Any attempt to look away from the God of electing grace revealed in Jesus Christ in an effort to find a ground of the possibility of election must inevitably open the door to natural theology. This is a door I chose not to open. What God in fact *does* is clearly possible for God; more than this I cannot say.

why natural theology? I think the point is the being of God not natural theology unless by this he means analogia entis [handwritten note; "immanent" inserted above "being"]

37. Ibid., 54.
38. Ibid.
39. *CD* II/2:44–51.
40. *CD* II/2:45.

Conclusion

In concluding, I would like to issue a few challenges of my own. I would like to challenge my opponents in this debate to please explain to me and to our readers why Barth chose to locate his doctrine of election in his doctrine of God. Why not locate it where Reformed scholasticism always located it—with creation, as the first of God's works *ad extra*? And why does Barth say, in explaining his decision to locate election within the doctrine of God, that "there can be no Christian truth which does not from the very first contain with itself as its basis the fact that from and to all eternity God is the electing God. There can be no tenet of Christian doctrine which, if it is to be a Christian tenet, does not necessarily reflect both in form and content this divine electing. . . . There is no height or depth in which God can be God in any other way"?[41] Why does he say this? What does he mean by it? Surely van Driel's doctrine of the Trinity is the very sort of doctrine which would be ruled out of court by the prohibition set forth in this passage. Or again, why does Barth protest against Protestant scholasticism on the grounds that in "everything it says about aseity, simplicity, immutability, infinity, etc.," it does not retain its hold on "the living God"? Why does Barth say of the God of the scholastics that he "is not the God who lives in concrete decision"—that this God is the living God only "figuratively"? Why does he say, "God is not *in abstracto* Father, Son and Holy Ghost, the triune God. He is so with a definite purpose and reference: in virtue of the love and freedom in which in the bosom of the triune being He foreordained Himself from and to all eternity"?[42] What did Barth mean by this? Why does he say, "Nothing can precede his grace, whether in eternity or time"? What does he mean by it? Passages of this sort could easily be multiplied.

Again, I am quite happy to admit that my opponents can find numerous passages which I cannot easily explain when operating within the parameters of my line of interpreting Barth. But my reading has a most significant advantage over theirs at this precise point. My reading *affirms* inconsistency on the level of formulation due to shifts in focus; theirs does not. As a consequence, their obligation is greater. I don't need to explain the passages they would adduce, since I have always regarded them as less-than-fortunate inconsistencies. But since my opponents deny inconsistency, they have to explain passages of the sort I have just adduced.

Second, I would like to challenge my opponents to explain how the actualistic Christology of *CD* IV/1–3 relates to the Trinity of peace and perfection which they presuppose. I would like for them to explain how it is that Barth's actualism—which, again, is not an actualism in general but the highly concrete

41. *CD* II/2:77.
42. *CD* II/2:79.

actualism which is grounded in the history of Jesus Christ—can be reconciled with their doctrine of the Trinity. And connected with this, I would like for them to please explain what Barth meant when he said that he was fond of a "little Hegeling."[43] Where is there any evidence of anything remotely Hegelian in van Driel's account?

And third, I would like to challenge my opponents (and Molnar most especially) to dial down the temperature of this debate a bit. The question I have posed is not, to my knowledge, a question that has ever been posed in quite the same way before. Certainly, it is not a question that has ever been taken up by a church council. No question of "orthodoxy" hangs on the answers given to it. I believe, as they do, that the immanent Trinity is "complete" in pretemporal eternity, above and prior to creation. I believe, as they do, in the divine freedom. There is nothing in the Nicene-Constantinopolitan Creed which I could not affirm; my position is every bit as orthodox as theirs. If I have my differences with classical theism at decisive points, this again is not something ruled out by any creed or confession belonging to my ecclesial tradition of which I am aware. This is not at all to say that nothing of importance hangs in the balance in this debate over how best to understand Barth; it does! For me, what is at stake in this debate is the coherence of our affirmation of the full and complete deity of Jesus Christ—a point that my opponents have yet to address head-on. So, if anyone has a right to be exercised, I would think it would be me. But rarely is anything achieved through the use of heated rhetoric. So I would like to encourage my opponents to relax a bit, loosen up, and not take themselves quite so seriously. Karl Barth knew when it was time to give himself over to his self-deprecating sense of humor. May the same be said of us "Barthians"!

43. See above, n. 26.

Part 4

Occasional Writings

11

The Barth Renaissance in America

An Opinion

"Why are the Americans so interested in Karl Barth?" This question has been posed to me, directly or indirectly, by many European friends, some of whom seem to imply, by asking the question, that *they* have regarded Barth's theology as outdated for some time. So why should America be experiencing something of a renaissance of Barth's theology? Allowing for a certain amount of differentiation among those interested in Barth—there really is no such thing as a typical "Barthian"!—the following features of Barth's theology seem to me to excite the most interest.

1. *Barth's theology intends to be "comprehensive" in its engagement with the Bible and the history of Christian theology.* It is a theology which takes seriously Holy Scripture and what Catholics and Orthodox think of as Holy Tradition. Barth's theology takes up old problems and makes a serious effort to mediate their solutions in a changed situation. This effort at mediation is extremely important today. There are many today who are casting longing eyes towards Rome and the East because they find in Catholicism and Orthodoxy a stability and solidity that is lacking in their own denominations. They also find in these churches a rich tradition—which can be very impressive in a land where so many lack historical sensibility. A vital Protestant theology which will sustain the Protestant churches must match the Catholic and Orthodox doctrinal "systems" for rigor, breadth, and beauty. And it must be able to make a good case that it has not simply cut itself off from the Christian past—from

This essay was originally published in a slightly different form under the title "The Barth Renaissance in America: An Opinion," in *Princeton Seminary Bulletin* 23 (2002): 337–40. Reprinted by permission.

antiquity to the present. Seen in this light, it is my own personal opinion that Karl Barth's theology may be the best hope for a rebirth of a genuinely Protestant theology in America.

2. *Barth's dogmatics is "nondogmatic" in character.* This thesis might seem to contradict the first. In truth, it does not—but attention to it does help to explain why the more liberally inclined are still interested in Barth. In a cultural moment described by many in terms of the categories of "postmodernism," it is the open-endedness of Barth's theology that makes it attractive. I would explain this myself in terms of the basic conception of revelation which gives shape to but at the same time relativizes the whole of Barth's dogmatic edifice. The heartbeat of Barth's doctrine of revelation is the notion of indirect identity. God mediates knowledge of himself to human beings through certain creaturely media (viz., the humanity of Jesus, the witness of the Bible, and preaching that is based on the Bible). But in the process of this act of Self-mediation, God remains ontologically "other" than these media. God, who is the "content" of revelation in and for itself, never becomes directly identical with the media employed. Revelation is always only indirectly identical with the media employed. The net effect of this basic decision is that Christian doctrinal theology must always take the form of a witness to an "object" (or Subject) which never becomes an epistemic "given." No matter how "complete" a theology may be in its efforts to answer the full range of questions turned up by the various Christian traditions and by life in today's world, no matter how thorough the attempt to anticipate possible objections and to address them in advance, no matter how "complete" in these senses, Christian theology can always have only a fragmentary and unfinished character. Theology done under the conditions described by Barth's doctrine of revelation must always "begin again at the beginning." It must always be prepared to be corrected. This is what I mean by the "nondogmatic character" of Barth's dogmatics. And it is the sheer modesty and humility reflected in this stance which, I believe, draws a good many to Barth.

3. *Barth's theology understands itself to be bound at every point to God and to God's Self-revelation in Jesus Christ.* It is a theology of submission to God and, as such, naturally leads to worship. In saying this, I am also saying that it is not a science of culture or even of religion; it is christocentric dogmatics. The importance of this point lies in the fact that a theology such as Barth's can nourish church life in a way that some forms of academic theology cannot. For those attracted to Barth's theology, if a theology could continue to find a justification for its place in the universities in the absence of churches, if its methods and procedures would be unchanged by the complete demise of the Christian churches, then the object of its study is probably not the God worshiped by Christians. In America we have had a long experience with the attempt to locate the "scientific" study of religion among the humane sciences in our universities. And we have profited from sociological and cultural-

anthropological investigations of religion in general and Christianity in relation to other world religions. But such investigations do not and cannot take the place of a theology that deepens the worship life of a church, a theology that shapes faith in a living God and practices that bear witness to him.

4. *In Barth's theology, dogmatics and ethics belong together in the closest possible relation.* The reason for this lies ultimately in the theological ontology which is presupposed by Barth's dogmatics and regularly comes to expression in it. The being of God, on the one hand, and the being of human creatures, which mirror God's being, on the other, are a being-in-act. Obviously, there is a lot more to this than I can possibly describe here. But the decisive point is that there is a very real sense in which "we are what we do"—whether in obedience to the God who has entered into a covenant of grace with us or in disobedience to it does not change the basic point. But however we conceive of the reason for the integration of dogmatics and ethics, this much is clear. What attracts a good many Americans to Barth in the present moment is the fact of this integration. Barth's dogmatics are ordered to the ethical; his ethics are everywhere grounded in rigorous dogmatic reflection. At a time when ethical decisions are being made on every other conceivable ground but the theological, Barth's theology offers a clear alternative. Even more important, however, Barth's ethics of divine command—and the dialectical understanding of revelation which undergirds it—constitutes an effective antidote to the tendency towards ideological control and manipulation. Seen in this light, no political program can be judged to be "Christian" in an unqualified way. Even the best politics can never be anything more than a witness to the just and the good. They cannot attain, even on a descriptive level, to the thing itself. And they cannot bring into existence justice and goodness in a pure form. Therefore our commitments to political programs as Christians must always be provisional and never unreserved.

5. *Barth's theology makes the proper subject of theological existence to be the congregation in the first instance.* This is not to say that individual theologians and larger church structures do not serve as subjects of theological existence as well. But the congregation is for him the basic unit. And this I think offers a great deal of hope in a day when it is not clear whether the traditional denominations might not be replaced at some point in the near or distant future by looser confederations of congregations. Because Barth's center of gravity lies in common life, in that which can be said and done in concert with other Christians, there is a concreteness to his theology that has been missing for us during the years in which many ecclesial bureaucracies operated over the heads of people without sufficient accountability. What emerges from Barth's concentration on the congregation is a call for congregations to become more "mature" as unified bodies, with pastors and laity engaging together in the work of ministry rather than leaving such work to a professional class. Obviously, this challenge is not easily met. In a day when time itself seems increasingly to

be limited, when laity can find every reason possible for remaining uninvolved, the old tendency to professionalize ministry is being constantly strengthened, not lessened. But it is precisely here that Barth's theology calls for a shift in priorities. For the churches to flourish, the nurturing of common life in the churches must become a high priority.

Here I must stop. As a graduate student in the 1980s, I was told by my *Doktorvater* that he believed that the greatest period of Barth's influence in America still lay in the future. The Barth renaissance now under way in the United States has certainly proven the truth of this prediction. What becomes of this influence depends largely on efforts like the present one, to provide institutional resources for further research in the theology of Barth. With this in mind, I would like to offer my own personal word of thanks to Dr. Bernhard Christ and the members of the Karl Barth-Stiftung, Dieter Zellweger and the members of the Nachlaßkommission, and Hans-Anton Drewes and the members of the theological faculty of the University of Basel, for their willingness to enter into close cooperation with the Barth Center in Princeton in a work that all of us believe in very deeply.

12

Theology and Science

Karl Barth's Contribution to an Ongoing Debate

It is unfortunate in many ways that Barth's reflections on the idea of "science" came to be known and grappled with only as a consequence of his famous debate with Heinrich Scholz in the early 1930s—unfortunate because it is all too easy to come away from a reading of the contributions to that debate with the impression that Barth accepted the validity of Scholz's concept of "science" for every discipline but theology, thereby making theology alone to be exempt from principles which Barth, too, regarded as binding for the other disciplines. In such a view, the goal of the exercise was simply to argue that the "object" of theology was so unique in kind that the normal rules could not be applied to the study of it. And Barth does indeed make statements which are rightly taken in this direction.[1] But when he went so far as to question whether any particular science had the right to make itself the basis for elaborating a general concept of "science" to which all other disciplines must conform if they wished to be acknowledged as sciences, he was defending in principle the "rights" not only of theology but of all "sciences" against the totalizing effects of a unified theory elaborated on the basis of a single science (usually physics). "Ein Pachtrecht auf den Namen 'Wissenchaft' hat keine Wissenschaft und es

---

This essay was originally published in a slightly different form under the title "Theology and Science: Karl Barth's Contribution to an Ongoing Debate," in *Zeitschrift für dialektische Theologie* 22 (2006, *Sonderausgabe*): 56–59. Reprinted by permission.

    1. *CD* I/1:8: "The existence of other sciences, and the praiseworthy fidelity with which many of them at least pursue their own axioms and methods, can and must remind it that it must pursue its own task in due order and with the same fidelity. But it cannot allow itself to be told by them what this means concretely in its own case. As regards method, it has nothing to learn from them."

gibt auch keine Wissenschaftstheorie, die diesen Title mit letztinstanzlicher Vollmacht zu vergeben oder zu verweigern hätte."[2] With these words, Barth made it clear that what was at stake in this debate was not merely the uniqueness of the "object" of *theology* and therefore of the methods appropriate to this object; what was at stake was the concept of "science" itself.

To be sure, Barth gets at the concept of "science" through a consideration of the question of that which makes theology to be one. He writes, rather famously, "If theology allows itself to be called a science, and calls itself a 'science,' in so doing it declares: (1) that like all other so-called sciences it is a human concern with a definite object of knowledge; (2) that like all others it treads a definite and self-consistent path of knowledge; and (3) that like all others it must give an account of this path to itself and to all others who are capable of concern for this object and therefore of treading this path."[3] That Barth thought this definition might well apply to more than theology alone is made clear when he refers to the other sciences in point 1 as "so-called"— thereby indicating that he is conceding nothing to them in the way of primacy when it comes to defining that which is truly "scientific." But we will stay with theology a moment longer.

If the way taken to knowledge of the object of theology is determined by that object, then the logical question to ask is, What is the object in question? Barth's answer is God in his revelation, a revelation that entails a dialectic of veiling and unveiling.[4] God reveals himself by uniting himself to, or by taking up, certain creaturely media of his choosing. Such union does not result in a direct identity of God with any medium—even if that medium be the flesh of Jesus. The identity in question is indirect—a taking up of the medium in a way that remains imperceptible to external observation. Hence it is an act of concealment, of veiling. If God is nevertheless to be known, then something else must happen. There is a third moment in revelation, the moment in which the Holy Spirit gives to those he pleases the eyes to see or the ears to hear what is to be seen or heard in the divine act of Self-revelation. Now if this be an adequate description of the divine Self-revelation, then it follows that God is an "object" only to the extent that God remains the *unaufhebbare Subjekt*[5] of revelation. God is nowhere given to human beings directly; where God does give himself to be known, it is only indirectly.

2. *KD* I/1:9 (*CD* I/1:10–11).

3. *CD* I/1:7–8.

4. See, e.g., Karl Barth, *Unterricht in der christlichen Religion*, vol. 1, *Prolegomena, 1924*, ed. Hannelotte Reiffen (Zurich: Theologischer Verlag, 1985), 169–71; idem, "Schicksal und Idee," in *Vorträge und kleinere Arbeiten, 1925–1930*, ed. Hermann Schmidt (Zurich: Theologischer Verlag, 1994), 366.

5. Barth, *Prolegomena*, 120; idem, "Die dogmatische Prinzipienlehre bei Wilhelm Herrmann," in *Vorträge und kleinere Arbeiten, 1922–1925*, ed. Holger Finze (Zurich: Theologischer Verlag, 1990), 588.

A strange sort of an "object," is it not? No doubt, even Barth himself wondered from time to time whether this divine "object" stood in no analogy whatsoever to the objects studied by the other sciences. And yet the uniqueness of the object given in revelation does not mean that there is no analogy.

A relation of analogy, of course, embraces dissimilarity as well as similarity. And the dissimilarity in the relation of theology to the other sciences is such that it must prevent us from ever construing the "object" of theology as belonging to a continuum on which the objects of the other sciences are also to be found. What distinguishes the "object" known in theology from other objects is the fact that it must give itself *by an act of sovereign will* if it is to be known. Where divine election is in play, there something is taking place that is not true of human knowledge of any other object.[6] This is the element of dissimilarity in the analogy. The similarity, on the other hand, begins to emerge when we recognize that the knowledge of objects under investigation in the natural as well as the humane sciences is socially and linguistically mediated. No science (not even physics!) has an object directly available to it; no science has access to an "object in itself." The objects studied in the various sciences are available for study only to the extent that models have been constructed which help us to gain access to them. But such models are never perfect; they are subject to constant revision. And when they are revised, it is because the object to be known has, at some point at least, "resisted" the model constructed. The object has "presented" itself to the would-be knower in ways not anticipated by the model. So, however important our models are, it is still the case that the object must "give" itself to us if it is to be known. Knowledge in all the sciences is the result of a dialectical interaction between the mind and the real which takes place in communities and therefore intersubjectively. A dialectical interaction: the mind is never simply passive but always active. But the objects to be known are not simply inert either. They have the capacity to resist our more fanciful interpretations of them—even to make us pay a price if we miss the mark too widely![7]

If all knowledge in the sciences arises through the complex interplay of models and their confirmation or correction by the object under investigation, then it follows that that which is *Sachgemäß* in any given situation must not be decided in advance of engaging in the methods constructed and adapted for use in particular sciences. As the great American neopragmatist Hilary Putnam has put it: "There is no key to objectivity. Or rather, the idea of a kind of objectivity that does not spring from and is not corrected by a human

---

6. Barth, "Schicksal und Idee," 390–92.

7. The epistemology which I have in view here is best described in terms of a "critical realism." I have discussed these matters further in Bruce L. McCormack, "Die theologiegeschichtliche Ort Karl Barths," in *Karl Barth in Deutschland (1921–1935): Aufbruch–Klärung–Widerstand*, ed. Michael Beintker, Christian Link, and Michael Trowitzsch (Zurich: Theologischer Verlag, 2004).

practice is absurd. History, philosophy, sociology are human practices. Their standards of objectivity must be created, not found by some transcendental investigation."[8] Lest it be thought, however, that the malleability of "objectivity" as a concept should render it useless in defining what it means to be scientific, Putnam immediately added, "But creating standards of objectivity is not, for all that, a matter of proceeding at hazard; whenever we stand within one of these practices, instead of looking for an Olympus from which to look down on them, we know perfectly well that there is a difference between competent and incompetent, informed and uninformed, fruitful and fruitless, reasonable and unreasonable ways of proceeding."[9] The point is that what is truly scientific cannot be defined *in advance* of actually engaging in an inquiry of one sort or another. Sciences are human *practices* whose norms emerge only through carrying them out. That they have histories is not to be denied, and a history of success can contribute to giving norms an aura of invulnerability. But in truth, all we really have are agreements among practitioners that certain rules shall apply until further notice—until, that is, their utility has been so clearly called into question that revision has become necessary.

Given that sciences are practices whose norms emerge only through carrying them out, then the pursuit of a general *theory* of science has to be seen as a most dubious undertaking. And if there is no generally valid theory, then there can be no single, overarching conception capable of organizing all the sciences into an encyclopedic system—not this side of the eschaton, at any rate. This side of the eschaton, the "supposed academic cosmos [is], in reality, a confusion of individual leaves . . . which flutter above an abyss."[10] Barth's defense of the presence of a theological faculty in the university rests finally on its willingness to say what practitioners in the other sciences know to be true but are hesitant to say. "It is well known that it is precisely genuine science which is not certain of its subject matter. And not only here and there but fundamentally, it is uncertain of its ultimate presuppositions. Every individual science knows very well the minus which stands outside the brackets [by which it is contained]."[11] The justification for a faculty of theology in the university lies in its willingness to bear witness to an eschatological disclosure of the ultimate foundation of all the disciplines and, in so doing, to the meaningfulness of all the disciplines in spite of their inability to demonstrate their foundations.

Our scientists of religion will not be happy with this understanding of the relation of theology to science, of course. They would have us bring theology into

8. Hilary Putnam, "The Idea of Science," in *Word and Life* (Cambridge, MA: Harvard University Press, 1994), 490.

9. Ibid.

10. Karl Barth, "Das Wort Gottes als Aufgabe der Theologie," in *Vorträge und kleinere Arbeiten, 1922–1925,* 155.

11. Ibid.

a settled relation to an encyclopedia of sciences—either by placing theology outside the system as that which grounds the whole (in which case, theology is transformed into metaphysics) or by placing it within the system (in which case, theology is reduced to some other discipline—usually anthropology). That such outcomes do not serve the best interests of theology ought to be obvious. But such outcomes don't serve the best interests of the other sciences either. Theology does not serve the other sciences well by simply being a "good citizen" who is willing to find his place in a settled system. To the contrary (and this is Barth's greatest contribution to the theology and science debates), theology serves the other sciences best when it acts as a disruptive influence, when it reminds the other sciences of their inability to demonstrate their ultimate presuppositions, and of the fallibility not only of their propositions but even of their norms and methods. If faculties of theology could learn once again to perform this function, they will truly deserve their place at the table. If they do not, if they continue to allow theology to be transformed into metaphysics or reduced to anthropology, well, we ought not to be surprised if theology loses its place altogether.

13

Foreword to the German Edition of *Karl Barth's Critically Realistic Dialectical Theology*

It gives me great joy to see this book of mine appear in German translation.[1] Though written originally for an Anglo-American audience, it was conceived in Basel during a Fullbright year in 1984–1985, completed (in dissertation form) in Edinburgh, Scotland, in 1989, and revised and expanded during a sabbatical semester in Tübingen in 1992. Because its primary conversation partners are German-language Barth researchers, it seems more than appropriate that it should now return to Europe, in a language more accessible to the majority of Barth scholars there.

As eleven years have now elapsed since the first printing of this book in English, I thought it might be helpful to a German-speaking audience if I were to attempt here a brief overview of the literature which the book has spawned in the English-speaking world, including a few remarks on how what I have written since extends the argument first developed here.

The aim of this book when first published ten years ago was to overcome the "neoorthodox" misreading of Karl Barth's theology which had dominated the Anglo-American reception for several decades, a misreading made possible

---

This essay was originally published in a slightly different form as the foreword to *Theologische Dialektik und kritischer Realismus: Entstehung und Entwicklung von Karl Barths Theologie, 1909–1936* [Karl Barth's Critically Realistic Dialectical Theology: Its Genesis and Development, 1909–1936] (Zurich: TVZ, 2006). Reprinted by permission.

1. Bruce L. McCormack, *Theologische Dialektik und kritischer Realismus: Entstehung und Entwicklung von Karl Barths Theologie, 1909–1936*, trans. Matthias Gockel (Zurich: Theologischer Verlag, 2006); translation of *Karl Barth's Critically Realistic Dialectical Theology: Its Genesis and Development, 1909–1936* (Oxford: Clarendon, 1995).

by the von Balthasarian thesis that Barth took a "turn from dialectic to analogy" with the publication of the little book on Anselm in 1931. In this aim, the book succeeded wonderfully—though, it must be conceded, such success may have come too easily.

It is not altogether clear that those who happily promoted my paradigm for interpreting the development of Barth's theology were actually convinced by the arguments I advanced in support of it—or that they had fully understood the analysis which led to them. The conditions under which theology has been done in the United States and in the United Kingdom in the last ten years have made some, at least, quite happy to accept my claim that Karl Barth remained a dialectical theologian throughout all the phases of his development subsequent to, say, 1915—and to use such a claim for their own purposes. I have in mind here the "postmodern" readers of Karl Barth—above all, Graham Ward.[2] Ward's Barth is a man caught between a strong tendency towards apophaticism (left over from his *Romans* period) and the desire to formulate a theology of language by means of which he might explain the relation of the Word to human words. For Ward, the latter effort, centered in the concept of "analogy" which was elaborated in *CD* II/1, was less than successful. The solution to Barth's problems—problems created by what Ward calls the "crisis of representation"[3] which was taking place even as Barth constructed his understanding of "analogy"—is to be found, in his view, in Derridean deconstruction. Ward's approval of my work thus remains on a very formal level of analysis. I have never understood the early Barth as a theologian with apophatic tendencies. Apophaticism requires, in my judgment, a classical form of metaphysics to get up and running. One of Barth's central problems—both in *Romans* and in the *Church Dogmatics* as well—was a problem he shared with modern theology generally, namely, how to speak of the "otherness"

---

2. Ward's major work on Barth appeared simultaneously with my own. See Graham Ward, *Barth, Derrida and the Language of Theology* (Cambridge: Cambridge University Press, 1995). In the months that followed, he and I wrote reviews of each other's books. Ward's review of my book had already appeared in print before I sat down to write my own review of his book—which put me in a somewhat awkward position. It seemed an exercise in base ingratitude to respond to his very positive review of my book with a highly critical one of his. But after reading the book, I felt that I had little choice. See Graham Ward, "Map of Barth's Theology," *Expository Times* (December 1995): 88–89; Bruce L. McCormack, review of *Barth, Derrida and the Language of Theology*, by Graham Ward, *Scottish Journal of Theology* 49 (1996): 97–109. I followed up this article-length review with a rather lengthy critical evaluation of postmodern and postliberal readings of Barth in the following year: see ch. 5, "Beyond Nonfoundational and Postmodern Readings of Barth: Critically Realistic Dialectical Theology," in this volume. Though Ward himself has never responded to the critique which I advanced in either essay, his attempt to use Derridean categories to interpret Barth's theology of the Word has subsequently been defended by Garrett Green, "The Hermeneutics of Difference: Barth and Derrida on Words and the Word," in *Postmodern Philosophy and Christian Thought*, ed. Merold Westphal (Bloomington, IN: Indiana University Press, 1999), 91–108.

3. Ward, *Barth, Derrida and the Language of Theology*, 7.

of God *without resorting to metaphysics*. Postmodern readers of Barth will claim that they are engaged with the same problem. But if one cannot speak of God without first speaking of something else, one still hasn't escaped the net of metaphysical speculation—not even when one proceeds to *negate* that "something else." And so it is with apophaticism: it is an exercise in metaphysical thinking, one which contributed greatly to the elaboration of the "classical theism" which Barth was at pains to overcome. Already in *Romans*, Barth was seeking to overcome metaphysical accounts of the being of God. Granted, his success in this venture would remain only partial until he constructed his revised account of the doctrine of election in *CD* II/2. At no point, however, was he attracted to apophaticism—or to the Nestorian Christology which Ward thinks Barth needs in order to preserve the "alterity" of the divine even *in* the God-human.[4] Though Ward was pleased to announce—precisely on the basis of my work—the demise of the all-too-positive neoorthodox theologian of analogy, a close evaluation of the material content of our interpretations will show that we are headed in quite different directions.

In my judgment, the popularity of postmodern readings of Barth was limited, from the outset, to a fairly narrow circle of academics and is now waning. Of greater interest for me personally has been the reaction to my book on the part of Roman Catholics and Protestant theologians with Roman Catholic and/or Eastern Orthodox sympathies. After all, "Catholic" interpreters (of whatever shade) will still be with us long after postmodernism has passed from the scene!

Initially, the Roman Catholic reaction to my book took the form of a certain amount of defensiveness on behalf of Hans Urs von Balthasar[5]—defensiveness which was quite unnecessary, since I had rejected only *one* of von Balthasar's two models for interpreting Barth's development (the one made popular in the Anglo-American world by Hans Frei and Thomas F. Torrance) and had affirmed, in broad strokes at least, the second (less influential) model. What was becoming clear to me even at this early stage in the "Catholic" reception of my book, however, is that acceptance of my periodization of Barth's development did not mean that the full significance of the central interpretive tools which made it possible had been grasped. In fact, Fergus Kerr might have been speaking for a number of later interpreters when he claimed, "While McCormack's

---

4. Ibid., 32.

5. I am thinking here of Fergus Kerr, review of *Karl Barth's Critically Realistic Dialectical Theology: Its Genesis and Development, 1909–1936*, by Bruce L. McCormack, *New Blackfriars* 76 (1995): 462–64. More thoughtful though still supportive of von Balthasar was Reinhard Hütter, "Barth between von Balthasar and McCormack: A Dialectic," *Pro Ecclesia* 8 (1999): 105–9. I wish that I could say that such unnecessary defensiveness has disappeared, but it did resurface recently in Stephen Wigley, "The von Balthasar Thesis: A Re-examination of von Balthasar's Study of Barth in the Light of Bruce McCormack," *Scottish Journal of Theology* 56 (2003): 345–59.

documentation of the genesis of Barth's work is very convincing, he has yet to show us what difference it all makes to our reading of Barth."[6] My own conviction then and now was that the answer to this question had already been made clear. If, as I maintained in my book, the root of Barth's thinking in the early volumes of the *Church Dogmatics* was still the *Realdialektik* of the divine veiling and unveiling first elaborated in Göttingen, then the attempt to find in those volumes evidence of a "revelational positivism" must surely fail. And this means, too, that the neoorthodox project could not appeal to Barth as its guarantor. The followers of Frei and Torrance must look elsewhere for resources for their various projects.[7] At a minimum, I would have thought that this much should have been clear. However, more could be said in response to Kerr's question. So in a series of essays, I then attempted to draw out further consequences of my historical work for a systematic/constructive reception of Barth. The first one had to do with the relation of Barth's revised doctrine of election to his understanding of triunity in God.[8] The second had to do with shifts in Barth's Christology which took place within the bounds of the *Church Dogmatics*—again as a consequence of the doctrine of election.[9] The third had to do with the problem of the Christian's participation in Christ.[10] Taken together, these essays show that the final phase in Barth's theological development, inaugurated by his new doctrine of election, meant the final overcoming of residual elements of classical metaphysics which Barth had long intended and the emergence of a more historicized and hermeneutical account of the divine being. With the publication of *CD* II/2, Barth could say (in effect) that God is, in himself, the mode of his Self-revelation in time—and say it with greater self-consistency than heretofore. One of the obvious ways this development affects the way the *Church Dogmatics* is read is that it forbids drawing on Barth's reflections upon, let us say, any particular doctrinal theme at points scattered throughout the *Dogmatics* and treating them acontextually, as though Barth were incapable of changing his mind—even in matters of detail. Another difference made by the recognition that development has occurred within the bounds of the *Church Dogmatics* is that it forces us to read Barth's doctrine of God in *CD* II/1 somewhat critically in the light of the revision which occurs in *CD* II/2. Not everything Barth says in *CD* II/1 about God's being, power, and knowledge, for example, could still be said

6. Kerr, review of *Karl Barth's Critically Realistic Dialectical Theology*, 464.

7. I made all of this clear in an essay published two years after the book's release. See ch. 5, "Beyond Nonfoundational and Postmodern Readings of Barth: Critically Realistic Dialectical Theology," in this volume.

8. See ch. 7, "Grace and Being: The Role of God's Gracious Election in Karl Barth's Theological Ontology," in this volume.

9. See ch. 8, "Barth's Historicized Christology: Just How 'Chalcedonian' Is It?" in this volume.

10. See ch. 9, "Participation in God, Yes; Deification, No: Two Modern Protestant Responses to an Ancient Question," in this volume.

after *CD* II/2. As this foreword goes to the press, I am at work on an essay on Barth's doctrine of God which will at least hint at some of the corrections that would need to be registered against the understanding of that doctrine elaborated in *CD* II/1.[11]

Reading Barth as a "postmetaphysical theologian" has, however, called forth a new challenge from the Catholic side. In fact, it would not be going too far to say that the proposal advanced in *The Cambridge Companion* essay cited above[12] has incited a controversy which threatens to divide Barth scholars in the English-speaking world into two rival camps—the one camp representing Barth as a very traditional sort of theologian, completely at home with the classical theism and trinitarianism of the ancients, and the other camp representing the later Barth at least (after *CD* II/2) as a theologian more at home in the modern world with its problems and questions. At the heart of the controversy lies the suggestion I made in my *Cambridge Companion* essay that at least four consequences follow logically from the fact that Barth made *Jesus Christ* (rather than the "eternal Logos") to be the electing God, that is, the "subject" of election. First, there is no mode of being or existence in the triune life of God above and prior to the eternal act of Self-determination in which God "constitutes" himself as "God for us," and therefore there is no such thing as an "eternal Logos" in the abstract. The Logos appears already in the immanent Trinity as the *Logos incarnandus*. Put another way, the Father never had regard for the Son apart from the humanity "to be assumed." Second, the eternal act in which God gives to himself his own being as Father, Son, and Holy Spirit and the eternal act in which God chooses to be God in the covenant of grace with human beings are *one and the same act*. These are not two acts but one. Traditionally, of course, it was believed that the works of God *ad intra* precede and make possible the works of God *ad extra*—so that the eternal generation of the Son and the eternal procession of the Holy Spirit constitute an activity that is natural and necessary for God and therefore an activity that precedes and grounds all activity that is willed and contingent (which is what election was understood to be). To the extent that God also wills to be what he is naturally and necessarily, this is an act of Self-affirmation (rather than an act of Self-determination) and, as such, must be kept distinct from any subsequent act of Self-determination. To insist as I do, however, that both the *ad intra* relations and the *ad extra* relations are constituted in one and the same eternal event would set aside this traditional

---

11. Bruce L. McCormack, "The Actuality of God: Karl Barth in Conversation with Open Theism," in *Engaging the Doctrine of God: Contemporary Protestant Perspectives*, ed. Bruce L. McCormack (Grand Rapids: Baker Academic, 2008), 185–242. In ch. 8 of this volume, "Karl Barth's Historicized Christology: Just How 'Chalcedonian' Is It?" I try to demonstrate changes in Barth's Christology between *CD* I/2 and IV—changes which I explain by reference once again to his revision of election.

12. See above, n. 7.

understanding. What is "natural and necessary" in God is itself the consequence of the one eternal act of Self-determination. God may indeed be said to exist "necessarily," but *how* God exists, how his being is structured, is a function of his will. We may not interpret "necessity" in relation to God in absolute terms but only in contingent terms—as a necessity contingent upon God's utterly sovereign and free will. God, to put it another way, is so much the Lord that he is Lord even over his being and essence. Third, the triunity of God is a function of the divine election. Granted, neither precedes the other chronologically. But it is God's act of determining himself to be God for us in Jesus Christ which constitutes God as triune. Fourth and finally, there is no difference in content between the immanent Trinity and the economic Trinity. The *Logos incarnandus* is both *asarkos* (because not yet embodied) and *ensarkos* (by way of anticipation, on the basis of God's Self-determination in the act of electing); the *Logos incarnatus* is both *asarkos* (the so-called *extra Calvinisticum*) and *ensarkos* (having become embodied). Thus the identity of both the *Logos incarnandus* and the *Logos incarnatus* is the same. The Second Person of the Trinity has a name, and his name is "Jesus Christ" (the God-human in his divine-human unity).

The suggestions outlined here have elicited a sharp response from Paul Molnar, a Roman Catholic theologian at St. Johns University in New York and secretary of the Karl Barth Society of North America. According to Molnar, "the order between election and triunity cannot be logically reversed without in fact making creation, reconciliation and redemption necessary to God."[13] He acknowledges that "McCormack carefully distinguishes Barth's position from Hegel's, insisting that, for Barth, in opposition to Hegel, the incarnation is God's free act, that Barth sharply distinguished the creator-creature relation, that Barth insisted that God pre-existed creation, and that God's eternal actions could not be collapsed into history."[14] Nevertheless, Molnar is convinced that my reading of Barth leads ineluctably to Hegel anyway: "We cannot simply equate the immanent and economic Trinity in the manner suggested by McCormack, without actually making God dependent on the world in precisely the Hegelian way."[15] To my claim "If election is an eternal decision, then it has never not taken place," Molnar responds, "But if God's election has always taken place, how then can it be construed as a decision; does it not then become a necessity (a logical necessity at that), that is, the very opposite of what Barth intended with his doctrine of the immanent Trinity?"[16]

At least one of Molnar's suppositions here rests on a misunderstanding that is easily cleared up. To say that election "has never not taken place" may

---

13. Paul D. Molnar, *Divine Freedom and the Doctrine of the Immanent Trinity: In Dialogue with Karl Barth and Contemporary Theology* (London: T&T Clark, 2002), 63.

14. Ibid., 62.

15. Ibid., 64.

16. Ibid., 62.

logically be the same thing as saying that it has "always taken place." But it is not the same thing materially. The point of my statement was to suggest that the election of the human race (as the internal ground of creation) is, in fact, the act which *founds* time. Because this is the case, we must seek to avoid speaking of the being of God in any way which might suggest that there was a "time" before this act which founds time, a "time" in which the being of God was simply "indeterminate." But this is not at all the same thing as saying that the divine election has "always been"—as though this event of God's primal decision cannot really be described as an event at all since it is timeless in nature. No, the event which founds time is not itself timeless— and time as we know it is not simply alien to it. The event which founds time *comprehends* time, encloses and embraces it, and takes it up (ineffably) into itself. We would hardly expect it to be otherwise, given that the event in which God constitutes himself as triune is also the event in which God determines himself for the covenant of grace and therefore for the human experience of suffering and dying *in time*.

There is, however, a substantive issue dividing Molnar's understanding of Barth from my own which will not go away, no matter how well it is explained. Molnar believes it to be Barth's view that "God exists eternally as Father, Son and Holy Spirit and would so exist even if there had been no creation, reconciliation or redemption."[17] I, on the other hand, believe this to be true of the Barth of *CD* I/1 through II/1 only but that such a formulation is not finally compatible with the statement that "Jesus Christ is the electing God." What is at stake in this difference is not—as Molnar believes—the divine freedom. I am as convinced as he that God need not have created this world; God might have chosen to create a different world or to have created no world at all. What I question is the capacity of any human being to know what God would have been without us, to know, in fact, how the divine being would have been structured had God not determined to be God for us in Jesus Christ. But this is the error which Molnar commits in that he claims that God would be Father, Son, and Holy Spirit without us and would have been this with no definite goal or object in view.[18] The statement "God would be God without us" is a true statement and has a value in safeguarding the divine freedom. To say more than this, however, to say that God would have been this way or that way, is to enter into unwarranted speculation. And in truth, speculation must always be the result of opening up a gap in material content between the immanent and the economic Trinity—as Molnar does.

Before proceeding, I should note that Molnar's position has been taken up and more ably defended by Edwin Chr. van Driel in an essay entitled "Karl

17. Ibid., 63.
18. Cf. *KD* II/2:85 (*CD* II/2:79): "God is not *in abstracto* Father, Son, and Holy Ghost, the triune God. He is so with a definite purpose and reference."

Barth on the Eternal Existence of Jesus Christ."[19] My position has been given strong support by Paul Nimmo in an Edinburgh dissertation completed in 2005[20] as well as by Kevin Hector[21] and Aaron Smith.[22]

We come then finally to Reinhard Hütter. Hütter constitutes a special case among Catholic readers/critics of my book because of the fact that at the time he wrote his review and a subsequent essay in which he took up an oppositional stance to one of the central claims made in my book, he was still (institutionally) a Lutheran theologian. His conversion to Catholicism took place recently. But given the fact that his version of "evangelical Catholicism" has long prepared him for his conversion, he belongs here.

Hütter is convinced that it is a mistake to interpret the early Barth "exclusively in the triangle of his retrieval of classical Reformed theology, his ongoing (mainly negative) connectedness to liberal Protestantism, and his way of broadly presupposing the Kantian epistemological framework."[23] What he misses in my account of Barth's development is the recognition of "the central importance of Roman Catholicism as the main conversation partner for Barth's theology from the so-called 'Göttingen Dogmatics' on." Though he grants that I have interpreted "Barth's encounter with Catholicism in Münster in detail and very accurately," he claims that I have failed to understand "the *systematic* importance of this engagement for Barth's own constructive theological project."[24] Hütter does not elaborate further on the "systematic importance" of Barth's engagement with Roman Catholicism here in his review, however.

By 2000, it had become clear that Hütter's reading of Barth served an apologetical purpose, namely, that of promoting his own version of "evangelical catholicity." But even more was at stake than a merely theological program. Hütter was himself on a journey—and it was rapidly becoming very clear that Barth belonged more to his past than to his future. His much-read essay

---

19. Edwin C. van Driel, "Karl Barth on the Eternal Existence of Jesus Christ," *Scottish Journal of Theology* 60 (2007): 45–61. Bruce L. McCormack, "Seek God Where He May Be Found: A Response to Edwin Chr. van Driel," *Scottish Journal of Theology* 60 (2007): 62–79, was my response, which appears in a slightly different form as chapter 10 of this book.

20. Paul Nimmo, "Ethical Agency and Actualistic Ontology in the Theological Ethics of Karl Barth" (PhD diss., University of Edinburgh, 2005); published as *Being in Action: The Theological Shape of Barth's Ethical Vision* (London and New York: T&T Clark, 2007).

21. Kevin W. Hector, "God's Triunity and Self-Determinatism: A Conversation with Karl Barth, Bruce McCormack and Paul Molnar," *International Journal of Systematic Theology* 3 (2005): 246–61.

22. Aaron T. Smith, "The Specification of Divine Being: The Will of God as the Being of God in Karl Barth's Doctrine of Election," forthcoming in the *Scottish Journal of Theology*.

23. Reinhard Hütter, "Barth between McCormack and von Balthasar: A Dialectic," *Pro Ecclesia* 8 (1999): 108.

24. Ibid.

"Karl Barth's 'Dialectical Catholicity': *Sic et non*"[25] constituted, so to speak, the next-to-last stop on that journey before his arrival in Rome.[26]

The "dialectical Catholicity" referred to in the title is described by Hütter as "a fundamental methodological strategy"[27] in Barth's theology—a strategy of steering "a course between Neo-Protestantism on the one side and Roman Catholicism on the other."[28] The basis for this judgment is found by Hütter in a question posed by Barth in his 1928 essay "Der römische Katholizismus als Frage an die protestantische Kirche." There Barth had written,

> I would like to ask in all seriousness whether Protestantism can be a real answer to anyone to whom Catholicism never should be a real question. Whether we still have any real business with the church of the Reformation if in the meanwhile we should have indeed left alone the counterpart with which it struggled. And I would like to give warning of the unhappy awakening which might some day follow such detachment. Those who know Catholicism even a little know how deceiving its remoteness and strangeness are, how uncannily close it is to us in reality, how urgent and vital the questions it puts to us are, and how inherently impossible the possibility is, not to seriously listen to them after one has once heard them.[29]

Parenthetically, it may be observed that talk of steering a course *between* neo-Protestantism and Catholicism is impossible. Why would Barth want to mediate between what he explicitly referred to as "two evils"?[30] Still, Hütter is on to something here—though, ironically, his efforts to describe it fall short of doing justice to what he has only just glimpsed. What Hütter could not have known at the time—since he had access only to Barth's published lectures on Roman Catholicism from the Münster period—is that Barth's ecumenical engagement with the Catholics went far beyond anything one might have imagined on the basis of these essays. We now know that in the unpublished portions of Barth's "Münster Dogmatics," he made an effort to identify the valid theological concerns which came to expression even in the Catholic preoccupation with "natural theology" and to do justice to those

25. Reinhard Hütter, "Karl Barth's 'Dialectical Catholicity': *Sic et non*," *Modern Theology* 16 (2000): 137–57.

26. The last stop before Rome is Reinhard Hütter, *Suffering Divine Things* (Grand Rapids: Eerdmans, 1997).

27. Ibid., 143.

28. Ibid., 142.

29. Hütter, "Karl Barth's 'Dialectical Catholicity,'" 137, here citing Karl Barth, "Der römische Katholizismus als Frage an die protestantische Kirche," in *Vorträge und kleinere Arbeiten, 1925–1930*, ed. Hermann Schmidt (Zurich: Theologischer Verlag, 1994), 313; translated as "Roman Catholicism: A Question to the Protestant Church," in *Theology and Church: Shorter Writings, 1920–1928*, trans. L. P. Smith (London: SCM Press, 1962), 310.

30. Barth, "Der römische Katholizismus," 318 n. c ("Roman Catholicism," 314n1).

concerns within his own theological frame of reference.[31] Whether the phrase "dialectical Catholicity" has sufficient explanatory value for describing this effort is a question for itself.[32] What is clear is that Barth's dialectical theology passed through an interlude on its way from its earliest dogmatic expression in Göttingen to the *Church Dogmatics*—an interlude in which Barth displayed a surprising amount of ecumenical openness. All of this came to an end with the political upheavals of the early 1930s and the breakup of the dialectical theologians. But! The fact that it was only an interlude bears directly on Hütter's efforts to tweak the genetic-historical paradigm set forth in my book.

As already noted, Hütter believes that engagement with Roman Catholicism was already a "methodological principle" of Barth's dogmatic work in Göttingen. This is surely an overstatement. Although it is true that Barth displayed an early interest in medieval Catholic theology—he audited Erik Peterson's lectures on the theology of Thomas Aquinas in 1923[33]—it is surely a bit odd and finally misleading, where an evaluation of Barth's sources in this period are concerned, to say as Hütter does that "Roman Catholicism was—at least abstractly—already a conversation partner in the 'Göttingen Dogmatics,' precisely because of the Reformers' own catholicity." During his time in Göttingen, Barth did indeed work "exclusively in the triangle"[34] created by his Kantian epistemological commitments, his retrieval of the older Protestantism, and his ongoing debate with neo-Protestantism. To the extent that he ever transcended this triangle of preoccupations, he did so only in Münster.

The importance of this question lies in the fact that if, as I contend, the most significant material decisions in Barth's dogmatics were already made in Göttingen, then the impact of Barth's later engagement with Roman Catholicism on the development of his theology as a whole would have been negligible. Hütter seems to have anticipated such a conclusion. But rather than arguing against it on the basis of concrete data from the Göttingen years, he shifts his ground and seeks instead to resurrect Eberhard Jüngel's theory regarding

31. See Amy E. Marga, "Karl Barth's Second Dogmatic Cycle, Münster, 1926–1928," *Zeitschrift für dialektische Theologie* 21 (2005): 135–37.

32. At the end of the day, Hütter is not all that interested in what he calls Barth's "dialectical Catholicity" anyway. He argues that Barth's dialectical Catholicity lacks sufficient "concreteness." Barth's talk of "genuine Protestantism" functions as a "critical principle" in his theology of a purely negative sort; "'genuine Protestantism' cannot really exist in an ecclesially embodied form" ("Karl Barth's 'Dialectical Catholicity,'" 147). More adequate for Hütter is Luther's "concrete catholicity, rooted in distinct practices that were understood as the Holy Spirit's work" (148). What Hütter is after, finally, is the notion that there are certain core doctrines and core practices which *constitute* the Christian church *as church*. In a later work, Hütter would expand the "pneumatological ecclesiology" he thinks himself to find in Luther through the adoption of the novel idea that the "core practices" of the church are *enhypostatic* in the Third Person of the Trinity (*Suffering Divine Things*, 132–33).

33. Marga, "Karl Barth's Second Dogmatic Cycle," 128.

34. See above, n. 22.

the impact of Erik Peterson's polemical essay against "dialectical theology" published in July 1925:[35]

> McCormack fails to understand the importance of Peterson's attack on Barth as well as the importance of Barth's response to Peterson. . . . What was primarily at stake between Peterson and Barth was not the "nature of dialectic" in theology as McCormack assumes. Rather, it was the nature of "dogma" and "doctrine" in relationship to theology. And in this regard Barth is precisely forced to specify publicly his understanding of the nature of doctrine to theology in a way he had not done heretofore. . . . Arguably it is precisely Peterson's question and the problematic he pressed, that forced Barth to concretize further his dogmatic method in a way that clarified his position and that made him increasingly appreciative of the challenge which Roman Catholic theology represents precisely in its dogmatic theology. Eberhard Jüngel's assessment of the importance of Peterson's attack for Barth's theology seems to me to be closer to the mark than McCormack's account of it.[36]

Hütter is quite right to say that Barth's response to Peterson set forth his first *public* declaration of his views on dogma and doctrine.[37] But that Barth was forced to "concretize his method" by Peterson's essay must remain doubtful. To Hütter's (somewhat oblique) suggestion that the material on "Das Dogma, die Dogmen und die Dogmatik" was new in *Die christliche Dogmatik im Entwurf* in 1927,[38] one can only respond that this material is not new in the least. It is to be found already in the 1924 Göttingen *Prolegomena*[39]—a full year prior to Peterson's attack. Certainly, it offers no evidence that Barth's engagement with a soon-to-be-Catholic theologian had any impact on the development of Barth's theology. And as for Jüngel, he did not have access to the "Göttingen Dogmatics" when he wrote his essay on Barth and Peterson.

Hütter's claims will not stand up to close scrutiny in the light of the available evidence—but they do tell us something rather important. I mentioned earlier that the spiritual and intellectual conditions under which Barth is studied in the Anglo-American world are quite different from the conditions under which Barth is studied in Europe—and here we catch sight of one important feature

35. Erik Peterson, "Was ist Theologie?" in *Theologische Traktate* (Munich: Kösel, 1951), 9–44.

36. Hütter, "Karl Barth's 'Dialectical Catholicity,'" 153n11, here referring to Eberhard Jüngel, "Von der Dialektik zur Analogie: Die Schule Kierkegaards und der Einspruch Petersons," in *Barth-Studien* (Zurich and Cologne: Benziger; Gütersloh: Gerd Mohn, 1982), 127–79.

37. Karl Barth, "Kirche und Theologie," in *Vorträge und kleinere Arbeiten, 1922–1925*, ed. Holger Finze (Zurich: Theologischer Verlag, 1990), 644–85.

38. Hütter, "Karl Barth's 'Dialectical Catholicity,'" 153n11, here citing Karl Barth, *Die christliche Dogmatik im Entwurf*, ed. Gerhard Sauter (Zurich: Theologischer Verlag, 1982), 159–64.

39. Karl Barth, *Unterricht in der christlichen Religion*, vol. 1, *Prologomena, 1924*, ed. Hannelotte Reiffen (Zurich: Theologischer Verlag, 1985), 30–37.

of that difference. The recent conversions to Roman Catholicism of Reinhard Hütter, Bruce Marshall, and R. R. Reno—the last two of whom were trained at Yale, a center of Barth studies in the last generation—are a symbol of the fact that it is getting harder and harder to do Protestant theology in the Protestant churches of America and harder and harder to read Karl Barth as a Protestant theologian without meeting resistance—precisely from Protestants!

The one Protestant response to my book worthy of mention here is that of Colin Gunton. Among the questions posed by Gunton, the one most pertinent to introducing this book and the issues it raises to a German-speaking audience is the first: "Professor McCormack's concern to distance himself from contemporary intellectual fashions leads him, I believe, to understate the continuities between Barth's theology and the world of contemporary philosophical culture. The reason is that modern critical realism, perhaps above all as it is seen in Polanyi's 'post-critical' philosophy, is itself attempting to come to terms with the legacy Kant bequeathed to the nineteenth century."[40] I have already responded to Gunton's critique in full and will not repeat that response here.[41] Suffice it to say that my use of the adjective "critically realistic" as a way of differentiating Barth's version of dialectical theology from other versions of the same (Bultmann et al.) was intended to point to the fact that Barth sought to overcome the limits imposed on human knowledge of God by the *philosophical* epistemology of the critical idealists (Cohen, Natorp, and Heinrich Barth) by means of an appeal to a divine *act* which was realistically conceived. The divine act in question is the act of taking up creaturely magnitudes to serve as the media of God's Self-revelation. That such "taking up" gives expression to divine *willing*, then, also means that the root of this activity in history is to be found in the divine election. And so it comes as no surprise that Barth should seek to resolve the conflicts created through his analysis of realism and idealism by means of an appeal to election at the end of his justly famous essay "Schicksal und Idee."[42] I had no intention of forbidding efforts to bring Barth's version of "critical realism" into conversation with philosophical variants of the same—though I wanted then, and would still want, to insist upon the thoroughly theological character of Barth's version.[43] And I wanted it to be clear that what I was seeking to describe with the adjective "critical" was a form of realism that

40. Colin Gunton, review of *Karl Barth's Critically Realistic Dialectical Theology: Its Genesis and Development, 1909–1936*, by Bruce L. McCormack, *Scottish Journal of Theology* 49 (1996): 488.

41. Bruce L. McCormack, "Barth in Context: A Response to Professor Gunton," *Scottish Journal of Theology* 49 (1996): 491–98.

42. Karl Barth, "Schicksal und Idee in der Theologie, 1929," in *Vorträge und kleinere Arbeiten, 1925–1930*, 344–92.

43. The best description of what I mean by "critical realism" in the German language is Eberhard Jüngel, "Laudatio," *Berliner theologische Zeitschrift* 16 (1999): 289–91.

is commensurate with the postmetaphysical outlook I have described above. Above all, I wanted to ensure that "critical realism" would not be confused with what is sometimes called "naive realism."

Though the intention of introducing German readers to the literature spawned by this book and the essays in which I have subsequently tried to extend its argument has left no room to engage German-language review, I do want to express my gratitude to my friends Dietrich Korsch[44] and Georg Pfleiderer[45] for their encouraging reviews of this book. Their response gives me every reason to believe that the full significance of the moves made in this book will be better understood in Germany.

It remains only to say a brief word about what I would do differently if I were undertaking the task of writing this book today. Certainly, I continue to believe that the paradigm set forth here for interpreting the development of Barth's theology is valid. However, the dating of the emergence of Barth's dialectical theology might require a bit of tweaking.[46] And the timing of the inauguration of the fourth phase in Barth's dialectical theology would need to be adjusted from 1936 to 1939. Matthias Gockel has succeeded in convincing me that although Barth's doctrine of election underwent a christological recentering in the aftermath of hearing Pierre Maury's lecture on predestination at the International Calvin Congress (Geneva, 1936), Barth's "mature" doctrine of election did not emerge until he advanced the thesis that Jesus Christ is the subject of election in his lectures on the material found in CD II/2 (winter semester 1939–1940).[47]

I should also mention two works which help to fill out the picture drawn in this book. Friedrich Lohmann has greatly enhanced our understanding of Barth's debt to neo-Kantianism.[48] And Matthias Freudenberg has filled a lacuna in my own research[49]—which was due to the fact that, when writing this book,

44. Dietrich Korsch, review of *Karl Barth's Critically Realistic Dialectical Theology: Its Genesis and Development, 1909–1936*, by Bruce L. McCormack, *Zeitschrift für dialektische Theologie* 12 (1996): 211–18.

45. Georg Pfleiderer, review of *Karl Barth's Critically Realistic Dialectical Theology: Its Genesis and Development, 1909–1936*, by Bruce L. McCormack, *Theologische Literaturzeitung* 123 (1998): 417–22.

46. In this book I have followed Ingrid Spieckermann in locating the turn to dialectical theology in August 1915. Having read the sermons of 1916, I have reasons now to ask questions about that dating. See Bruce L. McCormack, "Große und kleine 'Durchbrüche'—Predigten 1916," *Verkündigung und Forschung* 46 (2001): 21–26.

47. Matthias Gockel, *Barth and Schleiermacher on the Doctrine of Election* (Oxford: Oxford University Press, 2006), 159–64.

48. Johann Friedrich Lohmann, *Karl Barth und der Neukantianismus: Die Rezeption des Neukantianismus im "Römerbrief" und ihre Bedeutung für die weitere Ausarbeitung der Theologie Karl Barths* (Berlin and New York: Walter de Gruyter, 1995).

49. Matthias Freudenberg, *Karl Barth und die reformierte Theologie: Die Auseinandersetzung mit Calvin, Zwingli und den reformierten Bekenntnisschriften während seiner Göttinger Lehrtätigkeit* (Neukirchen-Vluyn: Neukirchener Verlag, 1997).

I did not have access to Barth's 1922 lectures on Zwingli or his 1923 lectures on the Reformed Confessions. I highly recommend both of these works.

Warm thanks are due Niklaus Peter of Theologischer Verlag Zurich for his support of this translation project and to Matthias Gockel, who spent untold hours doing the work of translation. I also wish to thank Princeton Theological Seminary and its former dean, James Armstrong, for its financial support of the translation work. The publication of the translation was made possible by a generous donation from Dr. Bernhard Christ on behalf of the Karl Barth-Stiftung. To Dr. Christ and the other members of the Stiftung go my sincerest thanks. As before, this book is dedicated to my wife of twenty-six years, Mary Schmitt McCormack, without whose steadfast support and loving encouragement over the years none of this would be possible.

14

Review of Johann Friedrich Lohmann's *Karl Barth und der Neukantianismus*

Theology, Karl Barth wrote in 1929, moves in "the same sphere" and along the same "tracks" as the idealistic mode of thinking; indeed, idealism provides theology with "a most important tool" for the presentation of Christian truth. Of course, he quickly added, "We should not overlook the fact that all thinking of this kind [i.e., the idealistic] . . . can in no way lead to Christian truth."[1] Still, there can be no question but that Barth found in idealism an ally, a fellow-traveller for at least part of the way in which he too wished to travel. But *which* form of idealism did he have in mind? The "dogmatic idealism" of the speculative philosophers, Hegel, Fichte, et al.? No, the form of idealism in whose school Barth entered as a student and by which even his mature theology was nourished was the "critical idealism" of Herrmann Cohen, Paul Natorp, and Heinrich Barth (the so-called Marburg neo-Kantians).

Barth's indebtedness to Marburg neo-Kantianism has long been noted, though few have fully grasped its extent. It is the lasting merit of Johann Friedrich Lohmann's study[2] to have shown just how extensive this influence was. Unlike Simon Fisher's 1988 study (the only other large monograph devoted

This essay was originally published in a slightly different form as a review of *Karl Barth und der Neukantianismus: Die Rezeption des Neukantianismus im "Römerbrief" und ihre Bedeutung für die weitere Ausarbeitung der Theologie Karl Barths*, by Johann Friedrich Lohmann, in *Journal of Religion* 78 (1998): 129–30. Reprinted by permission.

1. Karl Barth, *Ethik* (Zurich: Theologischer Verlag, 1978), 2:94–95.
2. Johann Friedrich Lohmann, *Karl Barth und der Neukantianismus: Die Rezeption des Neukantianismus im "Römerbrief" und ihre Bedeutung für die weitere Ausarbeitung der Theologie Karl Barths* (Berlin and New York: Walter de Gruyter, 1995).

to this theme), Lohmann does not rest content with showing the impact of the Marburg philosophy on the pre-war "liberal" theology of Barth; his goal is to trace the influence of neo-Kantianism right on through what is often (misleadingly) described as Barth's "dialectical phase" and into the *Church Dogmatics*. He does this through careful attention to three themes central to neo-Kantianism: (1) the antisubjectivism (or, alternatively, antipsychologism) of the epistemological theory advanced by the Marburgers; (2) the category of the *Ursprung* ("origin"); and (3) polemic against the "given" (together with all forms of positivism, empiricism, etc.).

The great strength of Lohmann's approach lies in its comprehensiveness. Where other interpreters have allowed themselves to be so bewitched by the category of the *Ursprung* that they have failed to notice other elements of neo-Kantian influence, Lohmann's three-pronged interpretive scheme opens up a number of new insights. The most important of these lies in his ability to show that Barth's actualism has its roots not in Hegel (as some have thought) but in the "dynamic" epistemological theory of Hermann Cohen.[3] Cohen held that the construction of "objects" of knowledge—and even of the "self"—was a never-completed task. Thus neither the "objects" known by the human mind nor the "self" which knows them has a finished, "given" character.

This is an important book, but it is not without its weaknesses. Lohmann believes that, of the three elements of neo-Kantian thought whose fortunes he traces, only the first is retained in the *Church Dogmatics*.[4] He is right with respect to the category of the *Ursprung*; it does disappear during the course of the 1920s. Less satisfactory is his treatment of the polemic against the "given." Lohmann claims that in the *Church Dogmatics* Barth turned back from the pointed rejection of the "given" and moved in the direction of a theological realism whose precise character is never defined.[5] Here it is necessary to register a sharp demurral. The defect in Lohmann's interpretation of Barth on this point has its roots in a misreading of the second *Romans*. In his reading, the Barth of the second edition of *Romans* is a finally "critical idealist," a theologian so heavily influenced by his brother Heinrich that the God-concept held by the two becomes virtually indistinguishable. In truth, however, the God of the second *Romans* is much more than the "principle of critical negation" advocated by H. Barth. Lohmann's single-minded pursuit of the influence of neo-Kantianism has caused him to miss the realistic elements in Barth's early dialectical theology. The result is that when he finally discovers theological realism in the later dogmatics, he thinks a "turn" has occurred. Worse still, failure to fully grasp the *critical realism* of Barth's early dialectical theology has rendered Lohmann incapable of comprehending the precise

3. Ibid., 310.
4. Ibid., 402.
5. Ibid., 392–99.

contours of Barth's later theological realism as well. He misses the ongoing *Realdialektik* which lies at the heart of Barth's later realism, and in doing so, he fails to realize the extent to which Barth's opposition to the "given" is still in place. Ironically, this also means that the influence of neo-Kantianism remained even more extensive in the later dogmatics than Lohmann dared to believe, since not just one but two of the three elements he examines continued to influence the later Barth.

15

Review of Karl Barth's *The Holy Spirit and the Christian Life*

The reprinting of R. Birch Hoyle's 1938 translation of Karl Barth's lecture "The Holy Spirit and the Christian Life" is a welcome event.[1] The lecture was originally given during the course of a "theological week"—a conference for pastors and students—in Elberfeld, Germany, on October 9, 1929, and published with a companion piece by Barth's philosopher brother Heinrich the following year. The lecture was composed towards the end of a sabbatical semester, during an irenic phase in Barth's theological existence. Though the fundamental material and methodological decisions set forth in this lecture were the same as those which would later govern the *Church Dogmatics*, Barth felt a good deal freer at this time to take up categories and concepts favored by his critics and to give them a "spin" which made them commensurate with his own theology. Among these borrowed categories were the so-called orders of creation (which had been expansively employed by Friedrich Gogarten) and, surprisingly perhaps, the *analogia entis* (which had been elaborated by the Polish Jesuit Erich Pryzwara). In the not-too-distant future, Barth would polemicize against the use of such terms. The mounting criticisms of his own project in dogmatic theology from within the circle of dialectical theologians, the dramatic shift in political fortunes in Germany in the autumn of 1930, and the unwelcome spectacle of erstwhile colleagues such as Gogarten embracing

This essay was originally published in a slightly different form as a review of *The Holy Spirit and the Christian Life: The Theological Basis of Ethics*, by Karl Barth, in *Princeton Seminary Bulletin* 25 (1994): 312–14. Reprinted by permission.

1. Karl Barth, *The Holy Spirit and the Christian Life: The Theological Basis of Ethics*, trans. R. Birch Hoyle with a foreword by Robin W. Lovin (Louisville: Westminster/John Knox, 1993).

nationalist ideologies would induce Barth to distance himself from his former comrades and eventually to break off all relations with them. One of the consequences of this development was that Barth sought to clarify his position through the elimination of ambiguous concepts. He could have continued to speak of the "orders of creation" and even the *analogia entis* in his own way, but to do so in the new situation would only have created confusion. For now, however, he was under no such constraints.

The recognition that Barth had not turned his back on the position articulated in this 1929 essay is of great importance for the Barth scholar today. It allows us to see, for example, that the *analogia fidei* has ontological implications—indeed, that a "true *analogia entis*" is the consequence of a rightly ordered understanding of the *analogia fidei*. In the 1929 essay, Barth rejected Pryzwara's elaboration of the *analogia entis* in terms of a given (created) continuity between the being of God and the being of the creature, by virtue of which the creature could understand himself or herself as "open upward," that is, as containing within himself or herself an abiding revelation which made the knowledge of God a human possibility. Against Pryzwara's view, Barth held that human beings can know a great deal about themselves but they cannot know that they are *creatures* in the strict, theological sense of the term. "If the creature is to be strictly understood as a reality willed and placed by God in distinction from God's own reality, that is to say, as the wonder of a reality which by the power of God's love, has a place and persistence alongside God's own reality, then the continuity between God and it (the true *analogia entis*, by virtue of which he, the uncreated Spirit, can be revealed to the created spirit)—this continuity cannot belong to the creature itself but only to the Creator *in his relation* to the creature."[2] "In his relation" to the creature—this means the true *analogia entis* must be understood to be the consequence of a dynamic relation of God to the creature, a relation that is never simply a given (a *datum*) but is always, in every moment, to be given (a *dandum*). Thus the true *analogia entis* is never a predicate of the creature but is, rather, a predicate of God's ongoing act of relating to the creature. It is a relationship of correspondence between the act in which God has his being (grace) and the act in which the creature has his or her being (obedience as the response to grace). Being, in this view, is a function of decision and act and not the other way around (as occurred in Catholic theology). The importance of these observations lies in the fact that they provide an account of the ontology which Barth presupposed but never clarified in the prolegomena volumes of the *Church Dogmatics* and thereby make a more accurate understanding of those volumes possible.

Barth's essay is only indirectly about ethics (the subtitle was added by the editor of this new edition). It is a work in pneumatology. Indeed, it is

2. Ibid., 5.

a trinitarian discussion of pneumatology which considers the work of the Holy Spirit from the standpoint of creation, reconciliation, and redemption. Barth's central conviction is that the Holy Spirit, if indeed it is truly the *Holy Spirit* of which we wish to speak, is not human spirit. No synthesis of the two may be imagined; every attempt at a synthesis falls under the judgment that the spirit spoken of is the "Evil Spirit,"[3] against which the Holy Spirit strives in his efforts to reconcile and redeem fallen humanity. Even the sworn enemy of Pelagianism, Augustine himself, comes in for sharp criticism for advancing an understanding of grace as an infused love which grants to the creature a capacity for cooperating with the work of the Holy Spirit. Faith, for Barth, is never, at any point, a capacity of the creature. It is a response of the creature to a present action of the Holy Spirit; it is never a completed action which would allow the creature to say, "I have believed." Thus Barth's actualistic account of faith is the end of all synergism. In Barth's view, we will never have a truly Protestant understanding of grace until every last vestige of the "sweet poison" of the Augustinian conception has been stripped away.[4] This will undoubtedly strike some readers as stern stuff, but the drift of contemporary theology into the abyss of self-deification shows just how needed such a word is today.

The new foreword by Robin W. Lovin has much to commend it, but the reader should be warned that Lovin's assessment of Barth's relationship to German idealism, as well as to the philosophy of his brother Heinrich, is one-sidedly negative. Barth did indeed reject the starting-point of idealistic considerations of "spirit," but the elaboration of his own starting-point owed a great deal to the idealistic tradition—above all to Barth's perception that Kant's epistemology was correct insofar as it touched upon human knowledge of empirical reality. As for Barth's relationship to his brother (who, contra Lovin, was no longer a neo-Kantian by this point in time), it is a measure of the relative cordiality of the relationship during this period that the publication of their essays together was done at Karl's urging. It is to be regretted that Lovin chose to follow Hoyle's example in not providing a translation of Heinrich Barth's essay. Although undeniable differences are to be found in the opinions expressed in the two essays, Karl believed that there was enough agreement in essentials to warrant sending them into the public arena under the shared title "On the Doctrine of the Holy Spirit."

It is hard to come away from a fresh reading of this essay without a certain feeling of wistfulness. Barth's mastery of his subject matter, his acute analysis of neo-Protestant ("liberal") and Catholic theology, the ease with which he assembles pertinent data from the writings of Augustine and Luther, and, above all, the very clear lines he draws in setting forth his pneumatology—all

3. Ibid., 23.
4. Ibid., 22.

combine to awaken in the reader a profound respect for the spiritual depth and academic rigor which once characterized theology in the twentieth century. Theology, as Barth did it, was indeed a beautiful science. With the publication of books such as this one, helping to create a new audience for serious theology, it may become so again.

Index